SMALLVILLE™

SEASON ELEVEN

VOLUME FOUR

ARGO

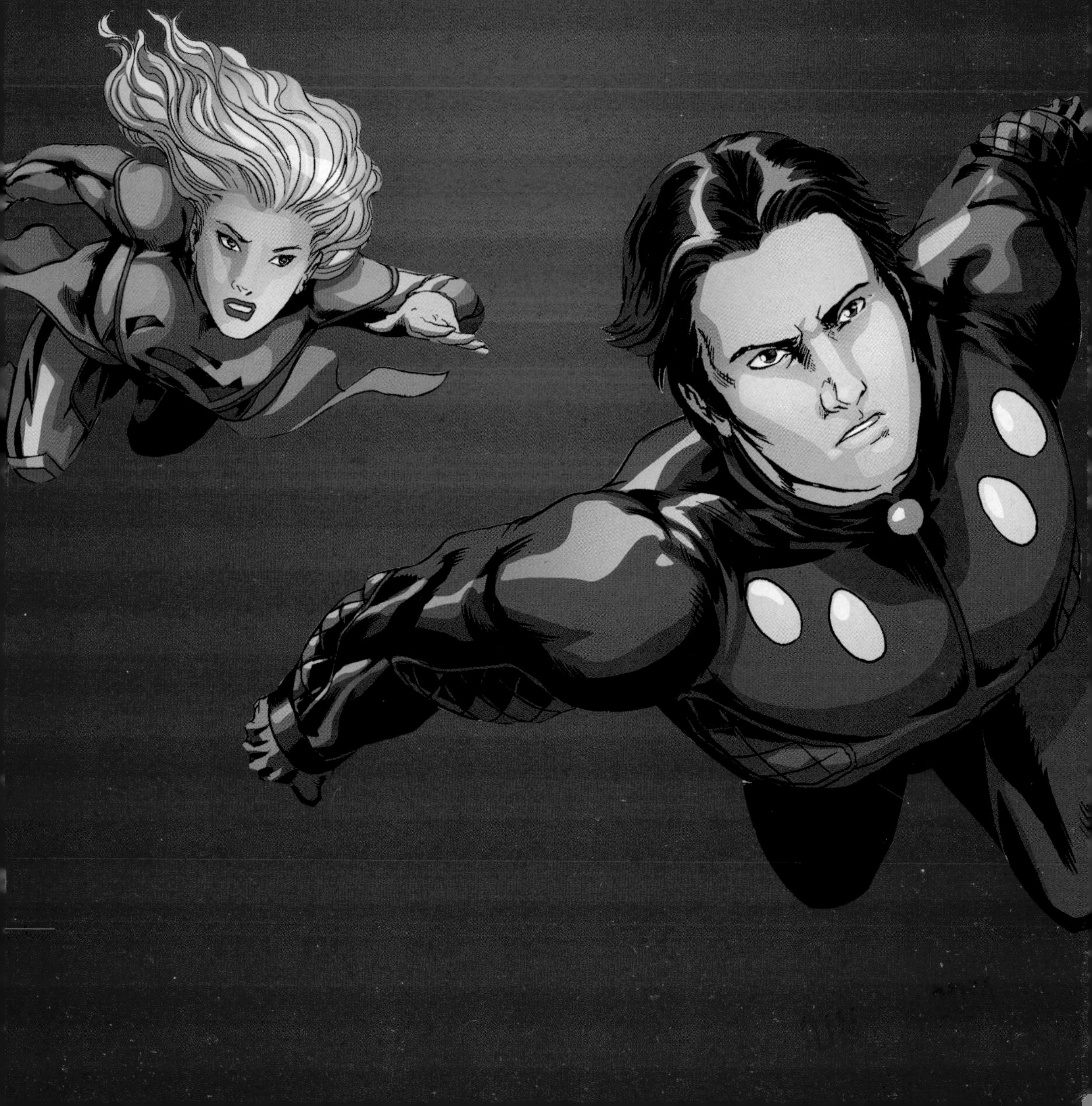

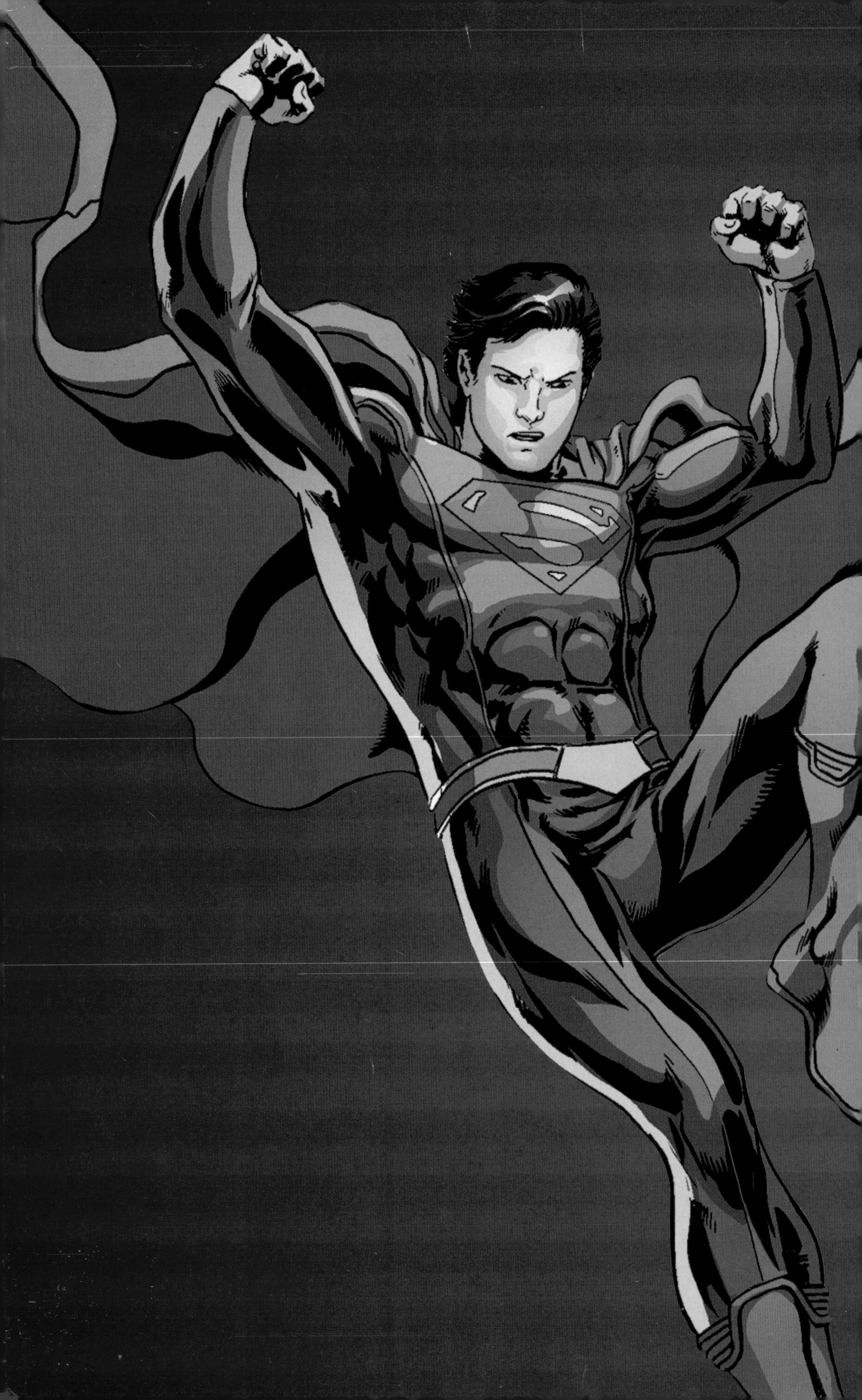

SMALLVILLE

SEASON ELEVEN

ARGO

BRYAN Q. MILLER
WRITER

DANIEL HDR
ARTIST – "ARGO"

RODNEY BUCHEMI
ADDITIONAL FINISHES – "ARGO"

CAT STAGGS
ARTIST – "VALKYRIE"

CARRIE STRACHAN

REX LOKUS
COLORISTS

SAIDA TEMOFONTE
LETTERER

PETE WOODS
COLLECTION COVER ARTIST

SPECIAL THANKS TO RODJER GOULART

KRISTY QUINN   Editor - Original Series
SARAH GAYDOS
JESSICA CHEN   Assistant Editors - Original Series
ROBIN WILDMAN   Editor
ROBBIN BROSTERMAN   Design Director - Books
DAMIAN RYLAND   Publication Design

HANK KANALZ   Senior VP - Vertigo and Integrated Publishing

DIANE NELSON   President
DAN DIDIO and JIM LEE   Co - Publishers
GEOFF JOHNS   Chief Creative Officer
JOHN ROOD   Executive VP - Sales, Marketing and Business Development
AMY GENKINS   Senior VP - Business and Legal Affairs
NAIRI GARDINER   Senior VP - Finance
JEFF BOISON   VP - Publishing Planning
MARK CHIARELLO   VP - Art Direction and Design
JOHN CUNNINGHAM   VP - Marketing
TERRI CUNNINGHAM   VP - Editorial Administration
ALISON GILL   Senior VP - Manufacturing and Operations
JAY KOGAN   VP - Business and Legal Affairs, Publishing
JACK MAHAN   VP - Business Affairs, Talent
NICK NAPOLITANO   VP - Manufacturing Administration
COURTNEY SIMMONS   Senior VP - Publicity
BOB WAYNE   Senior VP - Sales

SMALLVILLE SEASON ELEVEN VOLUME 4: ARGO

DC Comics, 1700 Broadway, New York, NY 10019
A Warner Bros. Entertainment Company.
Printed by RR Donnelley, Salem, VA, USA. 2/7/14. First Printing.
ISBN: 978-1-4012-4637-2

Library of Congress Cataloging-in-Publication Data

Miller, Bryan Q, author.
  Smallville season eleven. Volume 4, Argo / Bryan Q. Miller ; [illustrated by] Cat Staggs, Daniel
HDR.
       pages cm
  ISBN 978-1-4012-4637-2 (pbk.)
  1. Graphic novels. I. Title. II. Title: Argo.
  PN6728.S565M57 2014
  741.5'973—dc23
                                          2013046130

SUSTAINABLE
FORESTRY
INITIATIVE

Certified Chain of Custody
At Least 20% Certified Forest Content

www.sfiprogram.org
SFI-01042
APPLIES TO TEXT STOCK ONLY

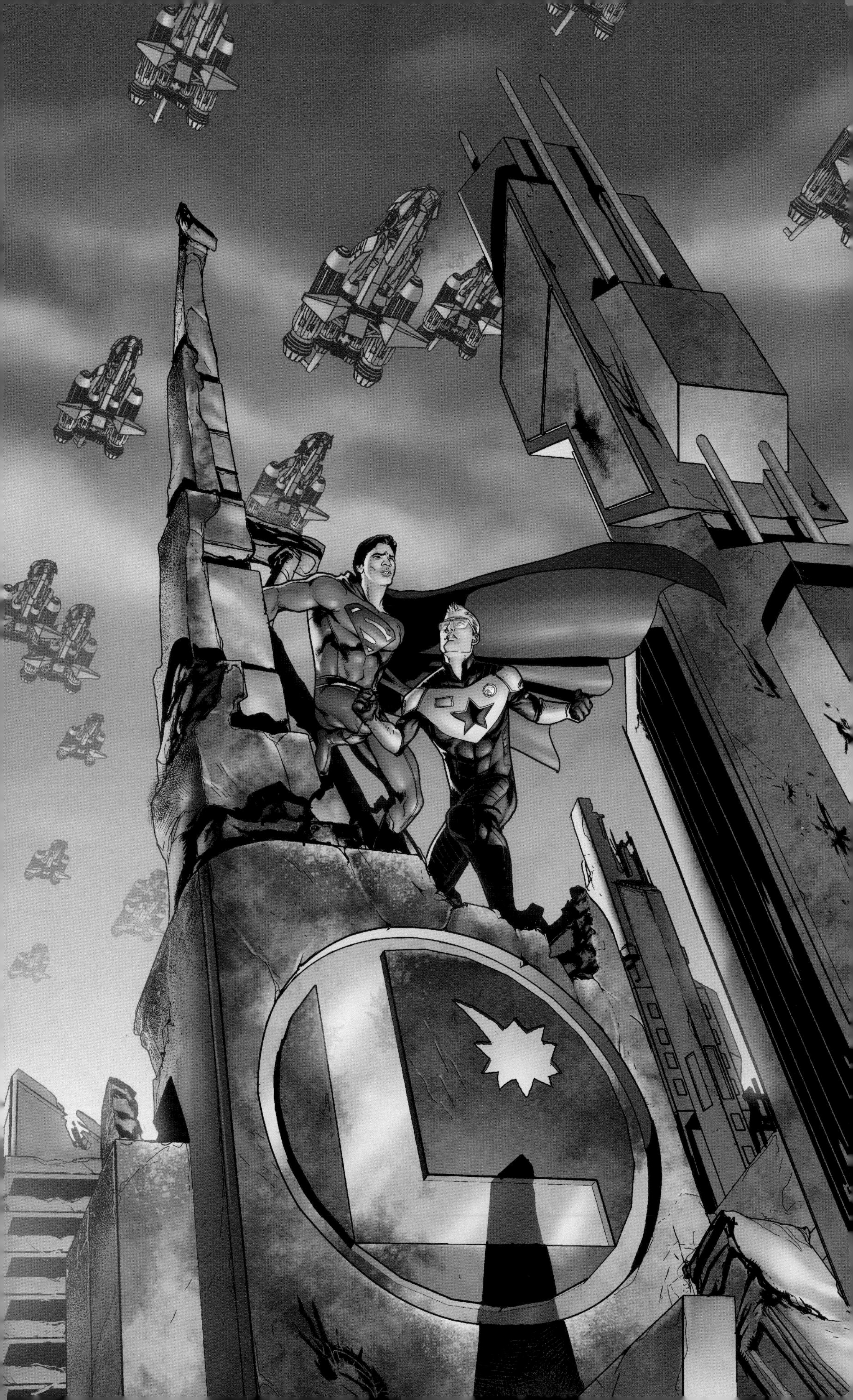

ARGO PART ONE
COVER BY PETE WOODS WITH RANDY MAYOR

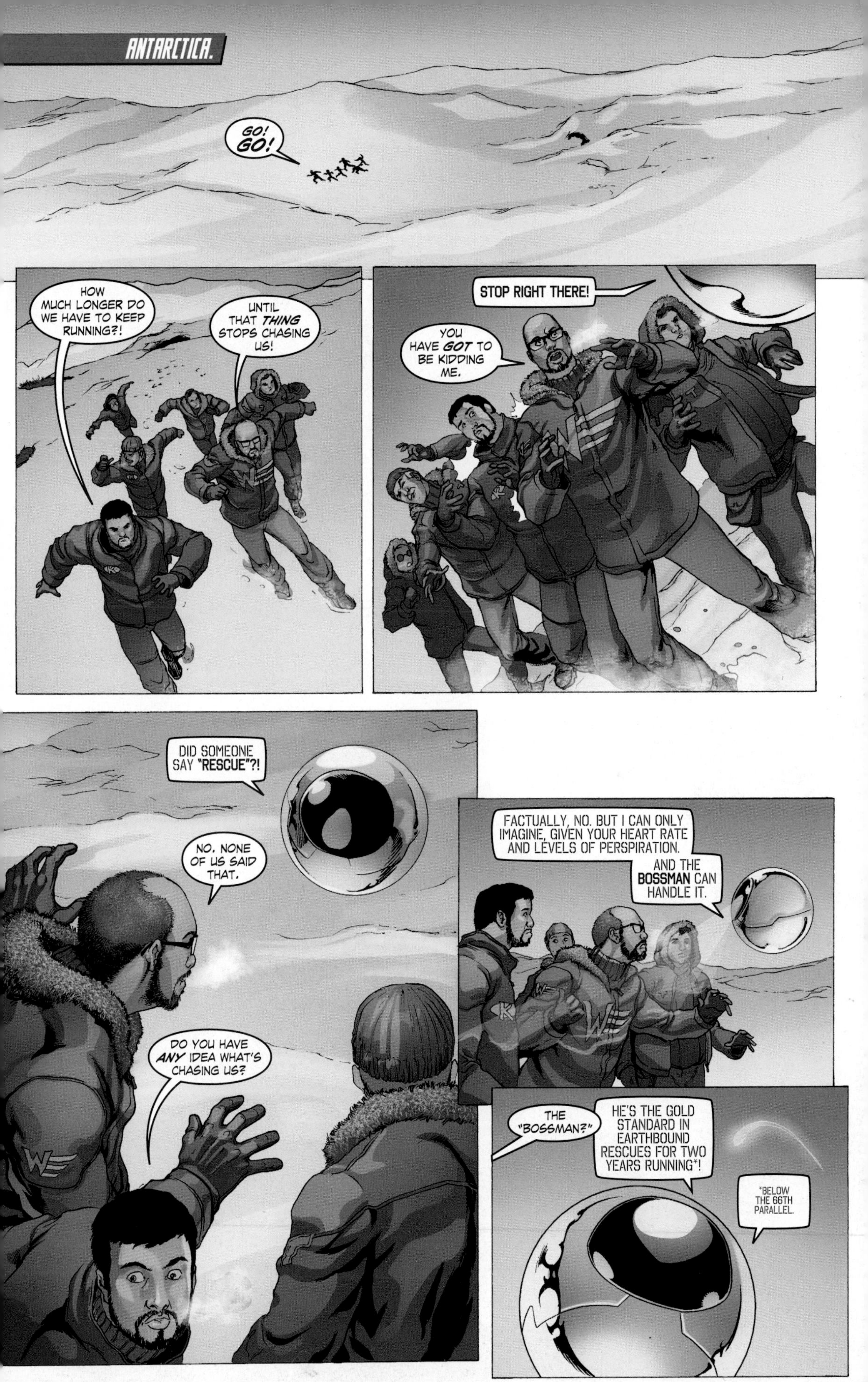
ANTARCTICA.
GO! GO!
HOW MUCH LONGER DO WE HAVE TO KEEP RUNNING?!
UNTIL THAT THING STOPS CHASING US!
STOP RIGHT THERE!
YOU HAVE GOT TO BE KIDDING ME.
DID SOMEONE SAY "RESCUE"?!
NO. NONE OF US SAID THAT.
DO YOU HAVE ANY IDEA WHAT'S CHASING US?
FACTUALLY, NO. BUT I CAN ONLY IMAGINE, GIVEN YOUR HEART RATE AND LEVELS OF PERSPIRATION.
AND THE BOSSMAN CAN HANDLE IT.
THE "BOSSMAN?"
HE'S THE GOLD STANDARD IN EARTHBOUND RESCUES FOR TWO YEARS RUNNING*!
*BELOW THE 66TH PARALLEL.

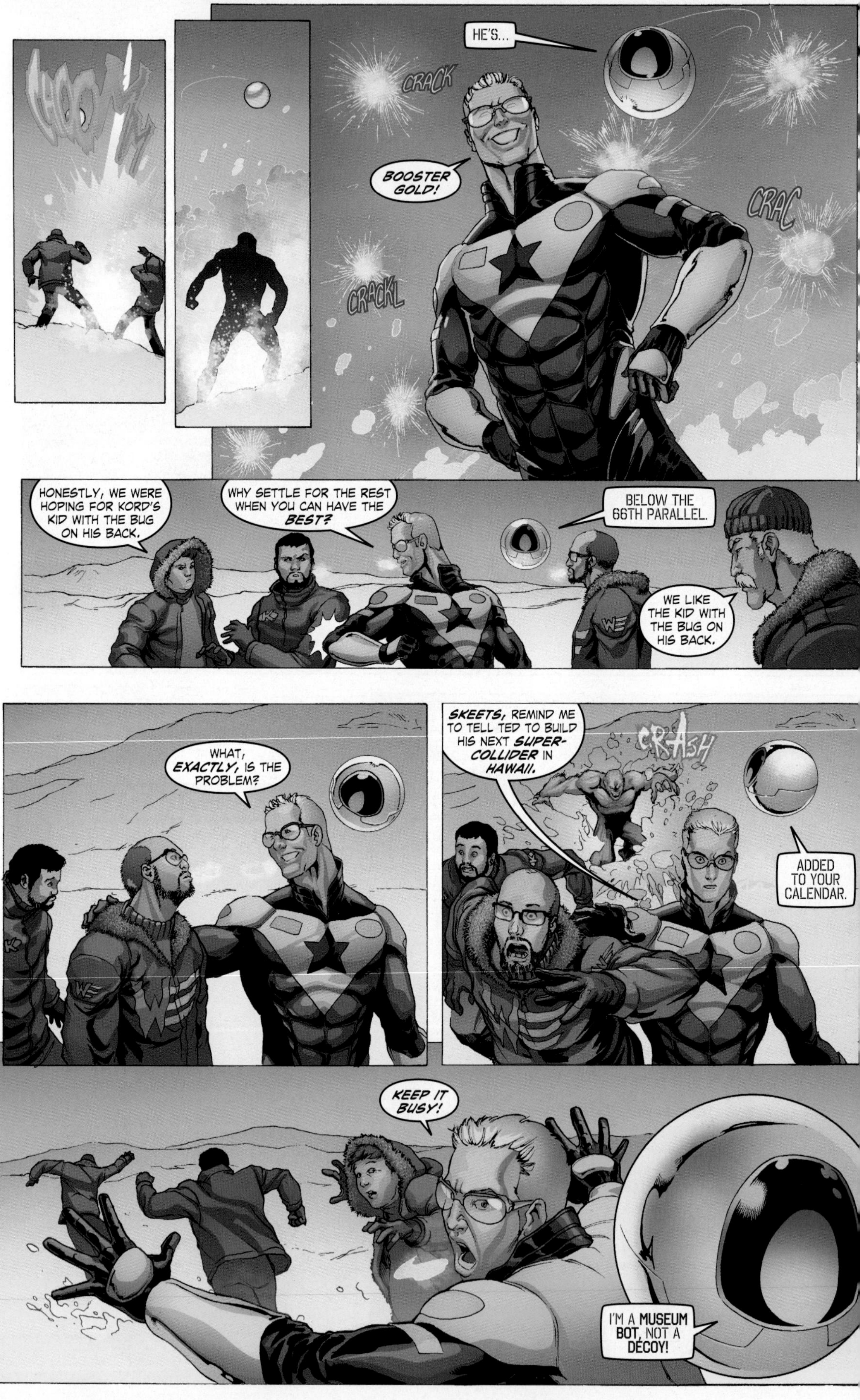
CHOOOM
HE'S...
CRACK
BOOSTER GOLD!
CRAC
CRACKL
HONESTLY, WE WERE HOPING FOR KORD'S KID WITH THE BUG ON HIS BACK.
WHY SETTLE FOR THE REST WHEN YOU CAN HAVE THE BEST?
BELOW THE 66TH PARALLEL.
WE LIKE THE KID WITH THE BUG ON HIS BACK.
WHAT, EXACTLY, IS THE PROBLEM?
SKEETS, REMIND ME TO TELL TED TO BUILD HIS NEXT SUPER-COLLIDER IN HAWAII.
CRASH
ADDED TO YOUR CALENDAR.
KEEP IT BUSY!
I'M A MUSEUM BOT, NOT A DECOY!

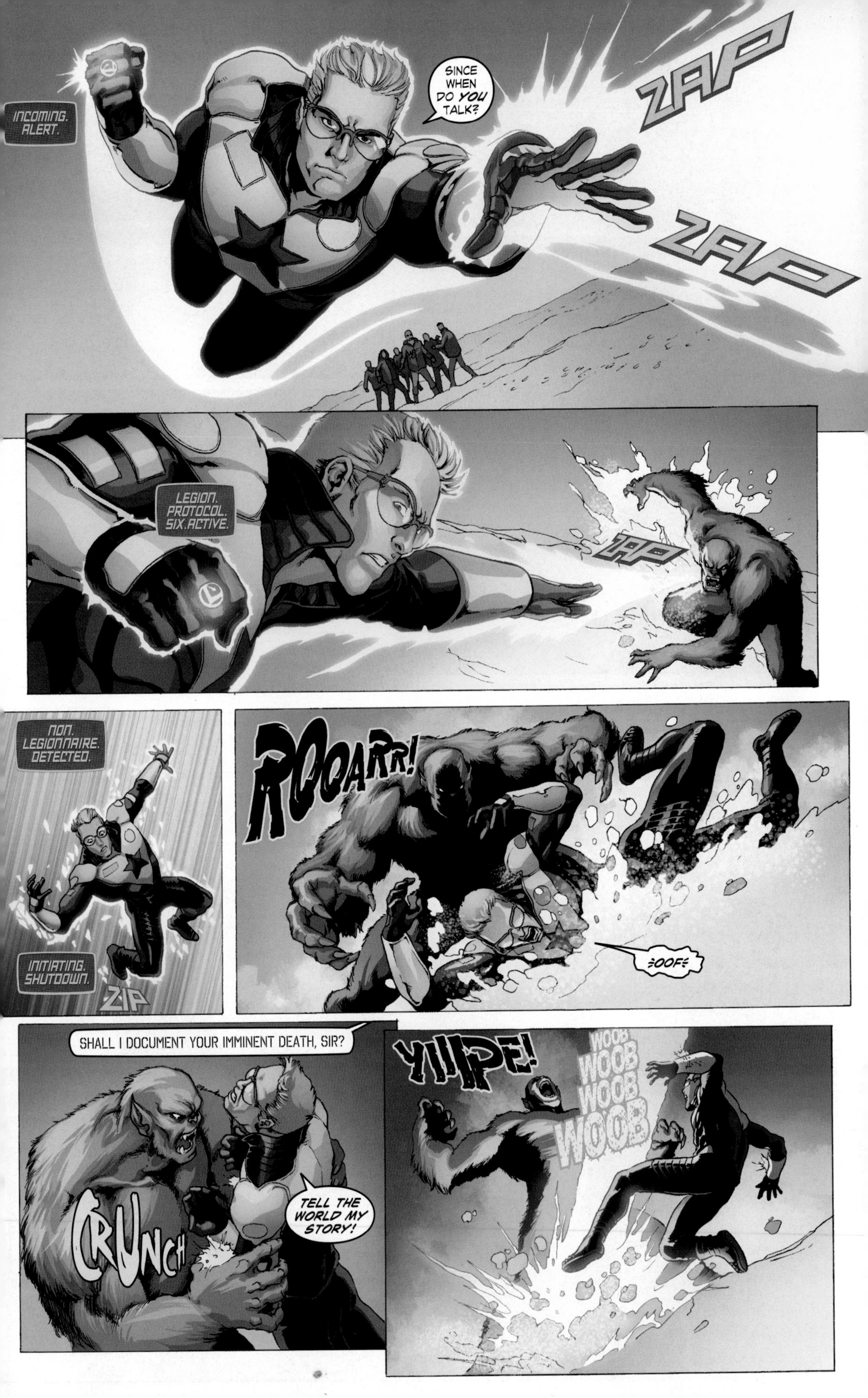
INCOMING. ALERT.
SINCE WHEN DO YOU TALK?
ZAP
ZAP
LEGION. PROTOCOL. SIX.ACTIVE.
ZAP
NON. LEGIONNAIRE. DETECTED.
INITIATING. SHUTDOWN.
ZIP
ROOARR!
OOF
SHALL I DOCUMENT YOUR IMMINENT DEATH, SIR?
CRUNCH
TELL THE WORLD MY STORY!
YIIIPE!
WOOB WOOB WOOB WOOB

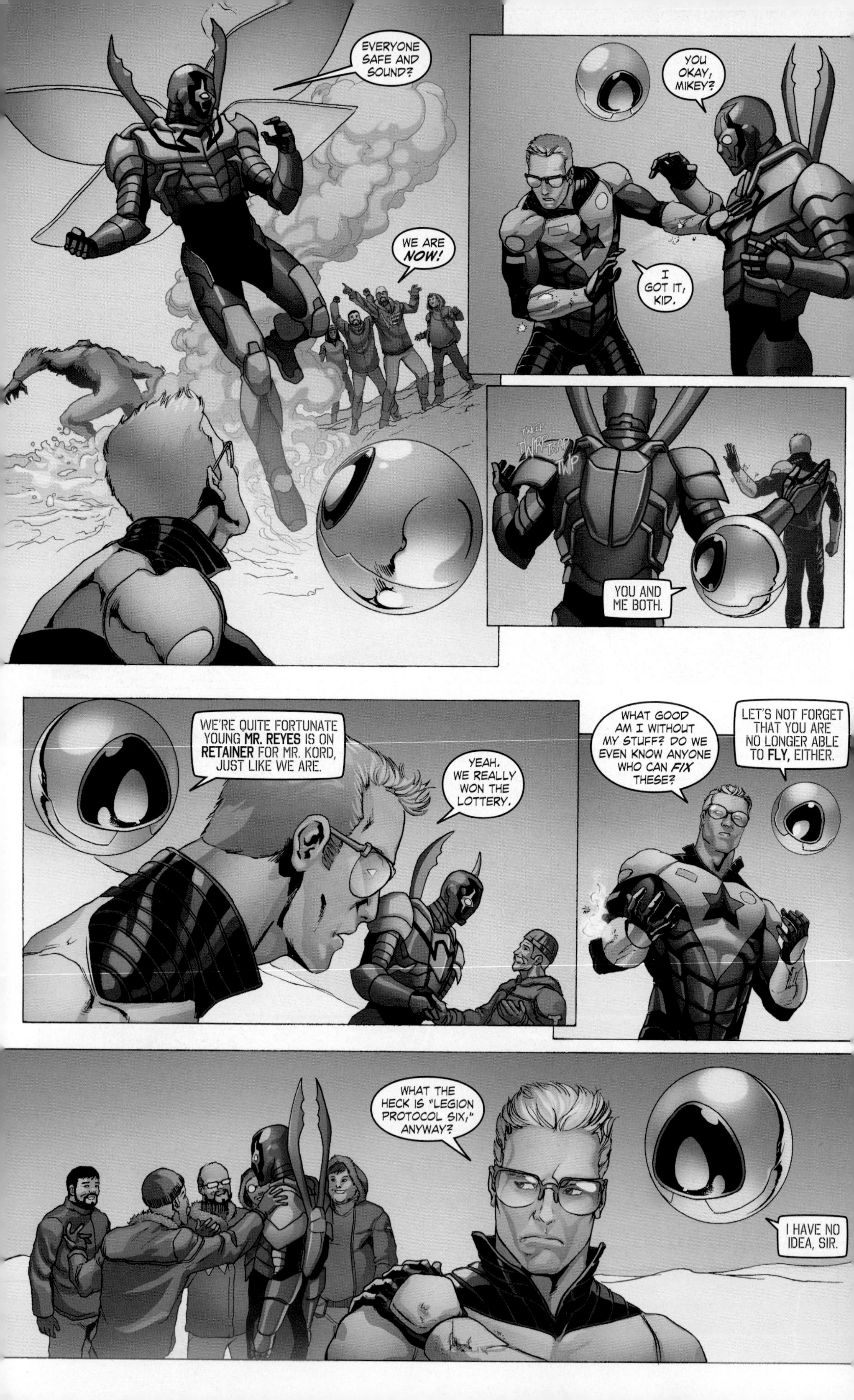
EVERYONE SAFE AND SOUND?
WE ARE NOW!
YOU OKAY, MIKEY?
I GOT IT, KID.
TWEEP TWIRP TWAP TWIP
YOU AND ME BOTH.
WE'RE QUITE FORTUNATE YOUNG MR. REYES IS ON RETAINER FOR MR. KORD, JUST LIKE WE ARE.
YEAH. WE REALLY WON THE LOTTERY.
WHAT GOOD AM I WITHOUT MY STUFF? DO WE EVEN KNOW ANYONE WHO CAN FIX THESE?
LET'S NOT FORGET THAT YOU ARE NO LONGER ABLE TO FLY, EITHER.
WHAT THE HECK IS "LEGION PROTOCOL SIX," ANYWAY?
I HAVE NO IDEA, SIR.

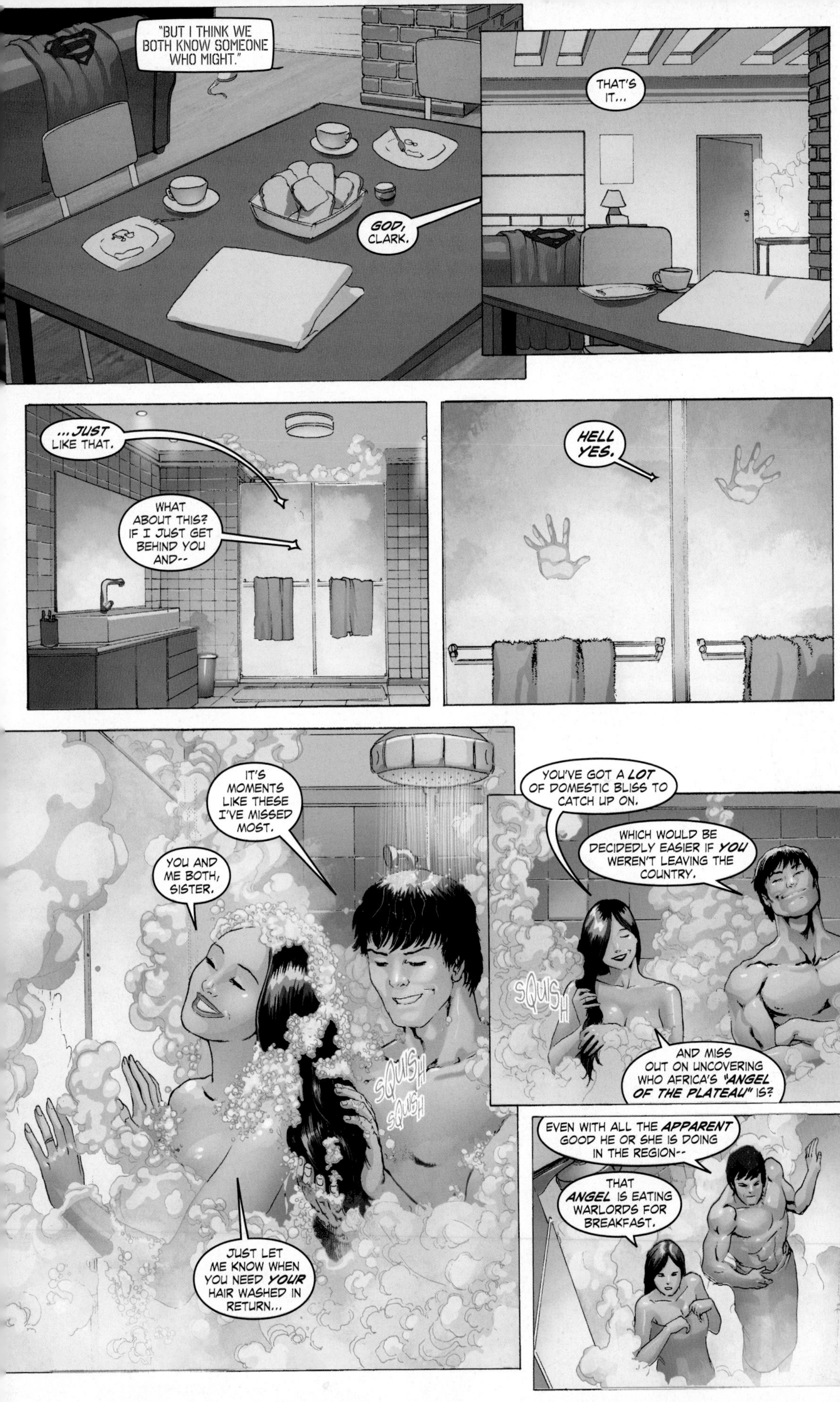
"BUT I THINK WE BOTH KNOW SOMEONE WHO MIGHT."
THAT'S IT...
GOD, CLARK.
...JUST LIKE THAT.
WHAT ABOUT THIS? IF I JUST GET BEHIND YOU AND--
HELL YES.
IT'S MOMENTS LIKE THESE I'VE MISSED MOST.
YOU AND ME BOTH, SISTER.
SQUISH
SQUISH
JUST LET ME KNOW WHEN YOU NEED YOUR HAIR WASHED IN RETURN...
YOU'VE GOT A LOT OF DOMESTIC BLISS TO CATCH UP ON.
WHICH WOULD BE DECIDEDLY EASIER IF YOU WEREN'T LEAVING THE COUNTRY.
SQUISH
AND MISS OUT ON UNCOVERING WHO AFRICA'S "ANGEL OF THE PLATEAU" IS?
EVEN WITH ALL THE APPARENT GOOD HE OR SHE IS DOING IN THE REGION--
THAT ANGEL IS EATING WARLORDS FOR BREAKFAST.

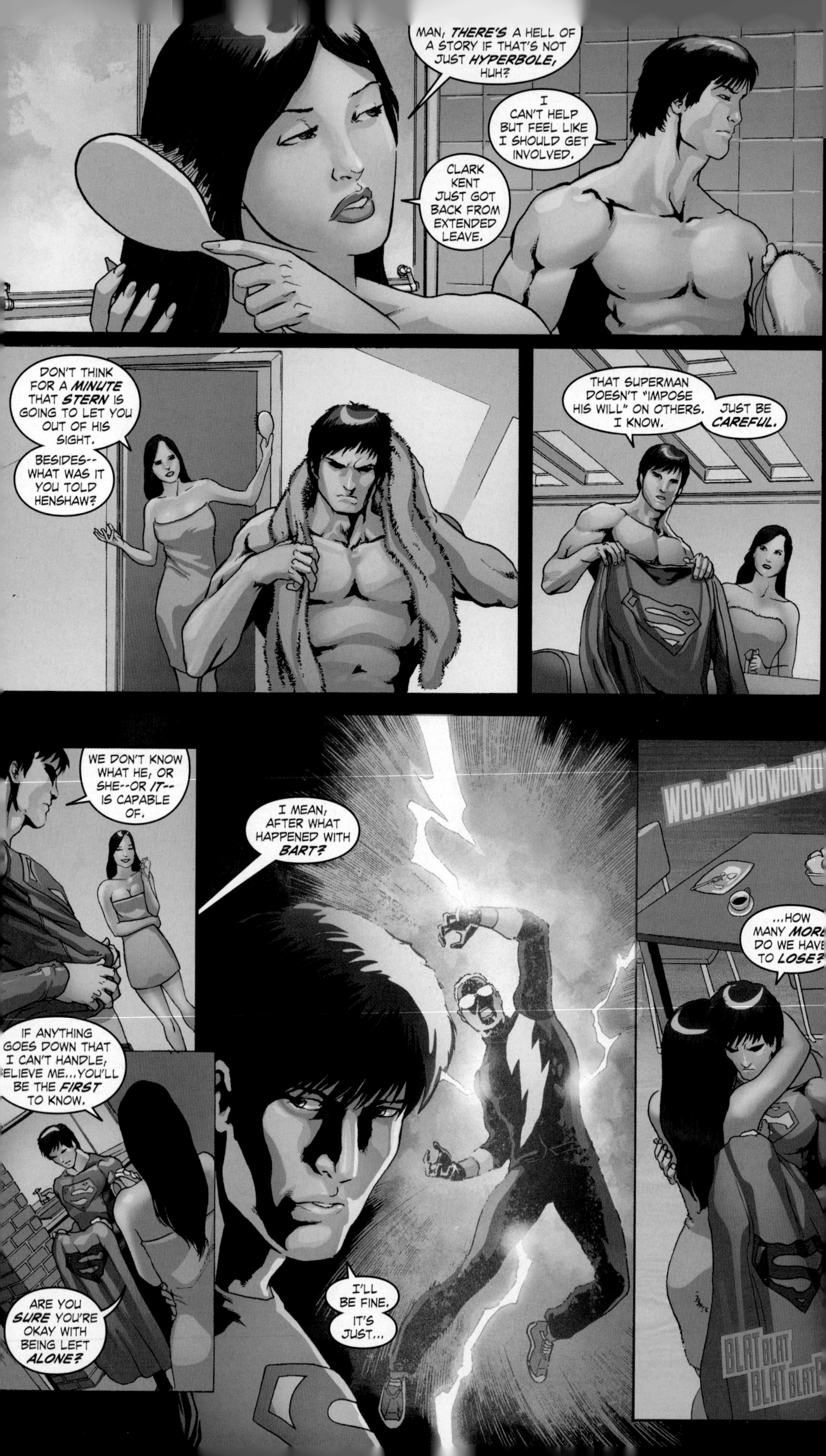
MAN, THERE'S A HELL OF A STORY IF THAT'S NOT JUST HYPERBOLE, HUH?
I CAN'T HELP BUT FEEL LIKE I SHOULD GET INVOLVED.
CLARK KENT JUST GOT BACK FROM EXTENDED LEAVE.
DON'T THINK FOR A MINUTE THAT STERN IS GOING TO LET YOU OUT OF HIS SIGHT.
BESIDES--WHAT WAS IT YOU TOLD HENSHAW?
THAT SUPERMAN DOESN'T "IMPOSE HIS WILL" ON OTHERS. I KNOW.
JUST BE CAREFUL.
WE DON'T KNOW WHAT HE, OR SHE--OR IT--IS CAPABLE OF.
IF ANYTHING GOES DOWN THAT I CAN'T HANDLE, BELIEVE ME...YOU'LL BE THE FIRST TO KNOW.
ARE YOU SURE YOU'RE OKAY WITH BEING LEFT ALONE?
I'LL BE FINE.
IT'S JUST...
I MEAN, AFTER WHAT HAPPENED WITH BART?
WOOwooWOOwooWO
...HOW MANY MORE DO WE HAVE TO LOSE?
BLAT BLAT
BLAT BLAT

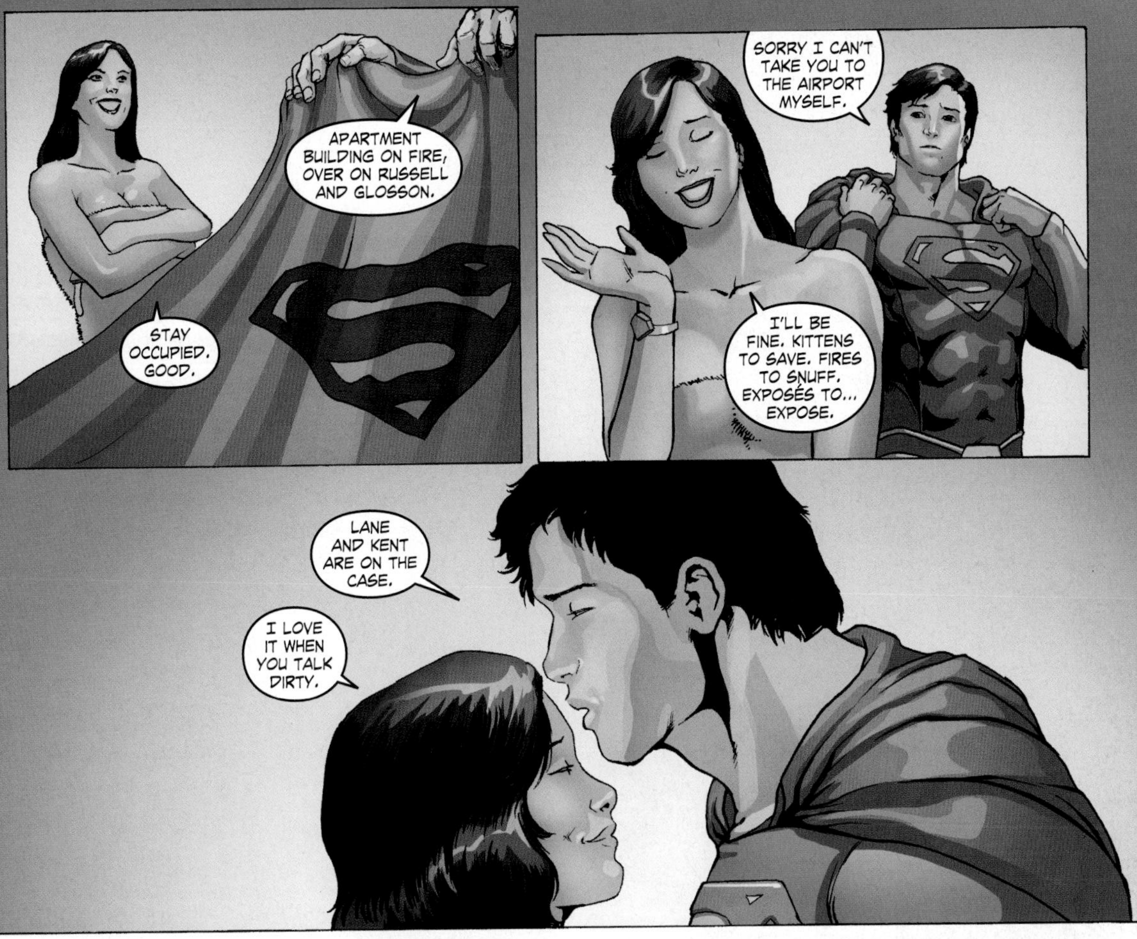
APARTMENT BUILDING ON FIRE, OVER ON RUSSELL AND GLOSSON.
STAY OCCUPIED. GOOD.
SORRY I CAN'T TAKE YOU TO THE AIRPORT MYSELF.
I'LL BE FINE. KITTENS TO SAVE. FIRES TO SNUFF. EXPOSÉS TO... EXPOSE.
LANE AND KENT ARE ON THE CASE.
I LOVE IT WHEN YOU TALK DIRTY.

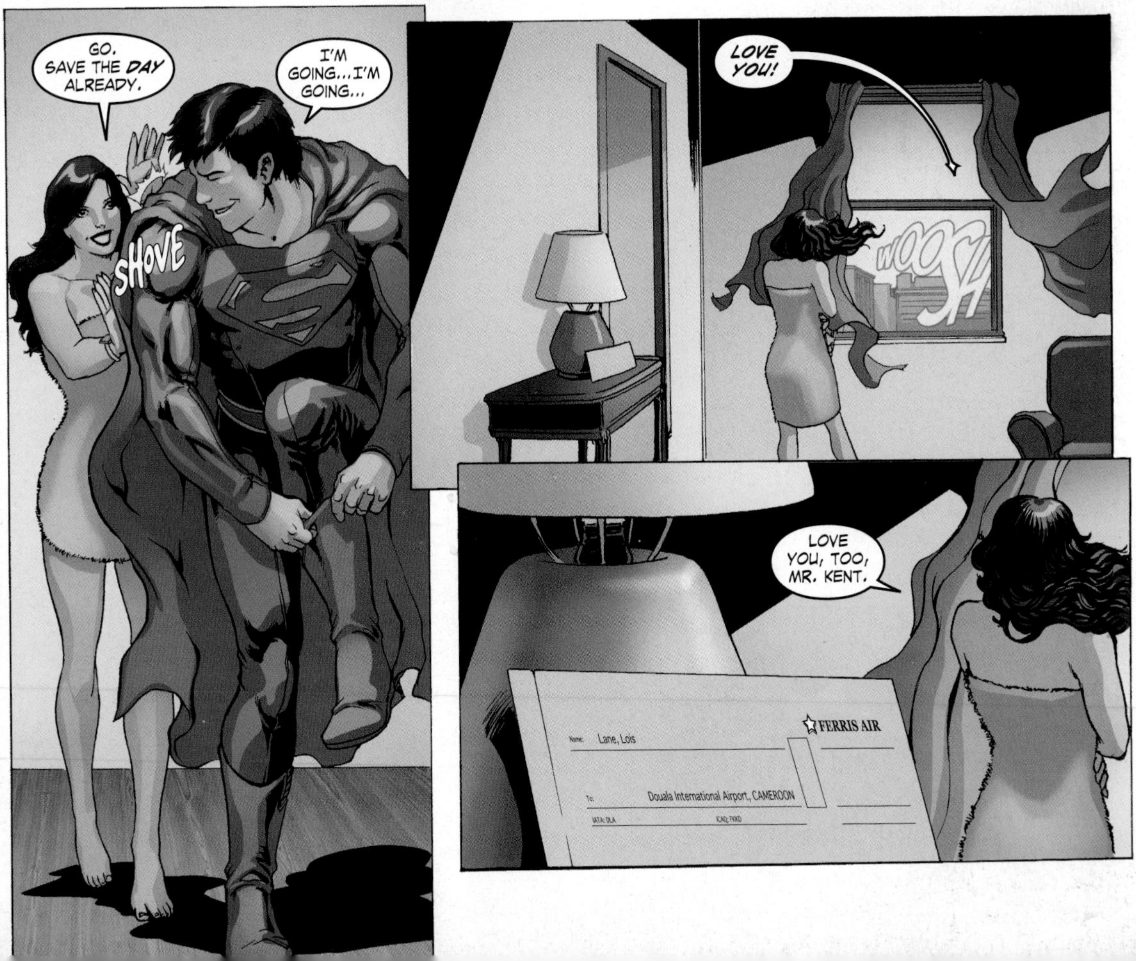
GO. SAVE THE *DAY* ALREADY.
I'M GOING...I'M GOING...
SHOVE
LOVE YOU!
LOVE YOU, TOO, MR. KENT.
Lane, Lois
FERRIS AIR
Douala International Airport, CAMEROON

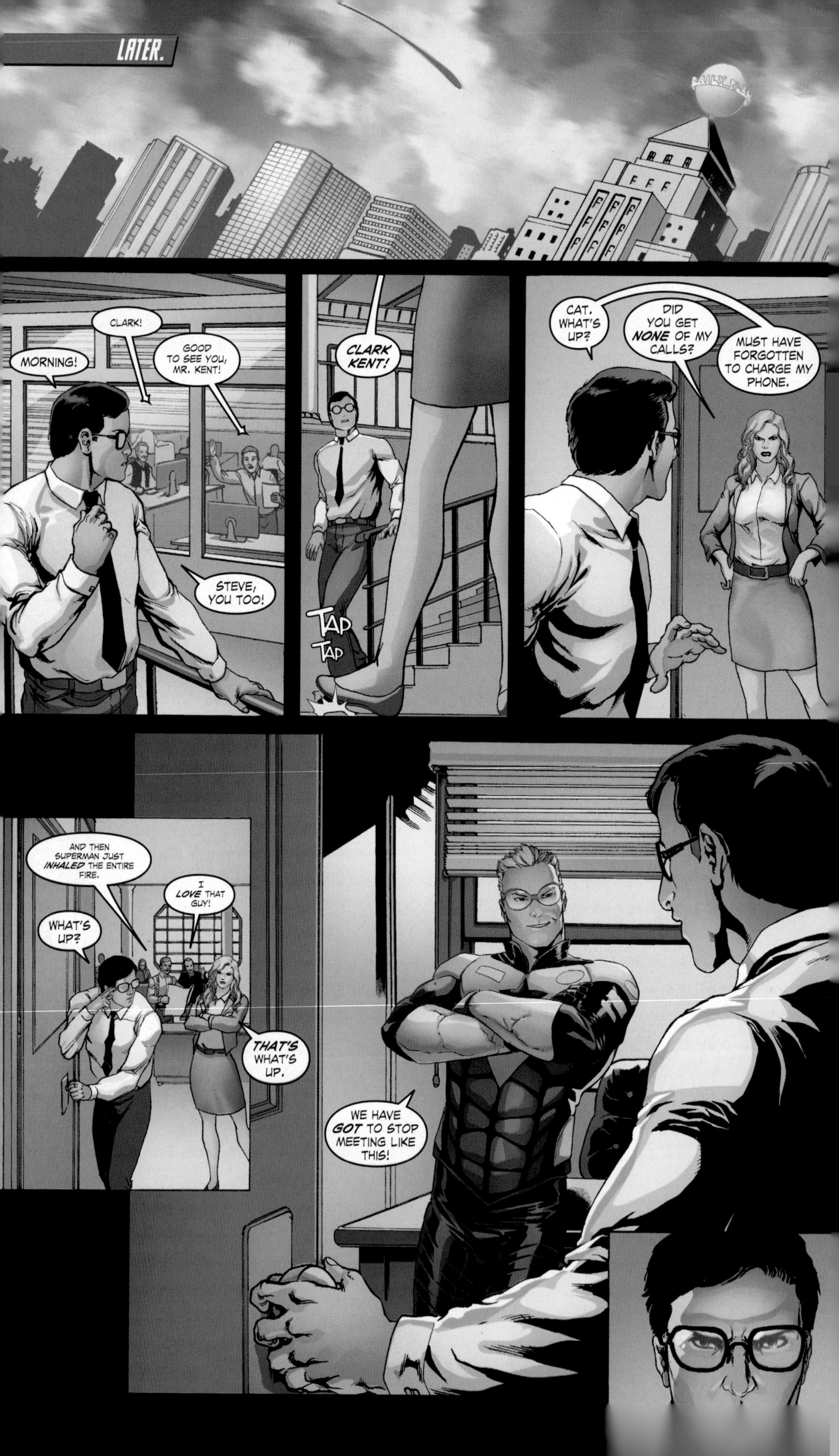
LATER.
MORNING!
CLARK!
GOOD TO SEE YOU, MR. KENT!
STEVE, YOU TOO!
CLARK KENT!
TAP TAP
CAT. WHAT'S UP?
DID YOU GET NONE OF MY CALLS?
MUST HAVE FORGOTTEN TO CHARGE MY PHONE.
AND THEN SUPERMAN JUST INHALED THE ENTIRE FIRE.
I LOVE THAT GUY!
WHAT'S UP?
THAT'S WHAT'S UP.
WE HAVE GOT TO STOP MEETING LIKE THIS!

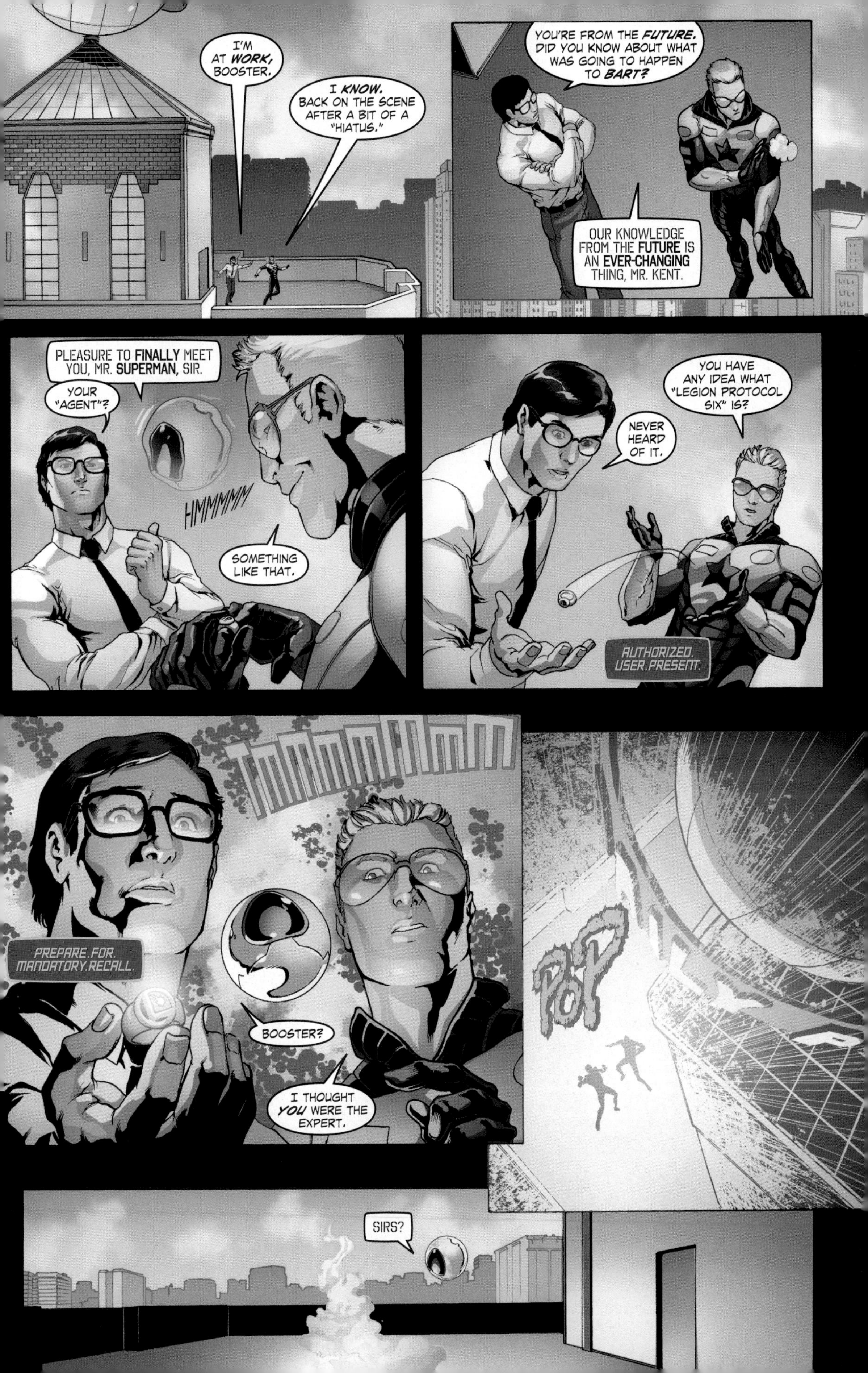
I'M AT WORK, BOOSTER.
I KNOW. BACK ON THE SCENE AFTER A BIT OF A "HIATUS."
YOU'RE FROM THE FUTURE. DID YOU KNOW ABOUT WHAT WAS GOING TO HAPPEN TO BART?
OUR KNOWLEDGE FROM THE FUTURE IS AN EVER-CHANGING THING, MR. KENT.
PLEASURE TO FINALLY MEET YOU, MR. SUPERMAN, SIR.
YOUR "AGENT"?
HMMMMM
SOMETHING LIKE THAT.
YOU HAVE ANY IDEA WHAT "LEGION PROTOCOL SIX" IS?
NEVER HEARD OF IT.
AUTHORIZED. USER.PRESENT.
TMMMMMMM
PREPARE.FOR. MANDATORY.RECALL.
BOOSTER?
I THOUGHT YOU WERE THE EXPERT.
POP
SIRS?

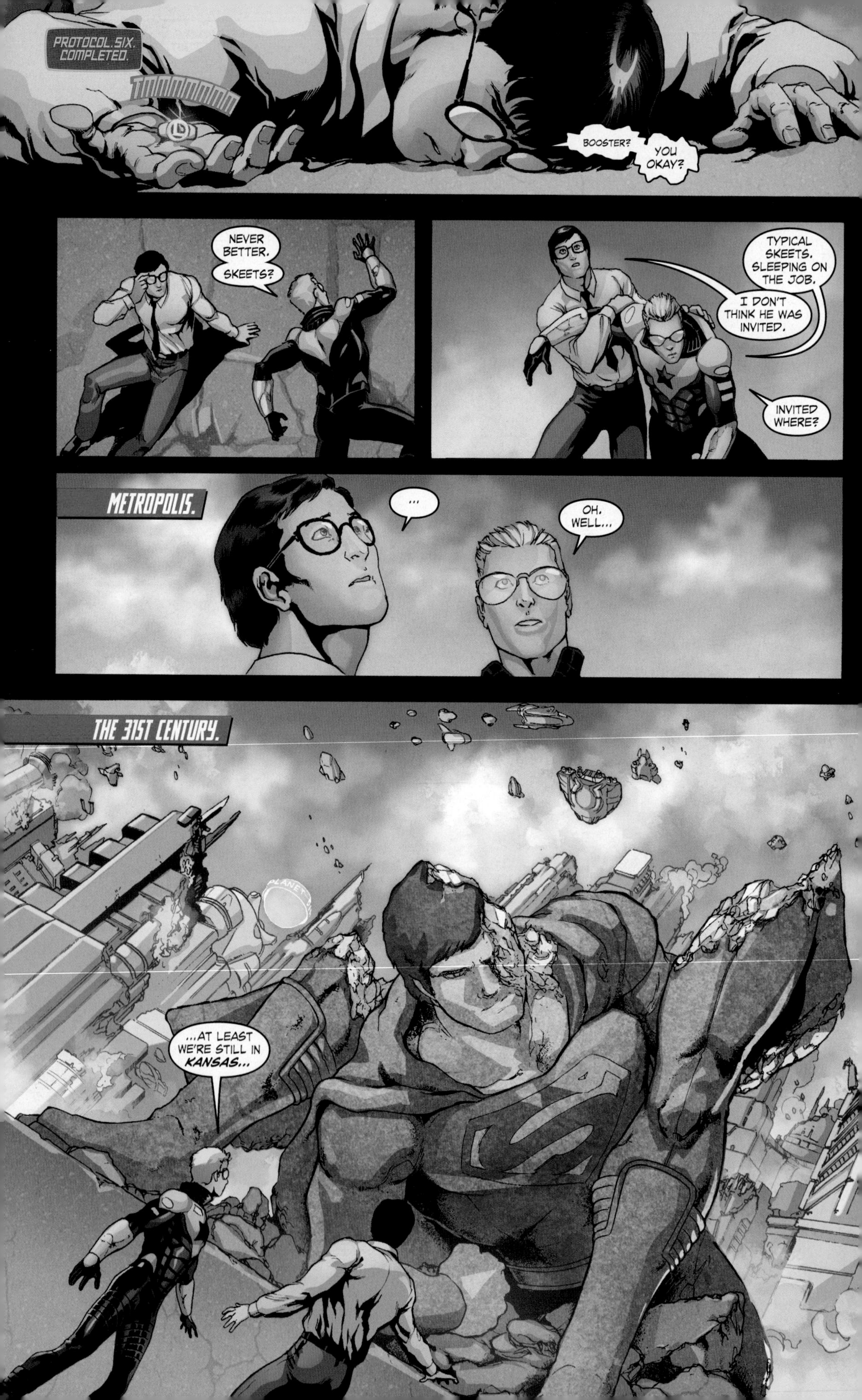
PROTOCOL.SIX.
COMPLETED.
TMMMMMM
BOOSTER?
YOU OKAY?
NEVER BETTER.
SKEETS?
TYPICAL SKEETS. SLEEPING ON THE JOB.
I DON'T THINK HE WAS INVITED.
INVITED WHERE?
METROPOLIS.
...
OH. WELL...
THE 31ST CENTURY.
...AT LEAST WE'RE STILL IN KANSAS...

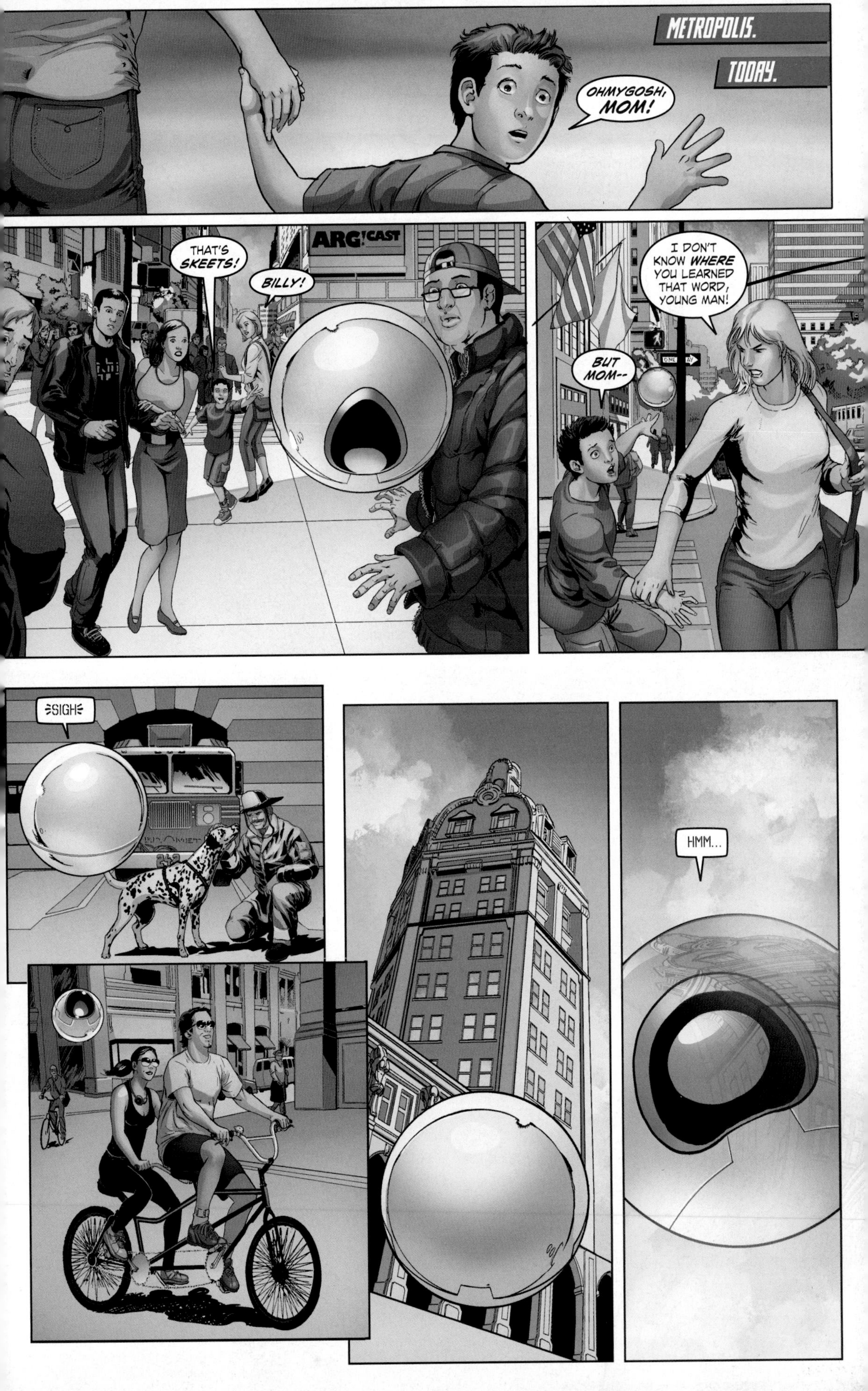
METROPOLIS.
TODAY.
OHMYGOSH, MOM!
THAT'S SKEETS!
BILLY!
ARG!CAST
I DON'T KNOW WHERE YOU LEARNED THAT WORD, YOUNG MAN!
BUT MOM--
ONE WAY
SIGH
HMM...

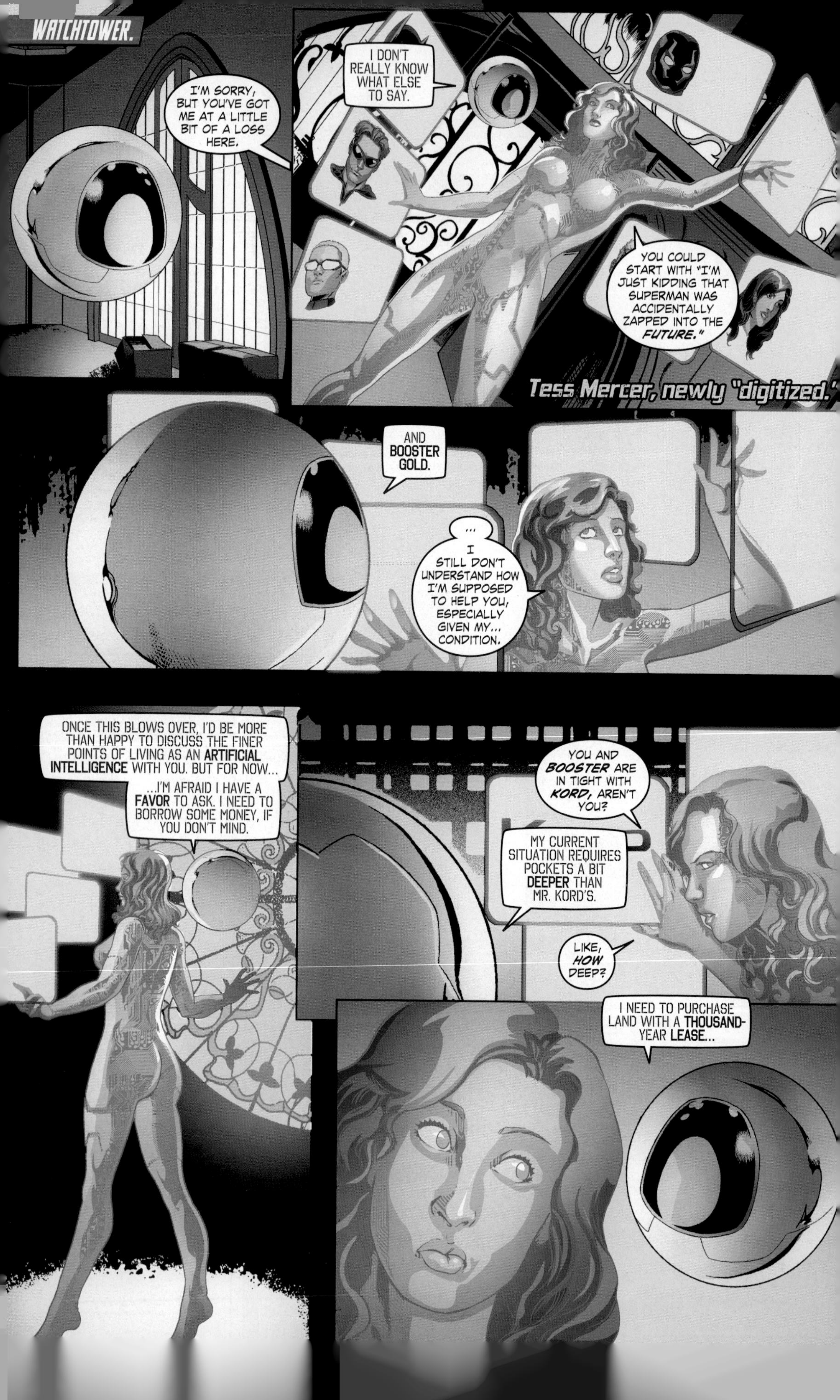
WATCHTOWER.
I'M SORRY, BUT YOU'VE GOT ME AT A LITTLE BIT OF A LOSS HERE.
I DON'T REALLY KNOW WHAT ELSE TO SAY.
YOU COULD START WITH "I'M JUST KIDDING THAT SUPERMAN WAS ACCIDENTALLY ZAPPED INTO THE FUTURE."
Tess Mercer, newly "digitized."
AND BOOSTER GOLD.
...
I STILL DON'T UNDERSTAND HOW I'M SUPPOSED TO HELP YOU, ESPECIALLY GIVEN MY... CONDITION.
ONCE THIS BLOWS OVER, I'D BE MORE THAN HAPPY TO DISCUSS THE FINER POINTS OF LIVING AS AN ARTIFICIAL INTELLIGENCE WITH YOU. BUT FOR NOW...
...I'M AFRAID I HAVE A FAVOR TO ASK. I NEED TO BORROW SOME MONEY, IF YOU DON'T MIND.
YOU AND BOOSTER ARE IN TIGHT WITH KORD, AREN'T YOU?
MY CURRENT SITUATION REQUIRES POCKETS A BIT DEEPER THAN MR. KORD'S.
LIKE, HOW DEEP?
I NEED TO PURCHASE LAND WITH A THOUSAND-YEAR LEASE...

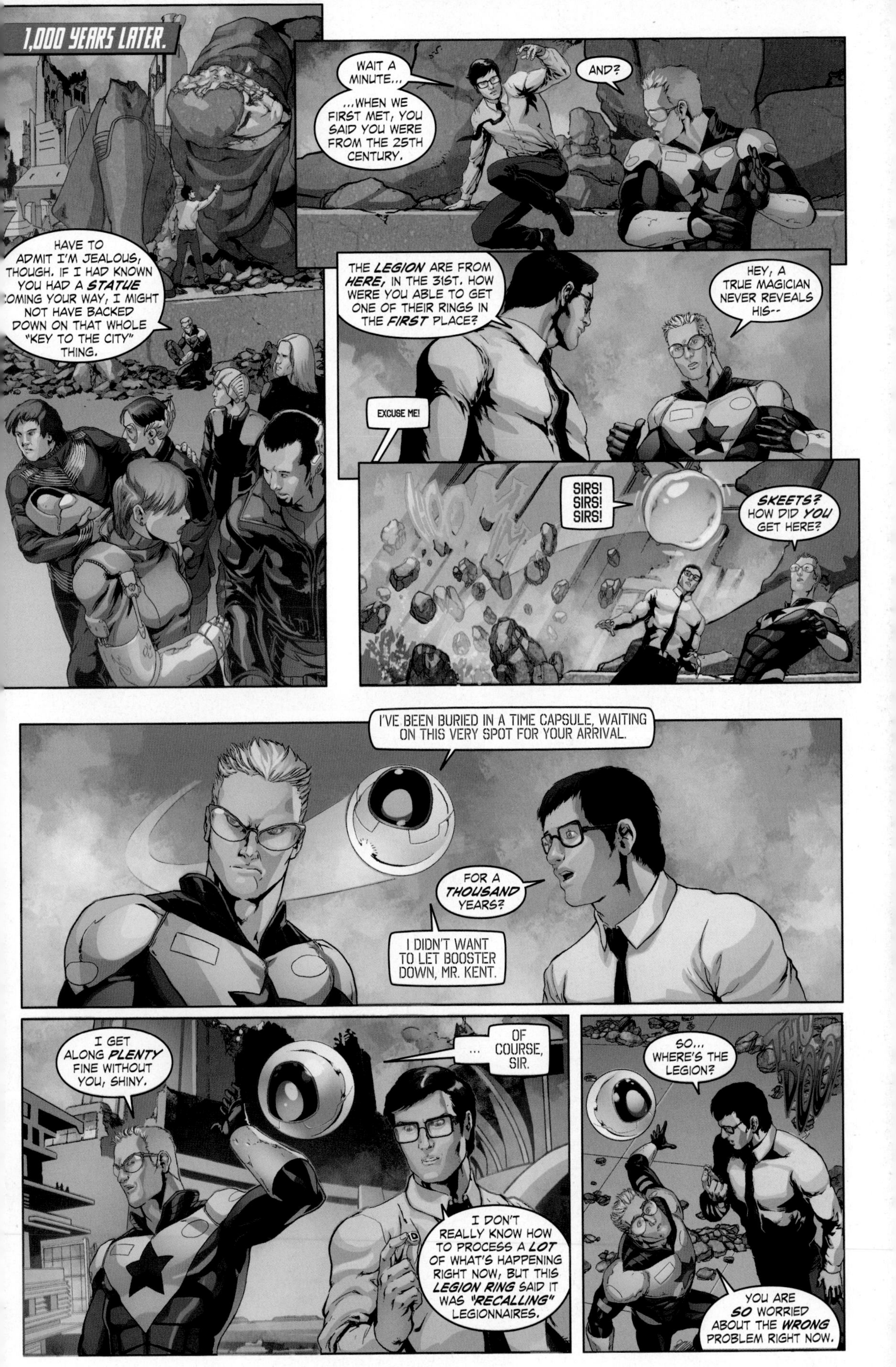
1,000 YEARS LATER.
WAIT A MINUTE...
...WHEN WE FIRST MET, YOU SAID YOU WERE FROM THE 25TH CENTURY.
AND?
HAVE TO ADMIT I'M JEALOUS, THOUGH. IF I HAD KNOWN YOU HAD A STATUE COMING YOUR WAY, I MIGHT NOT HAVE BACKED DOWN ON THAT WHOLE "KEY TO THE CITY" THING.
THE LEGION ARE FROM HERE, IN THE 31ST. HOW WERE YOU ABLE TO GET ONE OF THEIR RINGS IN THE FIRST PLACE?
HEY, A TRUE MAGICIAN NEVER REVEALS HIS--
EXCUSE ME!
SIRS! SIRS! SIRS!
SKEETS? HOW DID YOU GET HERE?
I'VE BEEN BURIED IN A TIME CAPSULE, WAITING ON THIS VERY SPOT FOR YOUR ARRIVAL.
FOR A THOUSAND YEARS?
I DIDN'T WANT TO LET BOOSTER DOWN, MR. KENT.
I GET ALONG PLENTY FINE WITHOUT YOU, SHINY.
... OF COURSE, SIR.
I DON'T REALLY KNOW HOW TO PROCESS A LOT OF WHAT'S HAPPENING RIGHT NOW, BUT THIS LEGION RING SAID IT WAS "RECALLING" LEGIONNAIRES.
SO... WHERE'S THE LEGION?
YOU ARE SO WORRIED ABOUT THE WRONG PROBLEM RIGHT NOW.

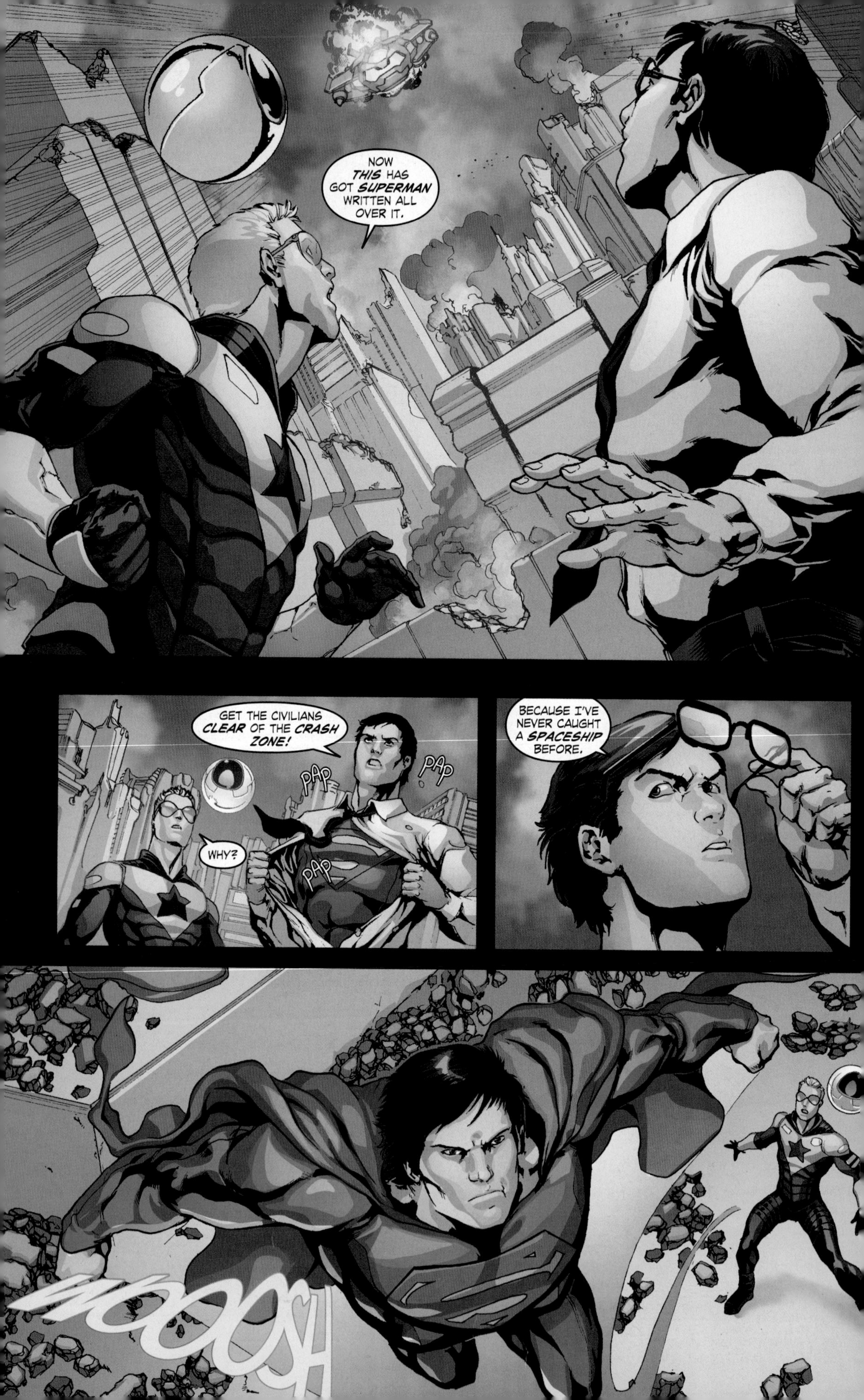
NOW THIS HAS GOT SUPERMAN WRITTEN ALL OVER IT.
GET THE CIVILIANS CLEAR OF THE CRASH ZONE!
PAP
PAP
PAP
WHY?
BECAUSE I'VE NEVER CAUGHT A SPACESHIP BEFORE.
WOOOSH

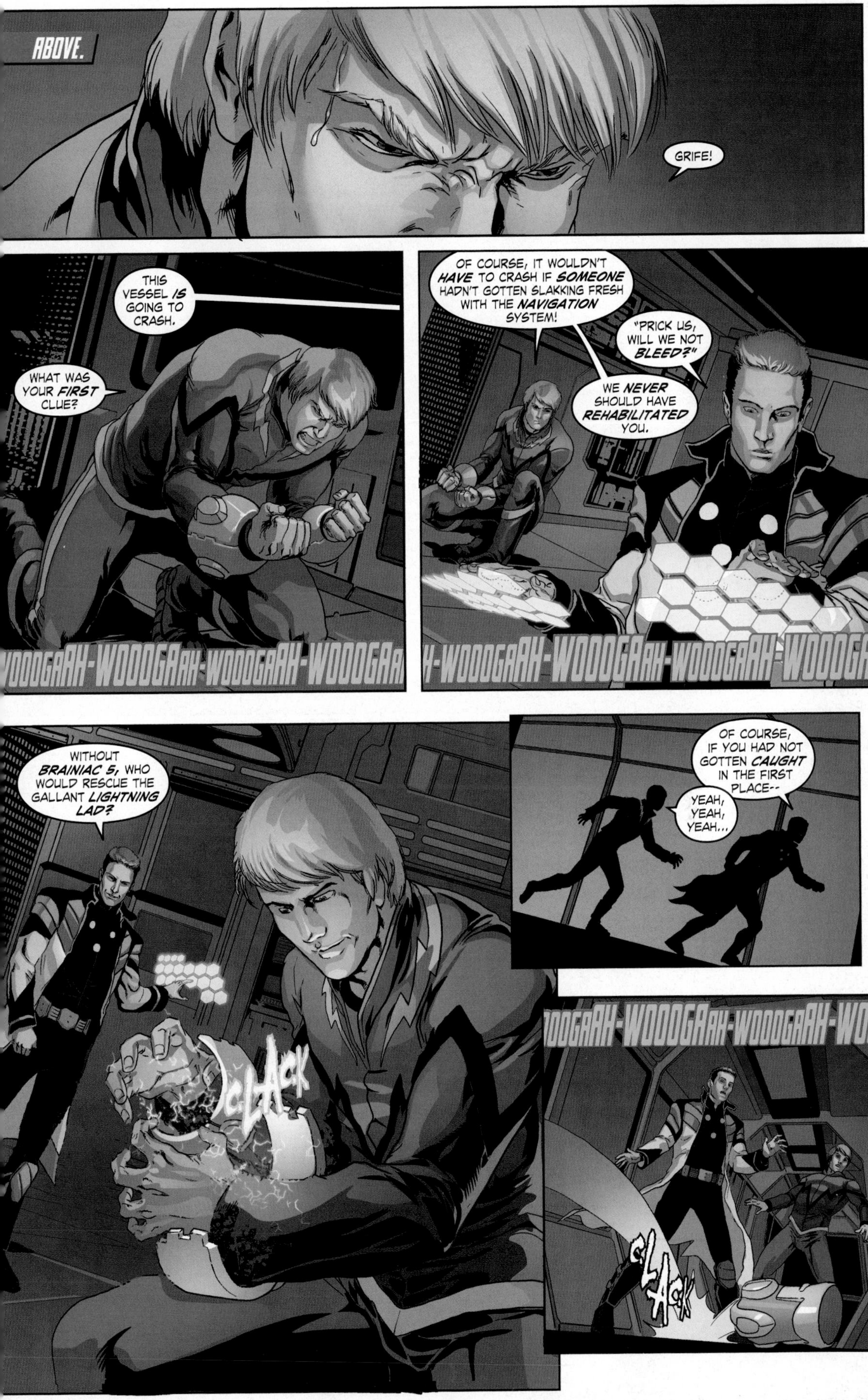
ABOVE.
GRIFE!
THIS VESSEL IS GOING TO CRASH.
WHAT WAS YOUR FIRST CLUE?
WOOOGAAH-WOOOGAAH-WOOOGAAH-WOOOGAA
OF COURSE, IT WOULDN'T HAVE TO CRASH IF SOMEONE HADN'T GOTTEN SLAKKING FRESH WITH THE NAVIGATION SYSTEM!
"PRICK US, WILL WE NOT BLEED?"
WE NEVER SHOULD HAVE REHABILITATED YOU.
WOOOGAAH-WOOOGAAH-WOOOGAAH-WOOOGA
WITHOUT BRAINIAC 5, WHO WOULD RESCUE THE GALLANT LIGHTNING LAD?
CLACK
OF COURSE, IF YOU HAD NOT GOTTEN CAUGHT IN THE FIRST PLACE--
YEAH, YEAH, YEAH...
OOGAAH-WOOOGAAH-WOOOGAAH-WOO
CLACK

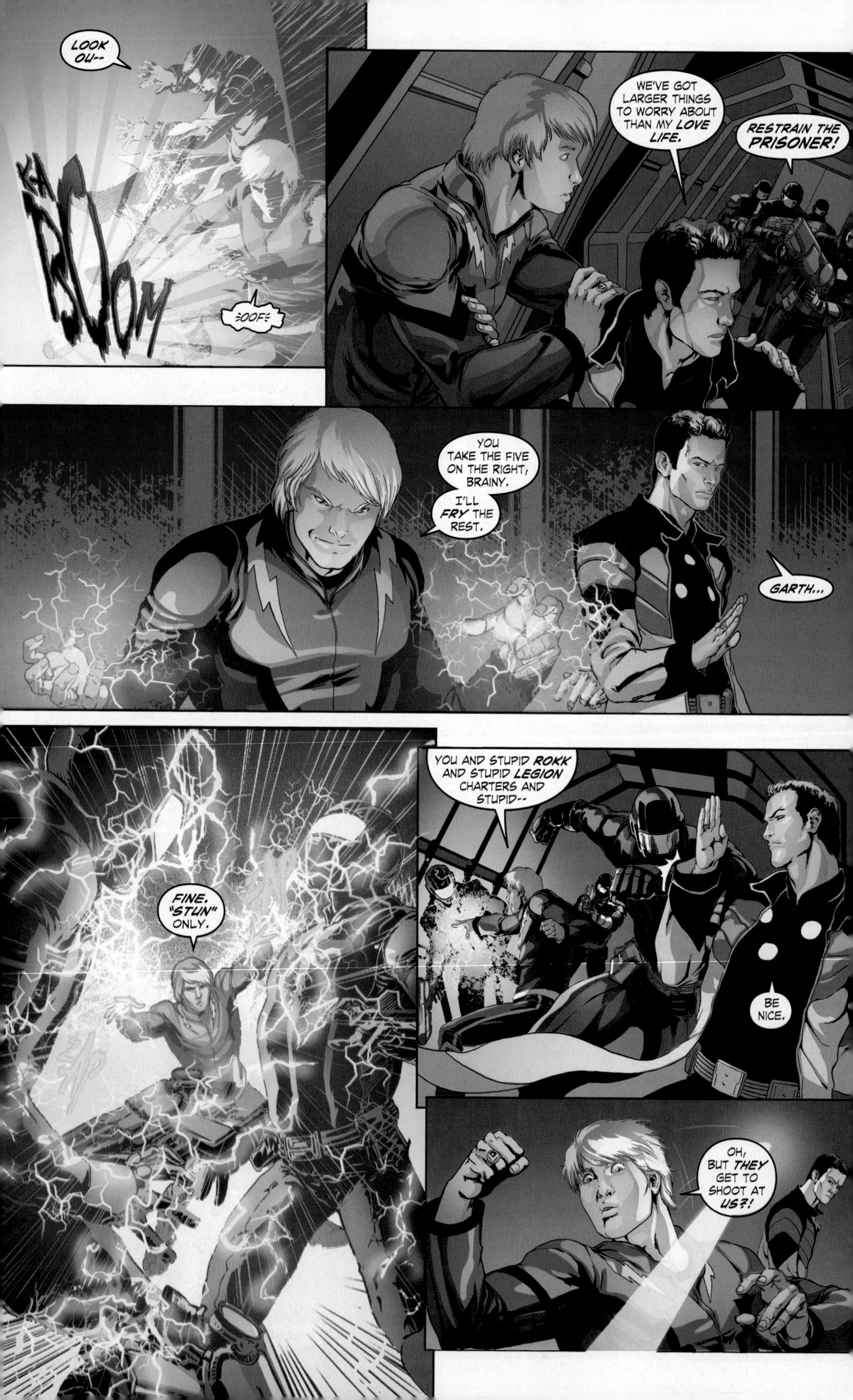
LOOK OU--
KA BOOM
OOF
WE'VE GOT LARGER THINGS TO WORRY ABOUT THAN MY LOVE LIFE.
RESTRAIN THE PRISONER!
YOU TAKE THE FIVE ON THE RIGHT, BRAINY.
I'LL FRY THE REST.
GARTH...
FINE. "STUN" ONLY.
YOU AND STUPID ROKK AND STUPID LEGION CHARTERS AND STUPID--
BE NICE.
OH, BUT THEY GET TO SHOOT AT US?!

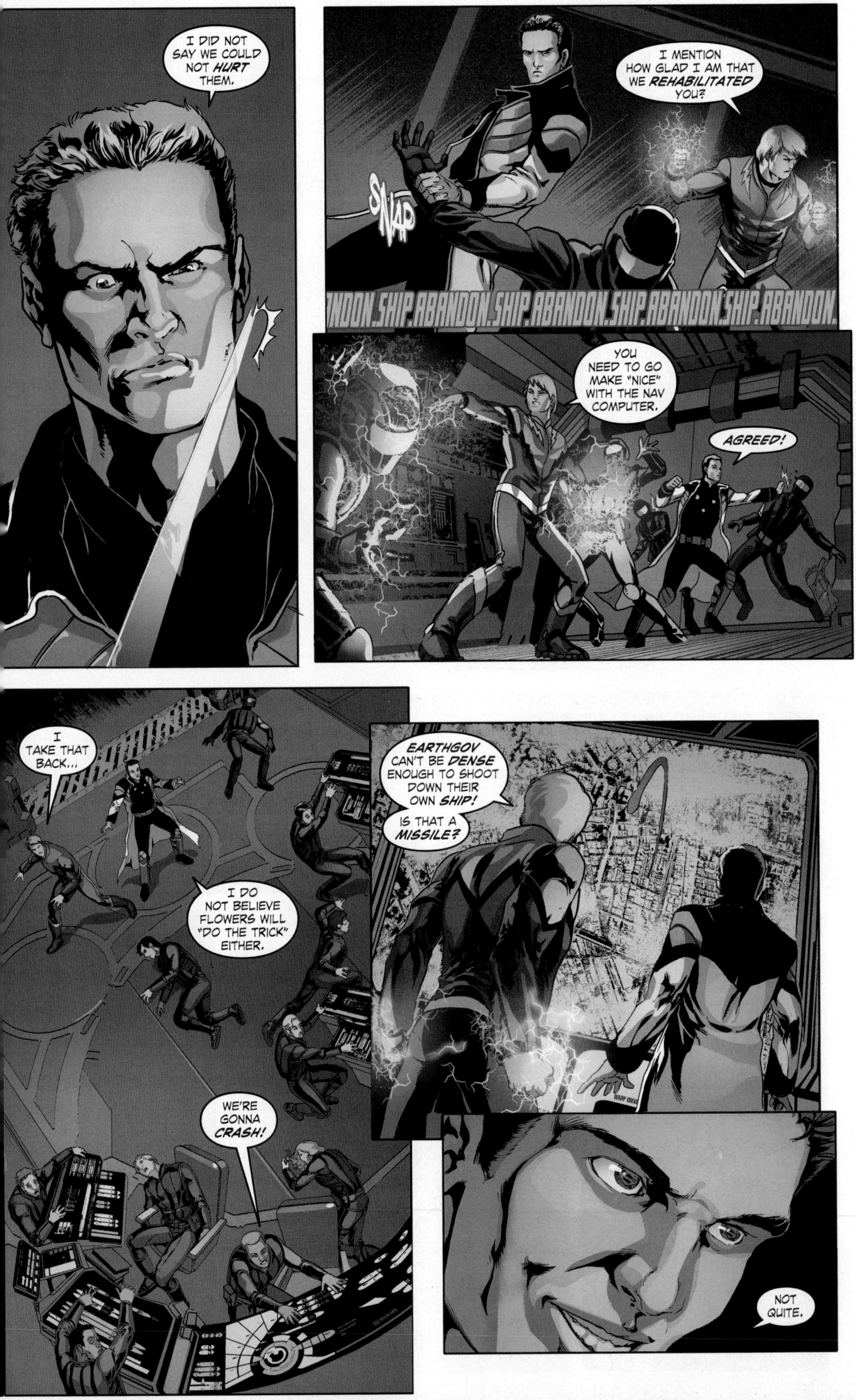
I DID NOT SAY WE COULD NOT *HURT* THEM.
I MENTION HOW GLAD I AM THAT WE *REHABILITATED* YOU?
SNAP
NDON.SHIP.ABANDON.SHIP.ABANDON.SHIP.ABANDON.SHIP.ABANDON.
YOU NEED TO GO MAKE "NICE" WITH THE NAV COMPUTER.
AGREED!
I TAKE THAT BACK...
I DO NOT BELIEVE FLOWERS WILL "DO THE TRICK" EITHER.
WE'RE GONNA *CRASH!*
EARTHGOV CAN'T BE *DENSE* ENOUGH TO SHOOT DOWN THEIR OWN *SHIP!*
IS THAT A *MISSILE?*
WARP DRIVE
NOT QUITE.

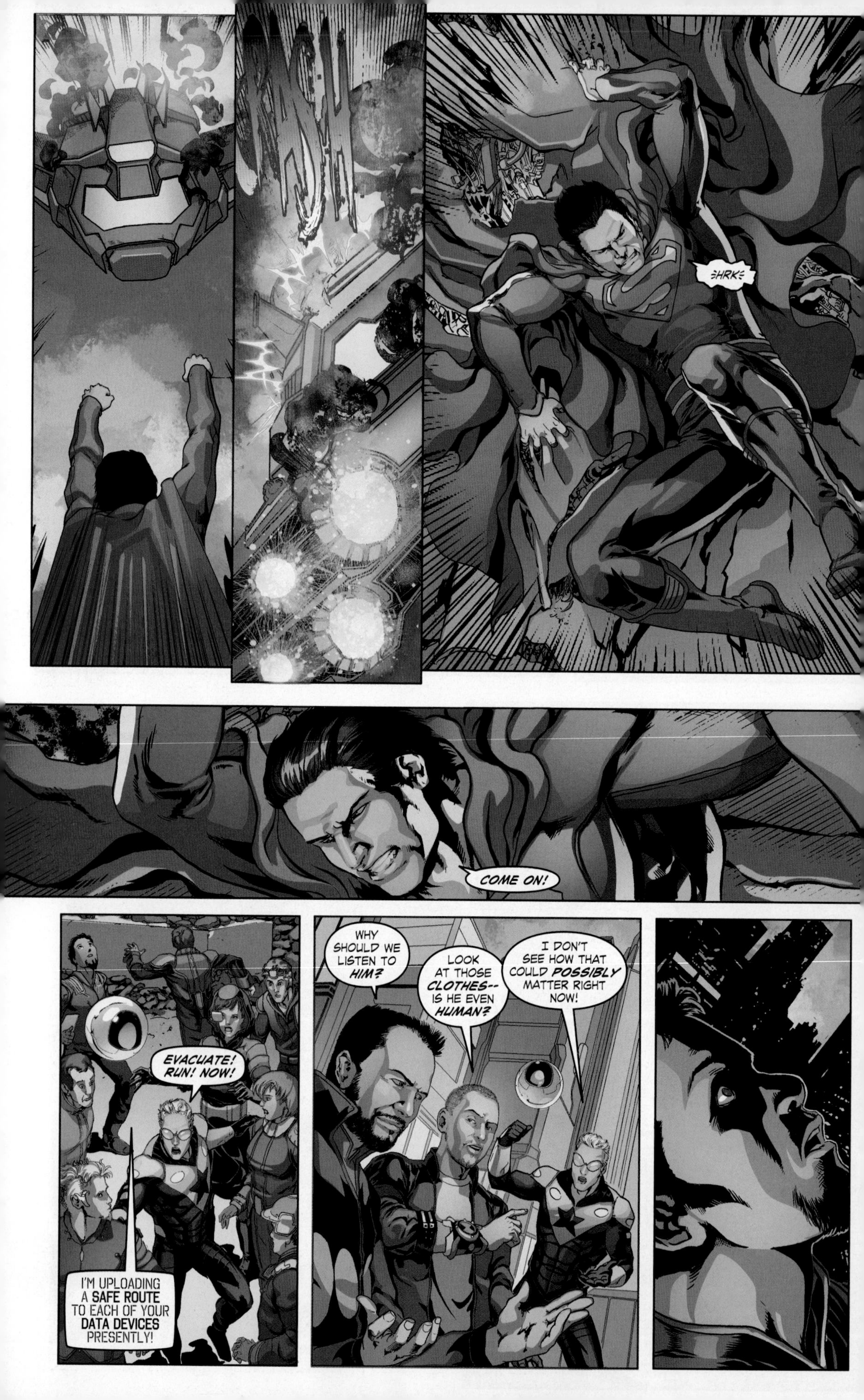
CRASH
HRK
COME ON!
EVACUATE! RUN! NOW!
I'M UPLOADING A SAFE ROUTE TO EACH OF YOUR DATA DEVICES PRESENTLY!
WHY SHOULD WE LISTEN TO HIM?
LOOK AT THOSE CLOTHES-- IS HE EVEN HUMAN?
I DON'T SEE HOW THAT COULD POSSIBLY MATTER RIGHT NOW!

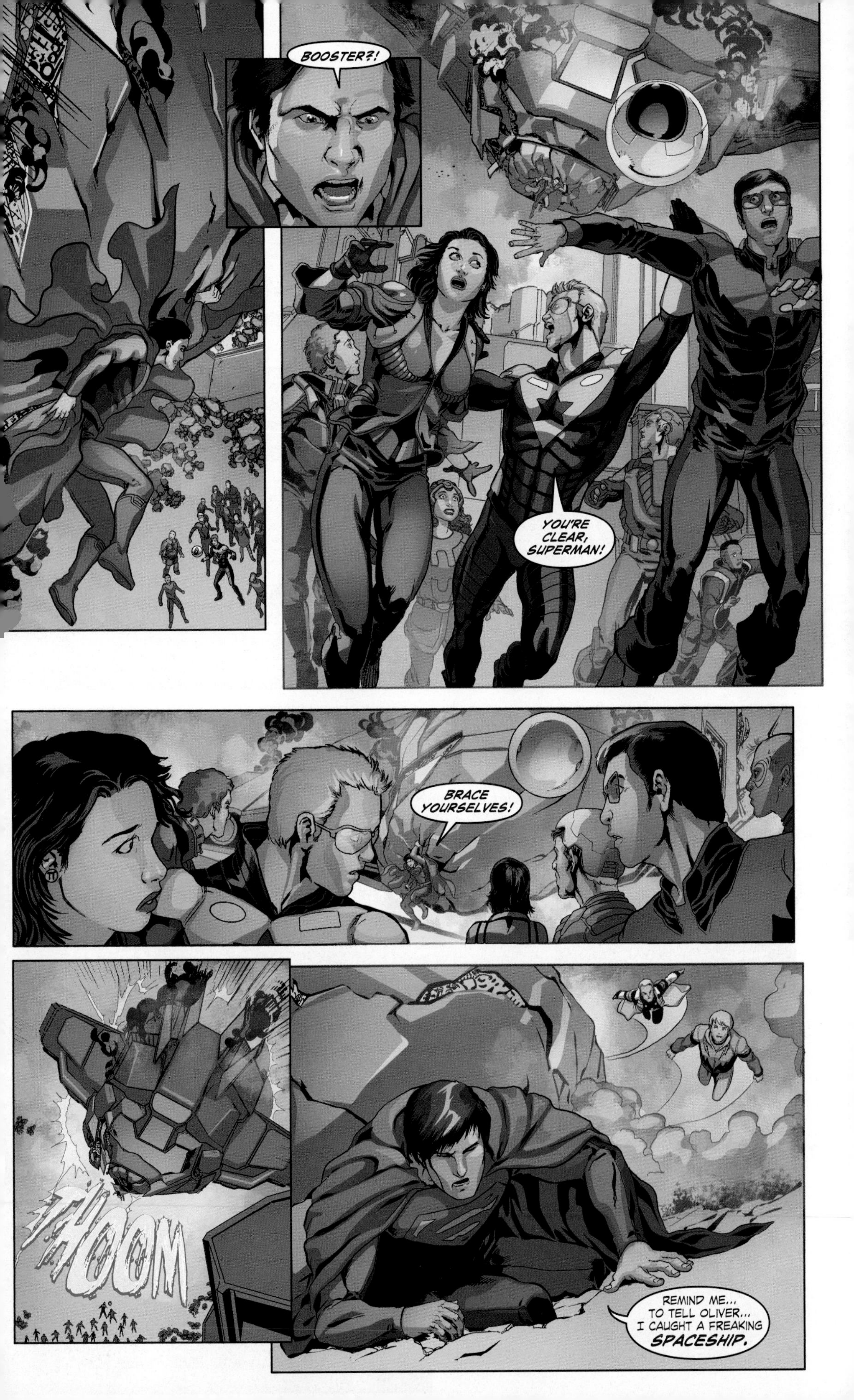
BOOSTER?!
YOU'RE CLEAR, SUPERMAN!
BRACE YOURSELVES!
THOOM
REMIND ME... TO TELL OLIVER... I CAUGHT A FREAKING SPACESHIP.

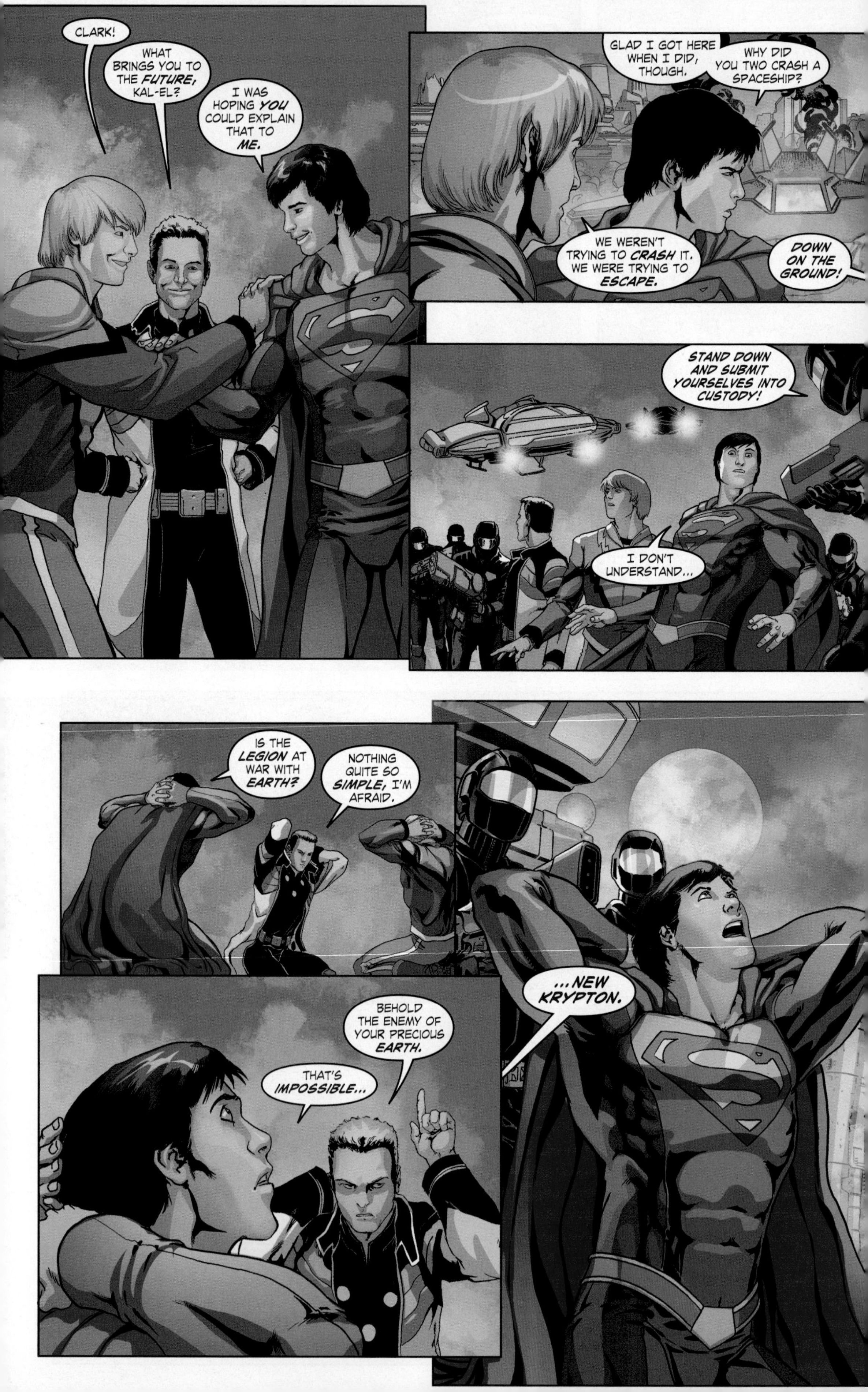
CLARK!
WHAT BRINGS YOU TO THE FUTURE, KAL-EL?
I WAS HOPING YOU COULD EXPLAIN THAT TO ME.
GLAD I GOT HERE WHEN I DID, THOUGH.
WHY DID YOU TWO CRASH A SPACESHIP?
WE WEREN'T TRYING TO CRASH IT. WE WERE TRYING TO ESCAPE.
DOWN ON THE GROUND!
STAND DOWN AND SUBMIT YOURSELVES INTO CUSTODY!
I DON'T UNDERSTAND...
IS THE LEGION AT WAR WITH EARTH?
NOTHING QUITE SO SIMPLE, I'M AFRAID.
BEHOLD THE ENEMY OF YOUR PRECIOUS EARTH.
THAT'S IMPOSSIBLE...
...NEW KRYPTON.

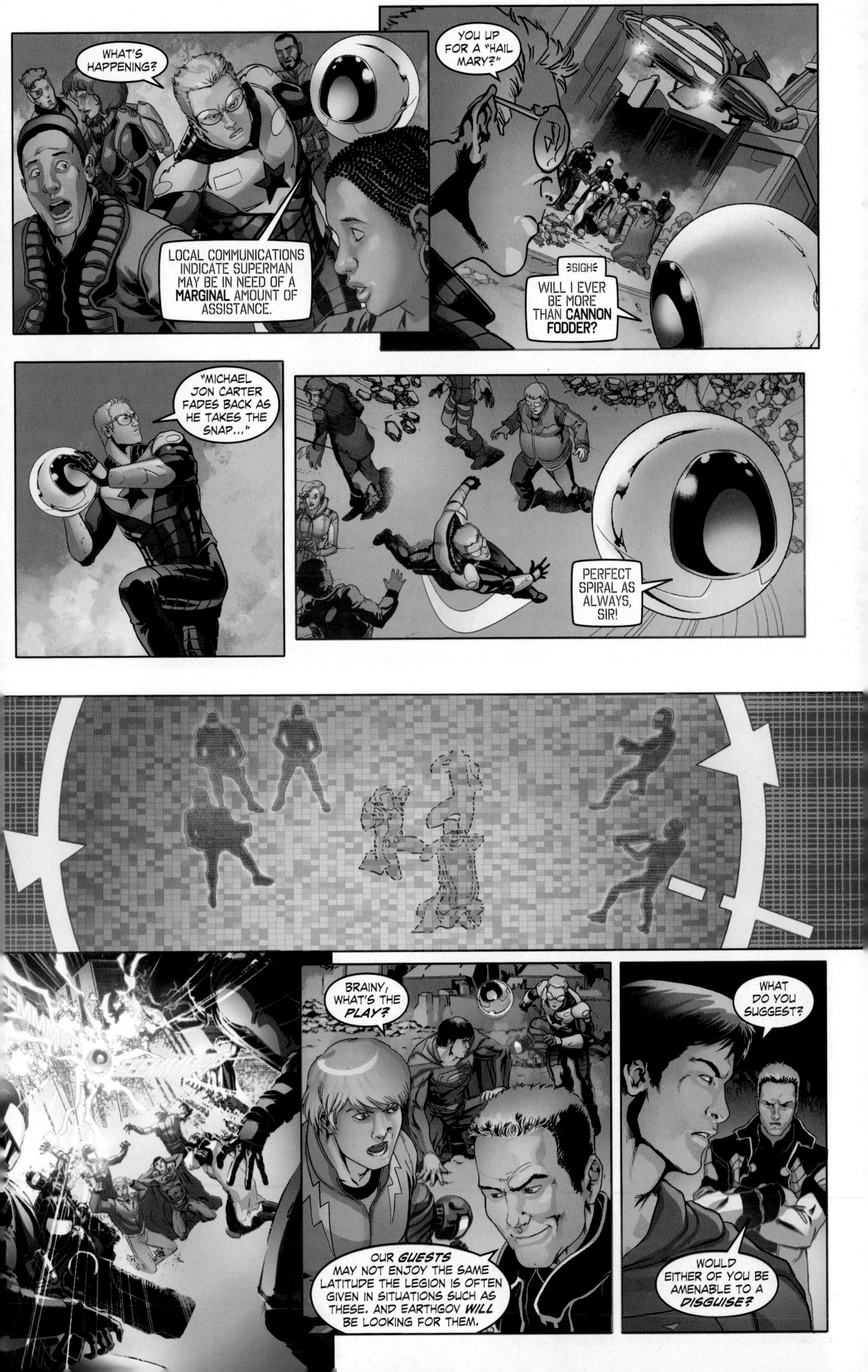
WHAT'S HAPPENING?
LOCAL COMMUNICATIONS INDICATE SUPERMAN MAY BE IN NEED OF A **MARGINAL** AMOUNT OF ASSISTANCE.
YOU UP FOR A "HAIL MARY?"
SIGH
WILL I EVER BE MORE THAN **CANNON FODDER?**
"MICHAEL JON CARTER FADES BACK AS HE TAKES THE SNAP..."
PERFECT SPIRAL AS ALWAYS, SIR!
BRAINY, WHAT'S THE ***PLAY?***
OUR ***GUESTS*** MAY NOT ENJOY THE SAME LATITUDE THE LEGION IS OFTEN GIVEN IN SITUATIONS SUCH AS THESE. AND EARTHGOV ***WILL*** BE LOOKING FOR THEM.
WHAT DO YOU SUGGEST?
WOULD EITHER OF YOU BE AMENABLE TO A ***DISGUISE?***

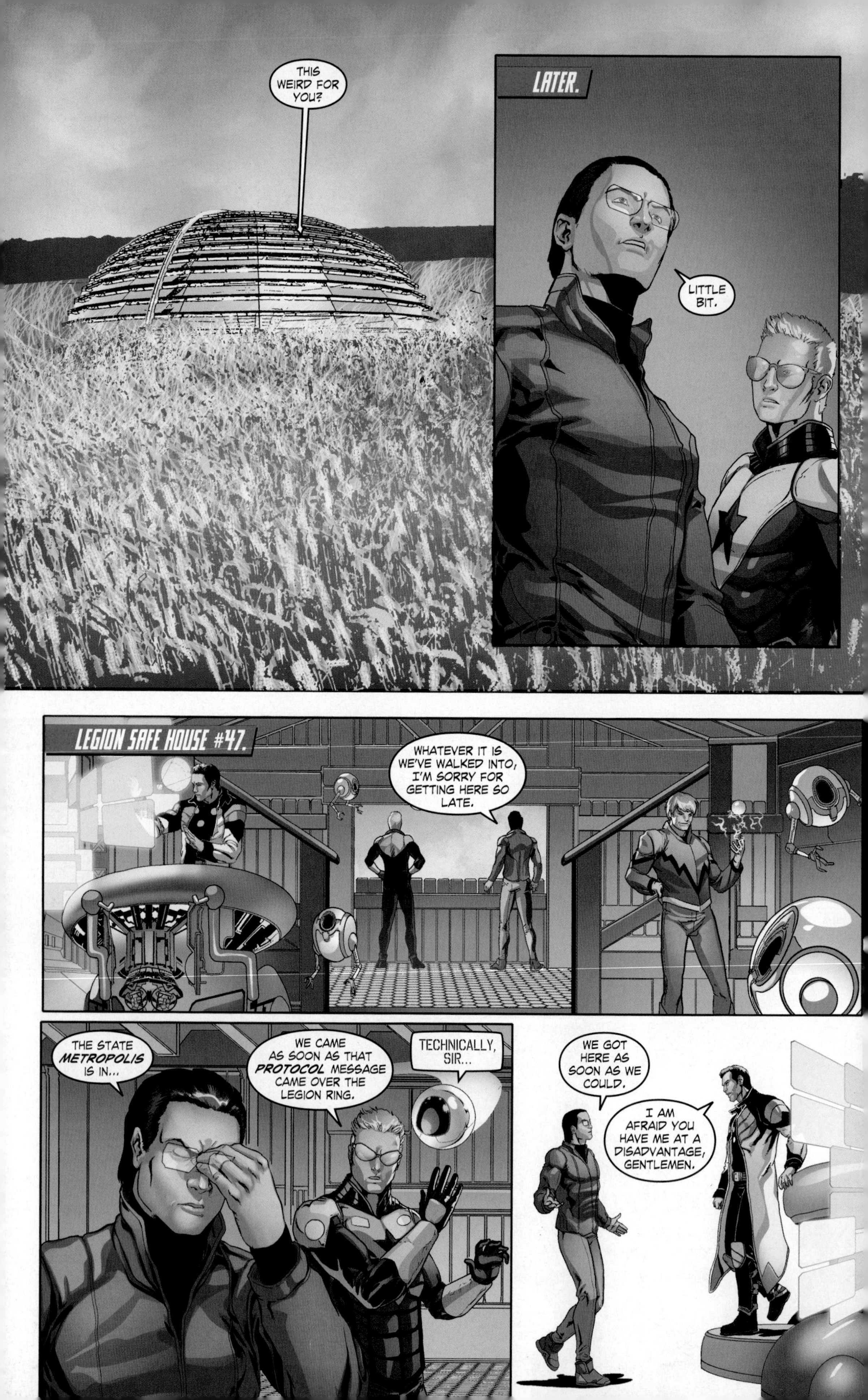
THIS WEIRD FOR YOU?
LATER.
LITTLE BIT.
LEGION SAFE HOUSE #47.
WHATEVER IT IS WE'VE WALKED INTO, I'M SORRY FOR GETTING HERE SO LATE.
THE STATE *METROPOLIS* IS IN...
WE CAME AS SOON AS THAT *PROTOCOL* MESSAGE CAME OVER THE LEGION RING.
TECHNICALLY, SIR...
WE GOT HERE AS SOON AS WE COULD.
I AM AFRAID YOU HAVE ME AT A DISADVANTAGE, GENTLEMEN.

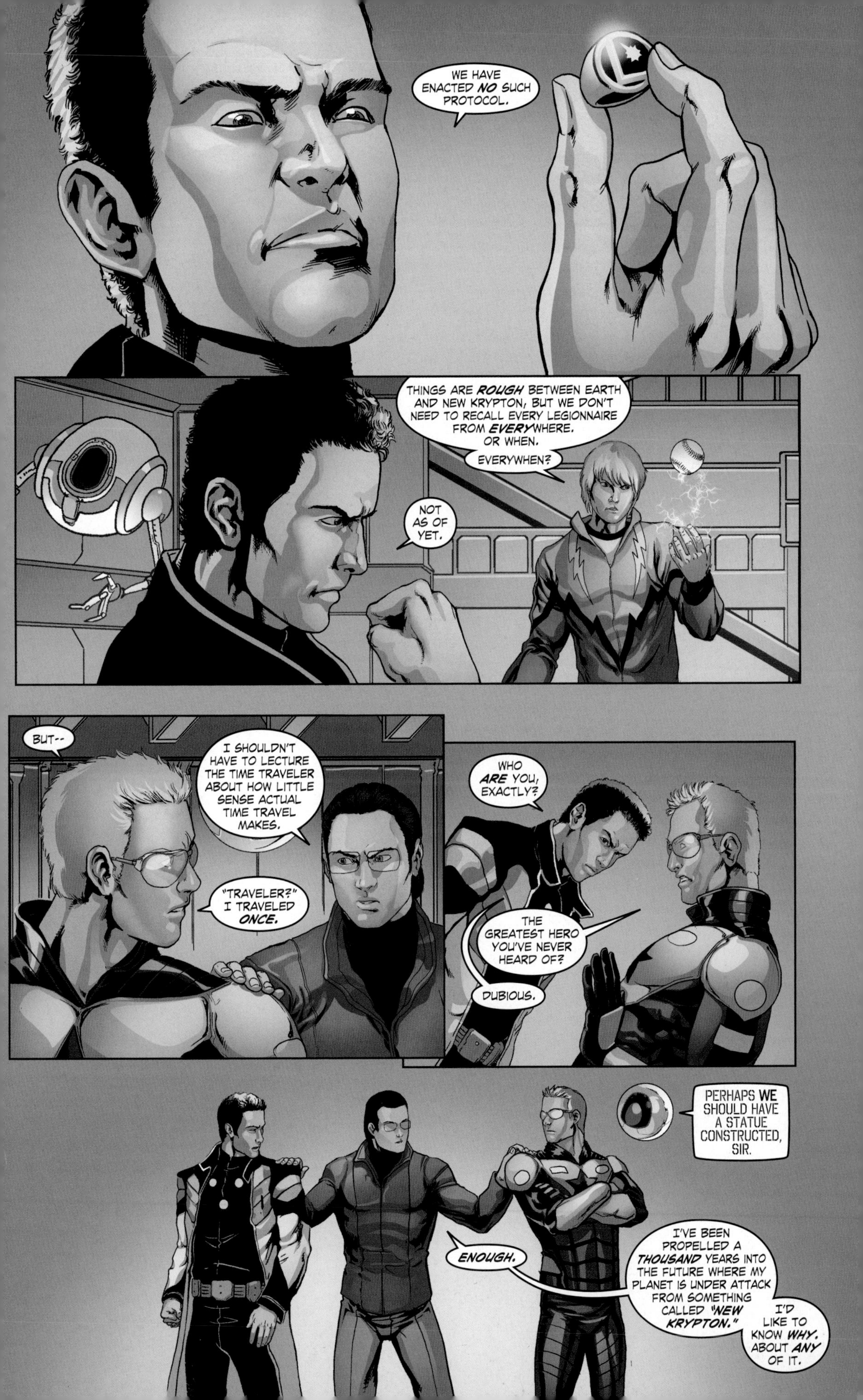
WE HAVE ENACTED NO SUCH PROTOCOL.
THINGS ARE ROUGH BETWEEN EARTH AND NEW KRYPTON, BUT WE DON'T NEED TO RECALL EVERY LEGIONNAIRE FROM EVERYWHERE. OR WHEN.
EVERYWHEN?
NOT AS OF YET.
BUT--
I SHOULDN'T HAVE TO LECTURE THE TIME TRAVELER ABOUT HOW LITTLE SENSE ACTUAL TIME TRAVEL MAKES.
"TRAVELER?" I TRAVELED ONCE.
WHO ARE YOU, EXACTLY?
THE GREATEST HERO YOU'VE NEVER HEARD OF?
DUBIOUS.
PERHAPS WE SHOULD HAVE A STATUE CONSTRUCTED, SIR.
ENOUGH.
I'VE BEEN PROPELLED A THOUSAND YEARS INTO THE FUTURE WHERE MY PLANET IS UNDER ATTACK FROM SOMETHING CALLED "NEW KRYPTON."
I'D LIKE TO KNOW WHY. ABOUT ANY OF IT.

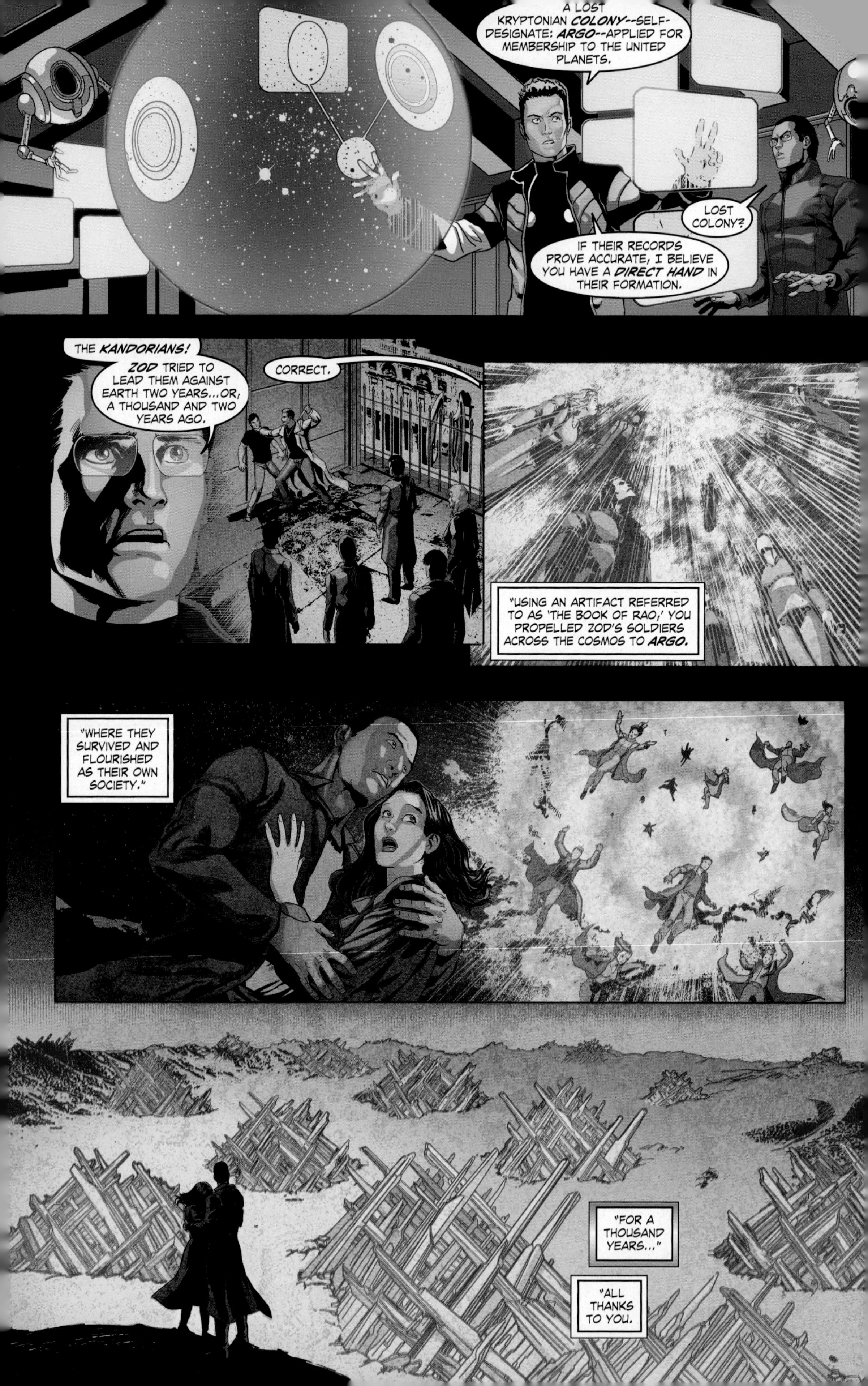
A LOST KRYPTONIAN COLONY--SELF-DESIGNATE: ARGO--APPLIED FOR MEMBERSHIP TO THE UNITED PLANETS.
LOST COLONY?
IF THEIR RECORDS PROVE ACCURATE, I BELIEVE YOU HAVE A DIRECT HAND IN THEIR FORMATION.
THE KANDORIANS!
ZOD TRIED TO LEAD THEM AGAINST EARTH TWO YEARS...OR, A THOUSAND AND TWO YEARS AGO.
CORRECT.
"USING AN ARTIFACT REFERRED TO AS 'THE BOOK OF RAO,' YOU PROPELLED ZOD'S SOLDIERS ACROSS THE COSMOS TO ARGO.
"WHERE THEY SURVIVED AND FLOURISHED AS THEIR OWN SOCIETY."
"FOR A THOUSAND YEARS..."
"ALL THANKS TO YOU.

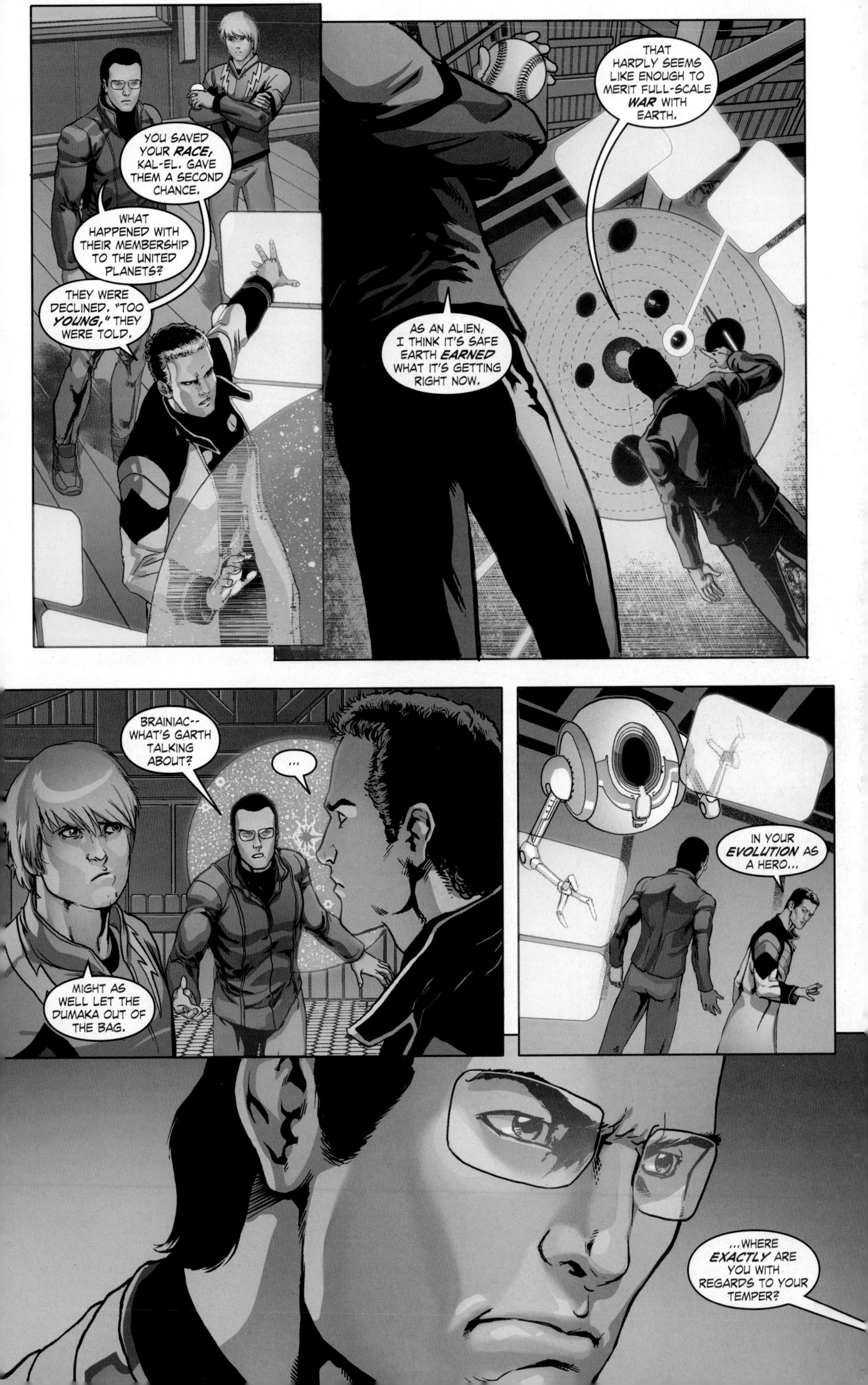
YOU SAVED YOUR RACE, KAL-EL. GAVE THEM A SECOND CHANCE.
WHAT HAPPENED WITH THEIR MEMBERSHIP TO THE UNITED PLANETS?
THEY WERE DECLINED. "TOO YOUNG," THEY WERE TOLD.
THAT HARDLY SEEMS LIKE ENOUGH TO MERIT FULL-SCALE WAR WITH EARTH.
AS AN ALIEN, I THINK IT'S SAFE EARTH EARNED WHAT IT'S GETTING RIGHT NOW.
BRAINIAC-- WHAT'S GARTH TALKING ABOUT?
...
MIGHT AS WELL LET THE DUMAKA OUT OF THE BAG.
IN YOUR EVOLUTION AS A HERO...
...WHERE EXACTLY ARE YOU WITH REGARDS TO YOUR TEMPER?

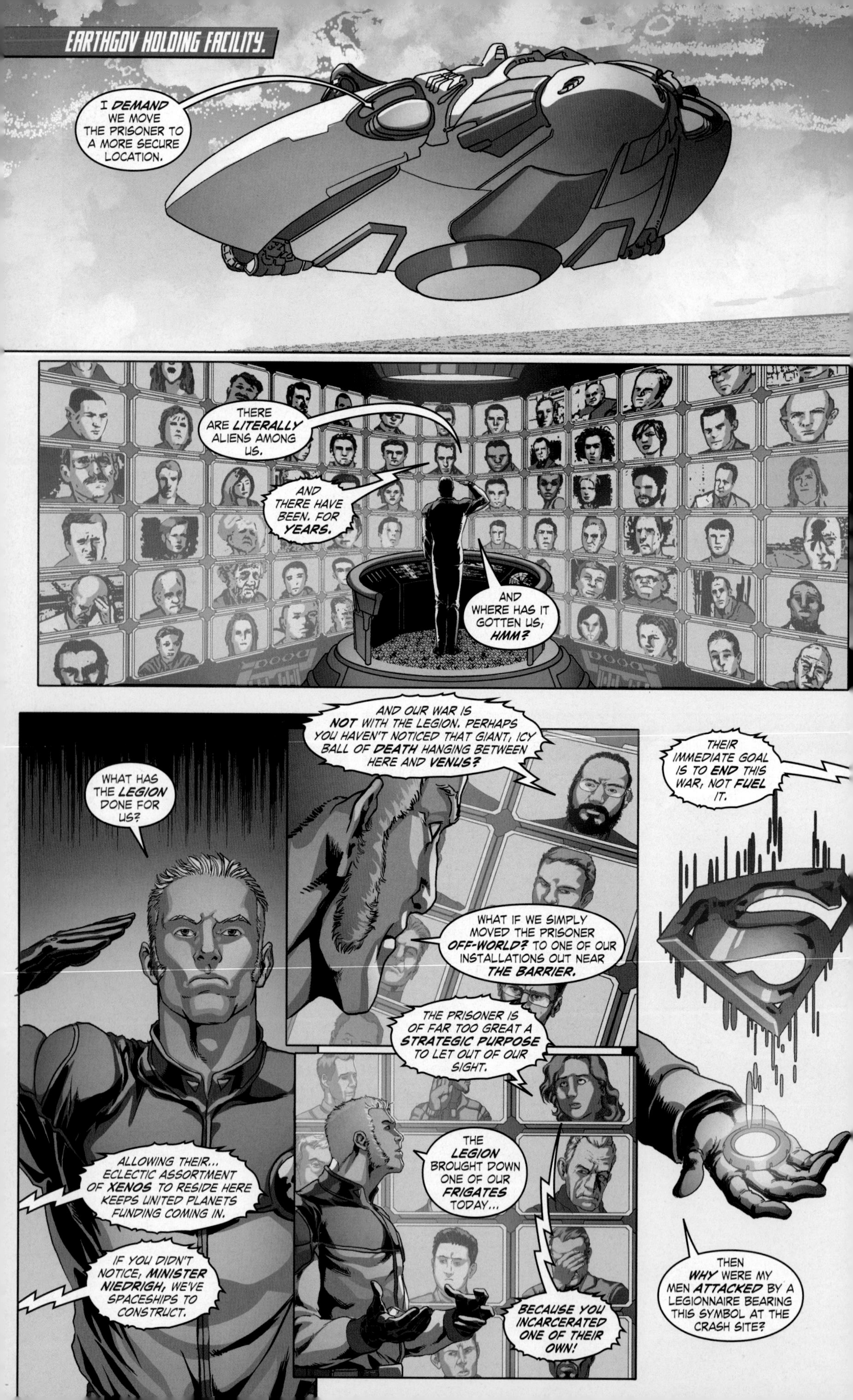
EARTHGOV HOLDING FACILITY.
I DEMAND WE MOVE THE PRISONER TO A MORE SECURE LOCATION.
THERE ARE LITERALLY ALIENS AMONG US.
AND THERE HAVE BEEN. FOR YEARS.
AND WHERE HAS IT GOTTEN US, HMM?
WHAT HAS THE LEGION DONE FOR US?
AND OUR WAR IS NOT WITH THE LEGION. PERHAPS YOU HAVEN'T NOTICED THAT GIANT, ICY BALL OF DEATH HANGING BETWEEN HERE AND VENUS?
THEIR IMMEDIATE GOAL IS TO END THIS WAR, NOT FUEL IT.
WHAT IF WE SIMPLY MOVED THE PRISONER OFF-WORLD? TO ONE OF OUR INSTALLATIONS OUT NEAR THE BARRIER.
THE PRISONER IS OF FAR TOO GREAT A STRATEGIC PURPOSE TO LET OUT OF OUR SIGHT.
ALLOWING THEIR... ECLECTIC ASSORTMENT OF XENOS TO RESIDE HERE KEEPS UNITED PLANETS FUNDING COMING IN.
IF YOU DIDN'T NOTICE, MINISTER NIEDRIGH, WE'VE SPACESHIPS TO CONSTRUCT.
THE LEGION BROUGHT DOWN ONE OF OUR FRIGATES TODAY...
BECAUSE YOU INCARCERATED ONE OF THEIR OWN!
THEN WHY WERE MY MEN ATTACKED BY A LEGIONNAIRE BEARING THIS SYMBOL AT THE CRASH SITE?

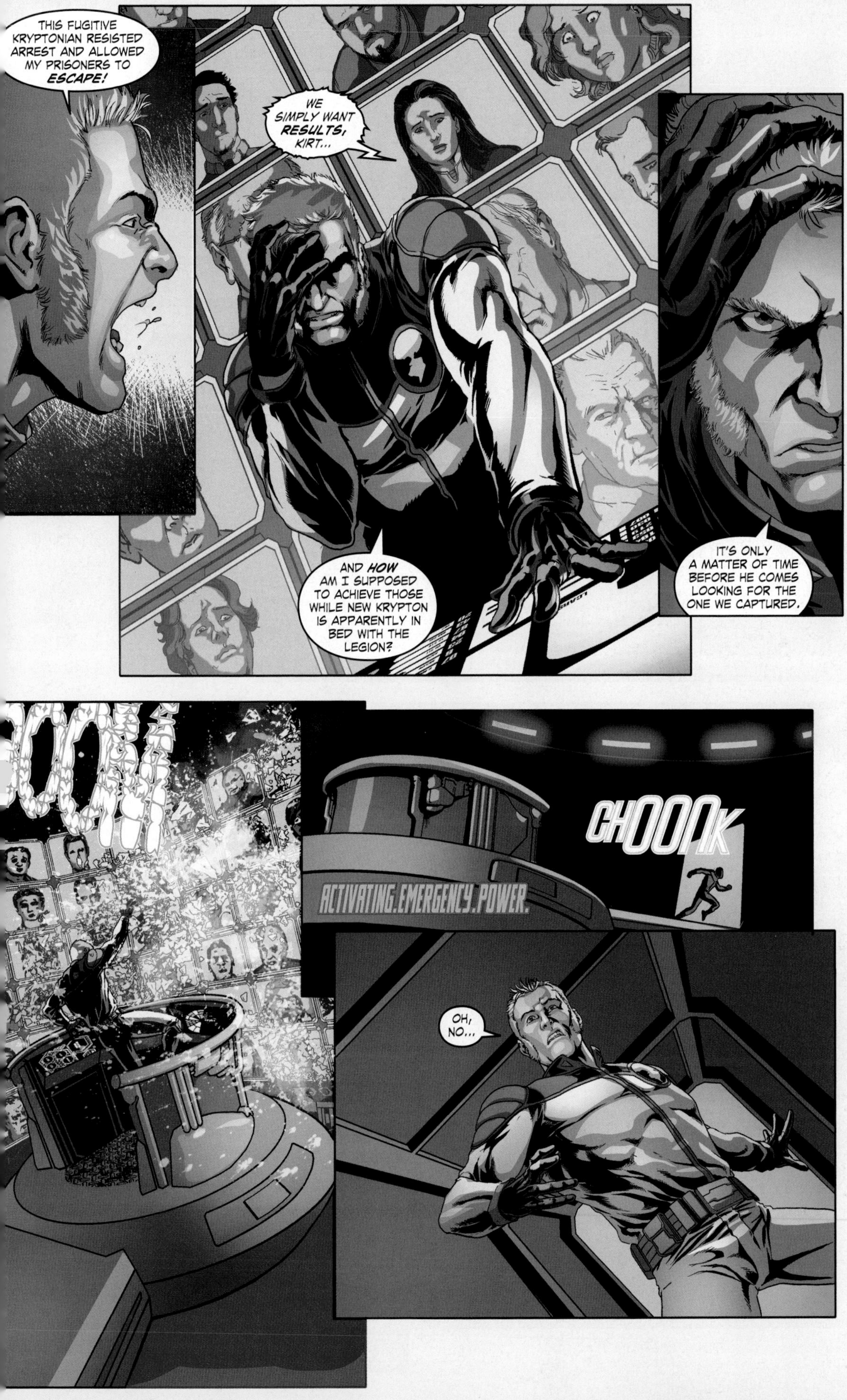
THIS FUGITIVE KRYPTONIAN RESISTED ARREST AND ALLOWED MY PRISONERS TO *ESCAPE!*
WE SIMPLY WANT *RESULTS,* KIRT...
AND *HOW* AM I SUPPOSED TO ACHIEVE THOSE WHILE NEW KRYPTON IS APPARENTLY IN BED WITH THE LEGION?
IT'S ONLY A MATTER OF TIME BEFORE HE COMES LOOKING FOR THE ONE WE CAPTURED.
CHOONK
ACTIVATING.EMERGENCY.POWER.
OH, NO...

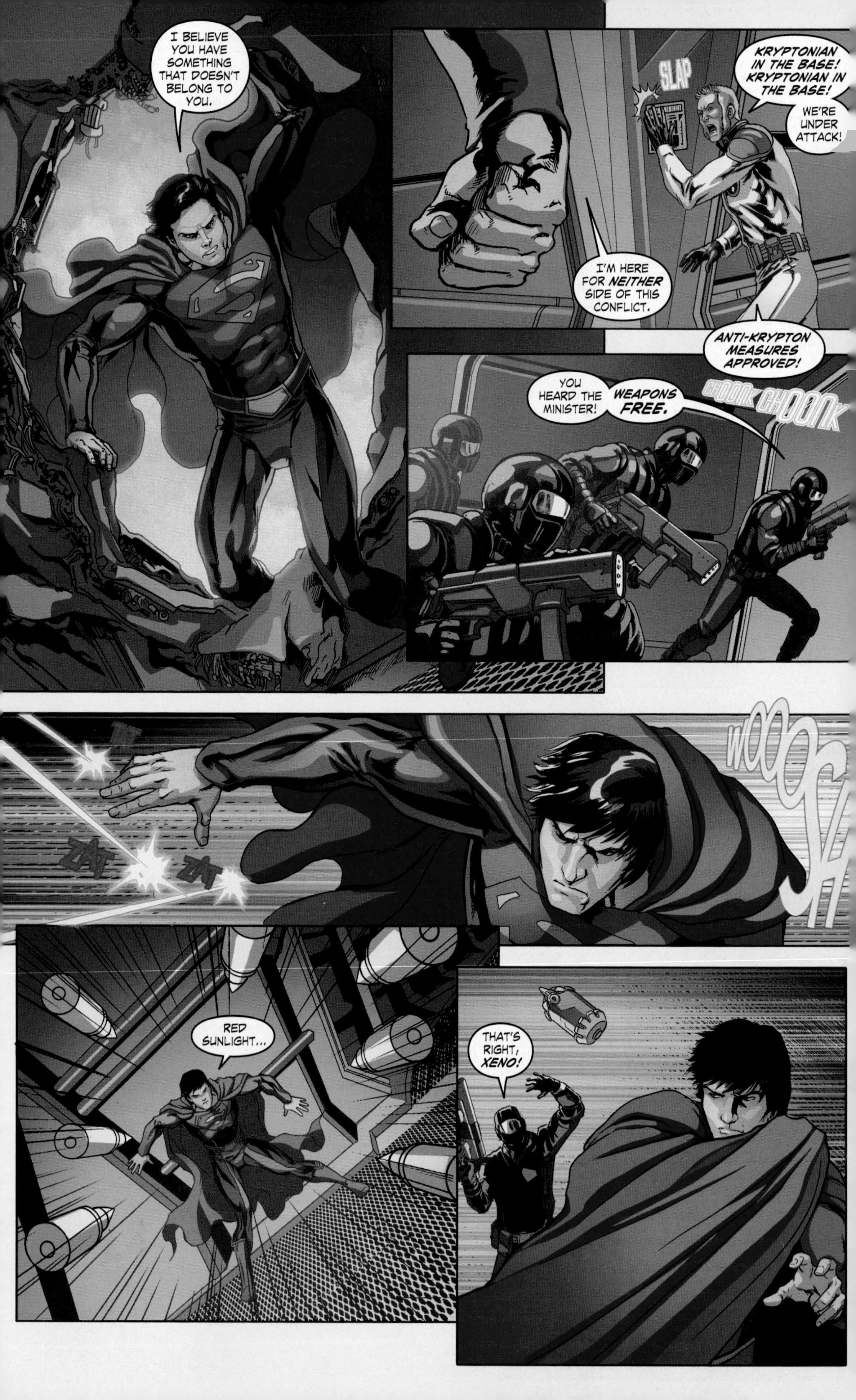
I BELIEVE YOU HAVE SOMETHING THAT DOESN'T BELONG TO YOU.
SLAP
KRYPTONIAN IN THE BASE! KRYPTONIAN IN THE BASE!
WE'RE UNDER ATTACK!
I'M HERE FOR NEITHER SIDE OF THIS CONFLICT.
ANTI-KRYPTON MEASURES APPROVED!
YOU HEARD THE MINISTER!
WEAPONS FREE.
CHOONK CHOONK
ZAT
ZAT
WOOOSH
RED SUNLIGHT...
THAT'S RIGHT, XENO!

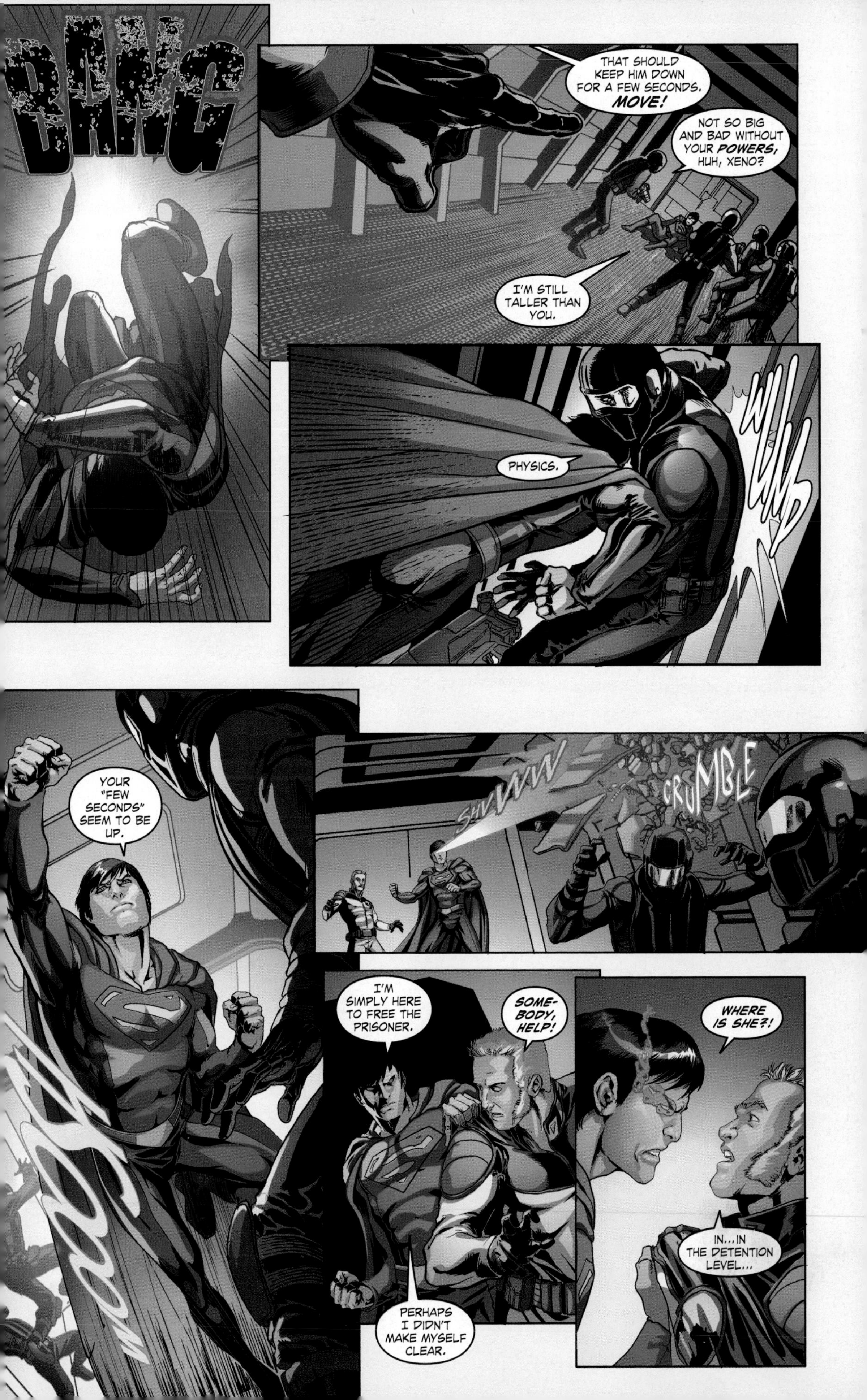
BANG
THAT SHOULD KEEP HIM DOWN FOR A FEW SECONDS. MOVE!
NOT SO BIG AND BAD WITHOUT YOUR POWERS, HUH, XENO?
I'M STILL TALLER THAN YOU.
PHYSICS.
WUMP
YOUR "FEW SECONDS" SEEM TO BE UP.
SHVVVVV
CRUMBLE
I'M SIMPLY HERE TO FREE THE PRISONER.
SOME-BODY, HELP!
PERHAPS I DIDN'T MAKE MYSELF CLEAR.
WHERE IS SHE?!
IN...IN THE DETENTION LEVEL...

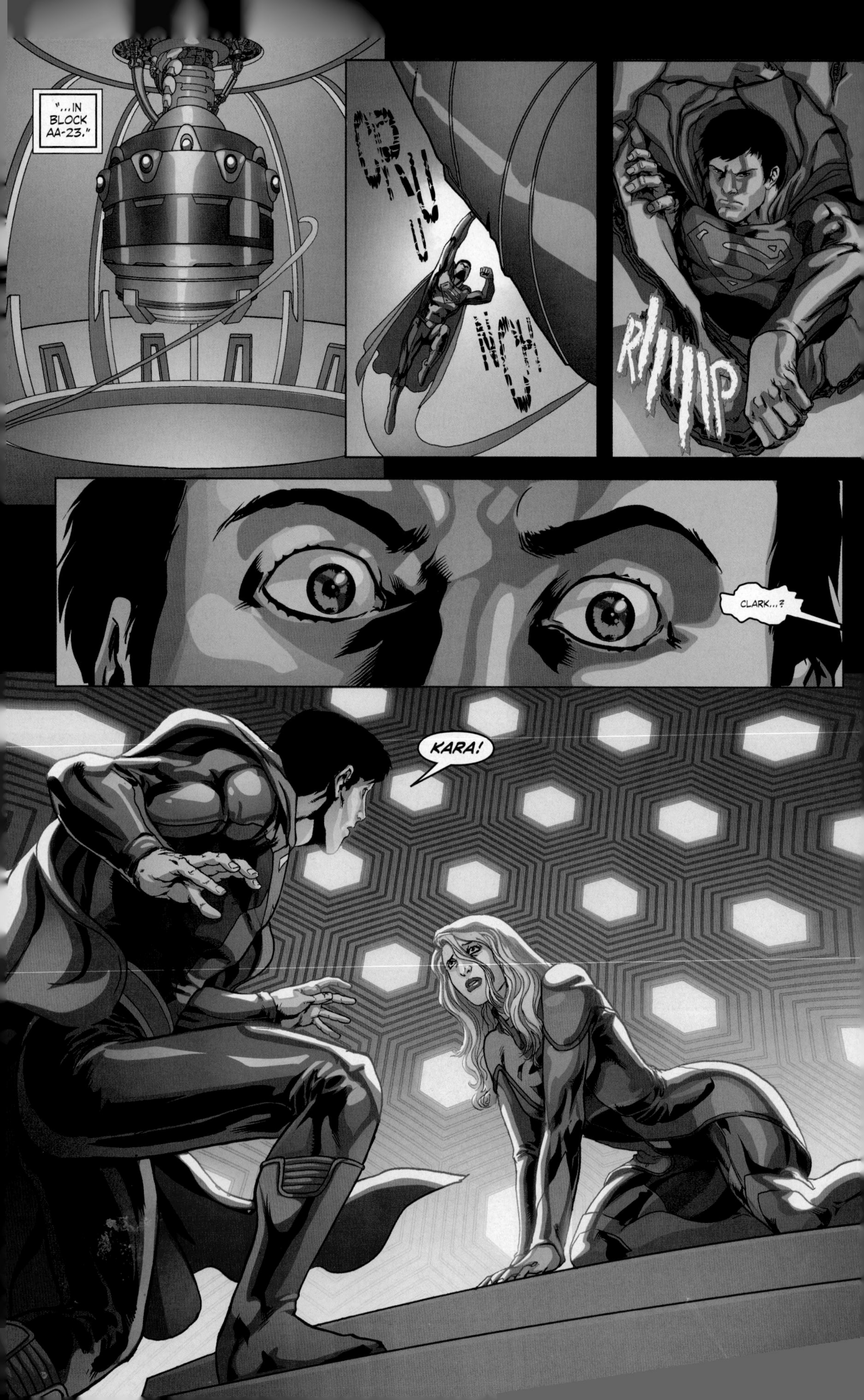
"...IN BLOCK AA-23."
CRUNCH
RIIIIP
CLARK...?
KARA!

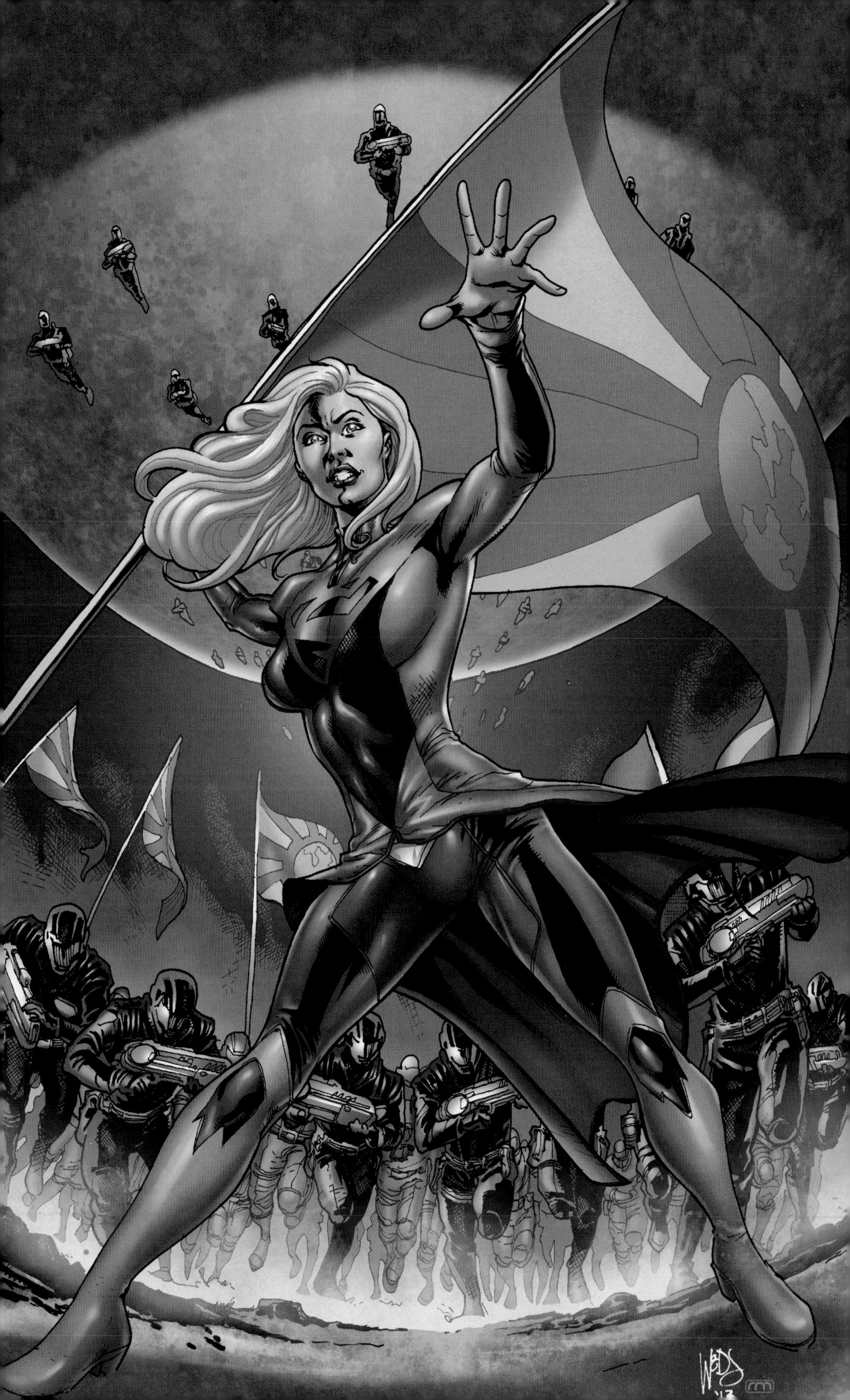

ARGO PART TWO
COVER BY PETE WOODS WITH RANDY MAYOR

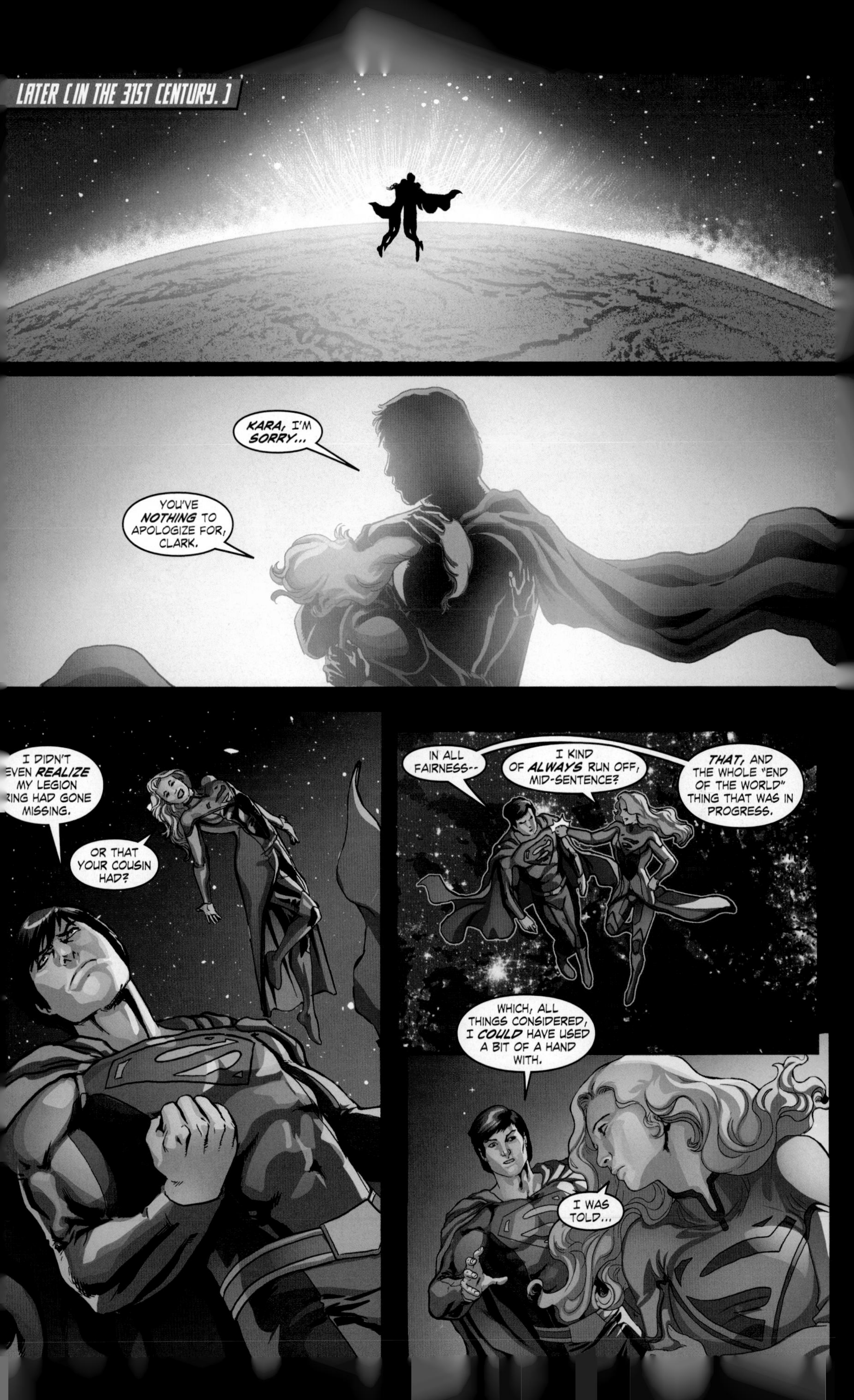
LATER (IN THE 31ST CENTURY.)
KARA, I'M SORRY...
YOU'VE NOTHING TO APOLOGIZE FOR, CLARK.
I DIDN'T EVEN REALIZE MY LEGION RING HAD GONE MISSING.
OR THAT YOUR COUSIN HAD?
IN ALL FAIRNESS--
I KIND OF ALWAYS RUN OFF, MID-SENTENCE?
THAT, AND THE WHOLE "END OF THE WORLD" THING THAT WAS IN PROGRESS.
WHICH, ALL THINGS CONSIDERED, I COULD HAVE USED A BIT OF A HAND WITH.
I WAS TOLD...

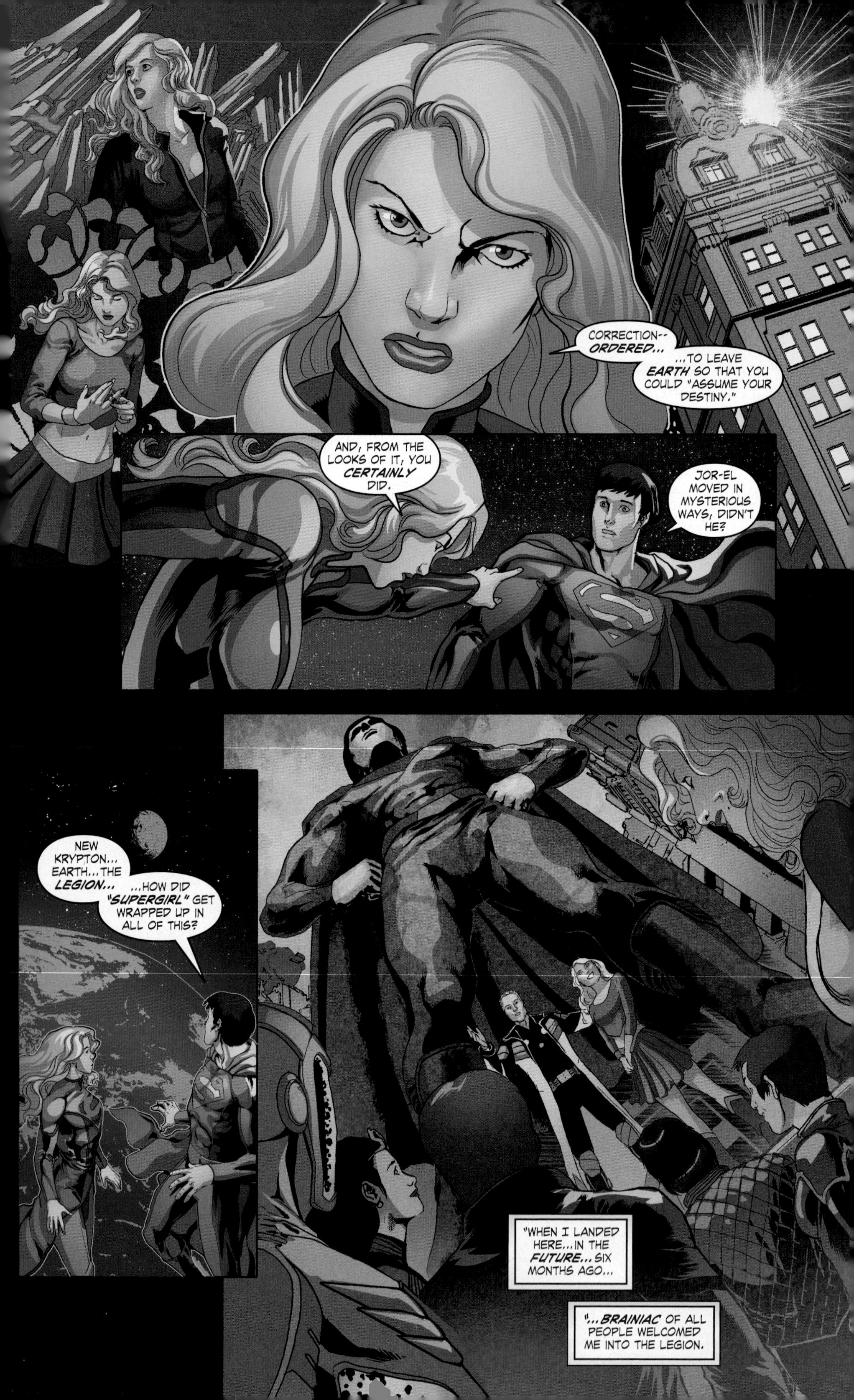
CORRECTION-- ORDERED...
...TO LEAVE EARTH SO THAT YOU COULD "ASSUME YOUR DESTINY."
AND, FROM THE LOOKS OF IT, YOU CERTAINLY DID.
JOR-EL MOVED IN MYSTERIOUS WAYS, DIDN'T HE?
NEW KRYPTON... EARTH... THE LEGION...
...HOW DID "SUPERGIRL" GET WRAPPED UP IN ALL OF THIS?
"WHEN I LANDED HERE... IN THE FUTURE... SIX MONTHS AGO...
"...BRAINIAC OF ALL PEOPLE WELCOMED ME INTO THE LEGION.

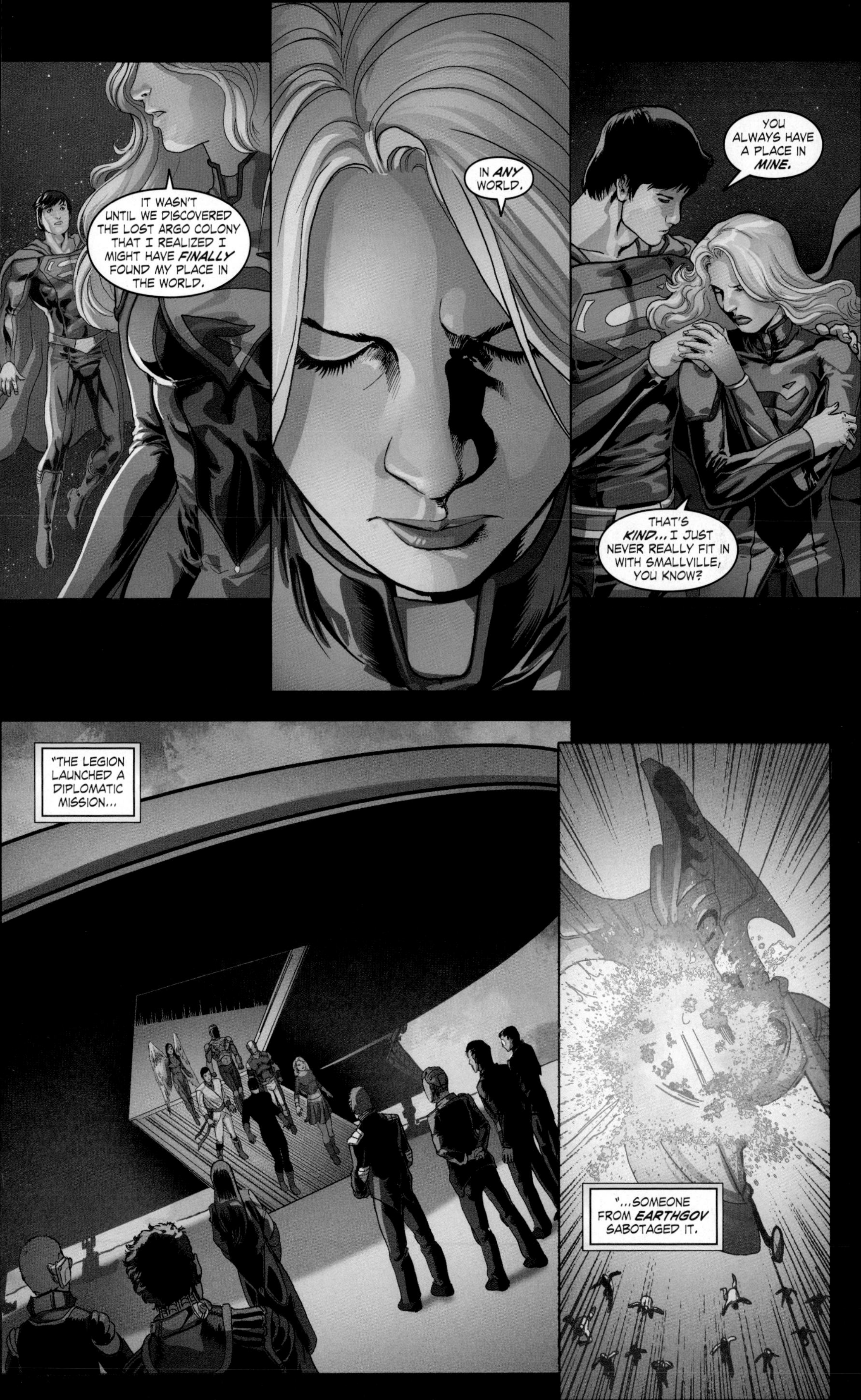
IT WASN'T UNTIL WE DISCOVERED THE LOST ARGO COLONY THAT I REALIZED I MIGHT HAVE *FINALLY* FOUND MY PLACE IN THE WORLD.
IN *ANY* WORLD.
YOU ALWAYS HAVE A PLACE IN *MINE.*
THAT'S *KIND...* I JUST NEVER REALLY FIT IN WITH SMALLVILLE, YOU KNOW?
"THE LEGION LAUNCHED A DIPLOMATIC MISSION...
"...SOMEONE FROM *EARTHGOV* SABOTAGED IT.

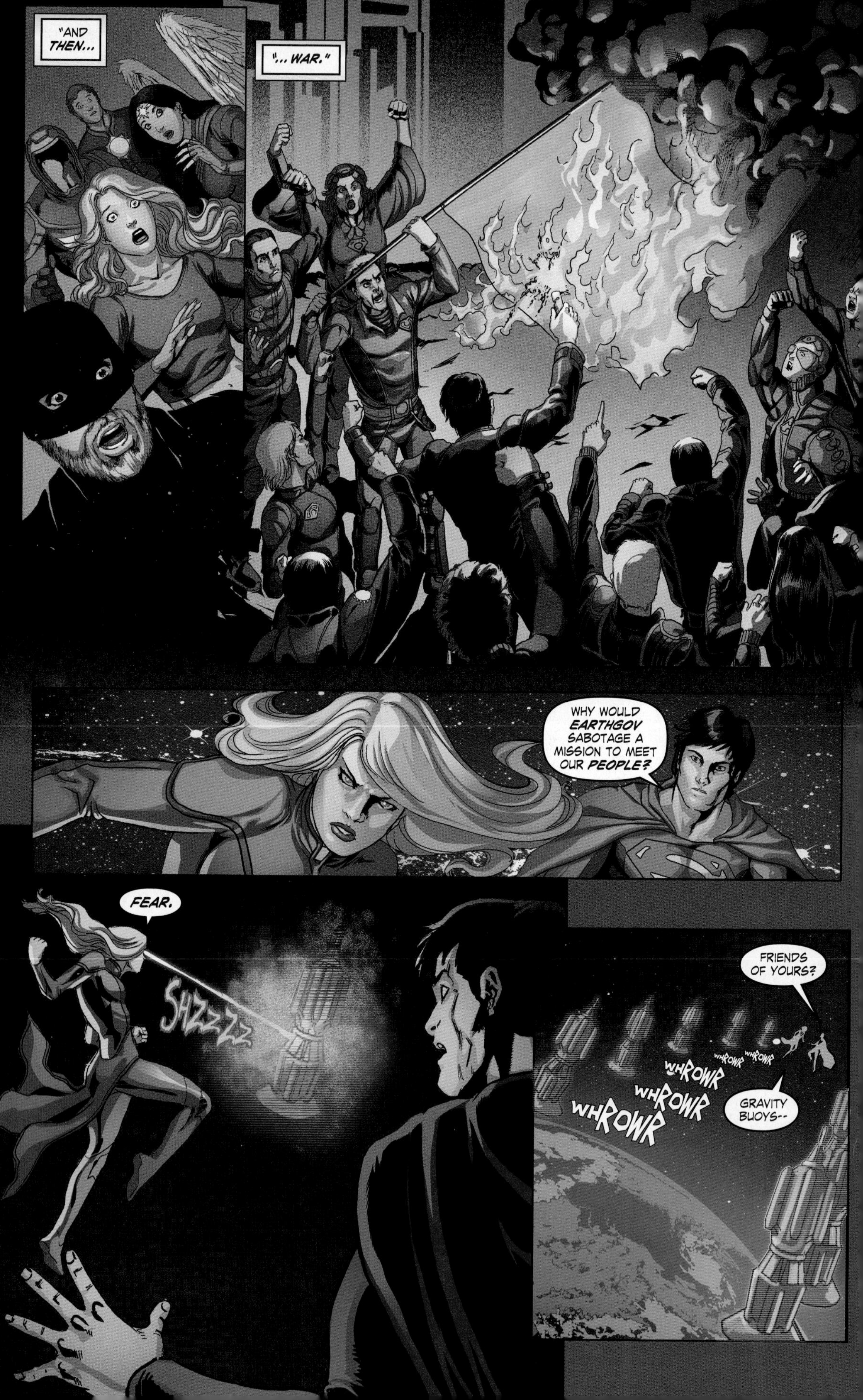
"AND THEN...
"... WAR."
WHY WOULD EARTHGOV SABOTAGE A MISSION TO MEET OUR PEOPLE?
FEAR.
SHZZZZ
FRIENDS OF YOURS?
WHROWR
WHROWR
WHROWR
WHROWR
WHROWR
GRAVITY BUOYS--

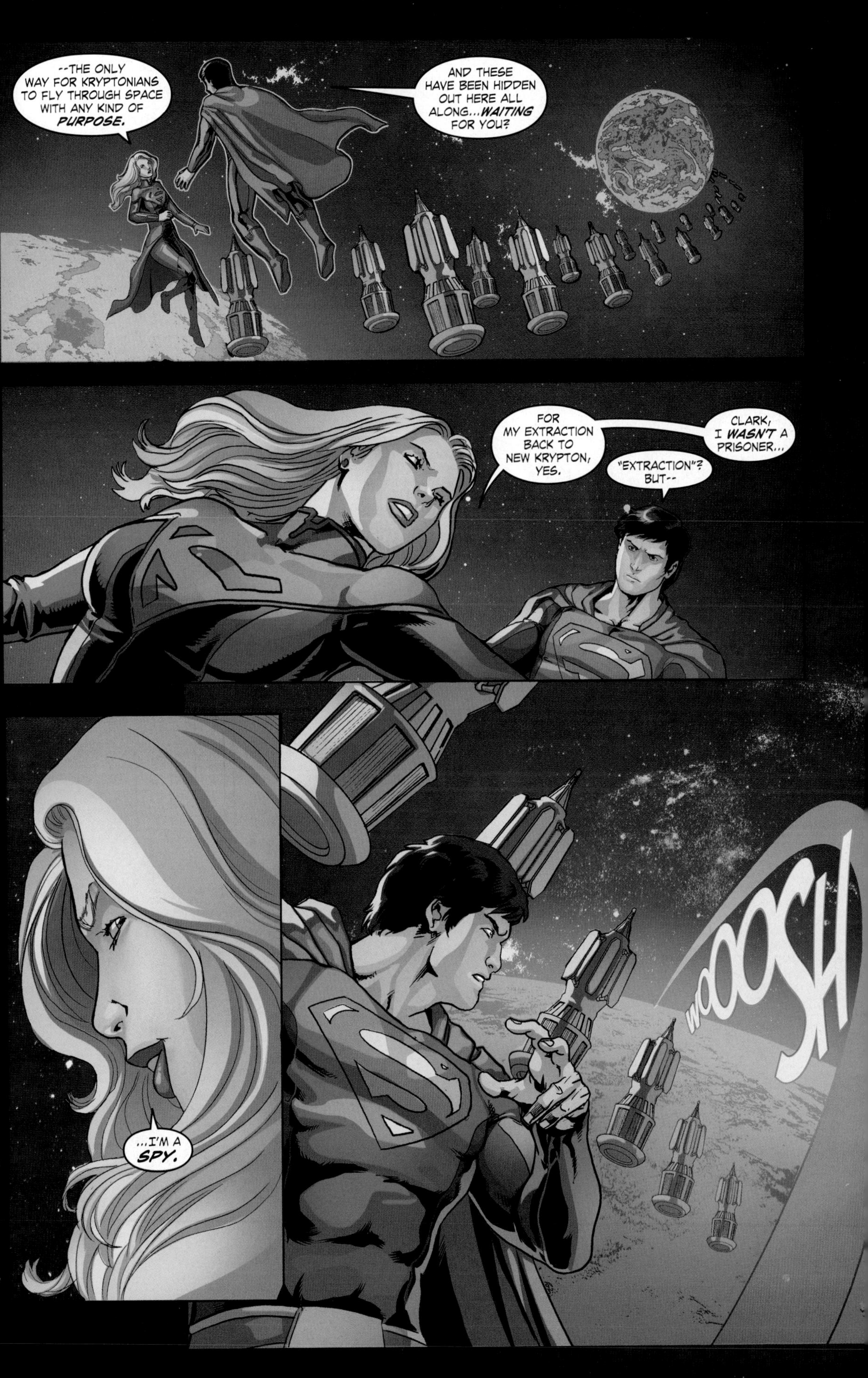

--THE ONLY WAY FOR KRYPTONIANS TO FLY THROUGH SPACE WITH ANY KIND OF PURPOSE.
AND THESE HAVE BEEN HIDDEN OUT HERE ALL ALONG...WAITING FOR YOU?
FOR MY EXTRACTION BACK TO NEW KRYPTON, YES.
"EXTRACTION"? BUT--
CLARK, I WASN'T A PRISONER...
...I'M A SPY.
WOOOSH

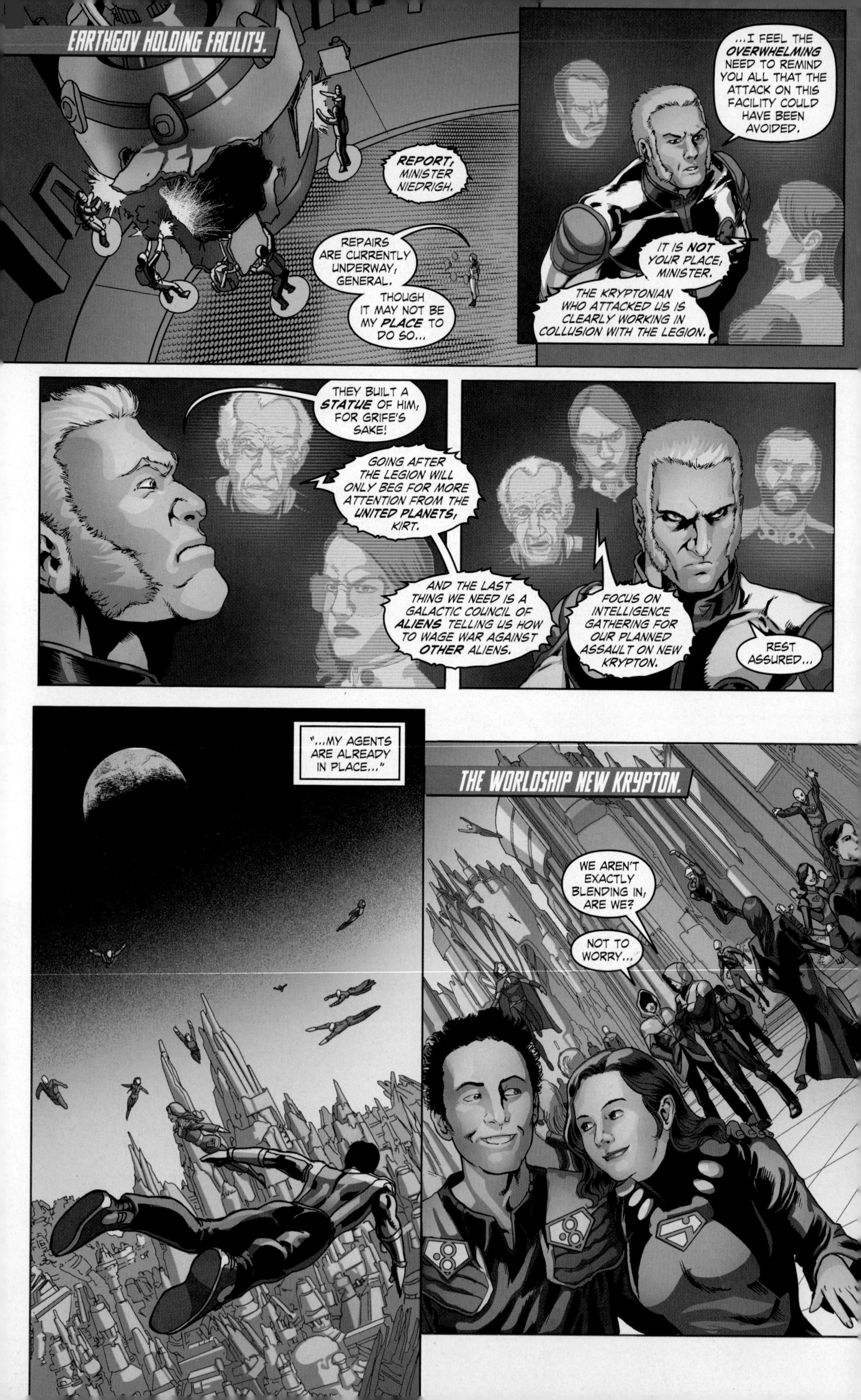
EARTHGOV HOLDING FACILITY.
REPORT, MINISTER NIEDRIGH.
REPAIRS ARE CURRENTLY UNDERWAY, GENERAL.
THOUGH IT MAY NOT BE MY PLACE TO DO SO...
...I FEEL THE OVERWHELMING NEED TO REMIND YOU ALL THAT THE ATTACK ON THIS FACILITY COULD HAVE BEEN AVOIDED.
IT IS NOT YOUR PLACE, MINISTER.
THE KRYPTONIAN WHO ATTACKED US IS CLEARLY WORKING IN COLLUSION WITH THE LEGION.
THEY BUILT A STATUE OF HIM, FOR GRIFE'S SAKE!
GOING AFTER THE LEGION WILL ONLY BEG FOR MORE ATTENTION FROM THE UNITED PLANETS, KIRT.
AND THE LAST THING WE NEED IS A GALACTIC COUNCIL OF ALIENS TELLING US HOW TO WAGE WAR AGAINST OTHER ALIENS.
FOCUS ON INTELLIGENCE GATHERING FOR OUR PLANNED ASSAULT ON NEW KRYPTON.
REST ASSURED...
"...MY AGENTS ARE ALREADY IN PLACE..."
THE WORLDSHIP NEW KRYPTON.
WE AREN'T EXACTLY BLENDING IN, ARE WE?
NOT TO WORRY...

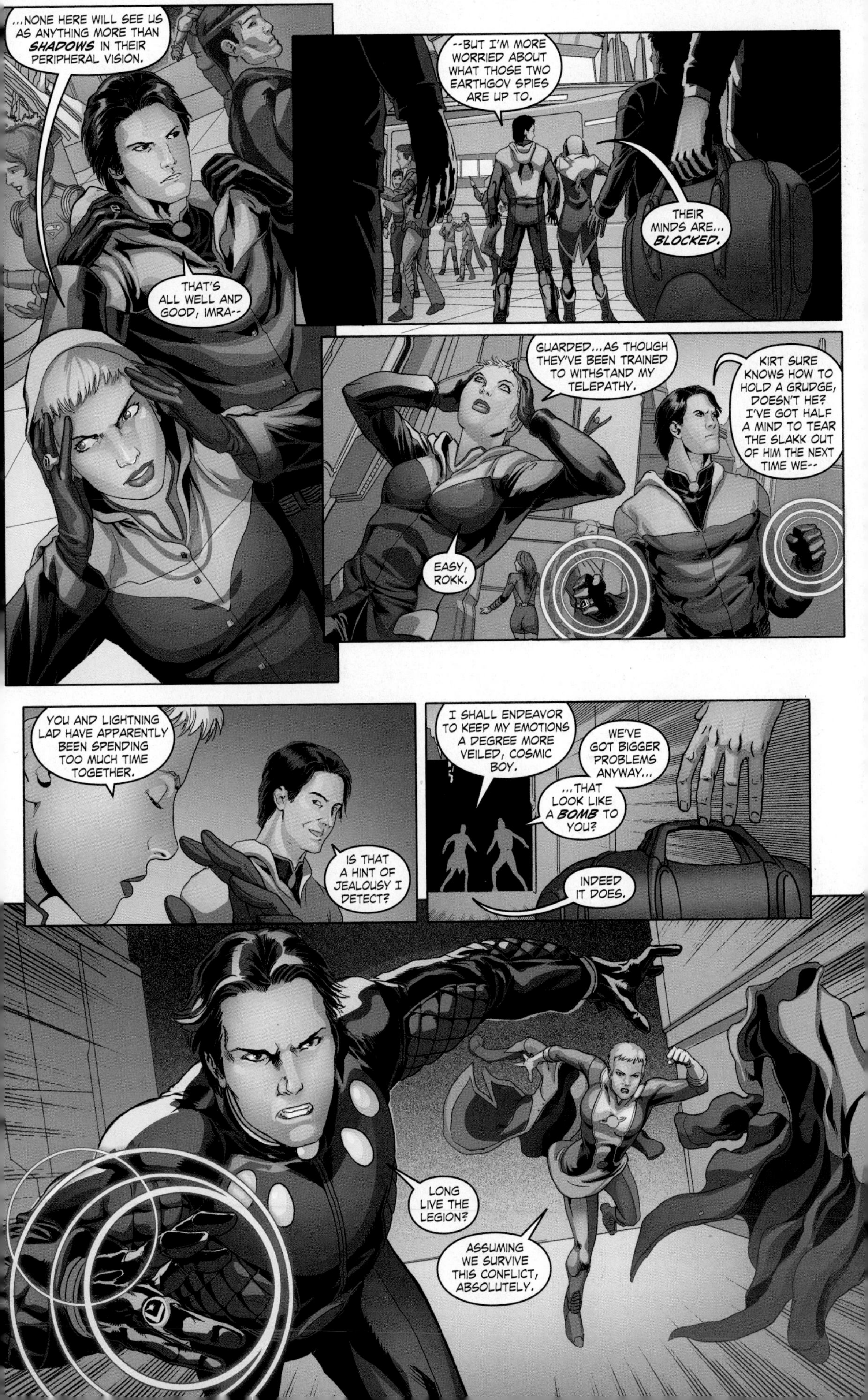

...NONE HERE WILL SEE US AS ANYTHING MORE THAN SHADOWS IN THEIR PERIPHERAL VISION.
THAT'S ALL WELL AND GOOD, IMRA--
--BUT I'M MORE WORRIED ABOUT WHAT THOSE TWO EARTHGOV SPIES ARE UP TO.
THEIR MINDS ARE... BLOCKED.
GUARDED...AS THOUGH THEY'VE BEEN TRAINED TO WITHSTAND MY TELEPATHY.
KIRT SURE KNOWS HOW TO HOLD A GRUDGE, DOESN'T HE? I'VE GOT HALF A MIND TO TEAR THE SLAKK OUT OF HIM THE NEXT TIME WE--
EASY, ROKK.
YOU AND LIGHTNING LAD HAVE APPARENTLY BEEN SPENDING TOO MUCH TIME TOGETHER.
IS THAT A HINT OF JEALOUSY I DETECT?
I SHALL ENDEAVOR TO KEEP MY EMOTIONS A DEGREE MORE VEILED, COSMIC BOY.
WE'VE GOT BIGGER PROBLEMS ANYWAY...
...THAT LOOK LIKE A BOMB TO YOU?
INDEED IT DOES.
LONG LIVE THE LEGION?
ASSUMING WE SURVIVE THIS CONFLICT, ABSOLUTELY.

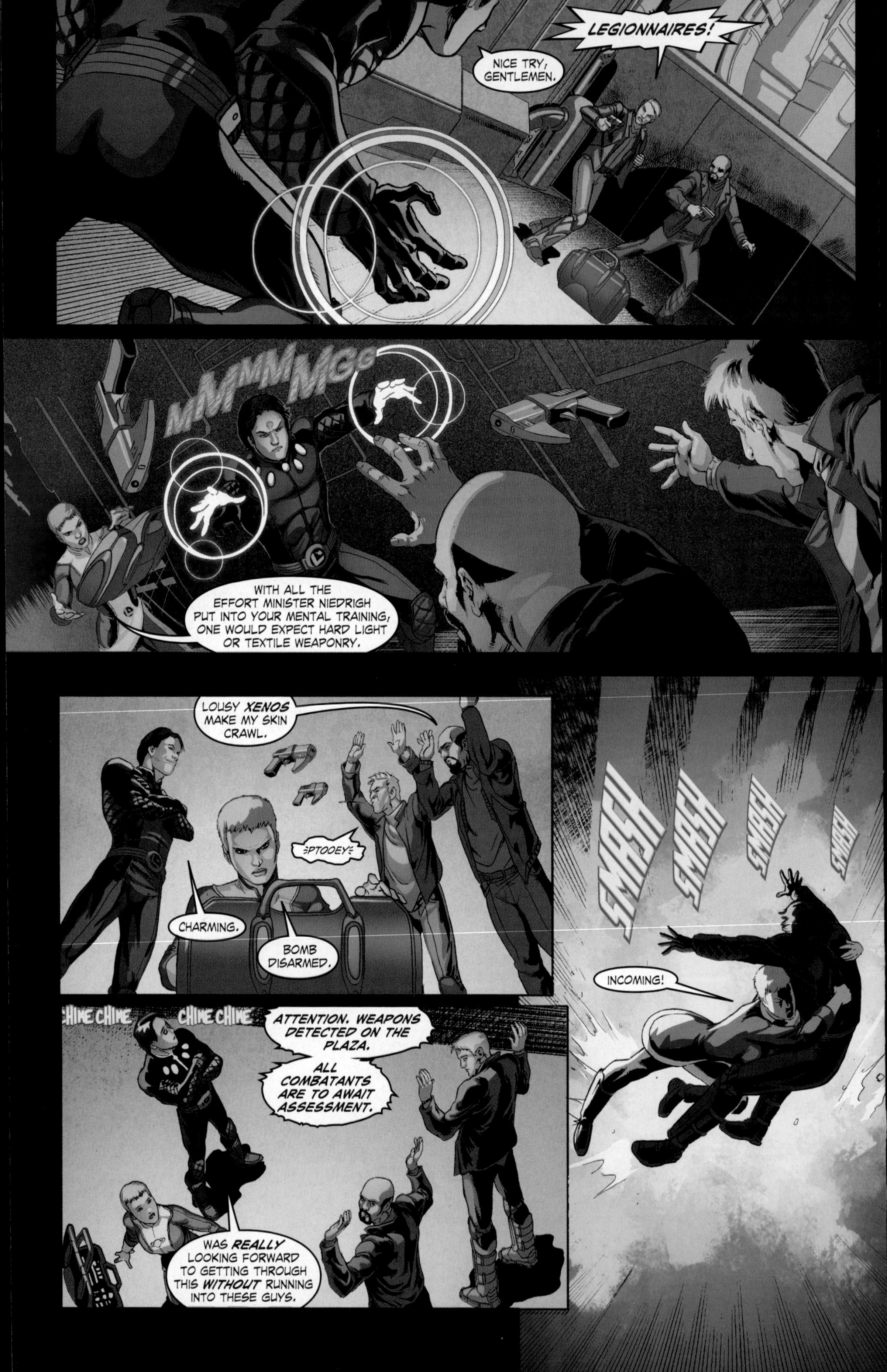
LEGIONNAIRES!
NICE TRY, GENTLEMEN.
MMMMMMG
WITH ALL THE EFFORT MINISTER NIEDRIGH PUT INTO YOUR MENTAL TRAINING, ONE WOULD EXPECT HARD LIGHT OR TEXTILE WEAPONRY.
LOUSY XENOS MAKE MY SKIN CRAWL.
PTOOEY
CHARMING.
BOMB DISARMED.
SMASH SMASH SMASH SMASH
INCOMING!
CHIME CHIME CHIME CHIME
ATTENTION. WEAPONS DETECTED ON THE PLAZA.
ALL COMBATANTS ARE TO AWAIT ASSESSMENT.
WAS REALLY LOOKING FORWARD TO GETTING THROUGH THIS WITHOUT RUNNING INTO THESE GUYS.

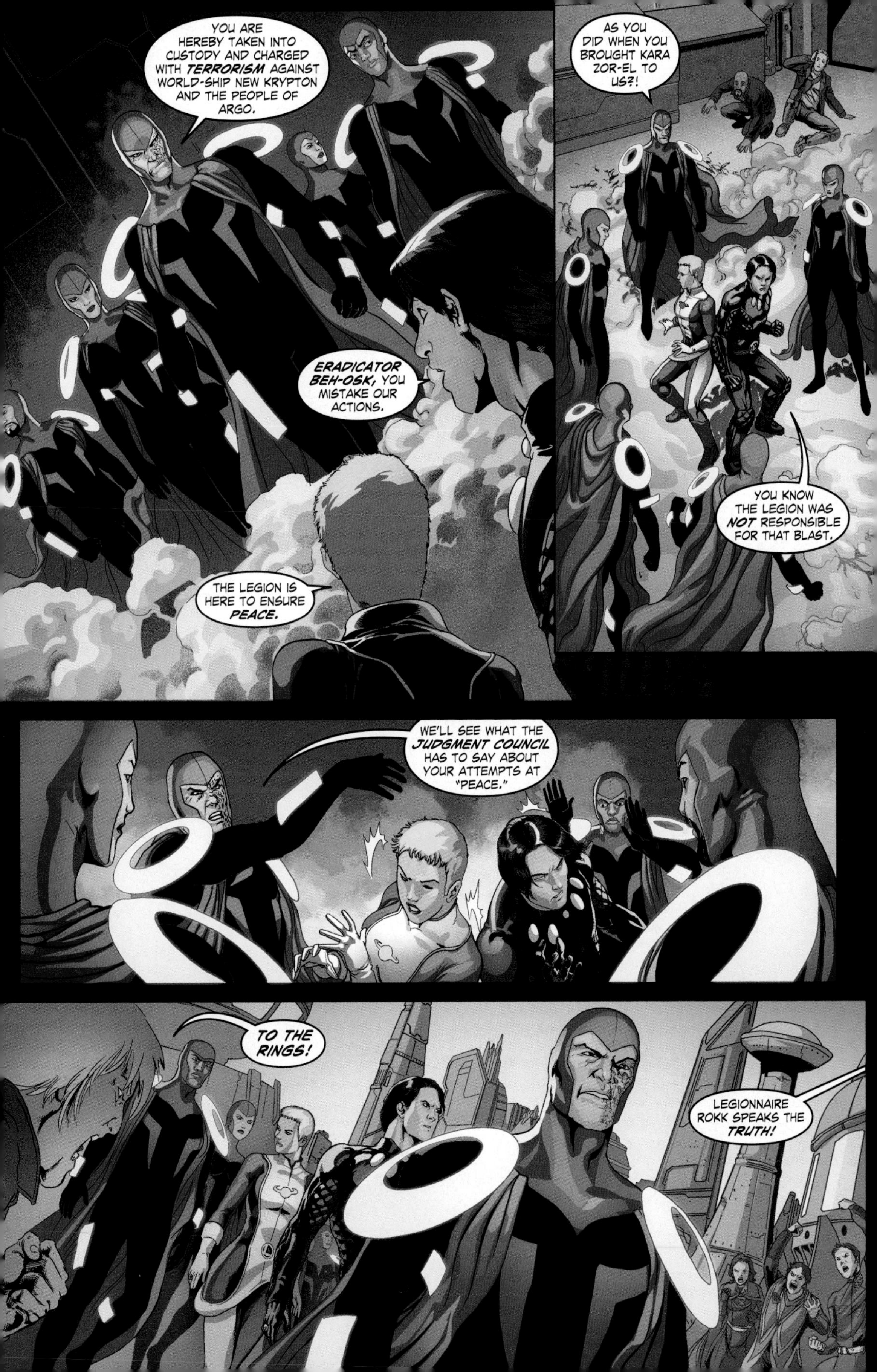
YOU ARE HEREBY TAKEN INTO CUSTODY AND CHARGED WITH TERRORISM AGAINST WORLD-SHIP NEW KRYPTON AND THE PEOPLE OF ARGO.
ERADICATOR BEH-OSK, YOU MISTAKE OUR ACTIONS.
THE LEGION IS HERE TO ENSURE PEACE.
AS YOU DID WHEN YOU BROUGHT KARA ZOR-EL TO US?!
YOU KNOW THE LEGION WAS NOT RESPONSIBLE FOR THAT BLAST.
WE'LL SEE WHAT THE JUDGMENT COUNCIL HAS TO SAY ABOUT YOUR ATTEMPTS AT "PEACE."
TO THE RINGS!
LEGIONNAIRE ROKK SPEAKS THE TRUTH!

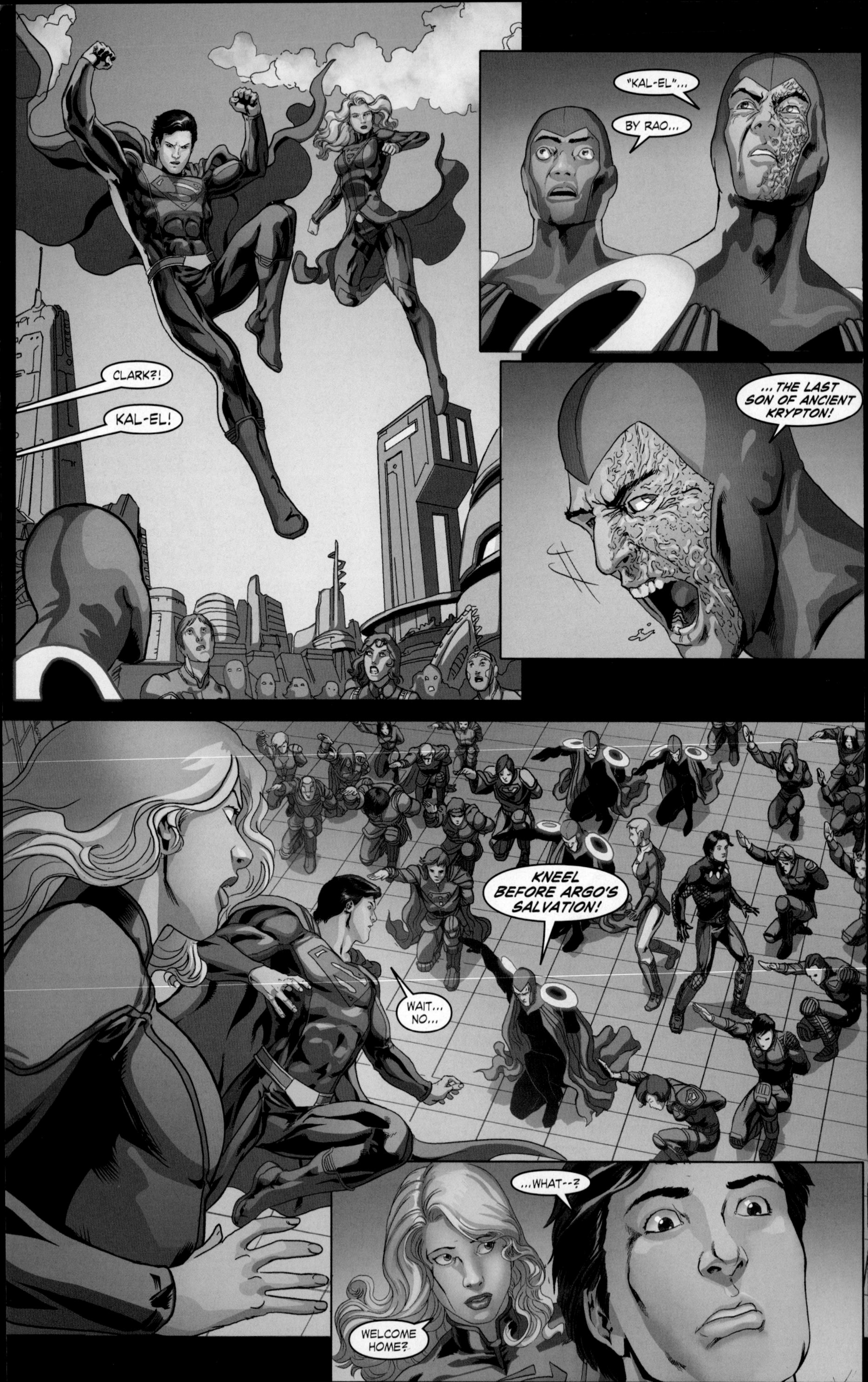
CLARK?!
KAL-EL!
"KAL-EL"...
BY RAO...
...THE LAST SON OF ANCIENT KRYPTON!
KNEEL BEFORE ARGO'S SALVATION!
WAIT... NO...
...WHAT--?
WELCOME HOME?

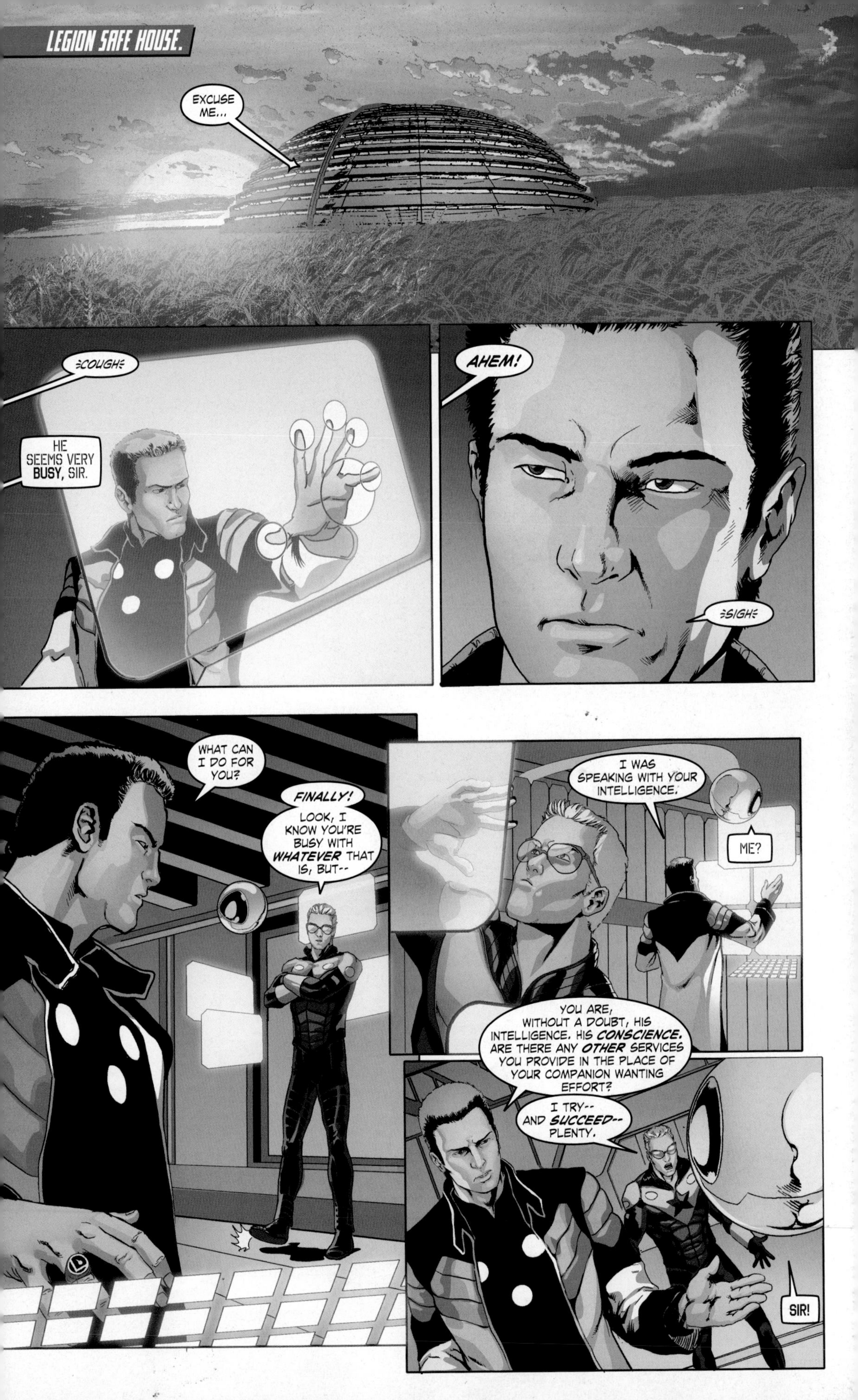
LEGION SAFE HOUSE.
EXCUSE ME...
=COUGH=
HE SEEMS VERY BUSY, SIR.
AHEM!
=SIGH=
WHAT CAN I DO FOR YOU?
FINALLY! LOOK, I KNOW YOU'RE BUSY WITH WHATEVER THAT IS, BUT--
I WAS SPEAKING WITH YOUR INTELLIGENCE.
ME?
YOU ARE, WITHOUT A DOUBT, HIS INTELLIGENCE. HIS CONSCIENCE. ARE THERE ANY OTHER SERVICES YOU PROVIDE IN THE PLACE OF YOUR COMPANION WANTING EFFORT?
I TRY-- AND SUCCEED-- PLENTY.
SIR!

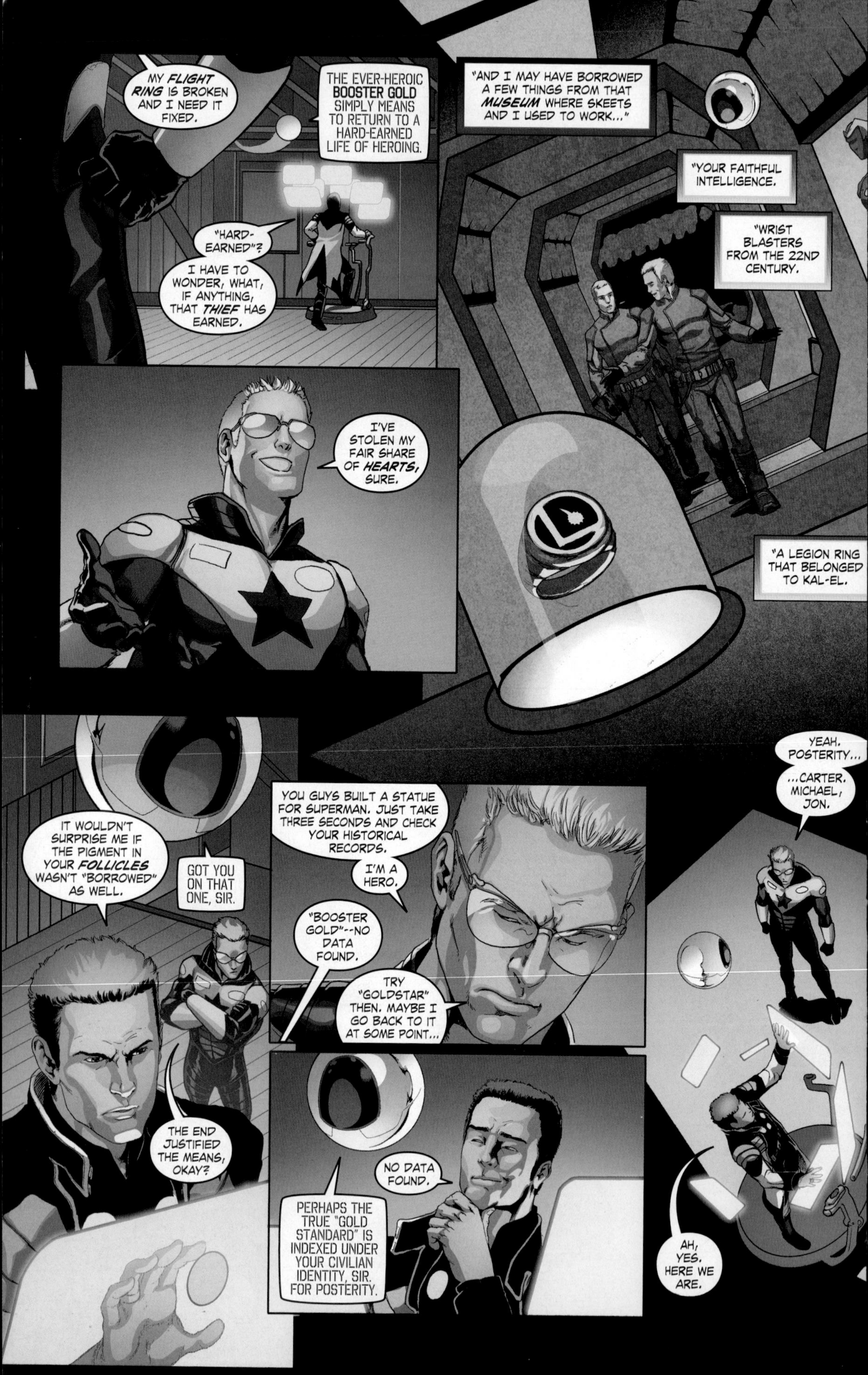
MY FLIGHT RING IS BROKEN AND I NEED IT FIXED.
THE EVER-HEROIC BOOSTER GOLD SIMPLY MEANS TO RETURN TO A HARD-EARNED LIFE OF HEROING.
"HARD-EARNED"?
I HAVE TO WONDER, WHAT, IF ANYTHING, THAT THIEF HAS EARNED.
"AND I MAY HAVE BORROWED A FEW THINGS FROM THAT MUSEUM WHERE SKEETS AND I USED TO WORK..."
"YOUR FAITHFUL INTELLIGENCE.
"WRIST BLASTERS FROM THE 22ND CENTURY.
I'VE STOLEN MY FAIR SHARE OF HEARTS, SURE.
"A LEGION RING THAT BELONGED TO KAL-EL.
IT WOULDN'T SURPRISE ME IF THE PIGMENT IN YOUR FOLLICLES WASN'T "BORROWED" AS WELL.
GOT YOU ON THAT ONE, SIR.
THE END JUSTIFIED THE MEANS, OKAY?
YOU GUYS BUILT A STATUE FOR SUPERMAN. JUST TAKE THREE SECONDS AND CHECK YOUR HISTORICAL RECORDS.
I'M A HERO.
"BOOSTER GOLD"--NO DATA FOUND.
TRY "GOLDSTAR" THEN. MAYBE I GO BACK TO IT AT SOME POINT...
NO DATA FOUND.
PERHAPS THE TRUE "GOLD STANDARD" IS INDEXED UNDER YOUR CIVILIAN IDENTITY, SIR. FOR POSTERITY.
YEAH. POSTERITY...
...CARTER. MICHAEL, JON.
AH, YES. HERE WE ARE.

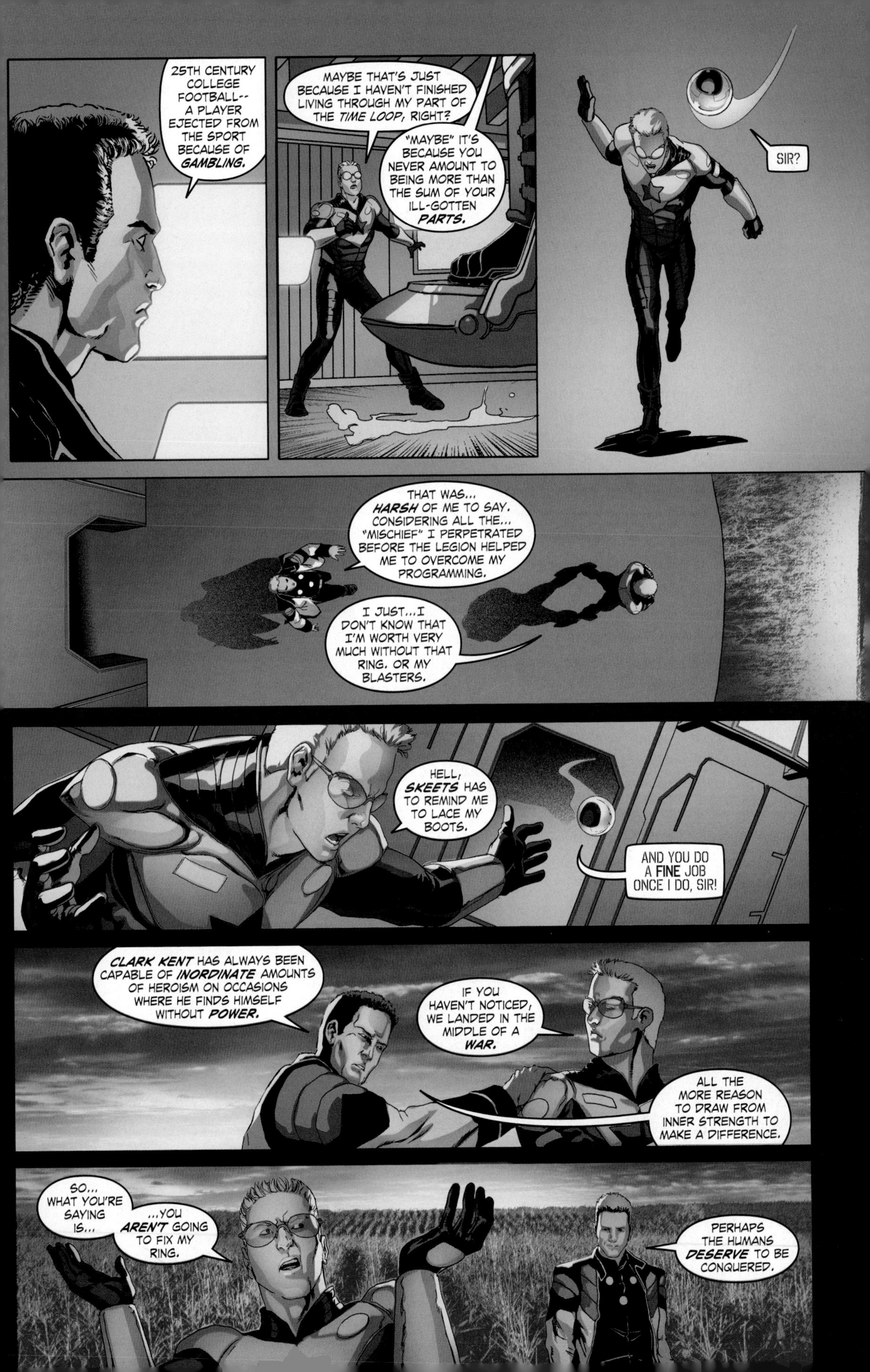
25TH CENTURY COLLEGE FOOTBALL-- A PLAYER EJECTED FROM THE SPORT BECAUSE OF GAMBLING.
MAYBE THAT'S JUST BECAUSE I HAVEN'T FINISHED LIVING THROUGH MY PART OF THE TIME LOOP, RIGHT?
"MAYBE" IT'S BECAUSE YOU NEVER AMOUNT TO BEING MORE THAN THE SUM OF YOUR ILL-GOTTEN PARTS.
SIR?
THAT WAS... HARSH OF ME TO SAY. CONSIDERING ALL THE... "MISCHIEF" I PERPETRATED BEFORE THE LEGION HELPED ME TO OVERCOME MY PROGRAMMING.
I JUST...I DON'T KNOW THAT I'M WORTH VERY MUCH WITHOUT THAT RING. OR MY BLASTERS.
HELL, SKEETS HAS TO REMIND ME TO LACE MY BOOTS.
AND YOU DO A FINE JOB ONCE I DO, SIR!
CLARK KENT HAS ALWAYS BEEN CAPABLE OF INORDINATE AMOUNTS OF HEROISM ON OCCASIONS WHERE HE FINDS HIMSELF WITHOUT POWER.
IF YOU HAVEN'T NOTICED, WE LANDED IN THE MIDDLE OF A WAR.
ALL THE MORE REASON TO DRAW FROM INNER STRENGTH TO MAKE A DIFFERENCE.
SO... WHAT YOU'RE SAYING IS...
...YOU AREN'T GOING TO FIX MY RING.
PERHAPS THE HUMANS DESERVE TO BE CONQUERED.

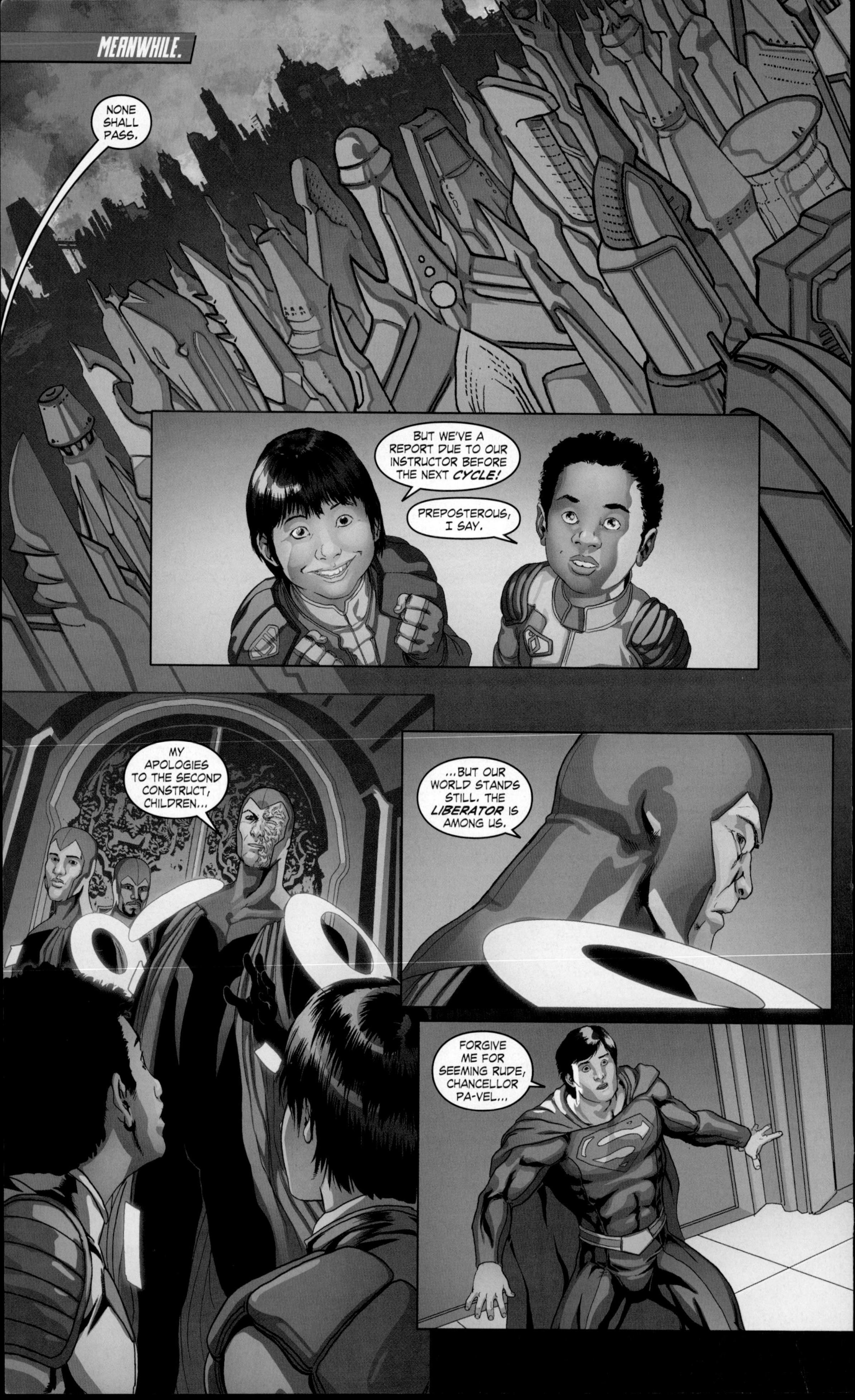
MEANWHILE.
NONE SHALL PASS.
BUT WE'VE A REPORT DUE TO OUR INSTRUCTOR BEFORE THE NEXT CYCLE!
PREPOSTEROUS, I SAY.
MY APOLOGIES TO THE SECOND CONSTRUCT, CHILDREN...
...BUT OUR WORLD STANDS STILL. THE LIBERATOR IS AMONG US.
FORGIVE ME FOR SEEMING RUDE, CHANCELLOR PA-VEL...

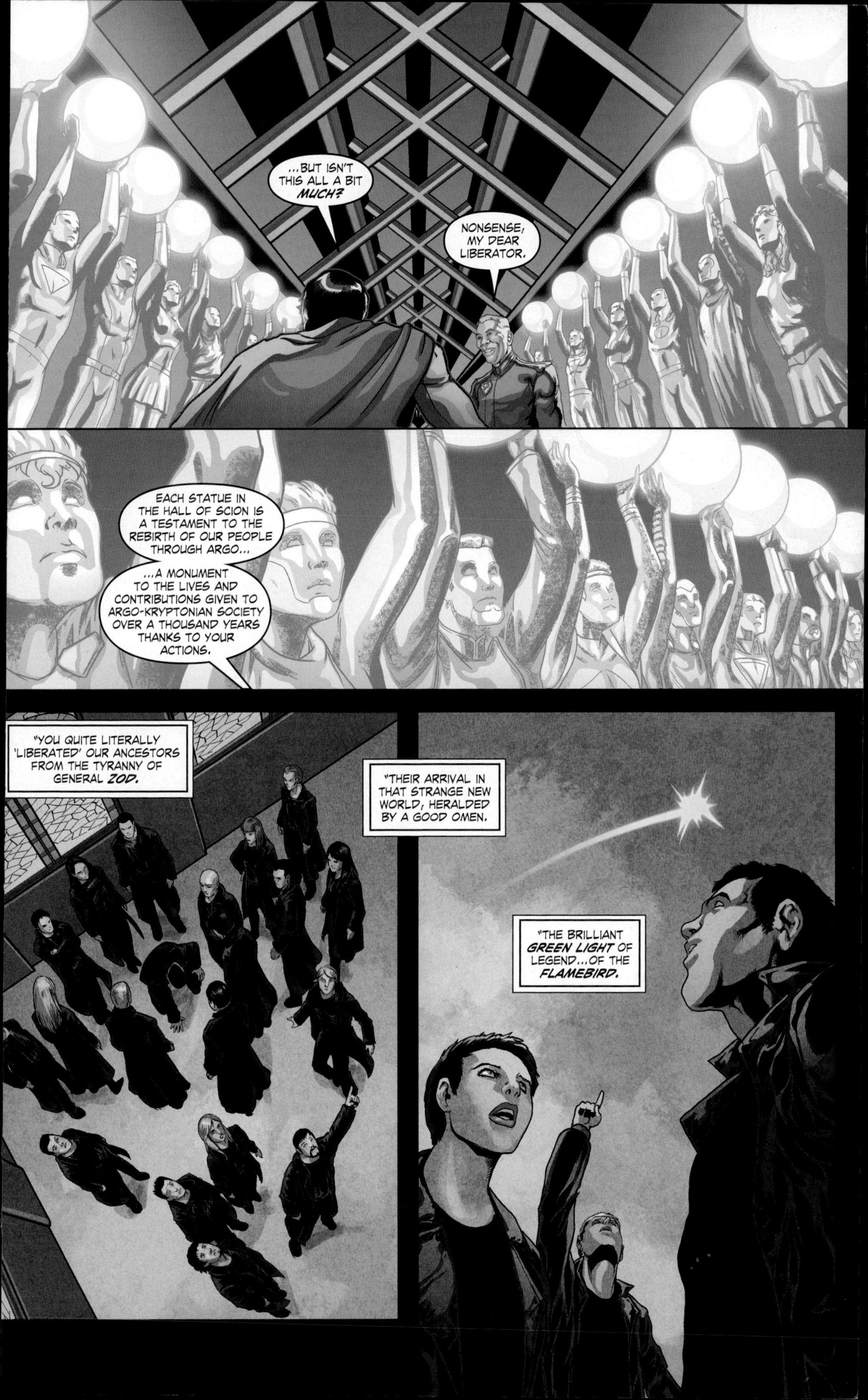
...BUT ISN'T THIS ALL A BIT MUCH?
NONSENSE, MY DEAR LIBERATOR.
EACH STATUE IN THE HALL OF SCION IS A TESTAMENT TO THE REBIRTH OF OUR PEOPLE THROUGH ARGO...
...A MONUMENT TO THE LIVES AND CONTRIBUTIONS GIVEN TO ARGO-KRYPTONIAN SOCIETY OVER A THOUSAND YEARS THANKS TO YOUR ACTIONS.
"YOU QUITE LITERALLY 'LIBERATED' OUR ANCESTORS FROM THE TYRANNY OF GENERAL ZOD.
"THEIR ARRIVAL IN THAT STRANGE NEW WORLD, HERALDED BY A GOOD OMEN.
"THE BRILLIANT GREEN LIGHT OF LEGEND...OF THE FLAMEBIRD.

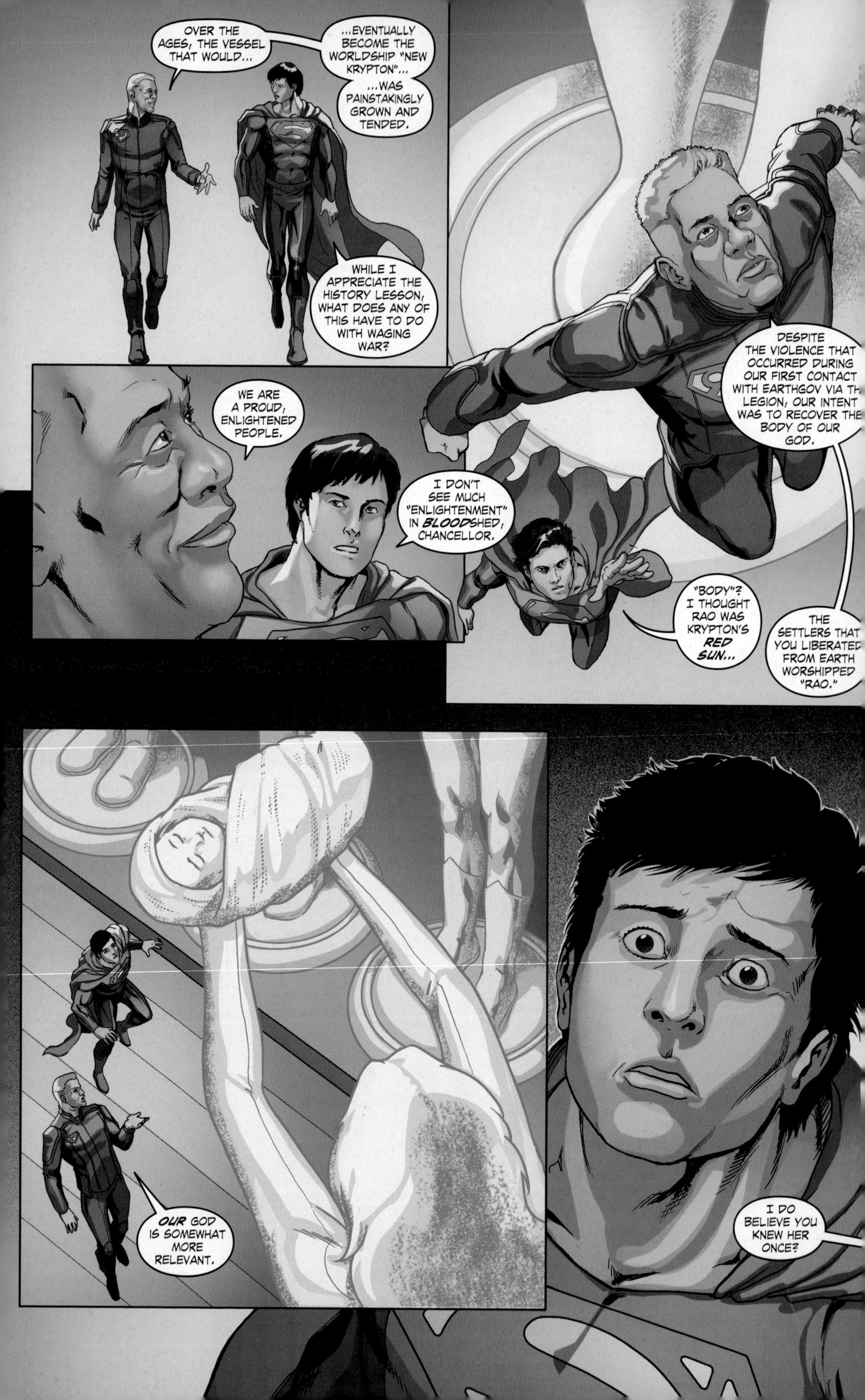
OVER THE AGES, THE VESSEL THAT WOULD...
...EVENTUALLY BECOME THE WORLDSHIP "NEW KRYPTON"...
...WAS PAINSTAKINGLY GROWN AND TENDED.
WHILE I APPRECIATE THE HISTORY LESSON, WHAT DOES ANY OF THIS HAVE TO DO WITH WAGING WAR?
WE ARE A PROUD, ENLIGHTENED PEOPLE.
I DON'T SEE MUCH "ENLIGHTENMENT" IN BLOODSHED, CHANCELLOR.
DESPITE THE VIOLENCE THAT OCCURRED DURING OUR FIRST CONTACT WITH EARTHGOV VIA TH LEGION, OUR INTENT WAS TO RECOVER THE BODY OF OUR GOD.
THE SETTLERS THAT YOU LIBERATED FROM EARTH WORSHIPPED "RAO."
"BODY"? I THOUGHT RAO WAS KRYPTON'S RED SUN...
OUR GOD IS SOMEWHAT MORE RELEVANT.
I DO BELIEVE YOU KNEW HER ONCE?

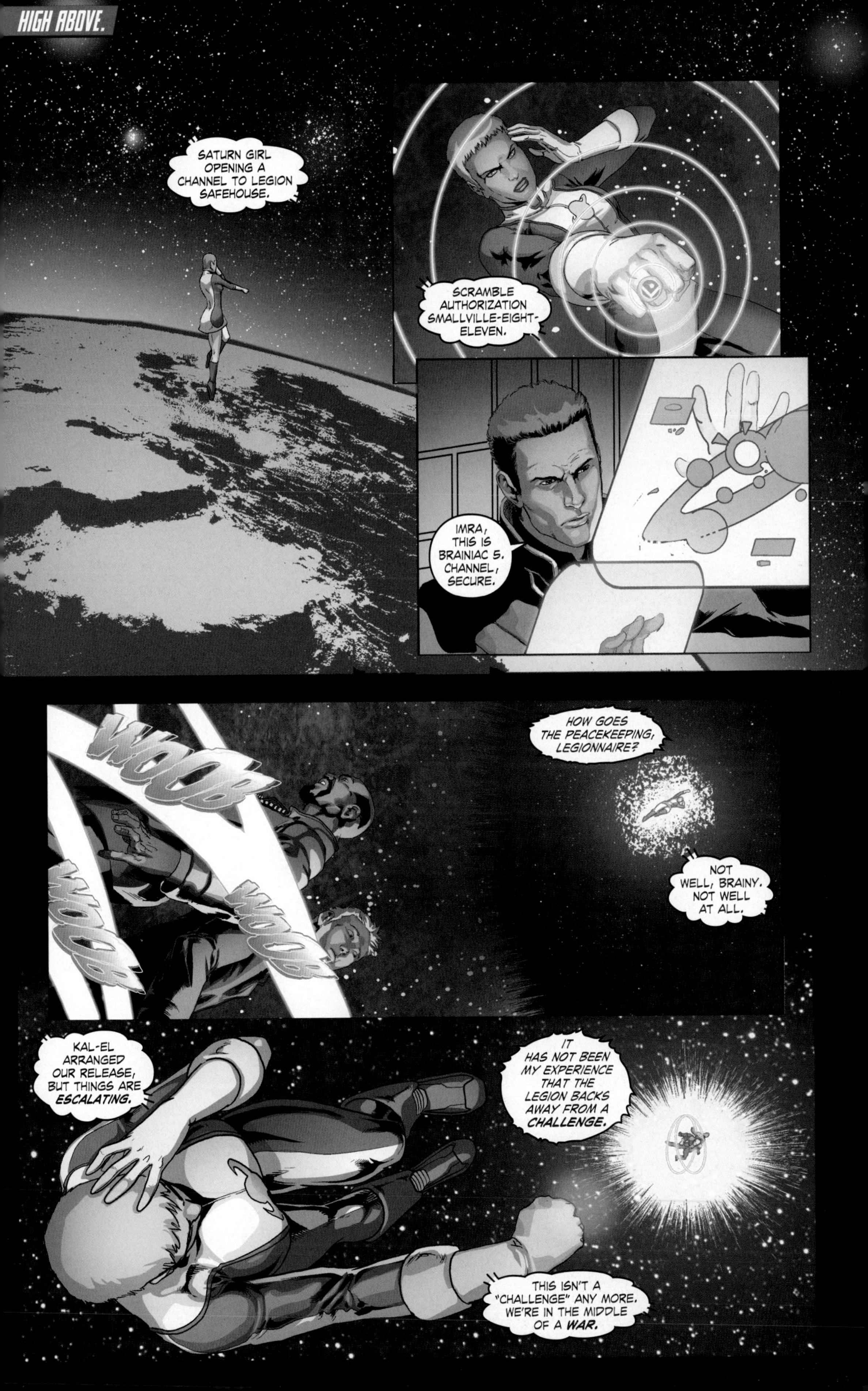
HIGH ABOVE.
SATURN GIRL OPENING A CHANNEL TO LEGION SAFEHOUSE.
SCRAMBLE AUTHORIZATION SMALLVILLE-EIGHT-ELEVEN.
IMRA, THIS IS BRAINIAC 5. CHANNEL, SECURE.
WOOB
HOW GOES THE PEACEKEEPING, LEGIONNAIRE?
WOOB
WOOB
NOT WELL, BRAINY. NOT WELL AT ALL.
KAL-EL ARRANGED OUR RELEASE, BUT THINGS ARE ESCALATING.
IT HAS NOT BEEN MY EXPERIENCE THAT THE LEGION BACKS AWAY FROM A CHALLENGE.
THIS ISN'T A "CHALLENGE" ANY MORE. WE'RE IN THE MIDDLE OF A WAR.

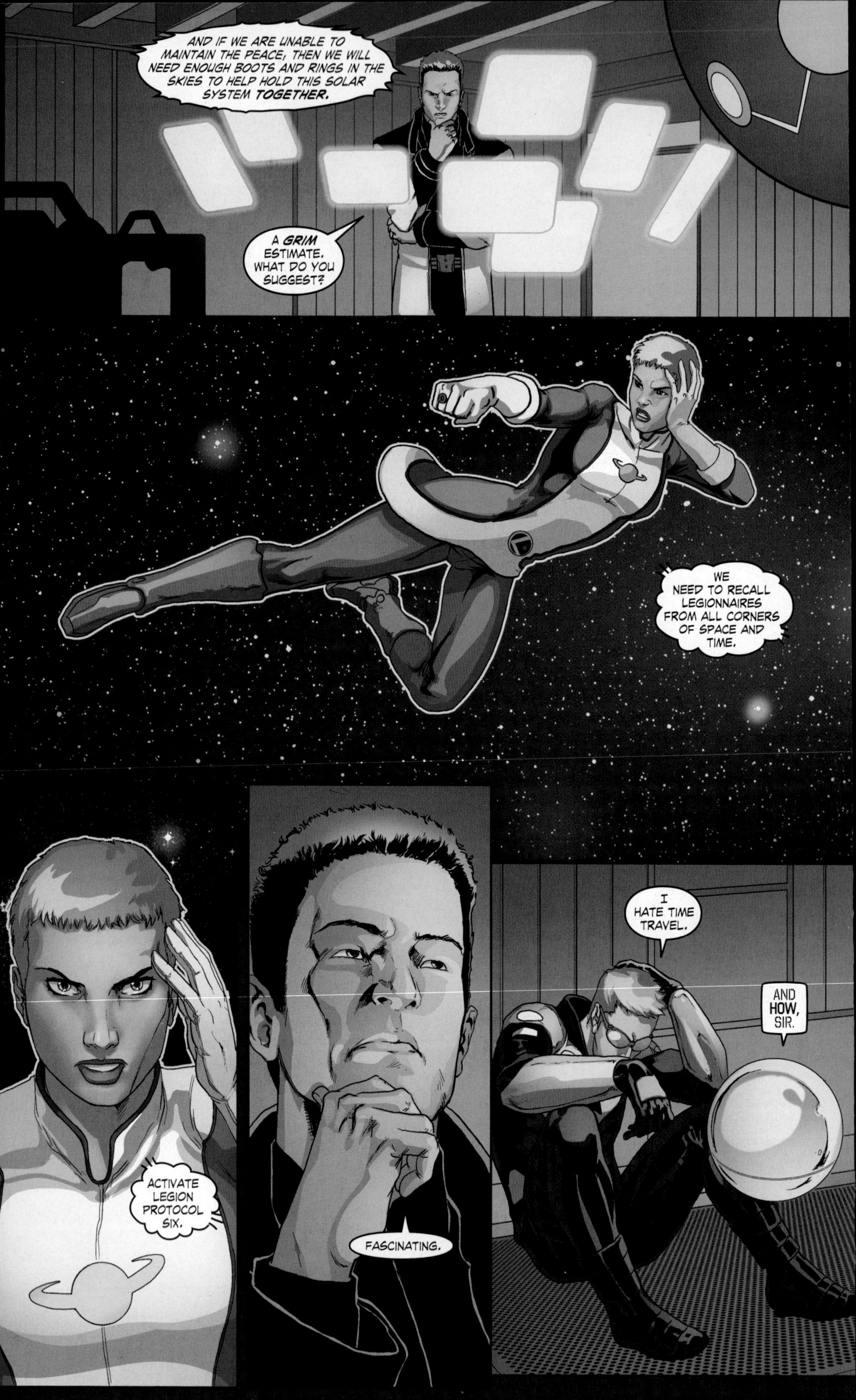
AND IF WE ARE UNABLE TO MAINTAIN THE PEACE; THEN WE WILL NEED ENOUGH BOOTS AND RINGS IN THE SKIES TO HELP HOLD THIS SOLAR SYSTEM TOGETHER.
A GRIM ESTIMATE. WHAT DO YOU SUGGEST?
WE NEED TO RECALL LEGIONNAIRES FROM ALL CORNERS OF SPACE AND TIME.
ACTIVATE LEGION PROTOCOL SIX.
FASCINATING.
I HATE TIME TRAVEL.
AND HOW, SIR.

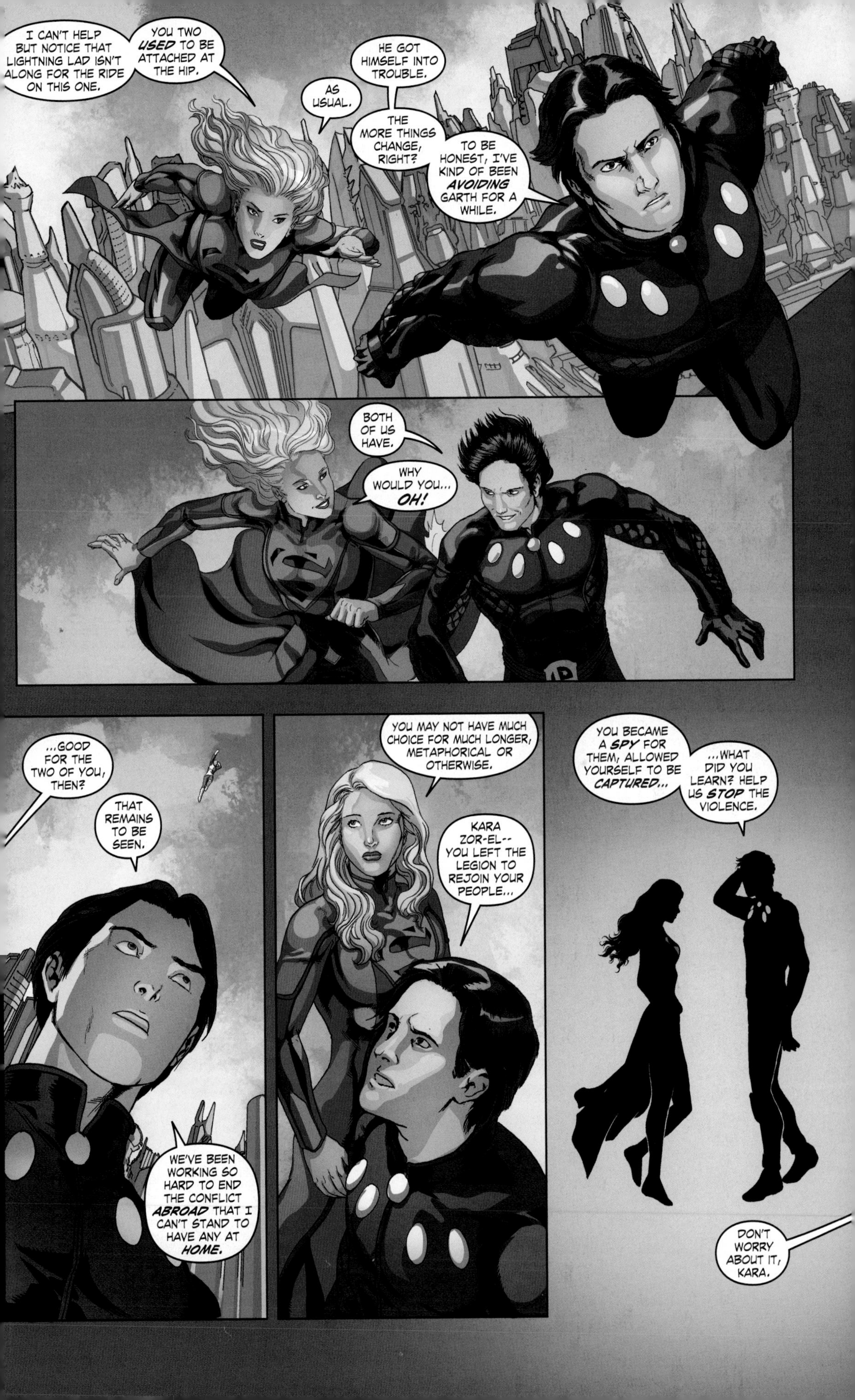
I CAN'T HELP BUT NOTICE THAT LIGHTNING LAD ISN'T ALONG FOR THE RIDE ON THIS ONE.
YOU TWO USED TO BE ATTACHED AT THE HIP.
AS USUAL.
HE GOT HIMSELF INTO TROUBLE.
THE MORE THINGS CHANGE, RIGHT?
TO BE HONEST, I'VE KIND OF BEEN AVOIDING GARTH FOR A WHILE.
BOTH OF US HAVE.
WHY WOULD YOU... OH!
...GOOD FOR THE TWO OF YOU, THEN?
THAT REMAINS TO BE SEEN.
WE'VE BEEN WORKING SO HARD TO END THE CONFLICT ABROAD THAT I CAN'T STAND TO HAVE ANY AT HOME.
YOU MAY NOT HAVE MUCH CHOICE FOR MUCH LONGER, METAPHORICAL OR OTHERWISE.
KARA ZOR-EL-- YOU LEFT THE LEGION TO REJOIN YOUR PEOPLE...
YOU BECAME A SPY FOR THEM, ALLOWED YOURSELF TO BE CAPTURED...
...WHAT DID YOU LEARN? HELP US STOP THE VIOLENCE.
DON'T WORRY ABOUT IT, KARA.

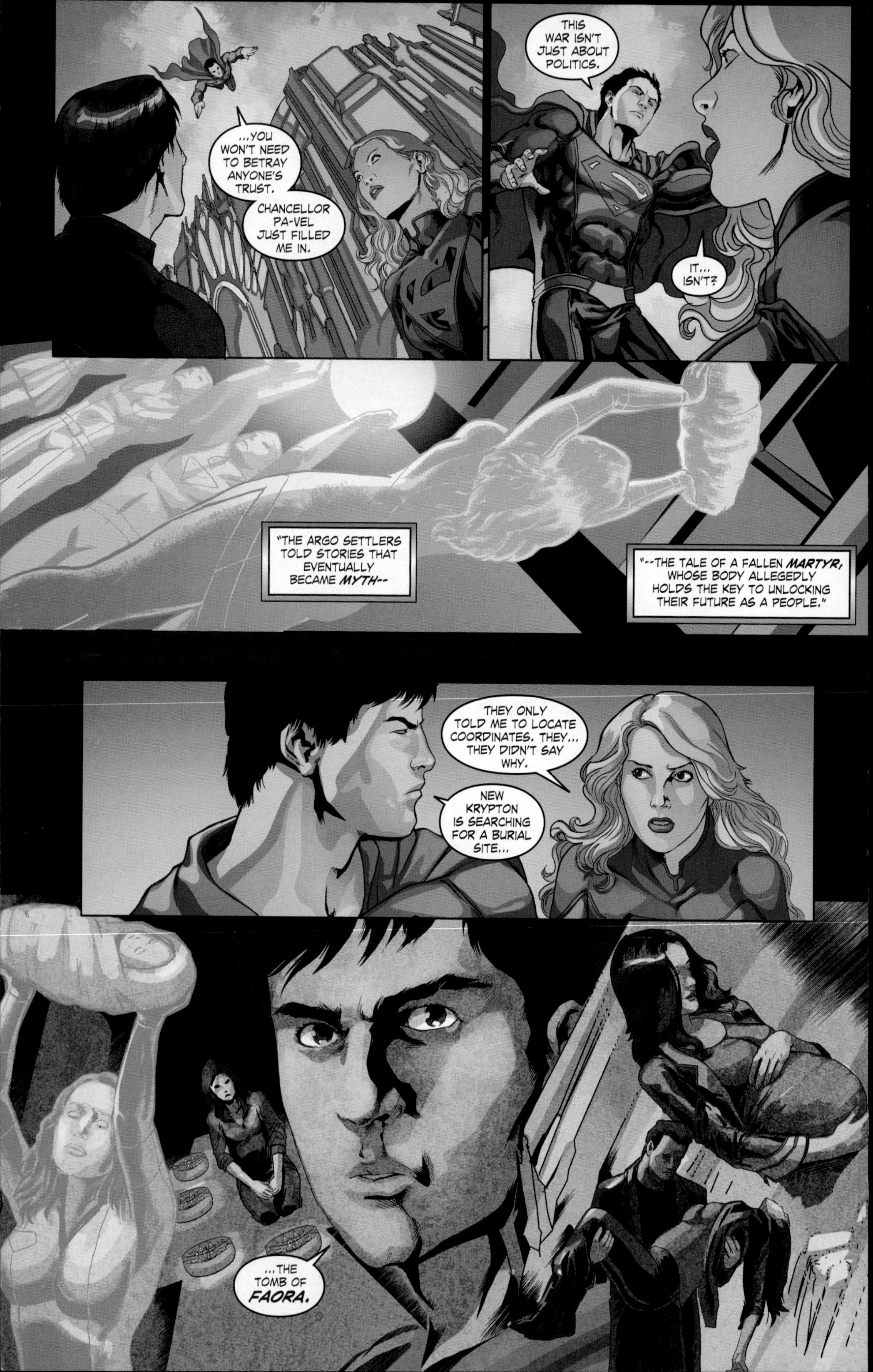
...YOU WON'T NEED TO BETRAY ANYONE'S TRUST.
CHANCELLOR PA-VEL JUST FILLED ME IN.
THIS WAR ISN'T JUST ABOUT POLITICS.
IT... ISN'T?
"THE ARGO SETTLERS TOLD STORIES THAT EVENTUALLY BECAME MYTH--
"--THE TALE OF A FALLEN MARTYR, WHOSE BODY ALLEGEDLY HOLDS THE KEY TO UNLOCKING THEIR FUTURE AS A PEOPLE."
THEY ONLY TOLD ME TO LOCATE COORDINATES. THEY... THEY DIDN'T SAY WHY.
NEW KRYPTON IS SEARCHING FOR A BURIAL SITE...
...THE TOMB OF FAORA.

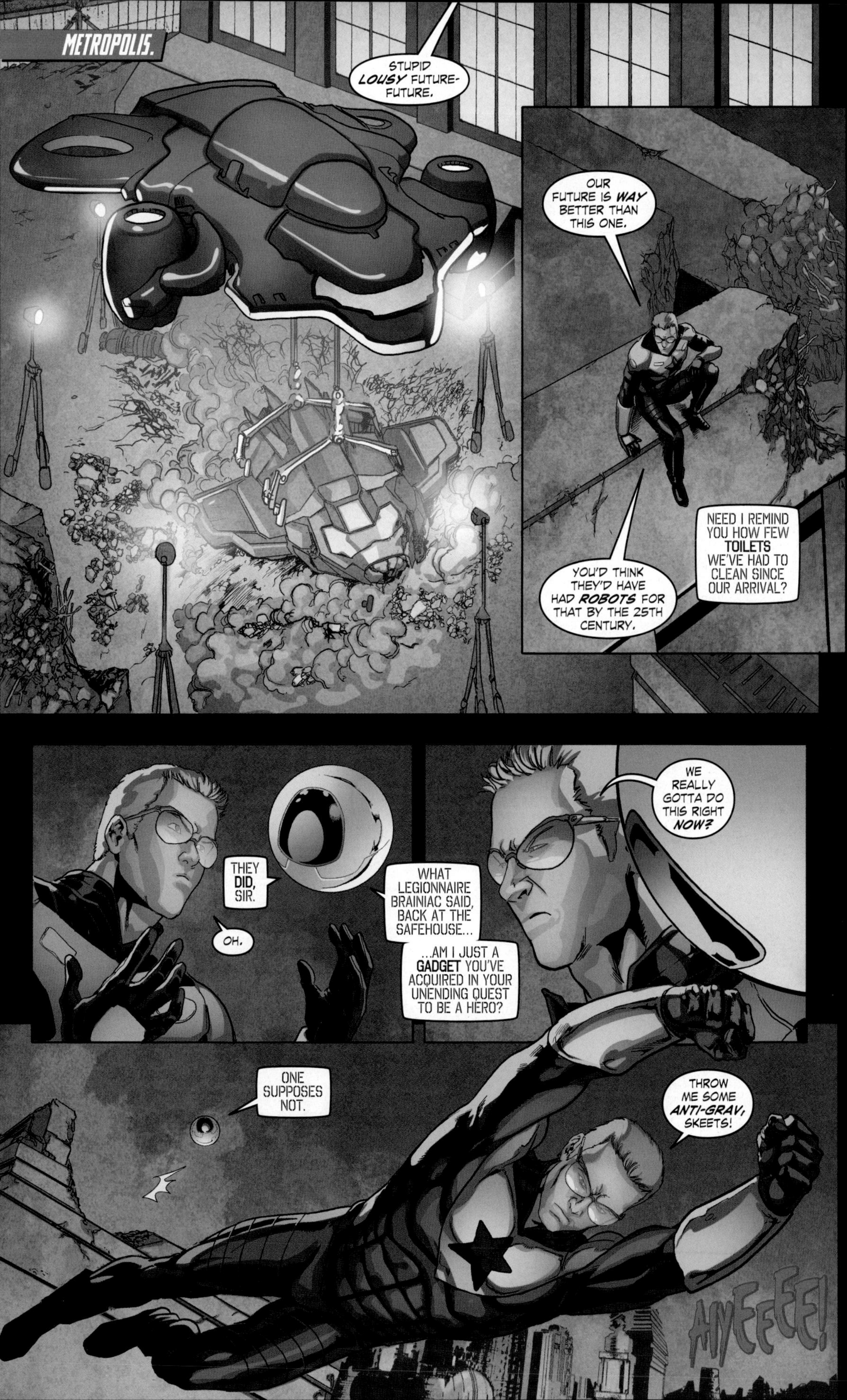
METROPOLIS.
STUPID LOUSY FUTURE-FUTURE.
OUR FUTURE IS WAY BETTER THAN THIS ONE.
YOU'D THINK THEY'D HAVE HAD ROBOTS FOR THAT BY THE 25TH CENTURY.
NEED I REMIND YOU HOW FEW TOILETS WE'VE HAD TO CLEAN SINCE OUR ARRIVAL?
THEY DID, SIR.
OH.
WHAT LEGIONNAIRE BRAINIAC SAID, BACK AT THE SAFEHOUSE...
...AM I JUST A GADGET YOU'VE ACQUIRED IN YOUR UNENDING QUEST TO BE A HERO?
WE REALLY GOTTA DO THIS RIGHT NOW?
ONE SUPPOSES NOT.
THROW ME SOME ANTI-GRAV, SKEETS!
AIYEEEE!

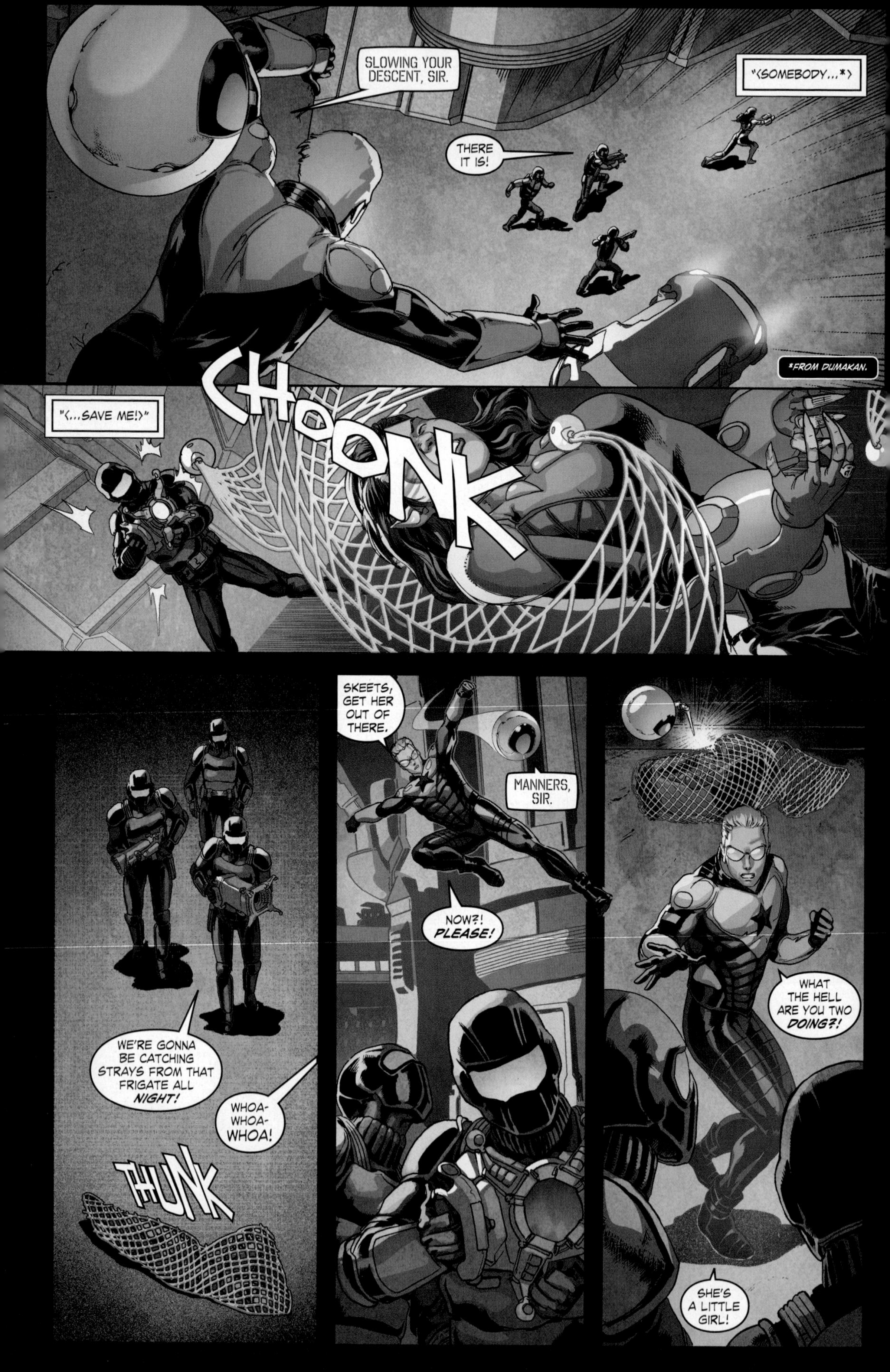
SLOWING YOUR DESCENT, SIR.
"‹SOMEBODY...*›
THERE IT IS!
*FROM DUMAKAN.
CHOONK
"‹...SAVE ME!›"
WE'RE GONNA BE CATCHING STRAYS FROM THAT FRIGATE ALL NIGHT!
WHOA-WHOA-WHOA!
THUNK
SKEETS, GET HER OUT OF THERE.
MANNERS, SIR.
NOW?! PLEASE!
WHAT THE HELL ARE YOU TWO DOING?!
SHE'S A LITTLE GIRL!

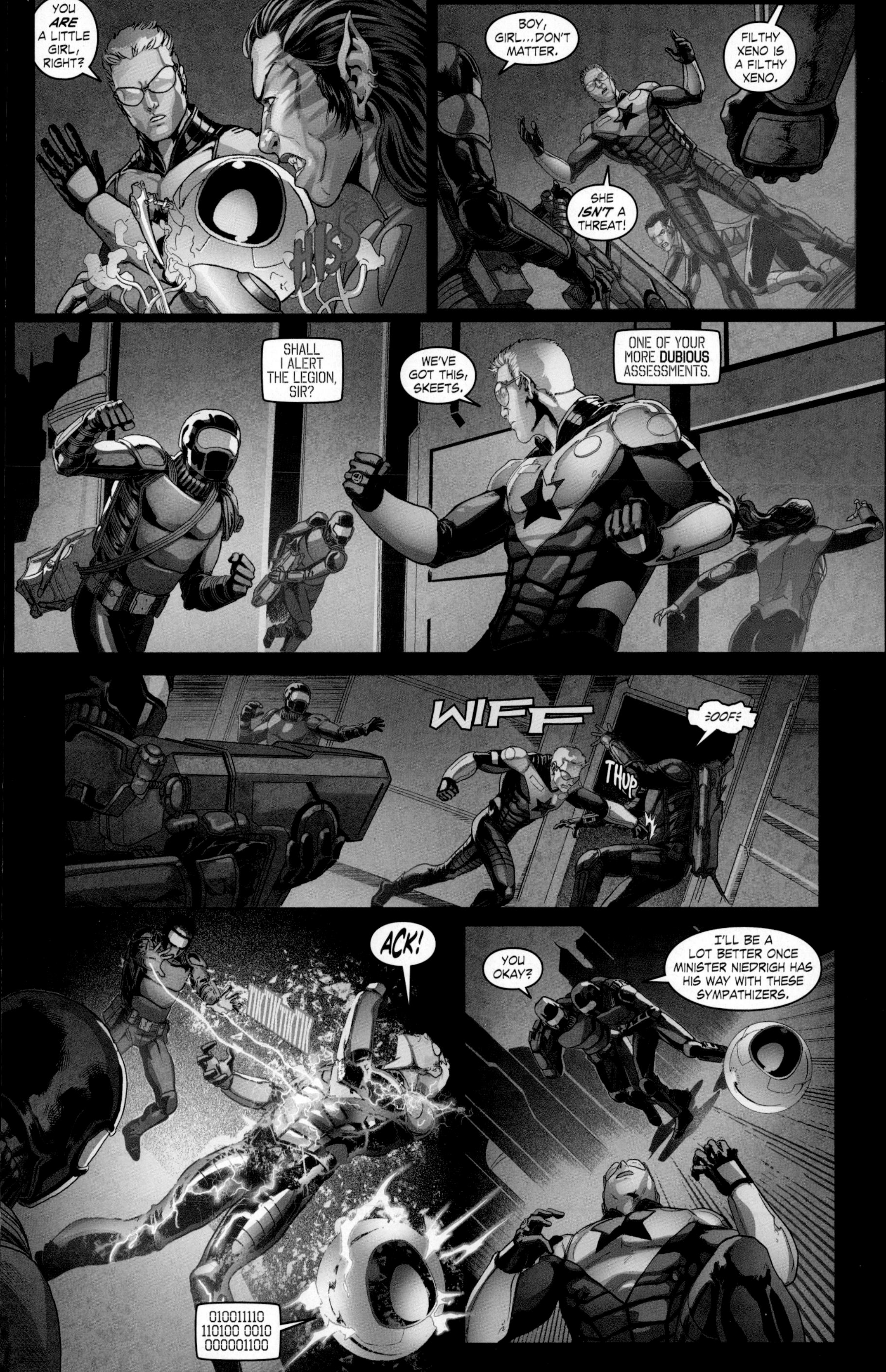

YOU *ARE* A LITTLE GIRL, RIGHT?
HISS
BOY, GIRL...DON'T MATTER.
FILTHY XENO IS A FILTHY XENO.
SHE *ISN'T* A THREAT!
SHALL I ALERT THE LEGION, SIR?
WE'VE GOT THIS, SKEETS.
ONE OF YOUR MORE **DUBIOUS** ASSESSMENTS.
WIFF
OOF
THUP
ACK!
YOU OKAY?
I'LL BE A LOT BETTER ONCE MINISTER NIEDRIGH HAS HIS WAY WITH THESE SYMPATHIZERS.
010011110 110100 0010 000001100

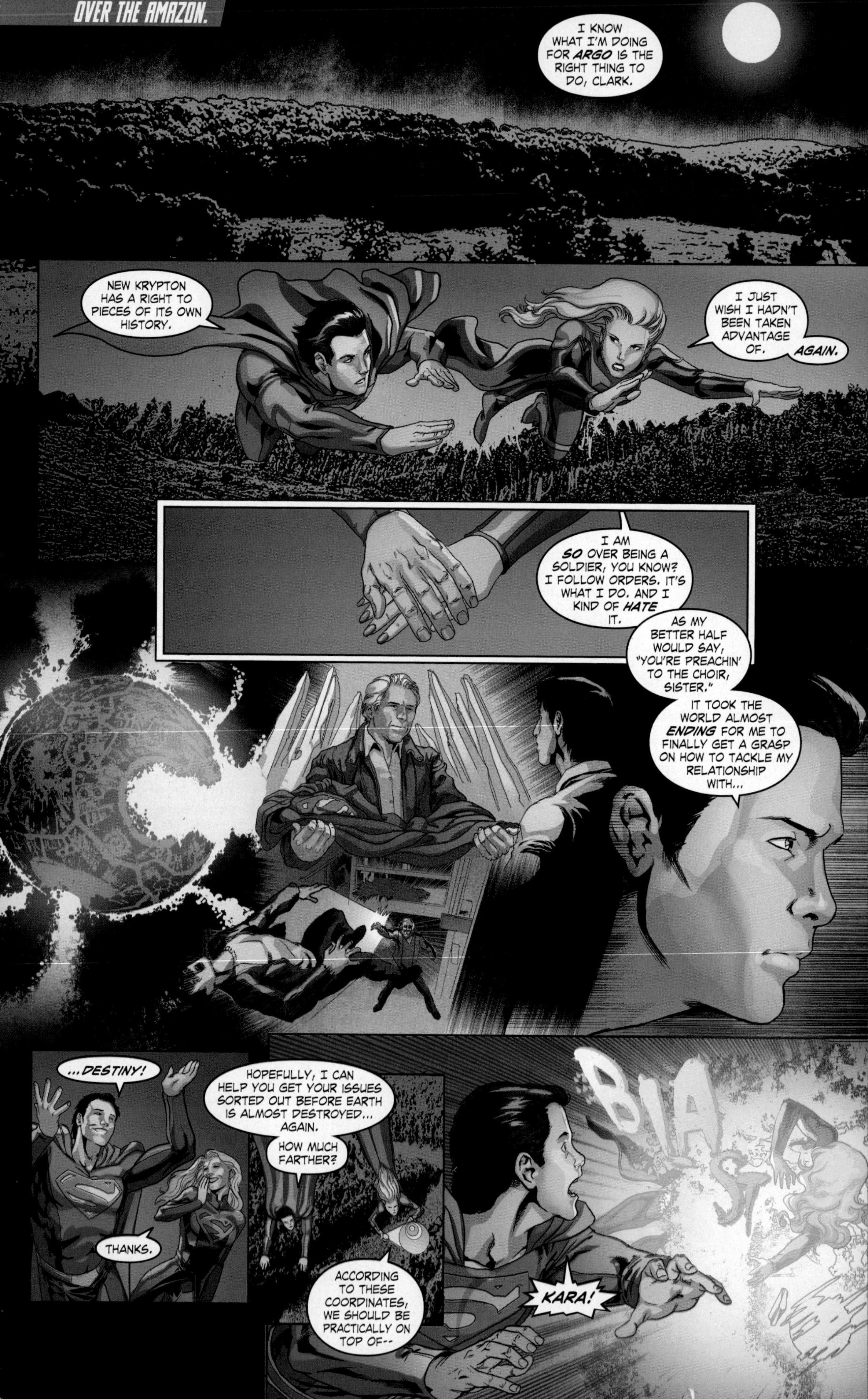
OVER THE AMAZON.
I KNOW WHAT I'M DOING FOR ARGO IS THE RIGHT THING TO DO, CLARK.
NEW KRYPTON HAS A RIGHT TO PIECES OF ITS OWN HISTORY.
I JUST WISH I HADN'T BEEN TAKEN ADVANTAGE OF. AGAIN.
I AM SO OVER BEING A SOLDIER, YOU KNOW? I FOLLOW ORDERS. IT'S WHAT I DO. AND I KIND OF HATE IT.
AS MY BETTER HALF WOULD SAY, "YOU'RE PREACHIN' TO THE CHOIR, SISTER."
IT TOOK THE WORLD ALMOST ENDING FOR ME TO FINALLY GET A GRASP ON HOW TO TACKLE MY RELATIONSHIP WITH...
...DESTINY!
THANKS.
HOPEFULLY, I CAN HELP YOU GET YOUR ISSUES SORTED OUT BEFORE EARTH IS ALMOST DESTROYED... AGAIN.
HOW MUCH FARTHER?
ACCORDING TO THESE COORDINATES, WE SHOULD BE PRACTICALLY ON TOP OF--
BLAST
KARA!

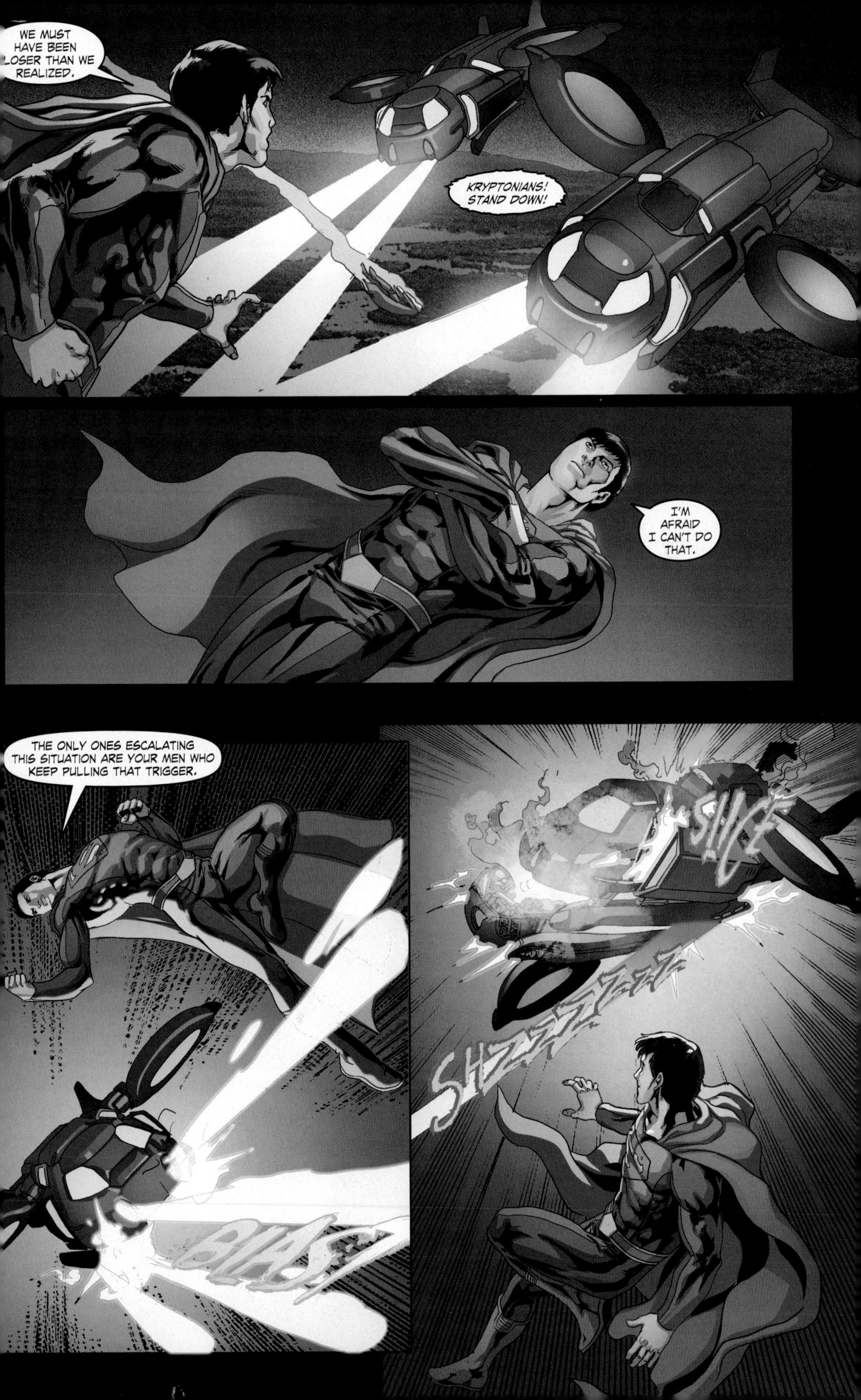
WE MUST HAVE BEEN LOSER THAN WE REALIZED.
KRYPTONIANS! STAND DOWN!
I'M AFRAID I CAN'T DO THAT.
THE ONLY ONES ESCALATING THIS SITUATION ARE YOUR MEN WHO KEEP PULLING THAT TRIGGER.

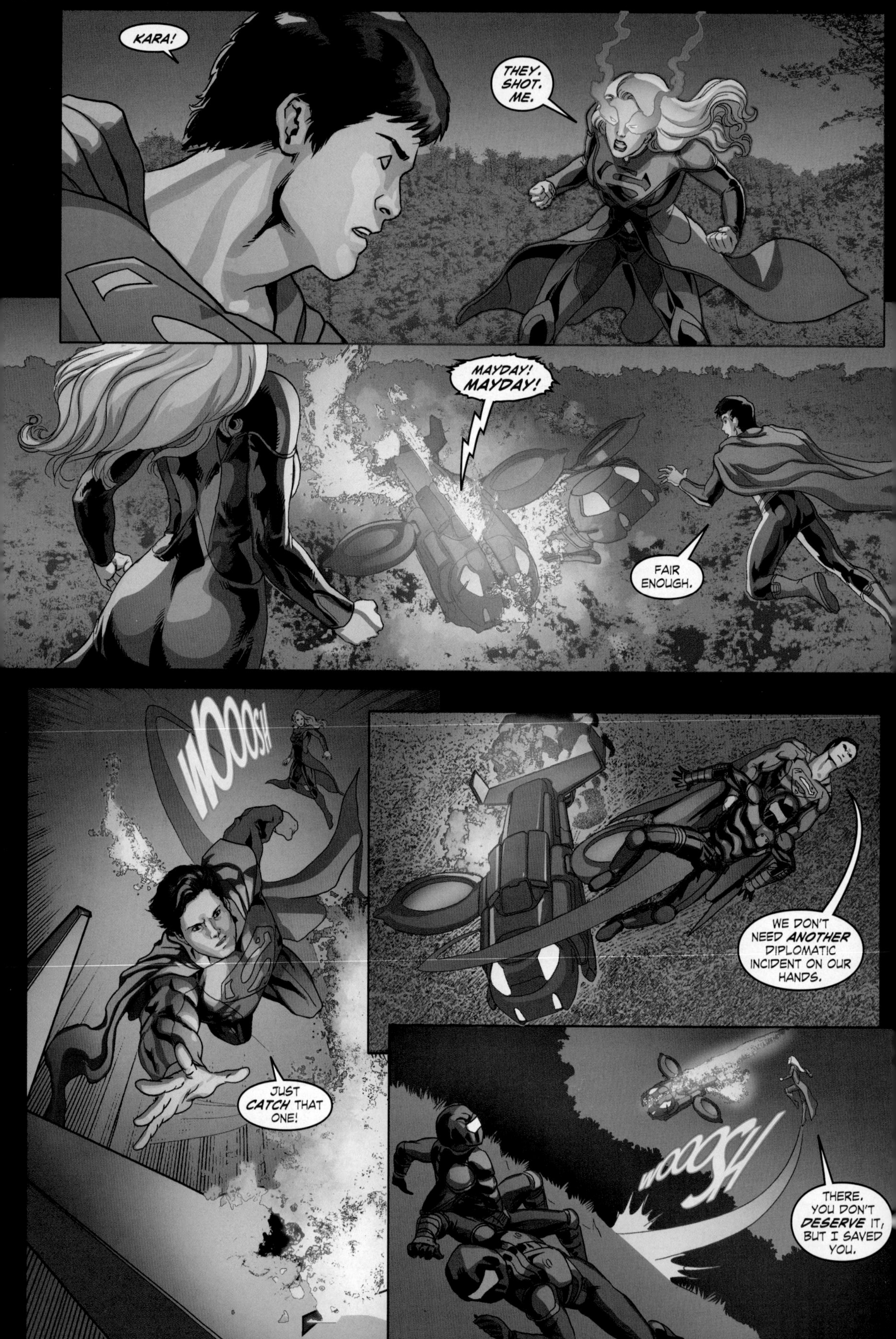
KARA!
THEY. SHOT. ME.
MAYDAY! MAYDAY!
FAIR ENOUGH.
WOOOSH
JUST CATCH THAT ONE!
WE DON'T NEED ANOTHER DIPLOMATIC INCIDENT ON OUR HANDS.
WOOOSH
THERE. YOU DON'T DESERVE IT, BUT I SAVED YOU.

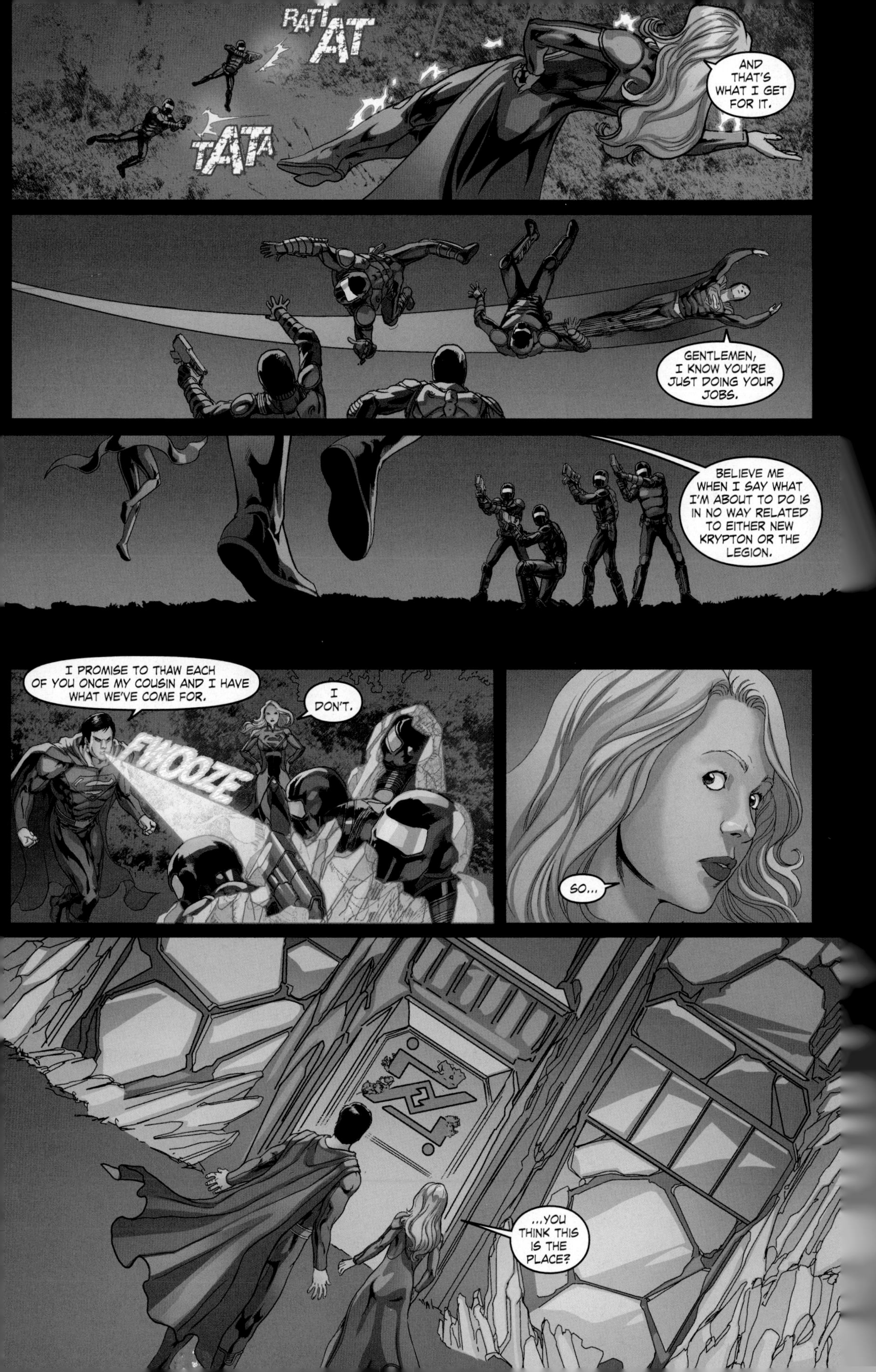

RATTAT
TATA
AND THAT'S WHAT I GET FOR IT.
GENTLEMEN, I KNOW YOU'RE JUST DOING YOUR JOBS.
BELIEVE ME WHEN I SAY WHAT I'M ABOUT TO DO IS IN NO WAY RELATED TO EITHER NEW KRYPTON OR THE LEGION.
I PROMISE TO THAW EACH OF YOU ONCE MY COUSIN AND I HAVE WHAT WE'VE COME FOR.
I DON'T.
FWOOZE
SO...
...YOU THINK THIS IS THE PLACE?

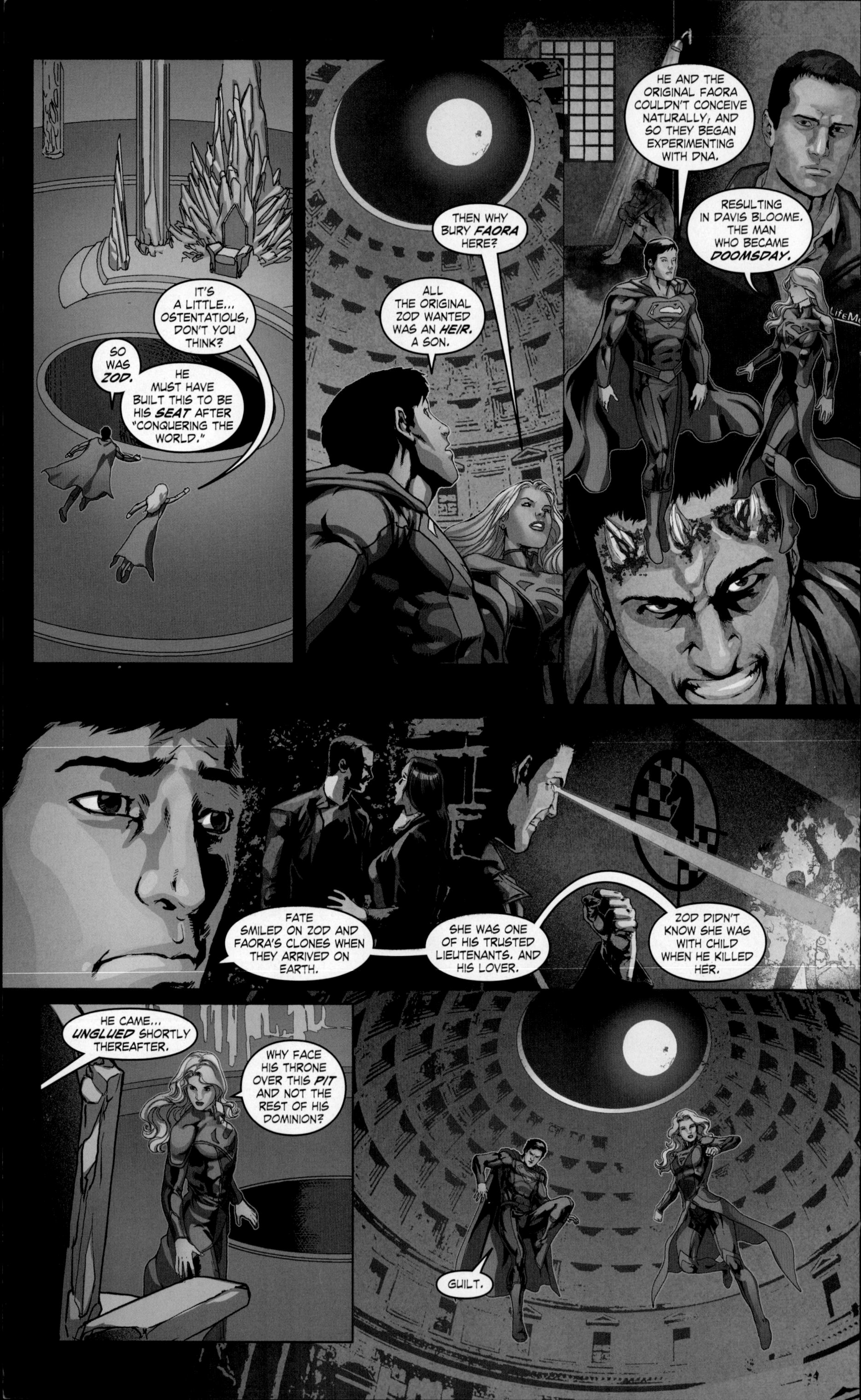
IT'S A LITTLE... OSTENTATIOUS, DON'T YOU THINK?
SO WAS ZOD.
HE MUST HAVE BUILT THIS TO BE HIS SEAT AFTER "CONQUERING THE WORLD."
THEN WHY BURY FAORA HERE?
ALL THE ORIGINAL ZOD WANTED WAS AN HEIR. A SON.
HE AND THE ORIGINAL FAORA COULDN'T CONCEIVE NATURALLY, AND SO THEY BEGAN EXPERIMENTING WITH DNA.
RESULTING IN DAVIS BLOOME. THE MAN WHO BECAME DOOMSDAY.
FATE SMILED ON ZOD AND FAORA'S CLONES WHEN THEY ARRIVED ON EARTH.
SHE WAS ONE OF HIS TRUSTED LIEUTENANTS. AND HIS LOVER.
ZOD DIDN'T KNOW SHE WAS WITH CHILD WHEN HE KILLED HER.
HE CAME... UNGLUED SHORTLY THEREAFTER.
WHY FACE HIS THRONE OVER THIS PIT AND NOT THE REST OF HIS DOMINION?
GUILT.

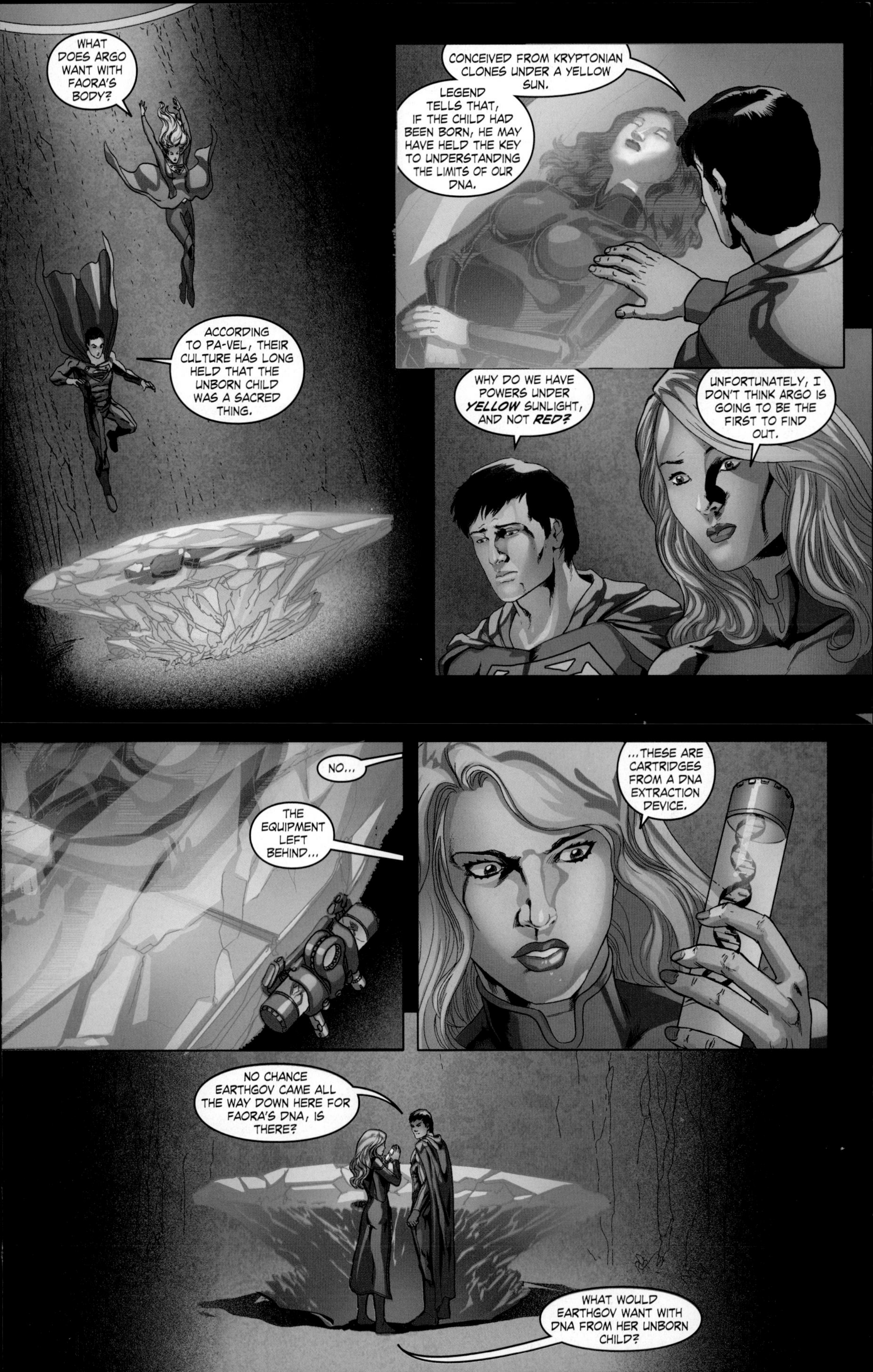
WHAT DOES ARGO WANT WITH FAORA'S BODY?
ACCORDING TO PA-VEL, THEIR CULTURE HAS LONG HELD THAT THE UNBORN CHILD WAS A SACRED THING.
CONCEIVED FROM KRYPTONIAN CLONES UNDER A YELLOW SUN.
LEGEND TELLS THAT, IF THE CHILD HAD BEEN BORN, HE MAY HAVE HELD THE KEY TO UNDERSTANDING THE LIMITS OF OUR DNA.
WHY DO WE HAVE POWERS UNDER YELLOW SUNLIGHT, AND NOT RED?
UNFORTUNATELY, I DON'T THINK ARGO IS GOING TO BE THE FIRST TO FIND OUT.
NO...
THE EQUIPMENT LEFT BEHIND...
...THESE ARE CARTRIDGES FROM A DNA EXTRACTION DEVICE.
NO CHANCE EARTHGOV CAME ALL THE WAY DOWN HERE FOR FAORA'S DNA, IS THERE?
WHAT WOULD EARTHGOV WANT WITH DNA FROM HER UNBORN CHILD?

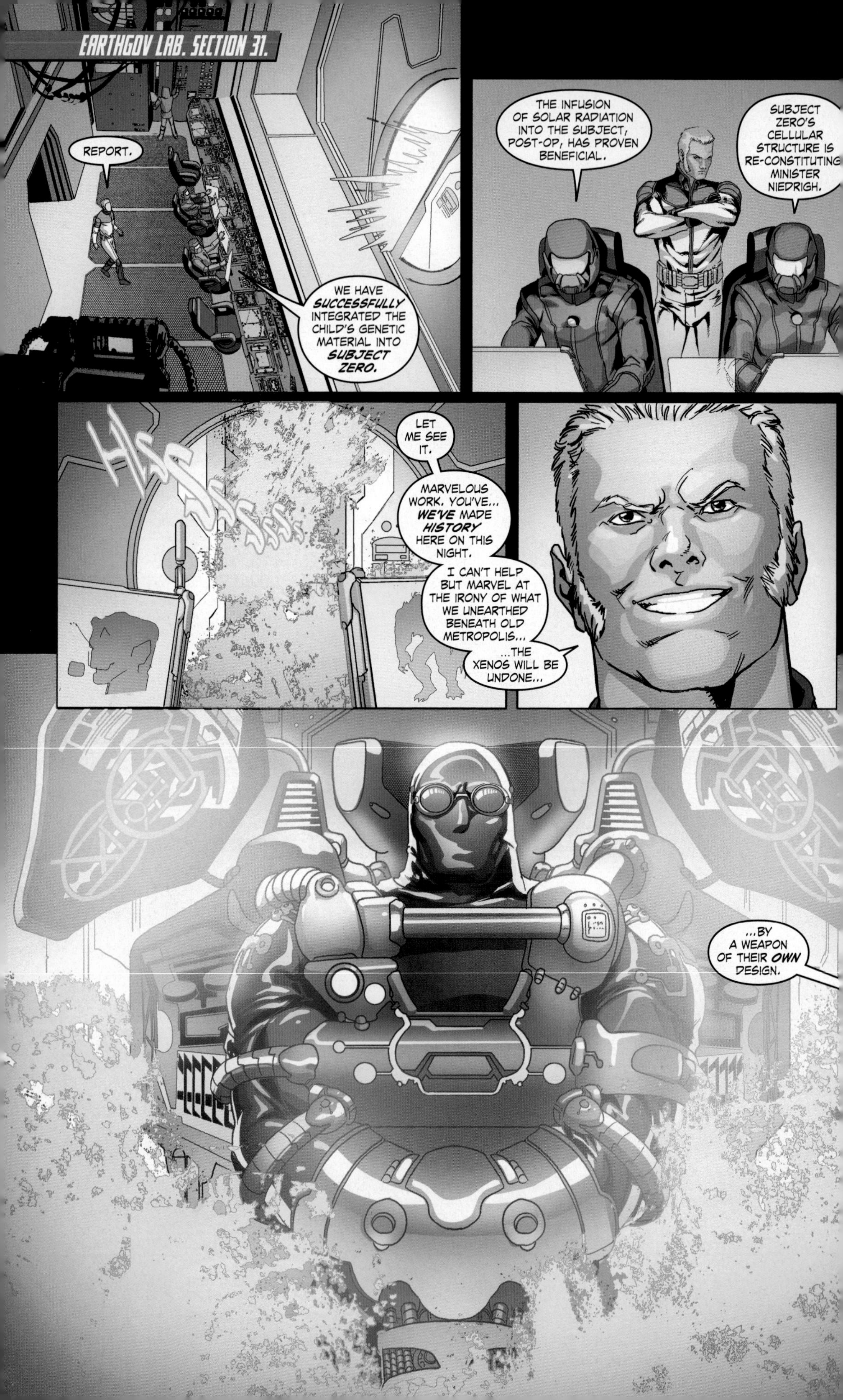
EARTHGOV LAB. SECTION 31.
REPORT.
WE HAVE SUCCESSFULLY INTEGRATED THE CHILD'S GENETIC MATERIAL INTO SUBJECT ZERO.
THE INFUSION OF SOLAR RADIATION INTO THE SUBJECT, POST-OP, HAS PROVEN BENEFICIAL.
SUBJECT ZERO'S CELLULAR STRUCTURE IS RE-CONSTITUTING MINISTER NIEDRIGH.
HISSSSSSSS
LET ME SEE IT.
MARVELOUS WORK. YOU'VE... WE'VE MADE HISTORY HERE ON THIS NIGHT.
I CAN'T HELP BUT MARVEL AT THE IRONY OF WHAT WE UNEARTHED BENEATH OLD METROPOLIS...
...THE XENOS WILL BE UNDONE...
...BY A WEAPON OF THEIR OWN DESIGN.

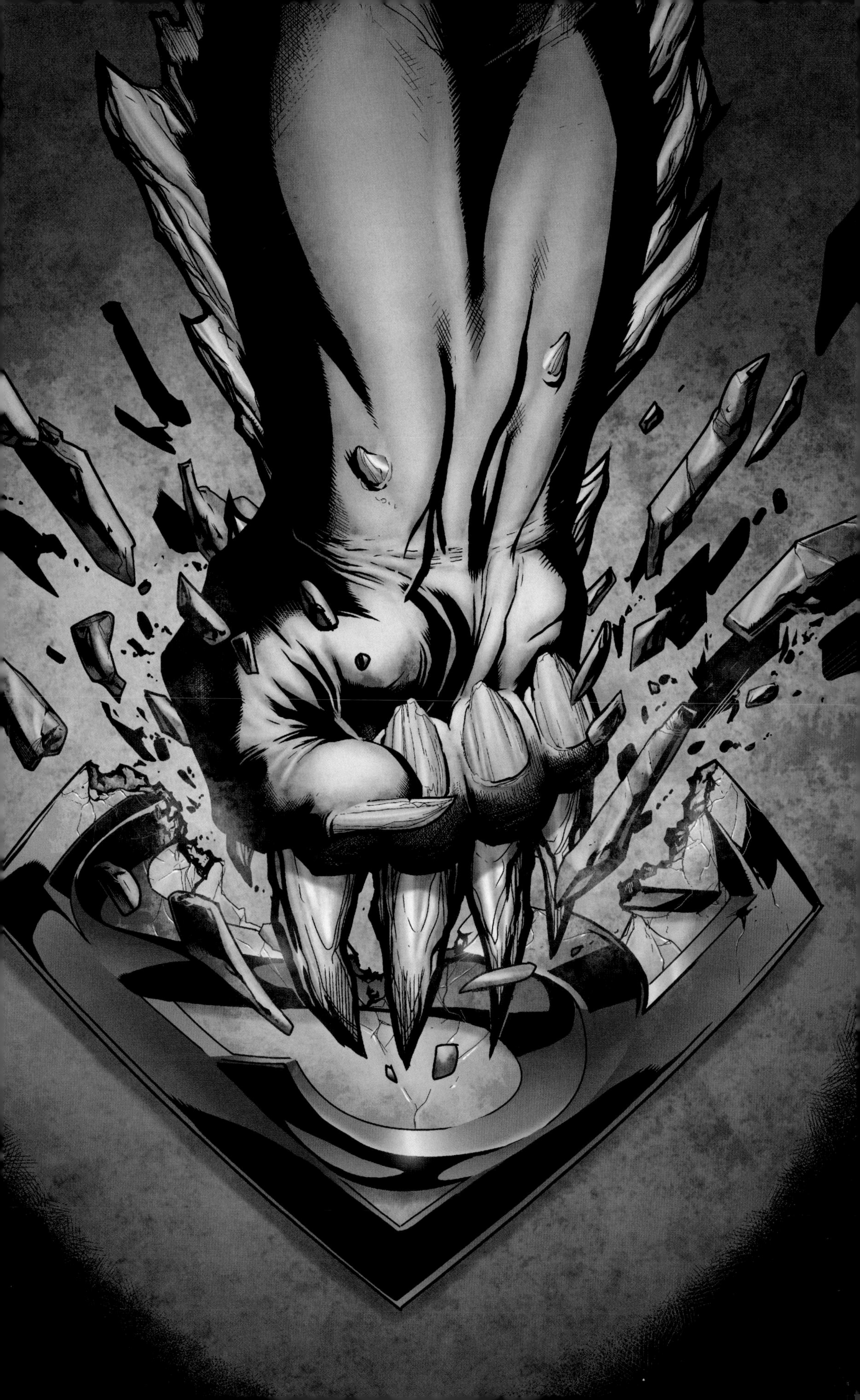

ARGO PART THREE
COVER BY PETE WOODS WITH RANDY MAYOR

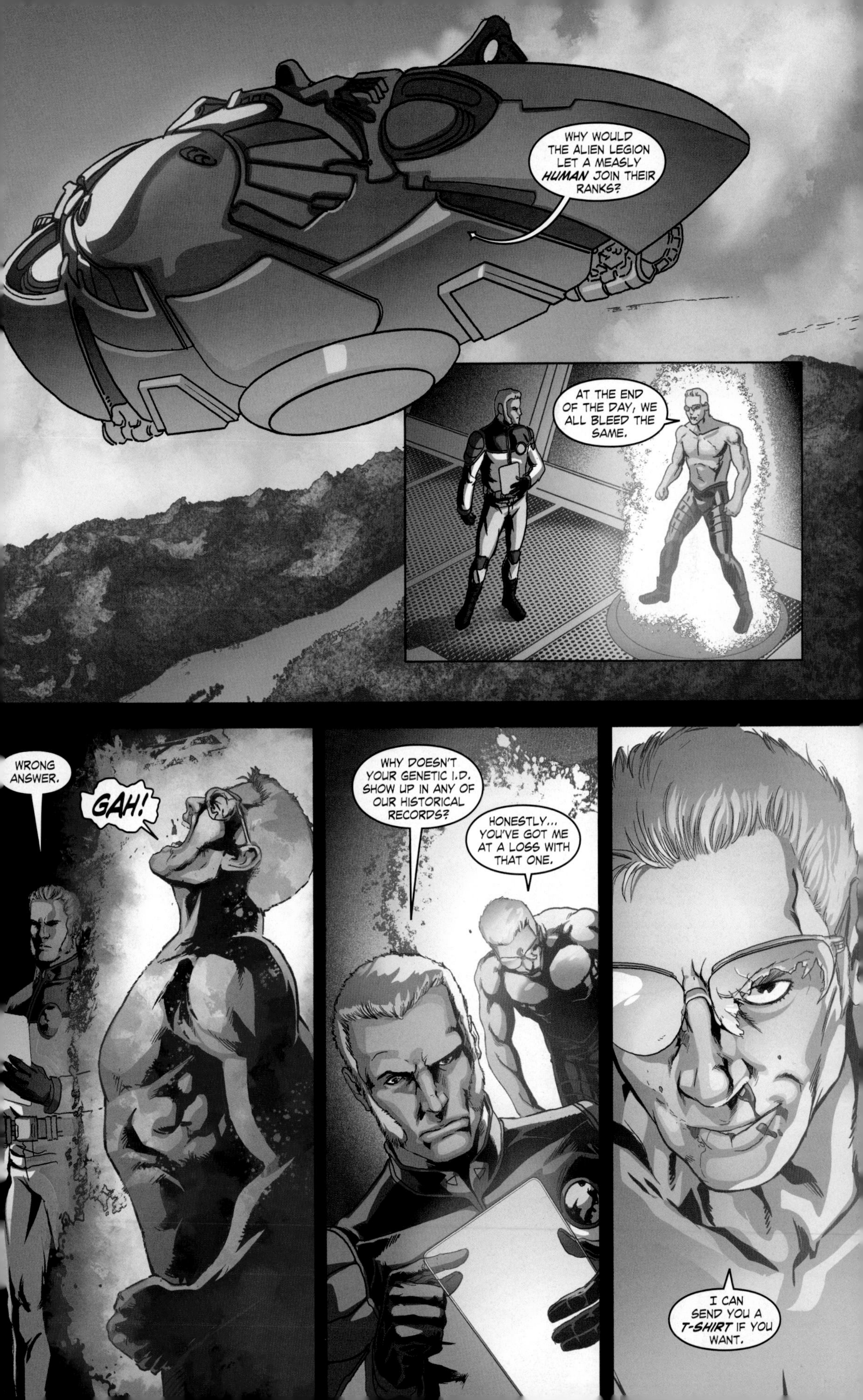
WHY WOULD THE ALIEN LEGION LET A MEASLY *HUMAN* JOIN THEIR RANKS?
AT THE END OF THE DAY, WE ALL BLEED THE SAME.
WRONG ANSWER.
GAH!
WHY DOESN'T YOUR GENETIC I.D. SHOW UP IN ANY OF OUR HISTORICAL RECORDS?
HONESTLY... YOU'VE GOT ME AT A LOSS WITH THAT ONE.
I CAN SEND YOU A *T-SHIRT* IF YOU WANT.

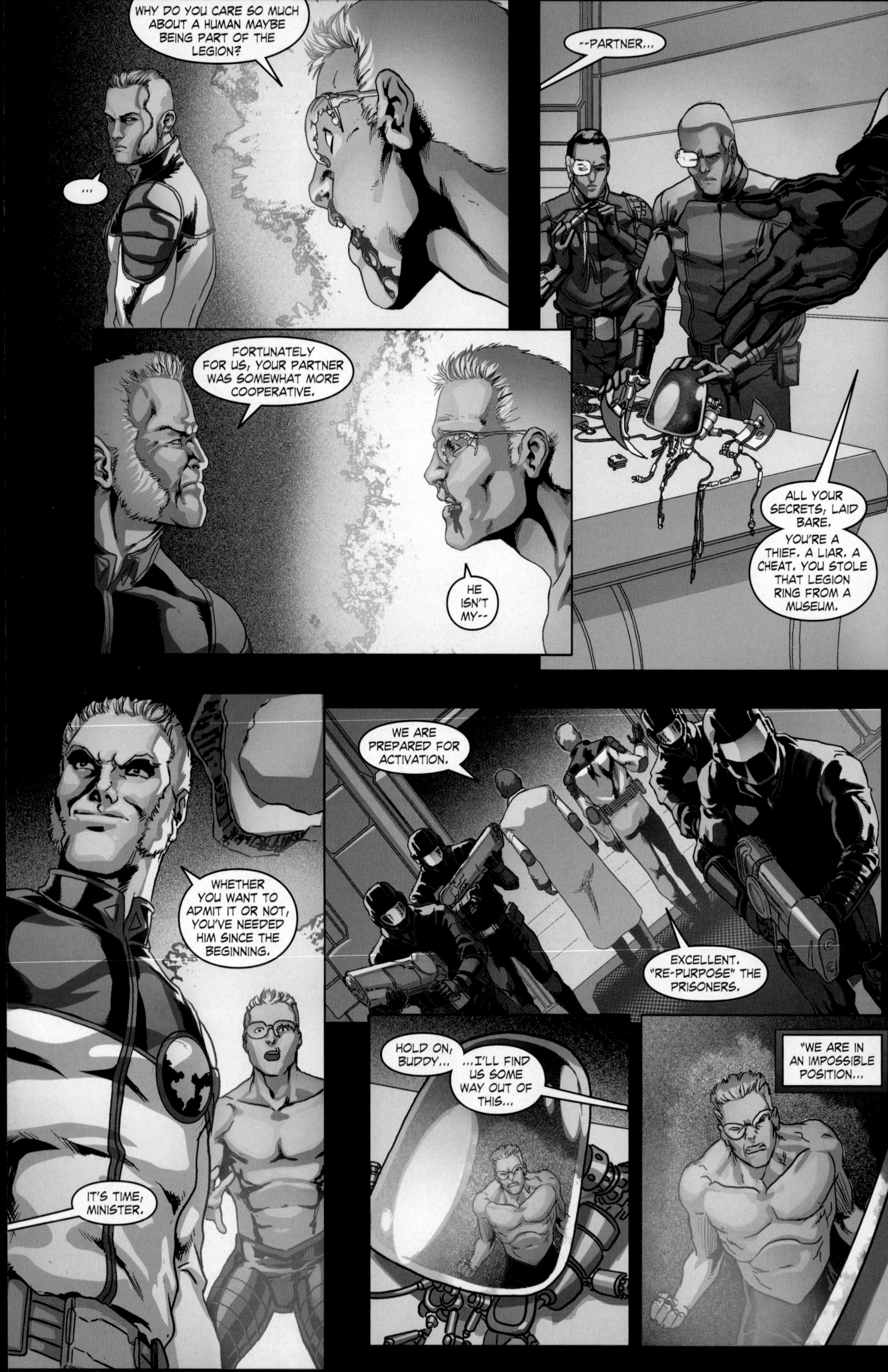
WHY DO YOU CARE SO MUCH ABOUT A HUMAN MAYBE BEING PART OF THE LEGION?
...
--PARTNER...
FORTUNATELY FOR US, YOUR PARTNER WAS SOMEWHAT MORE COOPERATIVE.
HE ISN'T MY--
ALL YOUR SECRETS, LAID BARE.
YOU'RE A THIEF. A LIAR. A CHEAT. YOU STOLE THAT LEGION RING FROM A MUSEUM.
WHETHER YOU WANT TO ADMIT IT OR NOT, YOU'VE NEEDED HIM SINCE THE BEGINNING.
IT'S TIME, MINISTER.
WE ARE PREPARED FOR ACTIVATION.
EXCELLENT. "RE-PURPOSE" THE PRISONERS.
HOLD ON, BUDDY...
...I'LL FIND US SOME WAY OUT OF THIS...
"WE ARE IN AN IMPOSSIBLE POSITION...

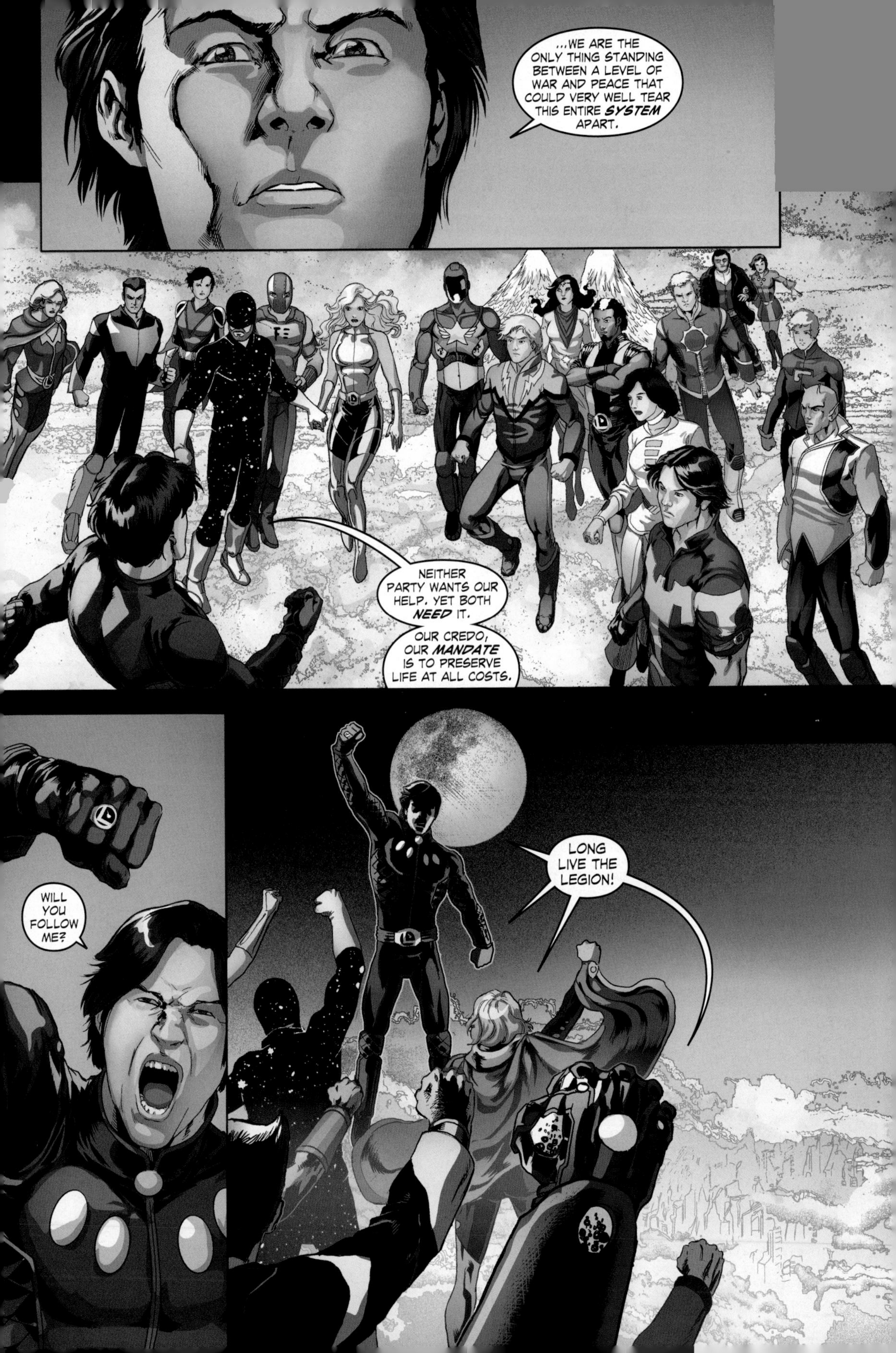
...WE ARE THE ONLY THING STANDING BETWEEN A LEVEL OF WAR AND PEACE THAT COULD VERY WELL TEAR THIS ENTIRE SYSTEM APART.
NEITHER PARTY WANTS OUR HELP. YET BOTH NEED IT.
OUR CREDO, OUR MANDATE IS TO PRESERVE LIFE AT ALL COSTS.
WILL YOU FOLLOW ME?
LONG LIVE THE LEGION!

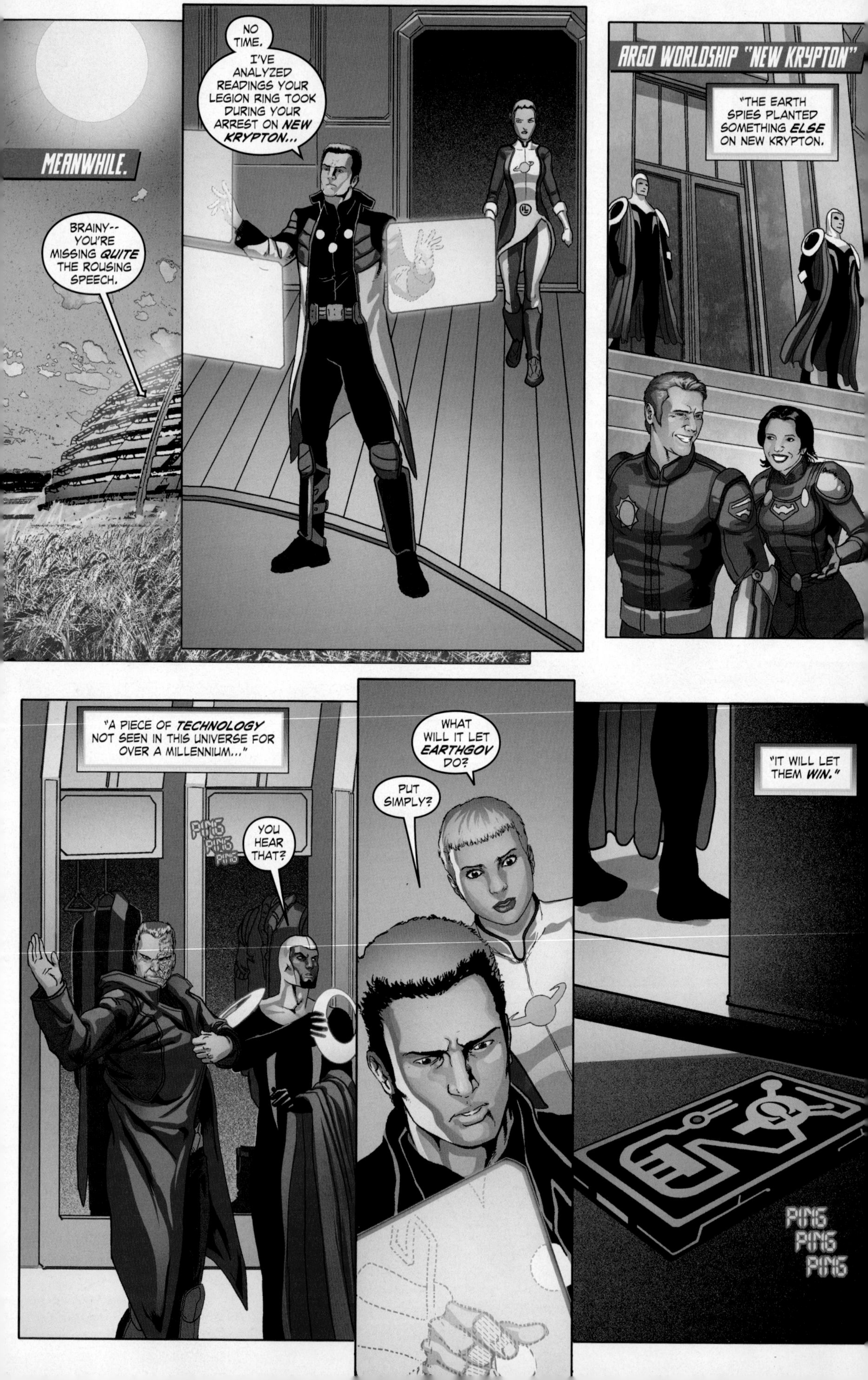
MEANWHILE.
BRAINY-- YOU'RE MISSING QUITE THE ROUSING SPEECH.
NO TIME. I'VE ANALYZED READINGS YOUR LEGION RING TOOK DURING YOUR ARREST ON NEW KRYPTON...
ARGO WORLDSHIP "NEW KRYPTON"
"THE EARTH SPIES PLANTED SOMETHING ELSE ON NEW KRYPTON.
"A PIECE OF TECHNOLOGY NOT SEEN IN THIS UNIVERSE FOR OVER A MILLENNIUM..."
PING PING PING
YOU HEAR THAT?
WHAT WILL IT LET EARTHGOV DO?
PUT SIMPLY?
"IT WILL LET THEM WIN."
PING PING PING

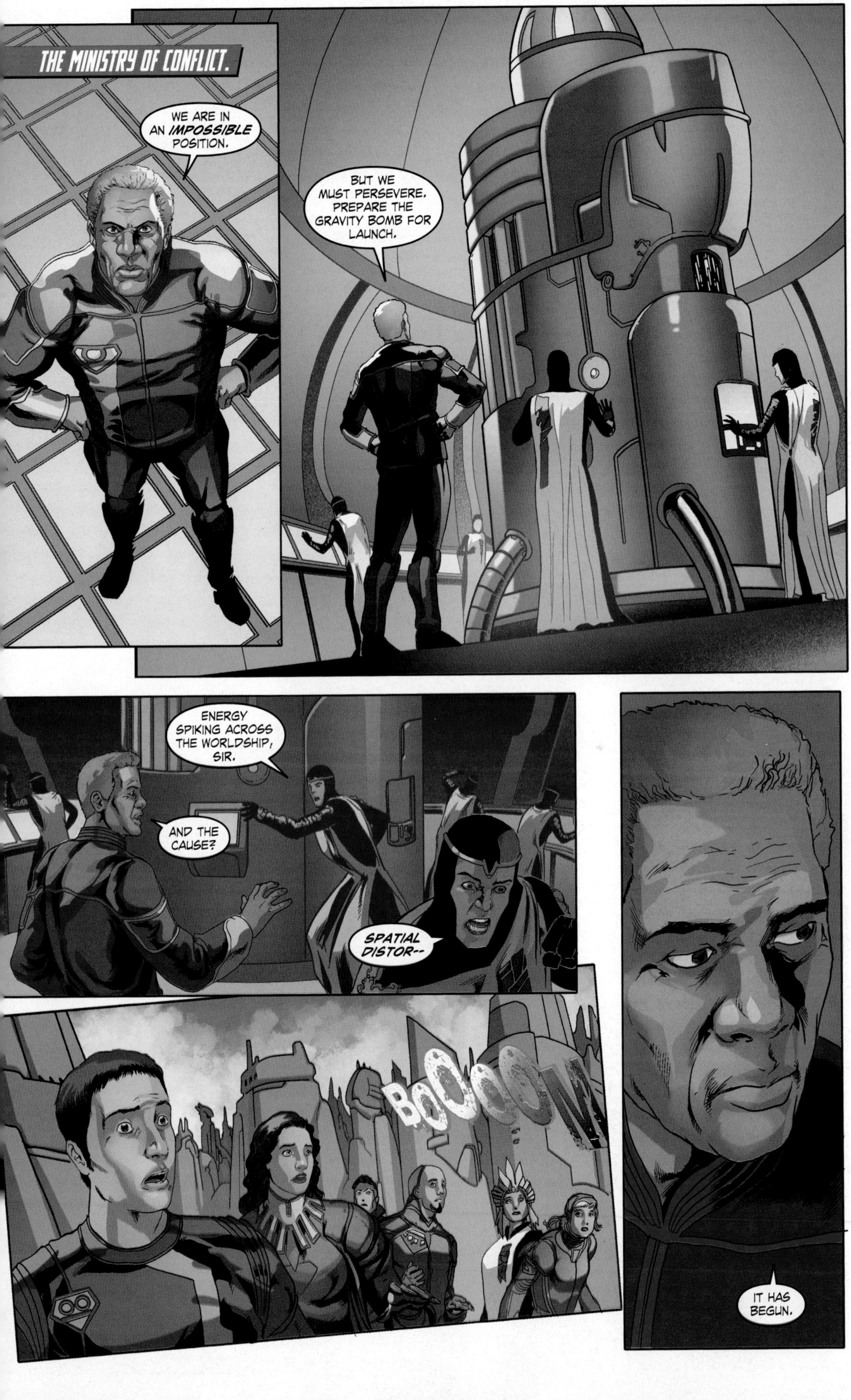
THE MINISTRY OF CONFLICT.
WE ARE IN AN *IMPOSSIBLE* POSITION.
BUT WE MUST PERSEVERE. PREPARE THE GRAVITY BOMB FOR LAUNCH.
ENERGY SPIKING ACROSS THE WORLDSHIP, SIR.
AND THE CAUSE?
SPATIAL DISTOR--
BOOOOOM
IT HAS BEGUN.

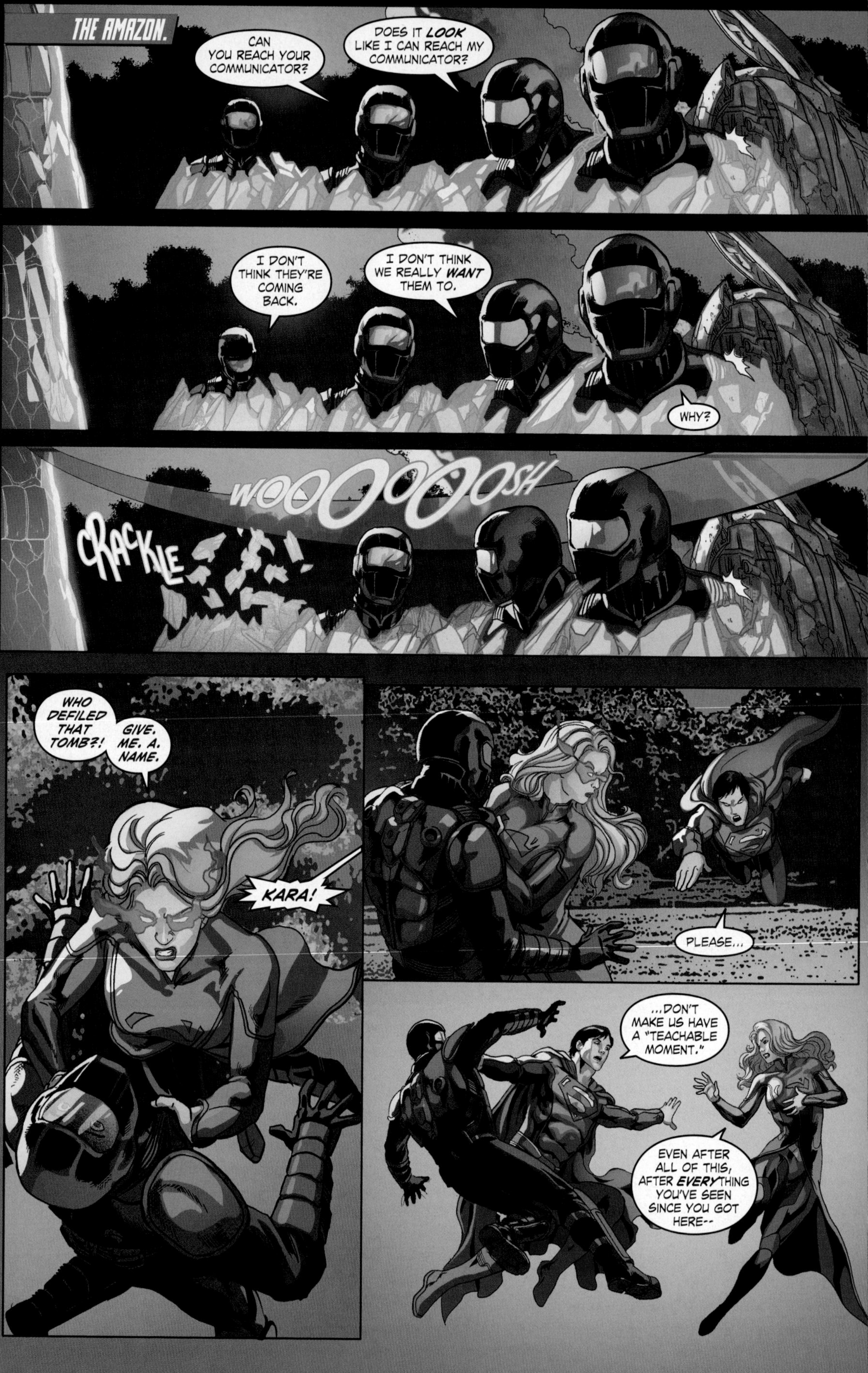
THE AMAZON.
CAN YOU REACH YOUR COMMUNICATOR?
DOES IT *LOOK* LIKE I CAN REACH MY COMMUNICATOR?
I DON'T THINK THEY'RE COMING BACK.
I DON'T THINK WE REALLY *WANT* THEM TO.
WHY?
WOOOOOOOSH
CRACKLE
WHO DEFILED THAT TOMB?!
GIVE. ME. A. NAME.
KARA!
PLEASE...
...DON'T MAKE US HAVE A "TEACHABLE MOMENT."
EVEN AFTER ALL OF THIS, AFTER *EVERY*THING YOU'VE SEEN SINCE YOU GOT HERE--

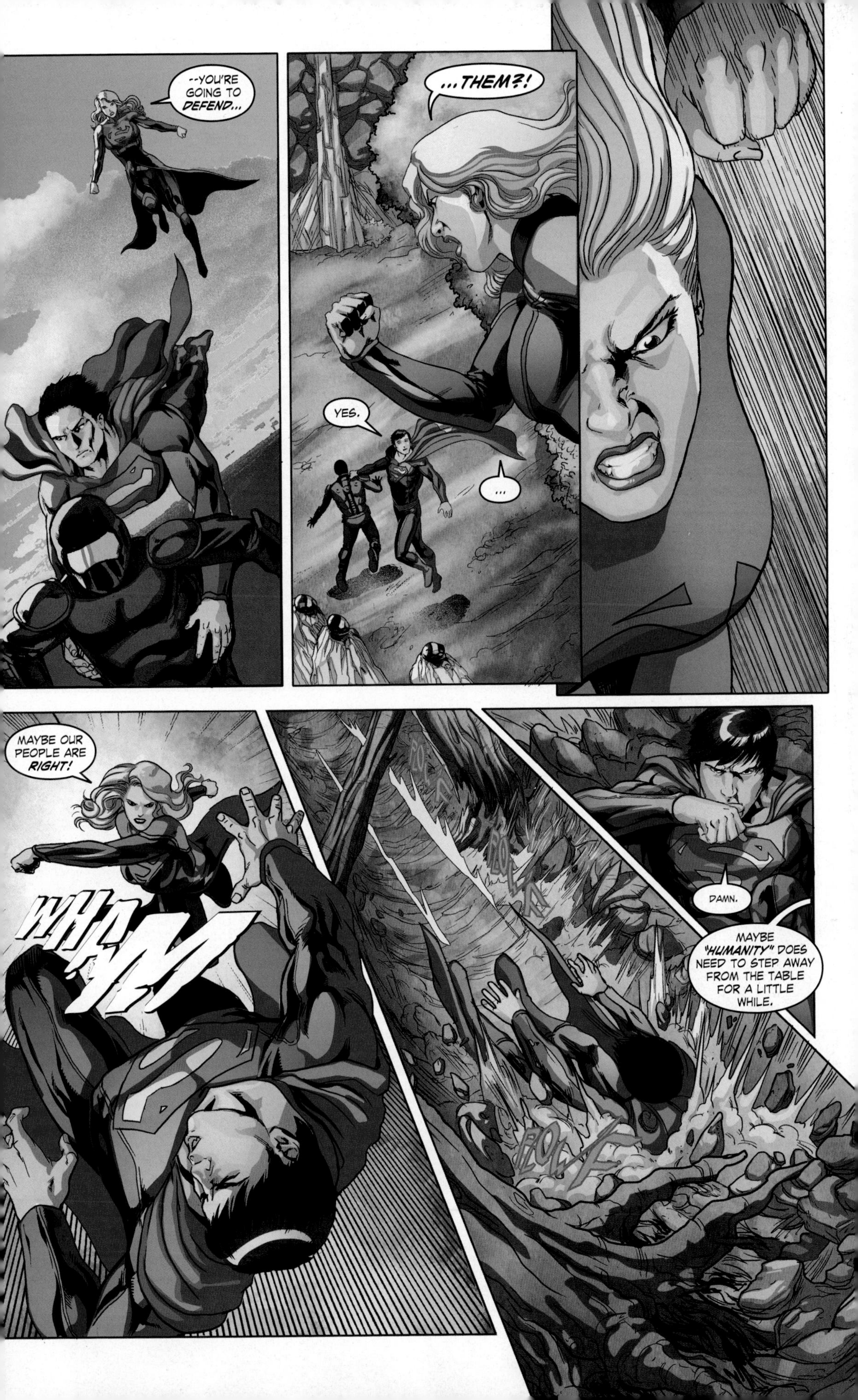
--YOU'RE GOING TO DEFEND...
...THEM?!
YES.
...
MAYBE OUR PEOPLE ARE RIGHT!
WHAM
DAMN.
MAYBE "HUMANITY" DOES NEED TO STEP AWAY FROM THE TABLE FOR A LITTLE WHILE.

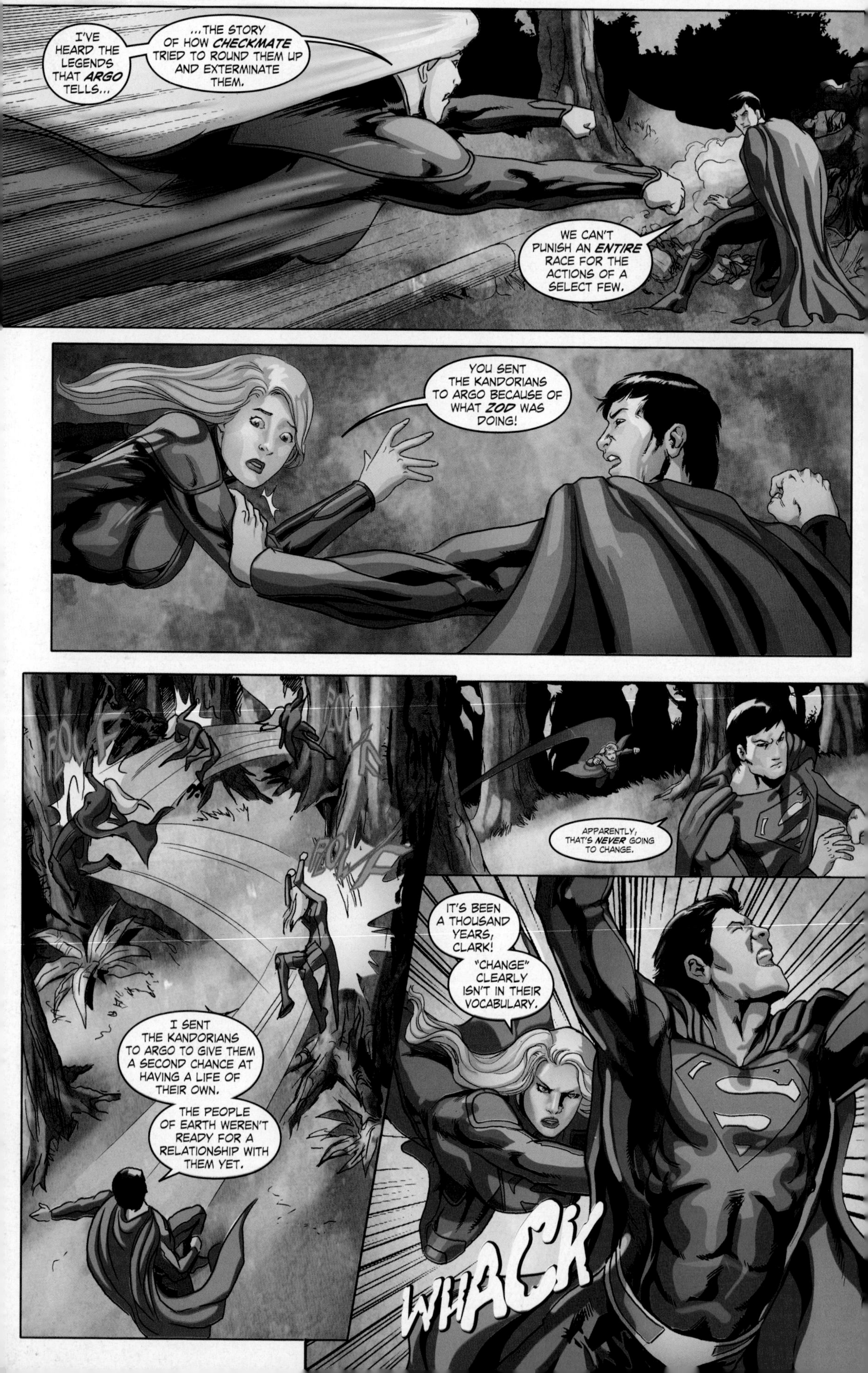
I'VE HEARD THE LEGENDS THAT ARGO TELLS...
...THE STORY OF HOW CHECKMATE TRIED TO ROUND THEM UP AND EXTERMINATE THEM.
WE CAN'T PUNISH AN ENTIRE RACE FOR THE ACTIONS OF A SELECT FEW.
YOU SENT THE KANDORIANS TO ARGO BECAUSE OF WHAT ZOD WAS DOING!
I SENT THE KANDORIANS TO ARGO TO GIVE THEM A SECOND CHANCE AT HAVING A LIFE OF THEIR OWN.
THE PEOPLE OF EARTH WEREN'T READY FOR A RELATIONSHIP WITH THEM YET.
APPARENTLY, THAT'S NEVER GOING TO CHANGE.
IT'S BEEN A THOUSAND YEARS, CLARK!
"CHANGE" CLEARLY ISN'T IN THEIR VOCABULARY.
WHACK

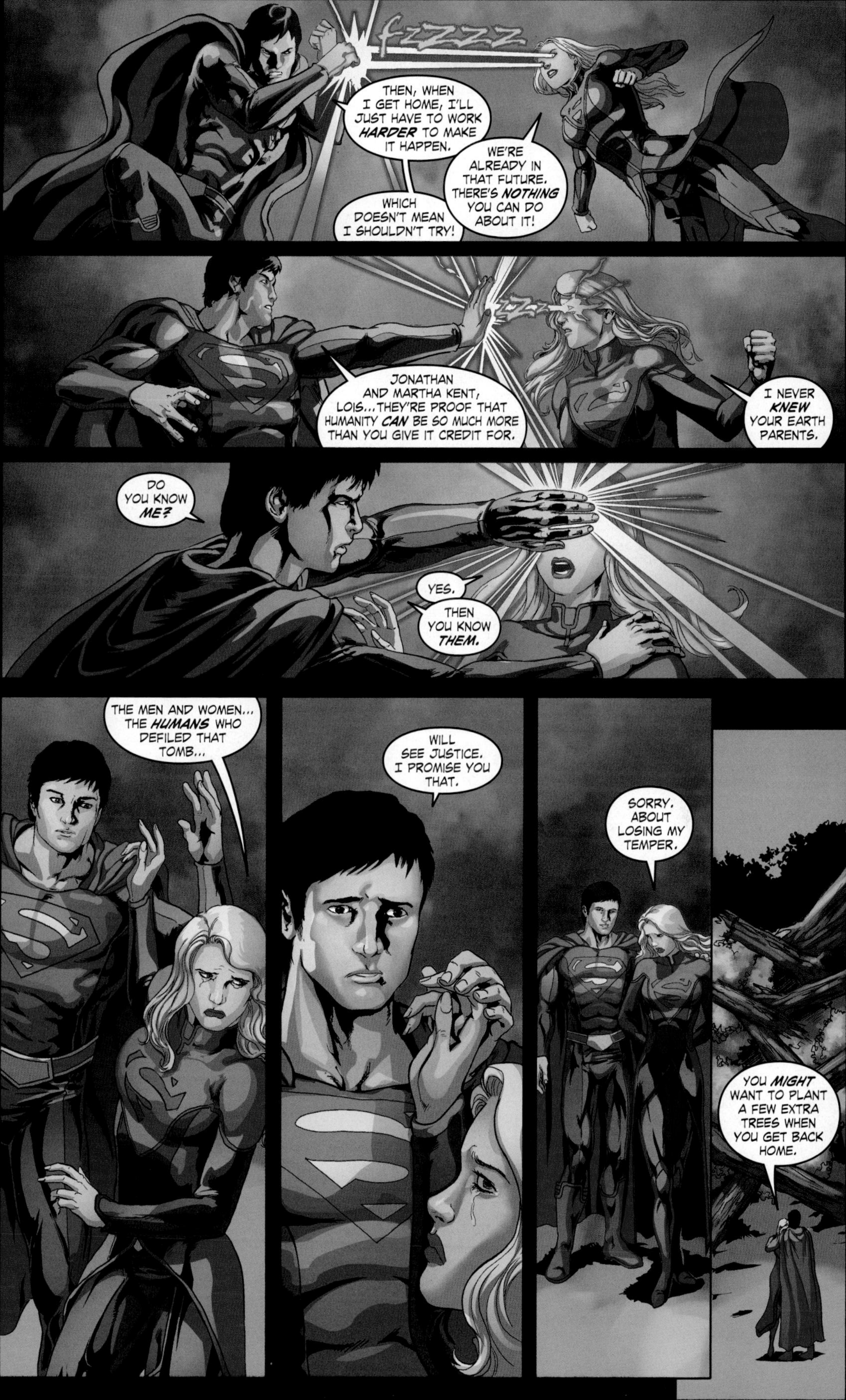
FZZZZ
THEN, WHEN I GET HOME, I'LL JUST HAVE TO WORK HARDER TO MAKE IT HAPPEN.
WHICH DOESN'T MEAN I SHOULDN'T TRY!
WE'RE ALREADY IN THAT FUTURE. THERE'S NOTHING YOU CAN DO ABOUT IT!
JONATHAN AND MARTHA KENT, LOIS...THEY'RE PROOF THAT HUMANITY CAN BE SO MUCH MORE THAN YOU GIVE IT CREDIT FOR.
I NEVER KNEW YOUR EARTH PARENTS.
DO YOU KNOW ME?
YES.
THEN YOU KNOW THEM.
THE MEN AND WOMEN... THE HUMANS WHO DEFILED THAT TOMB...
WILL SEE JUSTICE. I PROMISE YOU THAT.
SORRY. ABOUT LOSING MY TEMPER.
YOU MIGHT WANT TO PLANT A FEW EXTRA TREES WHEN YOU GET BACK HOME.

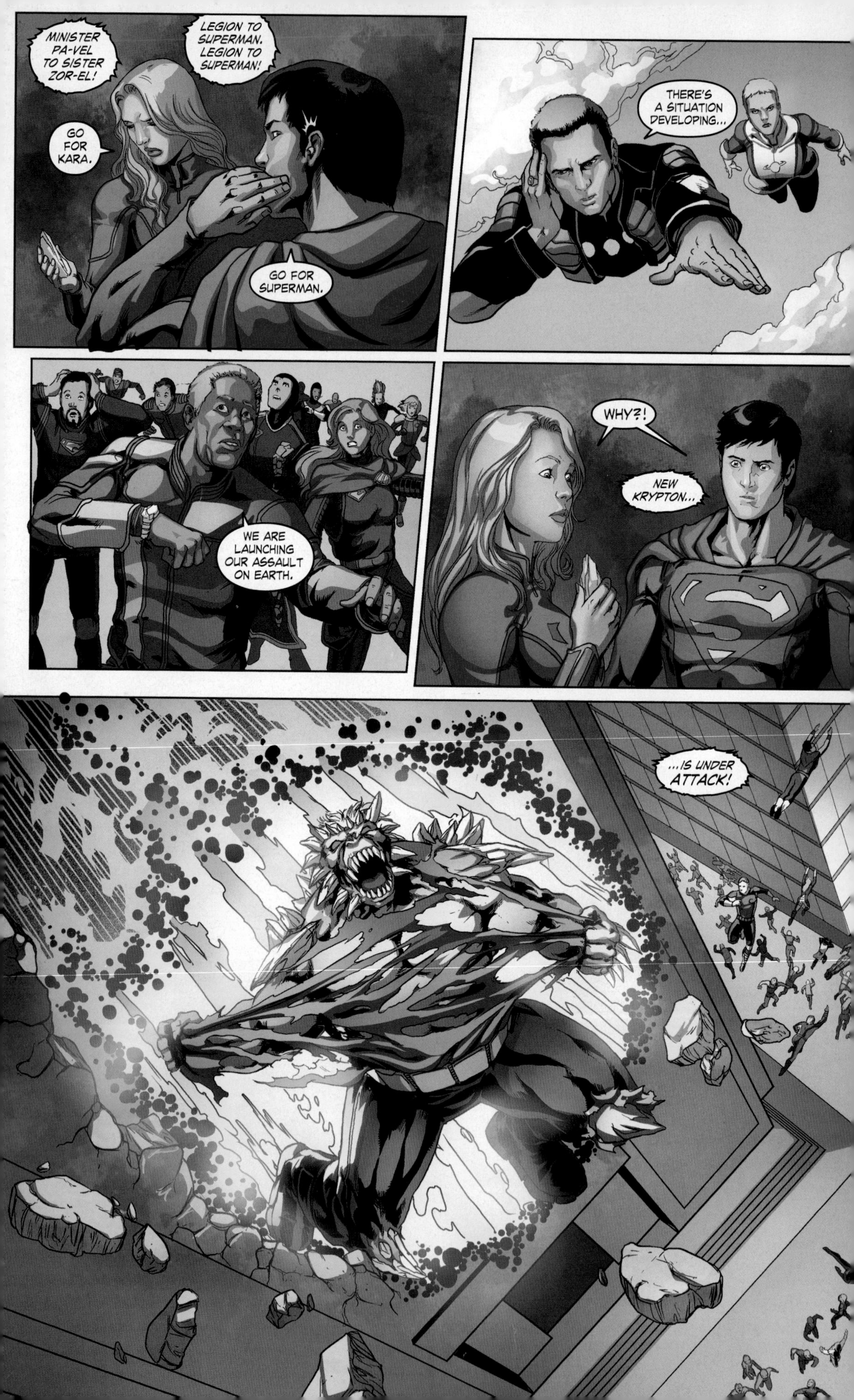
MINISTER PA-VEL TO SISTER ZOR-EL!
LEGION TO SUPERMAN. LEGION TO SUPERMAN!
GO FOR KARA.
GO FOR SUPERMAN.
THERE'S A SITUATION DEVELOPING...
WE ARE LAUNCHING OUR ASSAULT ON EARTH.
WHY?!
NEW KRYPTON...
...IS UNDER ATTACK!

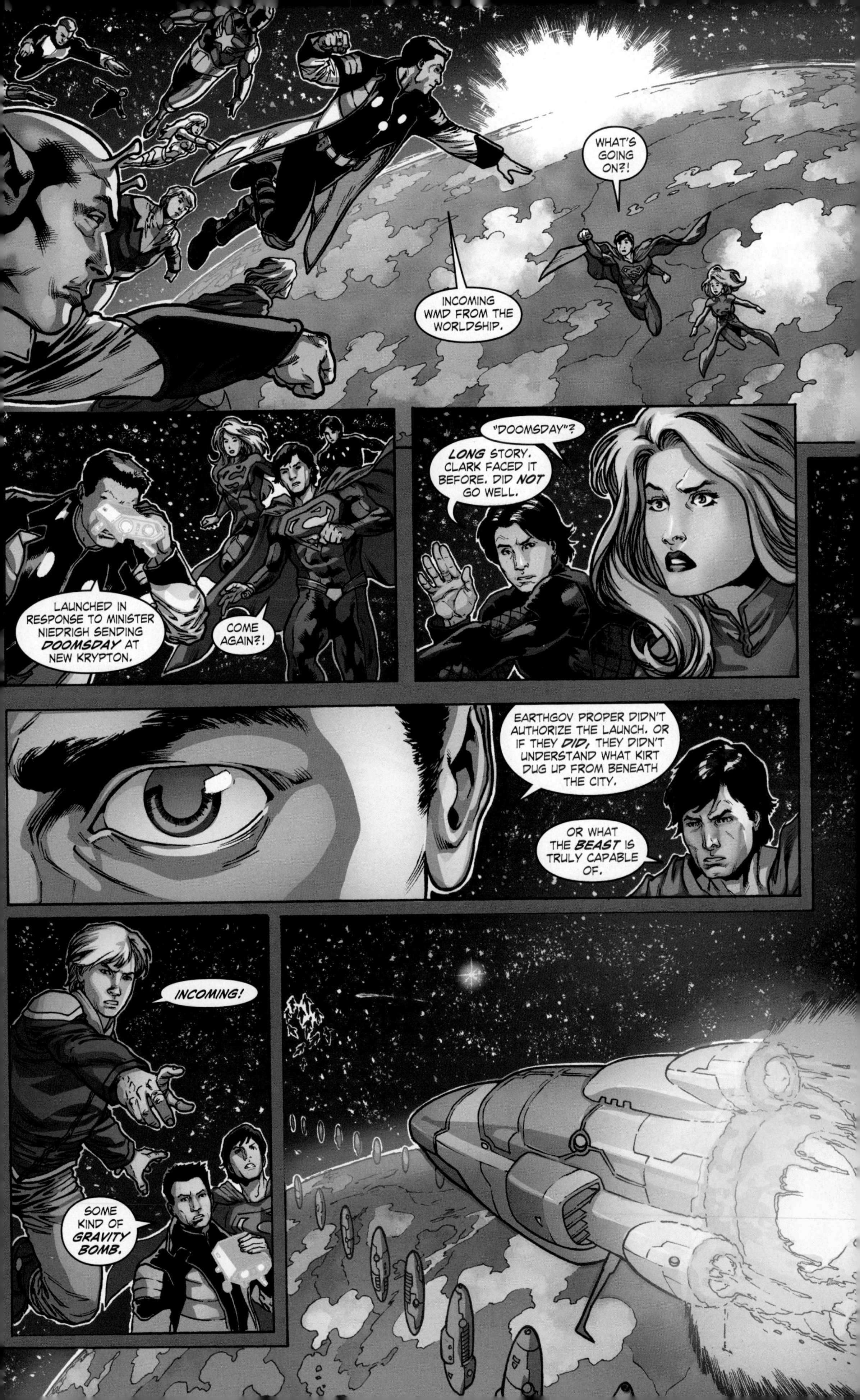

WHAT'S GOING ON?!
INCOMING WMD FROM THE WORLDSHIP.
LAUNCHED IN RESPONSE TO MINISTER NIEDRIGH SENDING DOOMSDAY AT NEW KRYPTON.
COME AGAIN?!
"DOOMSDAY"?
LONG STORY. CLARK FACED IT BEFORE. DID NOT GO WELL.
EARTHGOV PROPER DIDN'T AUTHORIZE THE LAUNCH. OR IF THEY DID, THEY DIDN'T UNDERSTAND WHAT KIRT DUG UP FROM BENEATH THE CITY.
OR WHAT THE BEAST IS TRULY CAPABLE OF.
INCOMING!
SOME KIND OF GRAVITY BOMB.

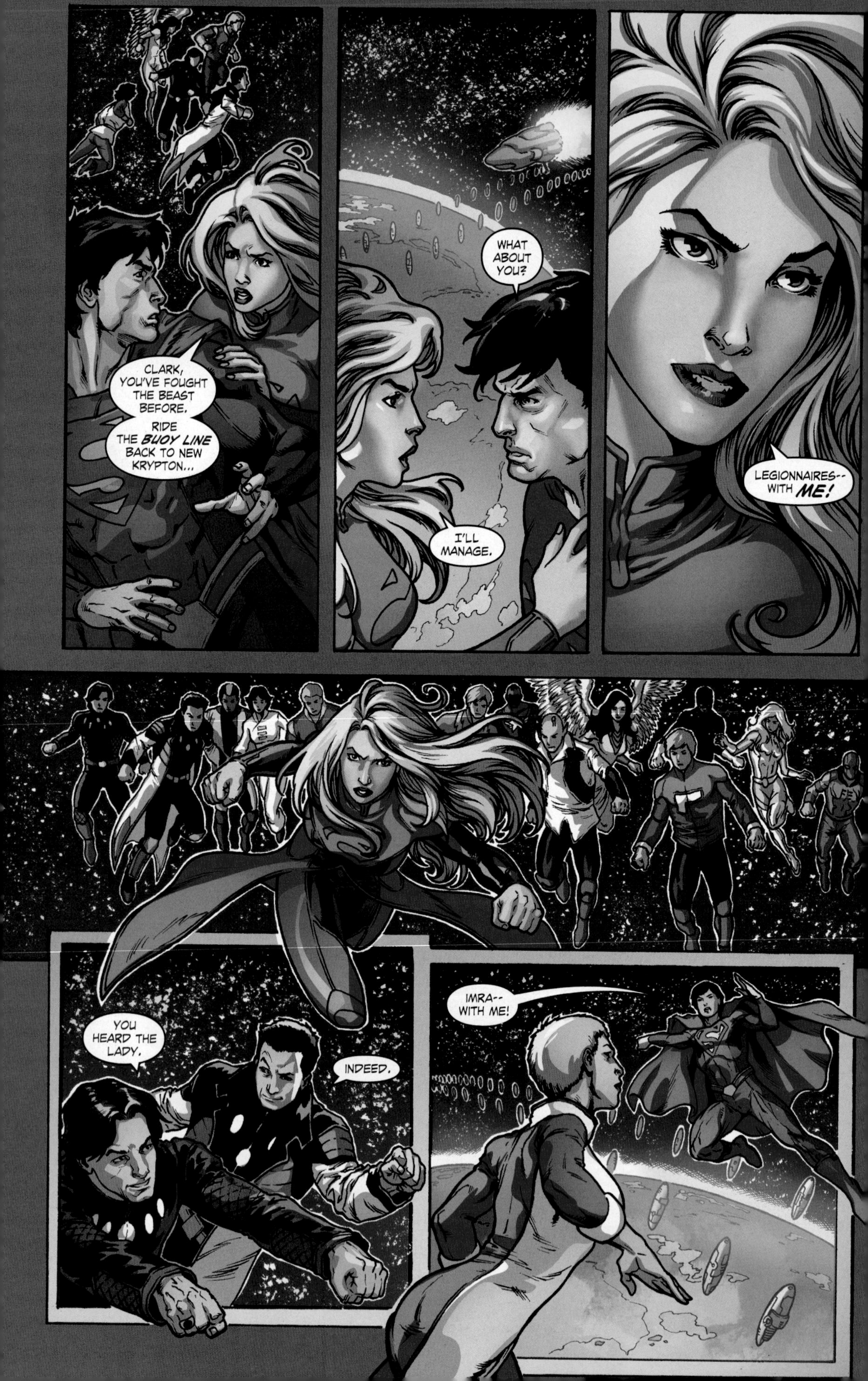
CLARK, YOU'VE FOUGHT THE BEAST BEFORE.
RIDE THE BUOY LINE BACK TO NEW KRYPTON...
WHAT ABOUT YOU?
I'LL MANAGE.
LEGIONNAIRES-- WITH ME!
YOU HEARD THE LADY.
INDEED.
IMRA-- WITH ME!

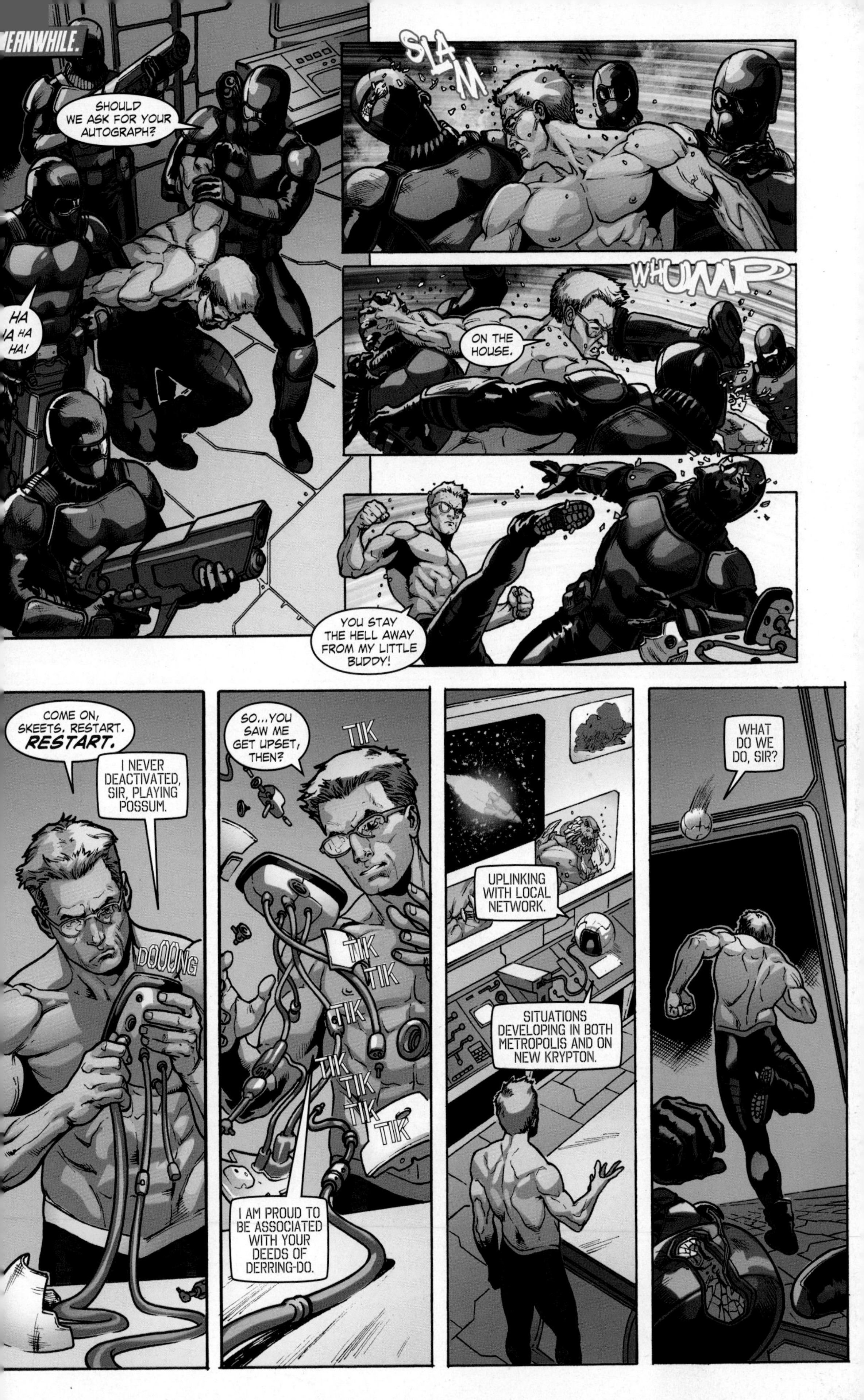
MEANWHILE.
SHOULD WE ASK FOR YOUR AUTOGRAPH?
HA HA HA HA!
SLAM
WHUMP
ON THE HOUSE.
YOU STAY THE HELL AWAY FROM MY LITTLE BUDDY!
COME ON, SKEETS. RESTART. RESTART.
I NEVER DEACTIVATED, SIR, PLAYING POSSUM.
DOOONG
SO...YOU SAW ME GET UPSET, THEN?
TIK
TIK TIK
TIK
TIK TIK TIK TIK
I AM PROUD TO BE ASSOCIATED WITH YOUR DEEDS OF DERRING-DO.
UPLINKING WITH LOCAL NETWORK.
SITUATIONS DEVELOPING IN BOTH METROPOLIS AND ON NEW KRYPTON.
WHAT DO WE DO, SIR?

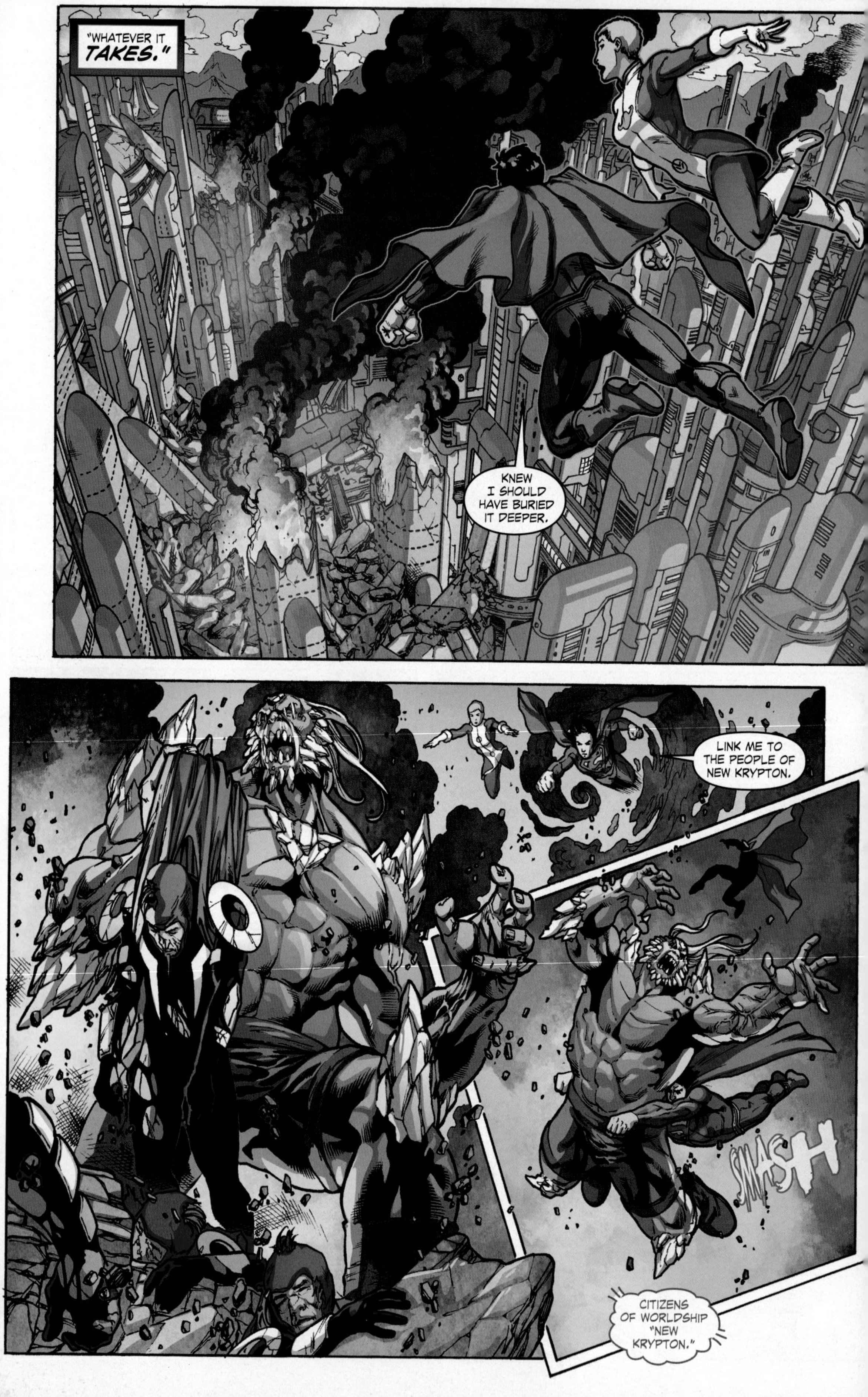
"WHATEVER IT TAKES."
KNEW I SHOULD HAVE BURIED IT DEEPER.
LINK ME TO THE PEOPLE OF NEW KRYPTON.
SMASH
CITIZENS OF WORLDSHIP "NEW KRYPTON."

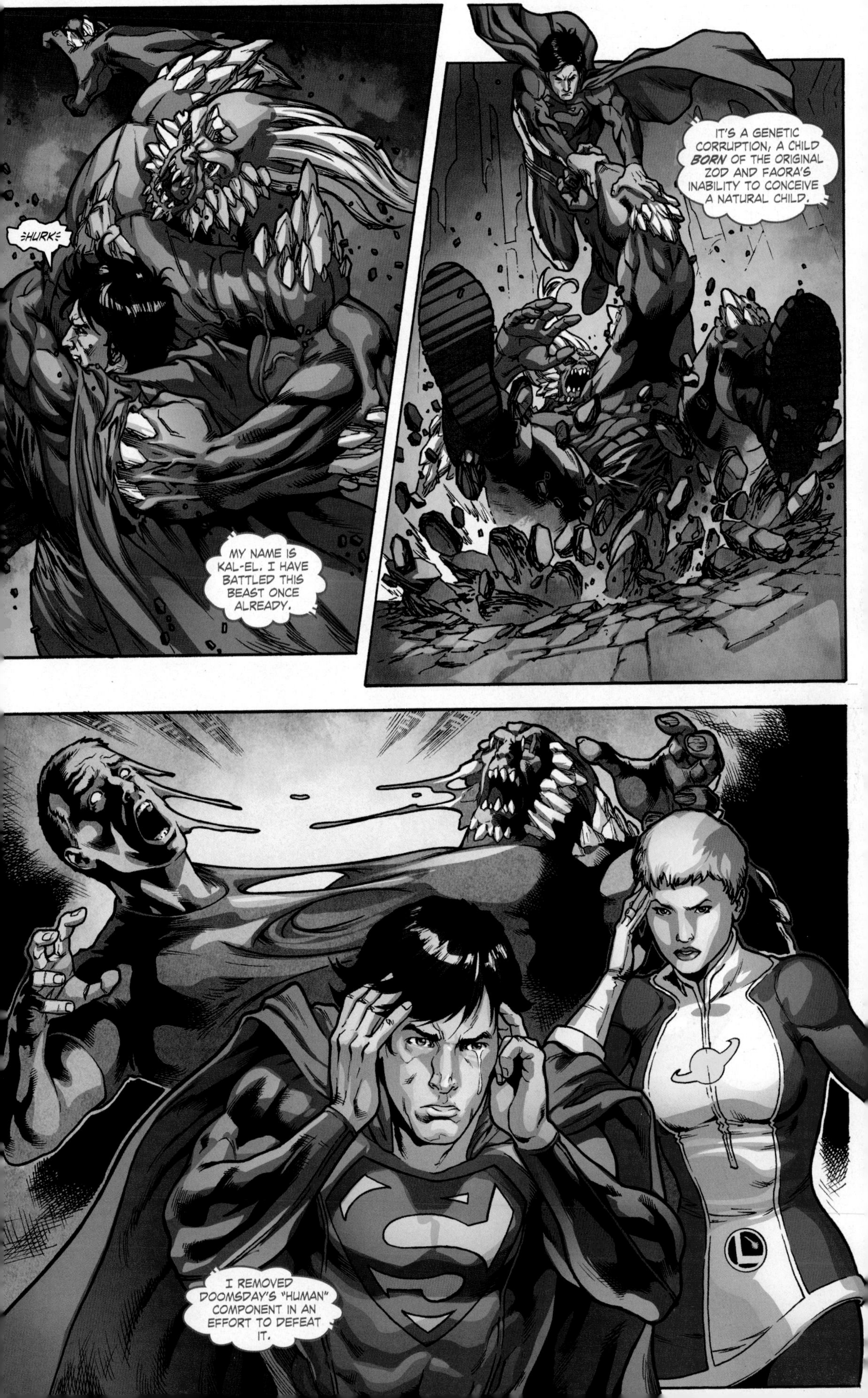
HURK
MY NAME IS KAL-EL. I HAVE BATTLED THIS BEAST ONCE ALREADY.
IT'S A GENETIC CORRUPTION, A CHILD BORN OF THE ORIGINAL ZOD AND FAORA'S INABILITY TO CONCEIVE A NATURAL CHILD.
I REMOVED DOOMSDAY'S "HUMAN" COMPONENT IN AN EFFORT TO DEFEAT IT.

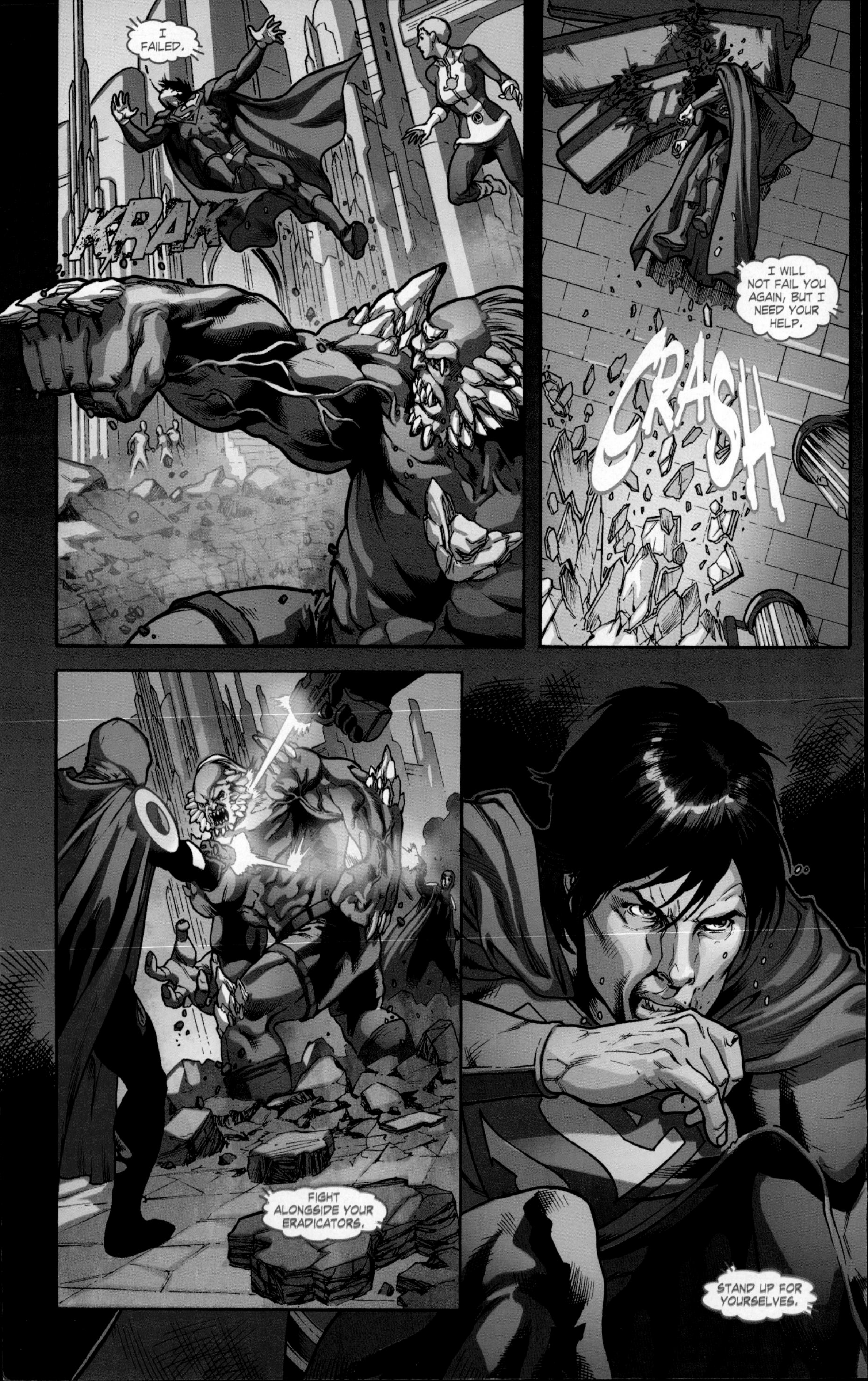
I FAILED.
KRAK
I WILL NOT FAIL YOU AGAIN, BUT I NEED YOUR HELP.
CRASH
FIGHT ALONGSIDE YOUR ERADICATORS.
STAND UP FOR YOURSELVES.

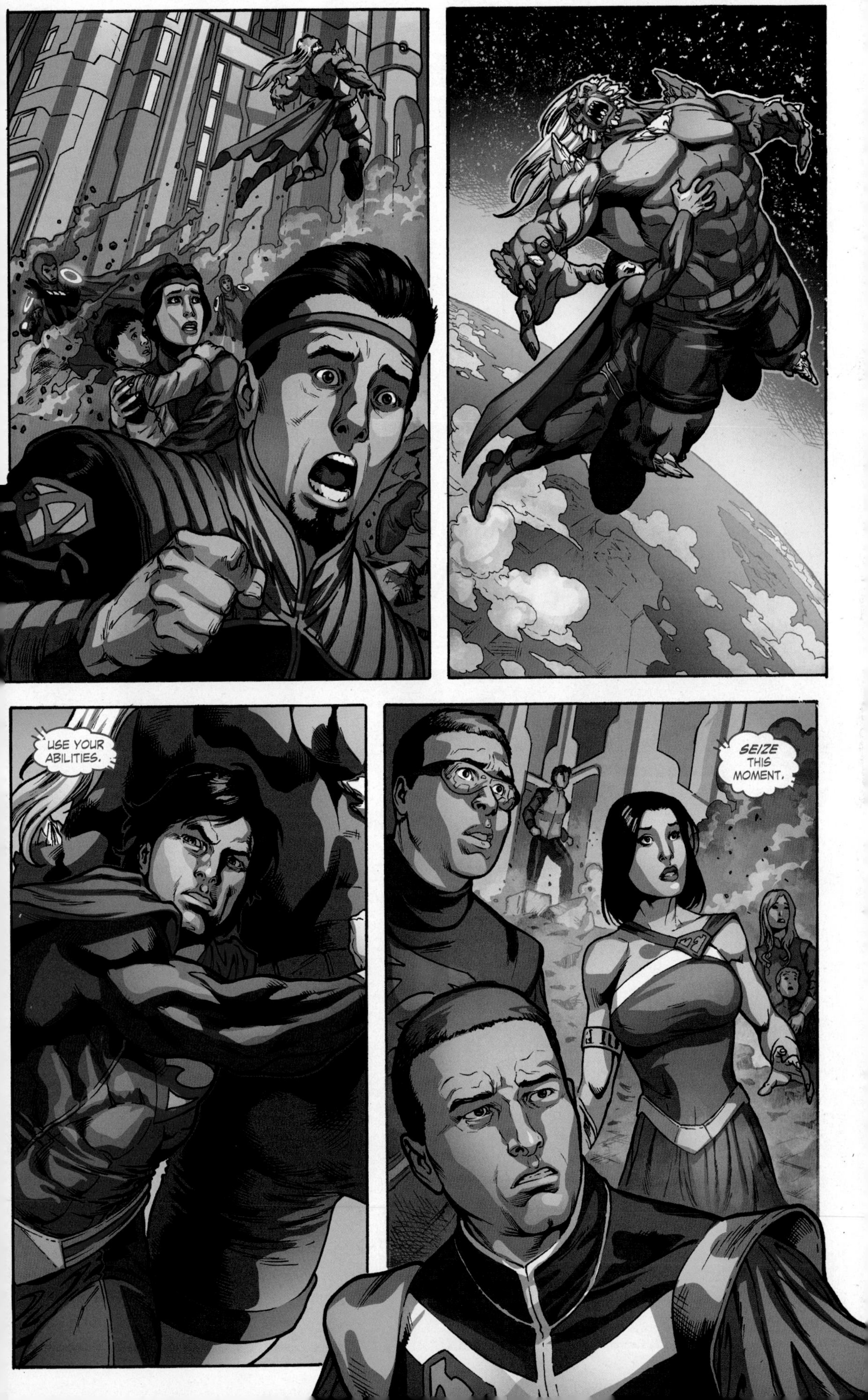
USE YOUR ABILITIES.
SEIZE THIS MOMENT.

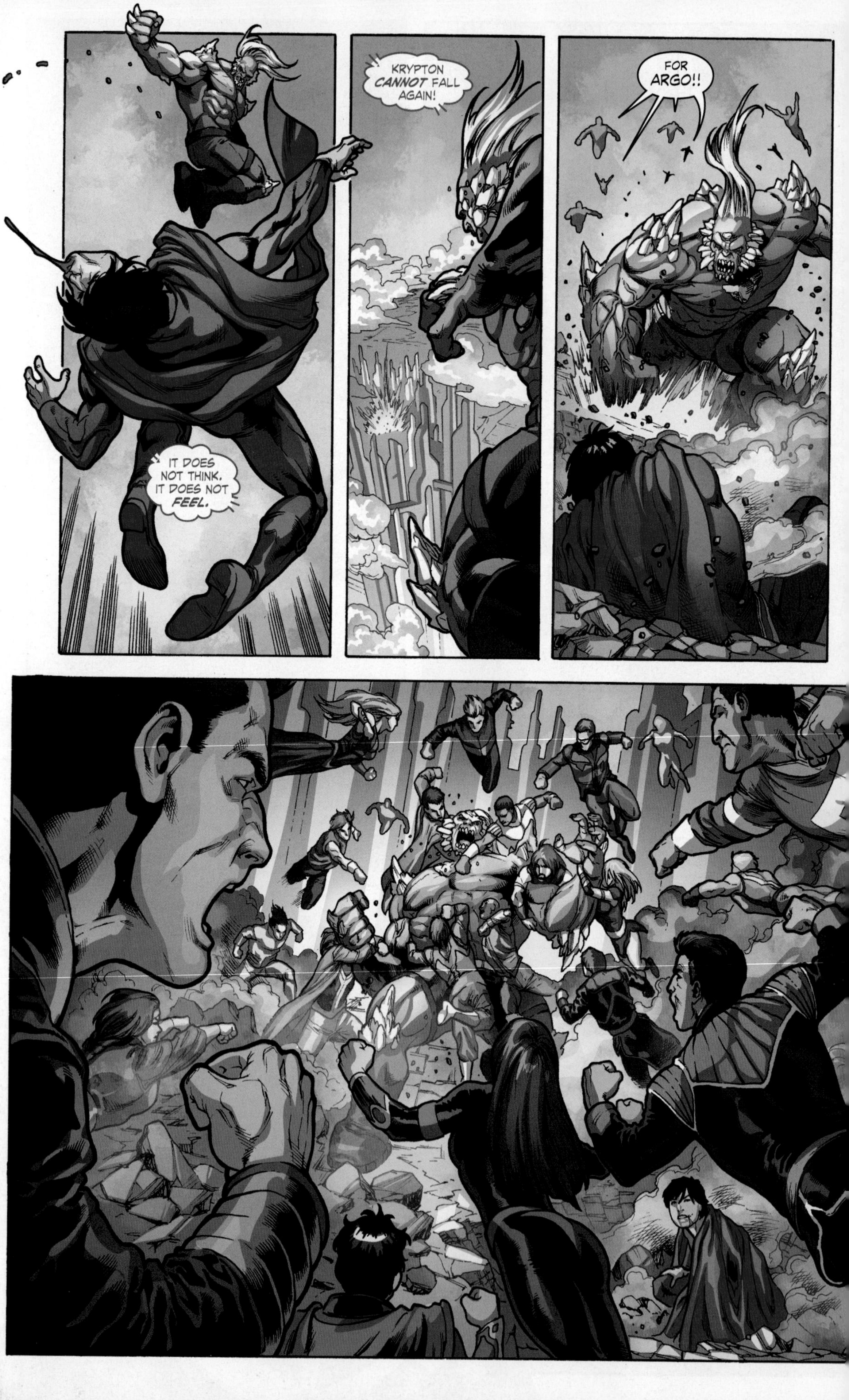
IT DOES NOT THINK. IT DOES NOT FEEL.
KRYPTON CANNOT FALL AGAIN!
FOR ARGO!!

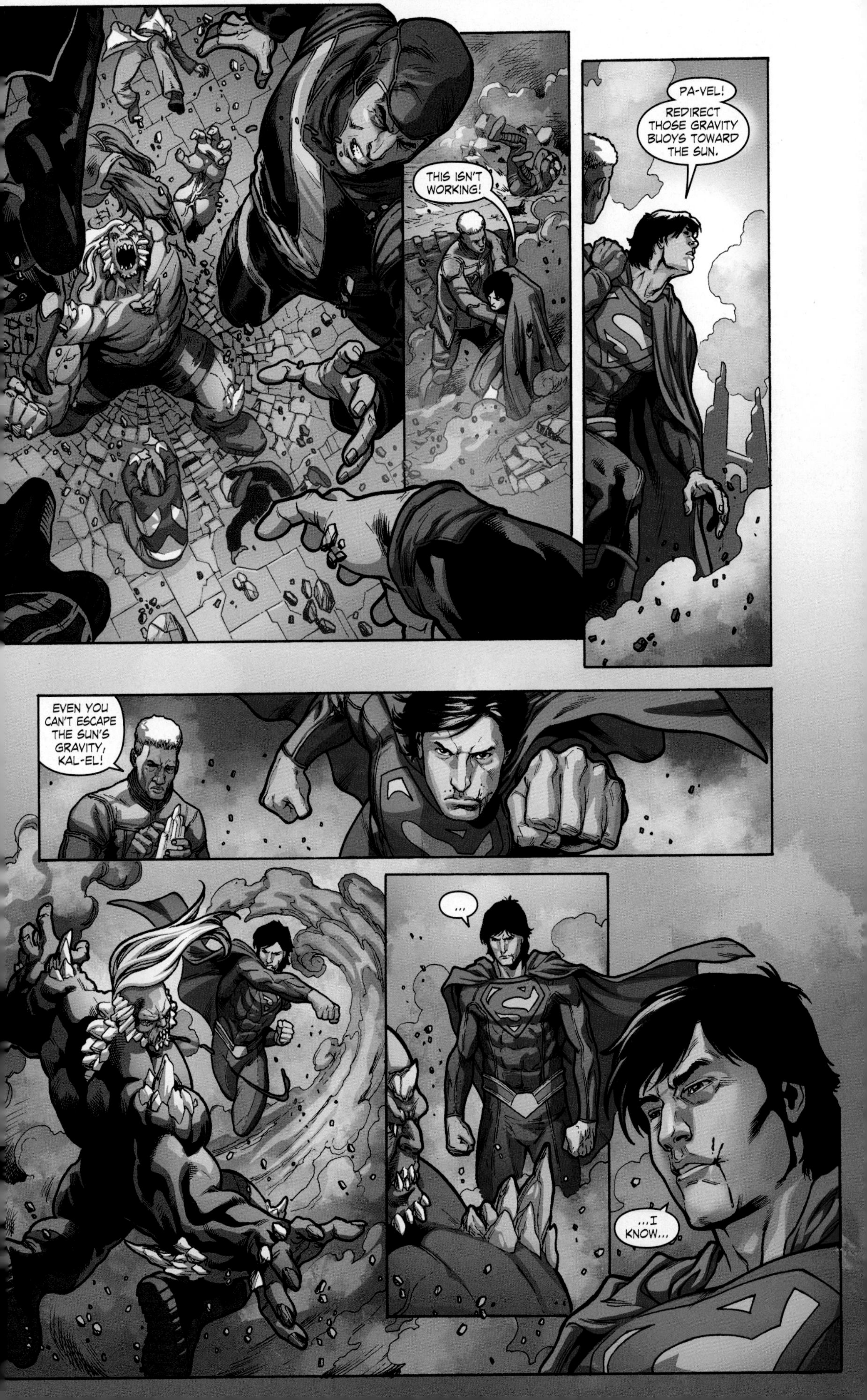
THIS ISN'T WORKING!
PA-VEL!
REDIRECT THOSE GRAVITY BUOYS TOWARD THE SUN.
EVEN YOU CAN'T ESCAPE THE SUN'S GRAVITY, KAL-EL!
...
...I KNOW...

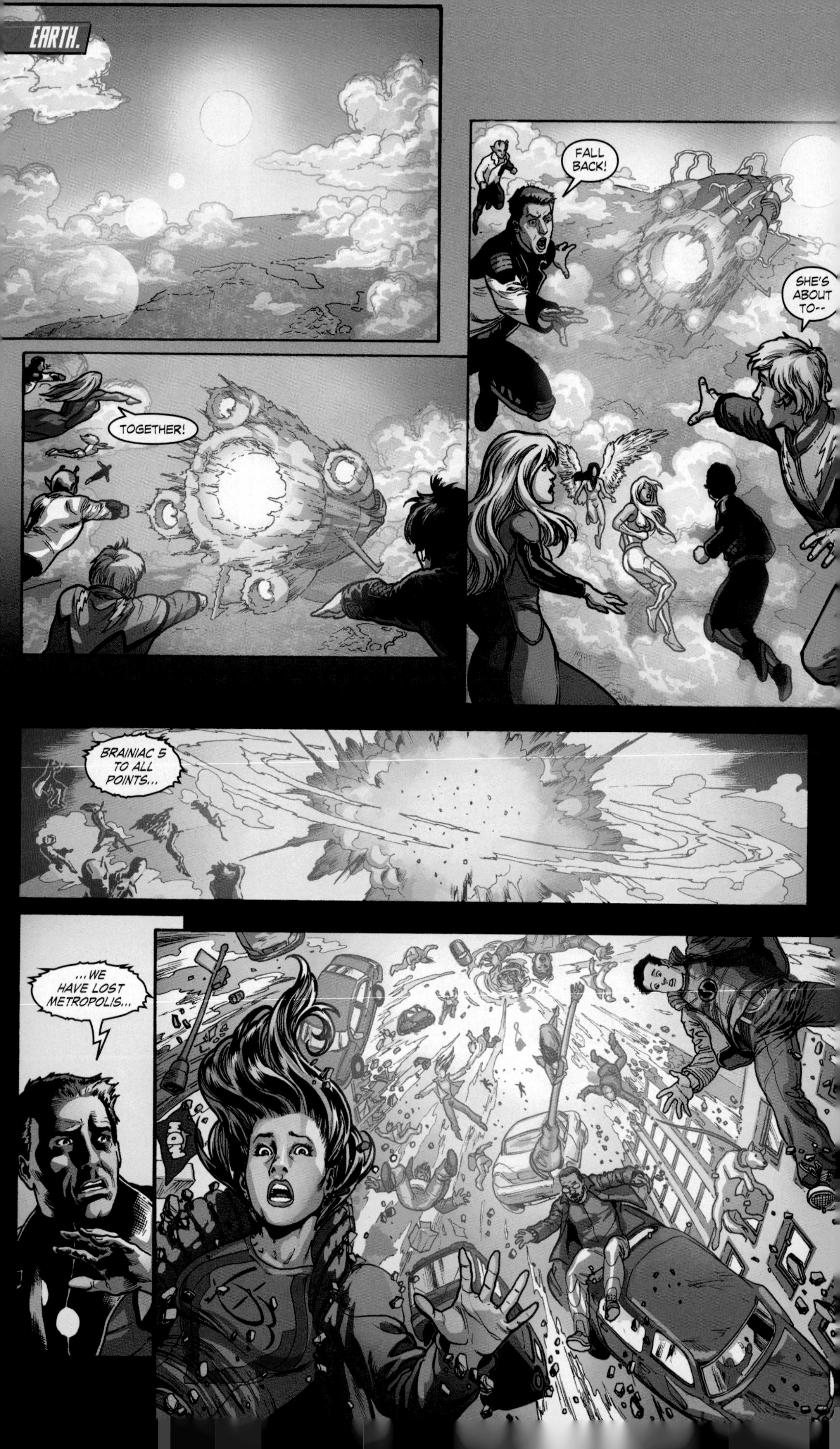
EARTH.
FALL BACK!
SHE'S ABOUT TO--
TOGETHER!
BRAINIAC 5 TO ALL POINTS...
...WE HAVE LOST METROPOLIS...

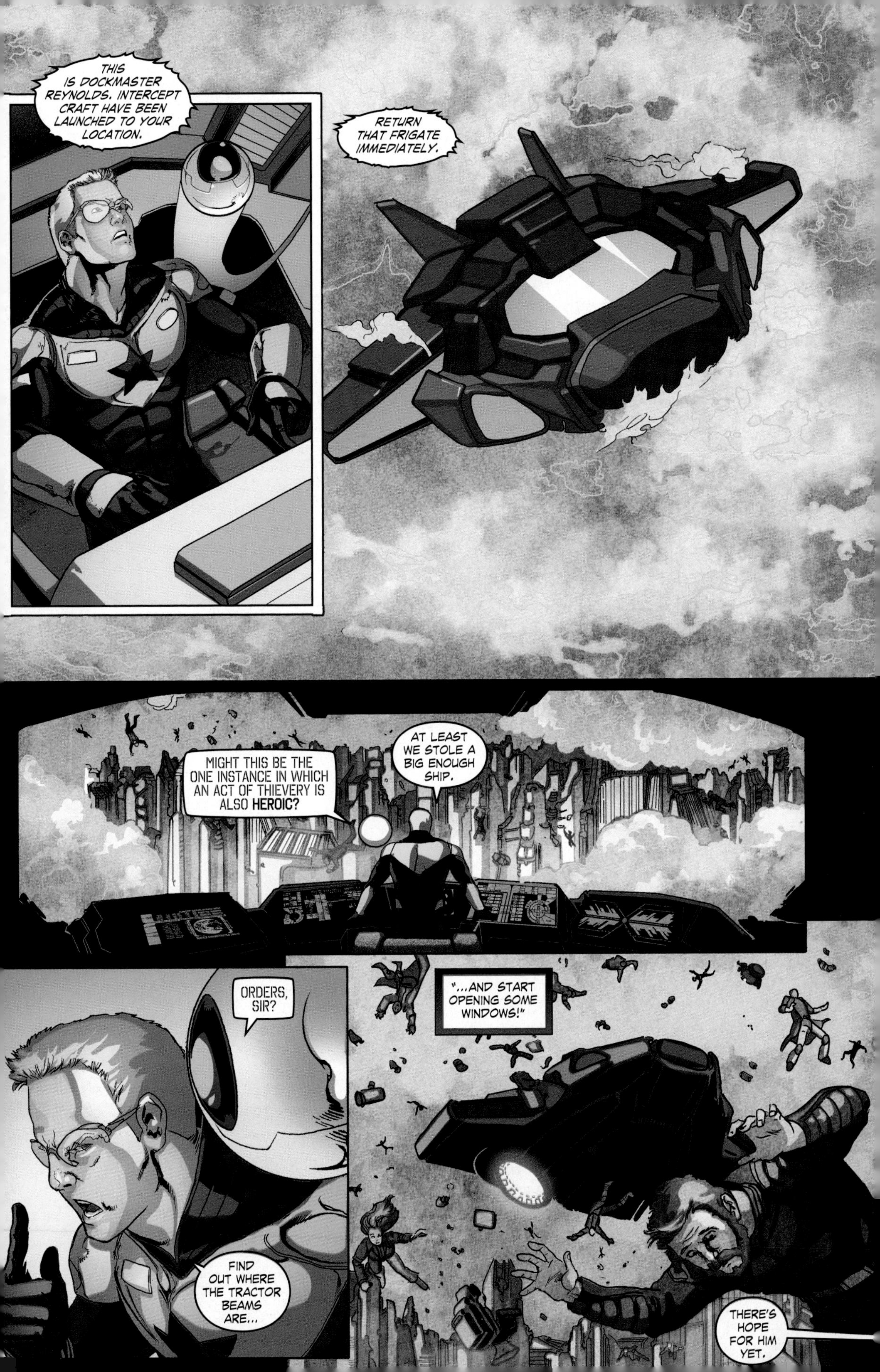
THIS IS DOCKMASTER REYNOLDS. INTERCEPT CRAFT HAVE BEEN LAUNCHED TO YOUR LOCATION.
RETURN THAT FRIGATE IMMEDIATELY.
MIGHT THIS BE THE ONE INSTANCE IN WHICH AN ACT OF THIEVERY IS ALSO HEROIC?
AT LEAST WE STOLE A BIG ENOUGH SHIP.
ORDERS, SIR?
FIND OUT WHERE THE TRACTOR BEAMS ARE...
"...AND START OPENING SOME WINDOWS!"
THERE'S HOPE FOR HIM YET.

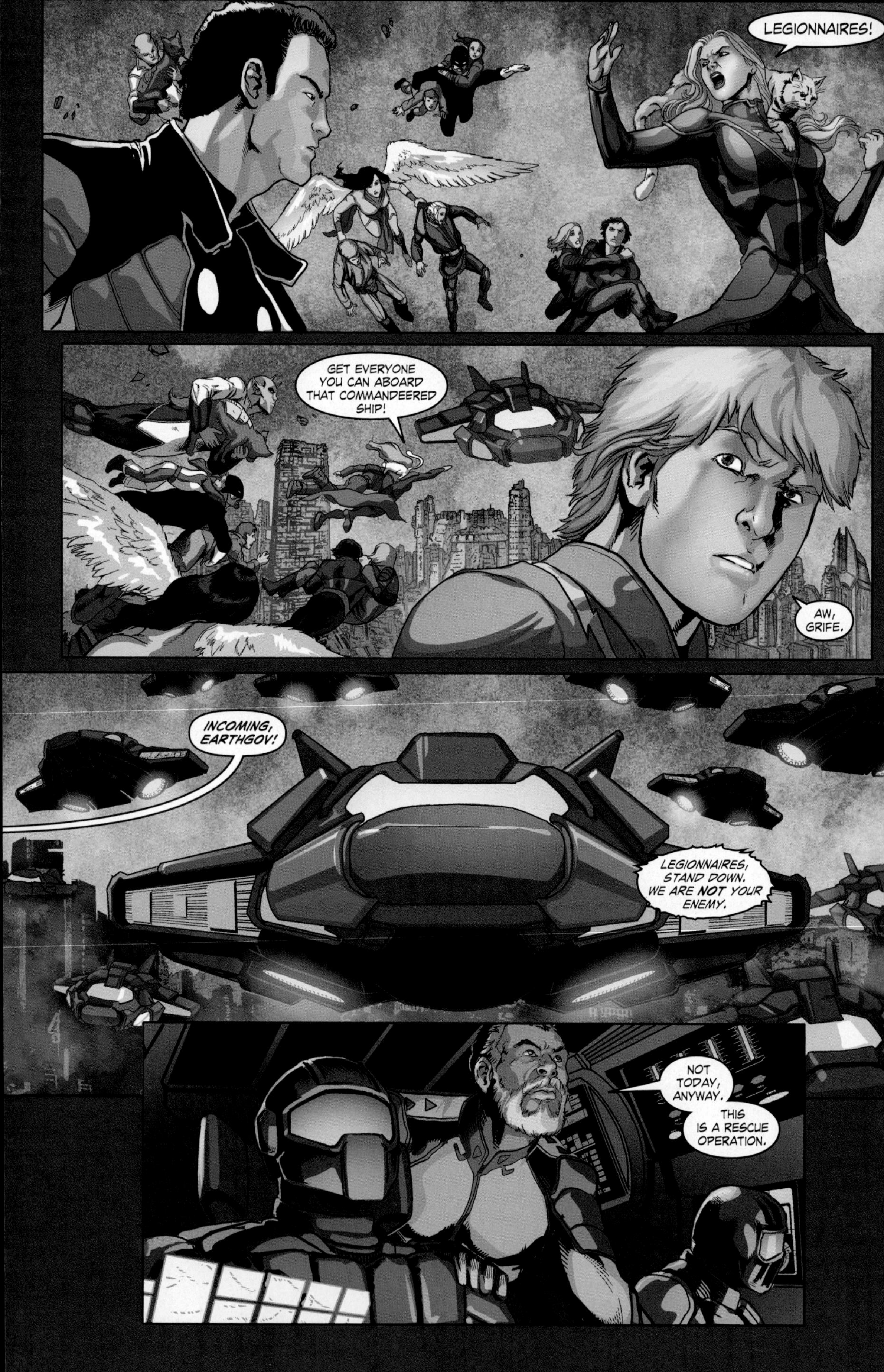
LEGIONNAIRES!
GET EVERYONE YOU CAN ABOARD THAT COMMANDEERED SHIP!
AW, GRIFE.
INCOMING, EARTHGOV!
LEGIONNAIRES, STAND DOWN. WE ARE NOT YOUR ENEMY.
NOT TODAY, ANYWAY.
THIS IS A RESCUE OPERATION.

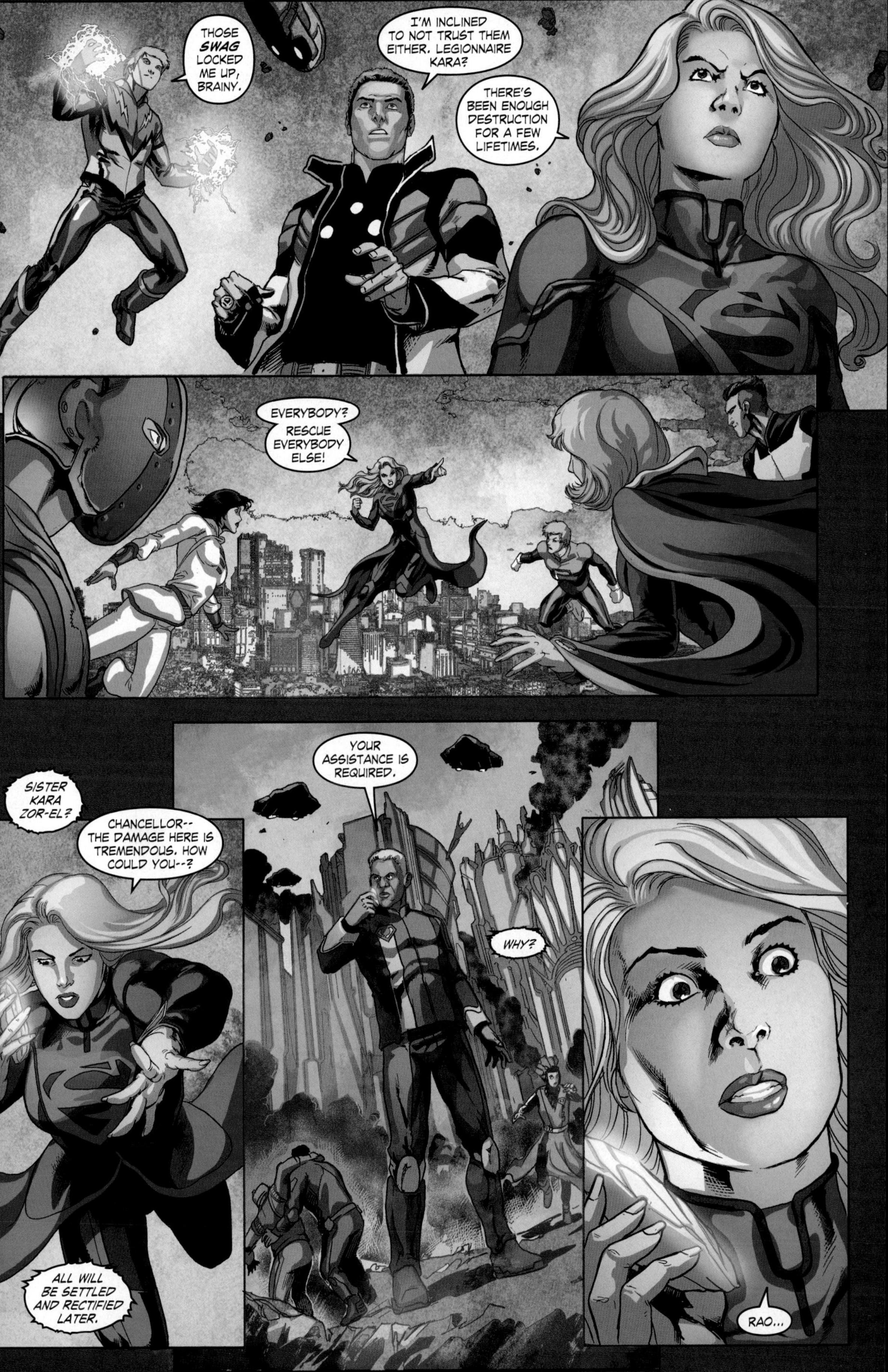
THOSE SWAG LOCKED ME UP, BRAINY.
I'M INCLINED TO NOT TRUST THEM EITHER. LEGIONNAIRE KARA?
THERE'S BEEN ENOUGH DESTRUCTION FOR A FEW LIFETIMES.
EVERYBODY? RESCUE EVERYBODY ELSE!
SISTER KARA ZOR-EL?
CHANCELLOR-- THE DAMAGE HERE IS TREMENDOUS. HOW COULD YOU--?
ALL WILL BE SETTLED AND RECTIFIED LATER.
YOUR ASSISTANCE IS REQUIRED.
WHY?
RAO...

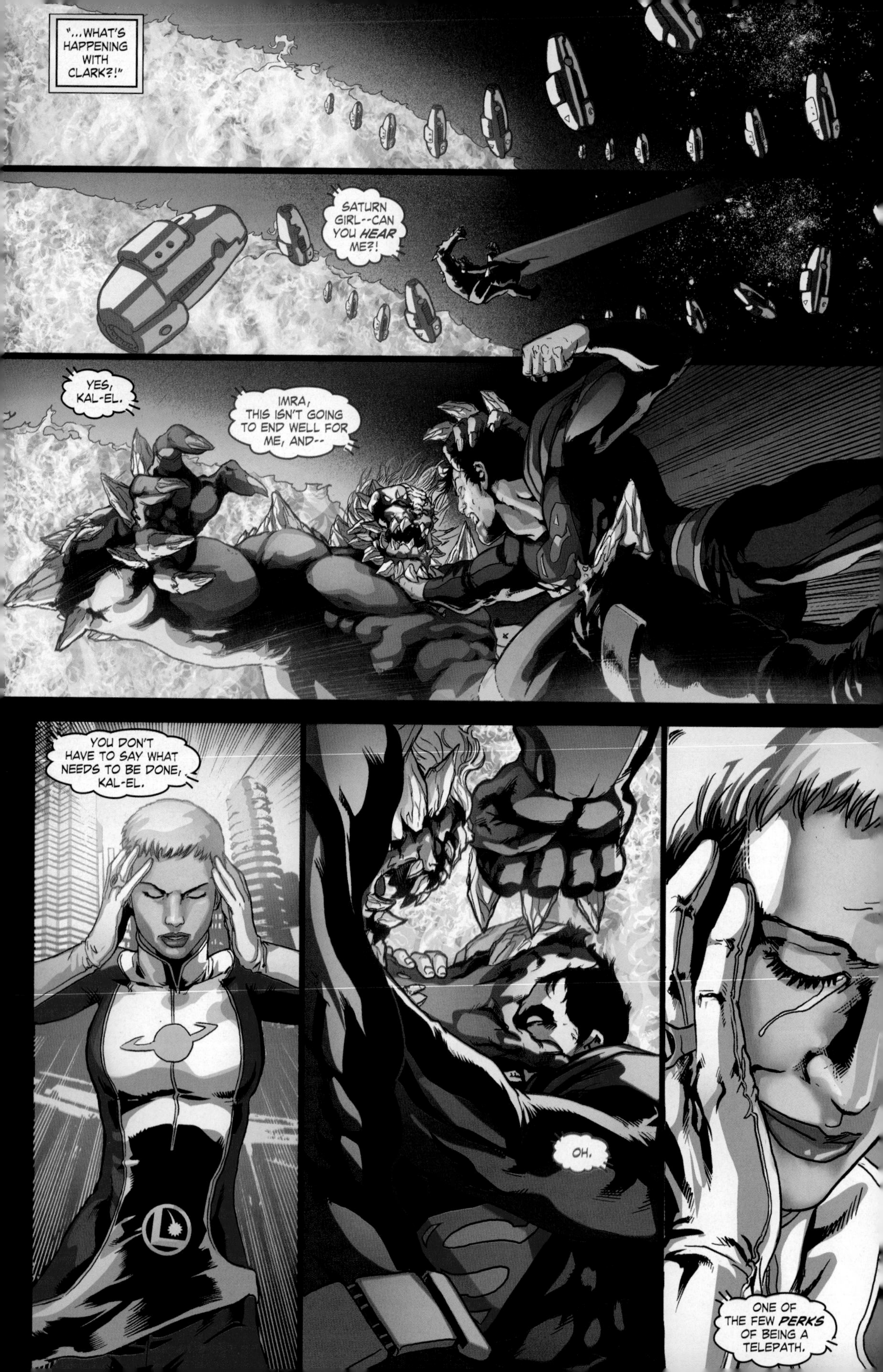
"...WHAT'S HAPPENING WITH CLARK?!"
SATURN GIRL--CAN YOU HEAR ME?!
YES, KAL-EL.
IMRA, THIS ISN'T GOING TO END WELL FOR ME, AND--
YOU DON'T HAVE TO SAY WHAT NEEDS TO BE DONE, KAL-EL.
OH.
ONE OF THE FEW PERKS OF BEING A TELEPATH.

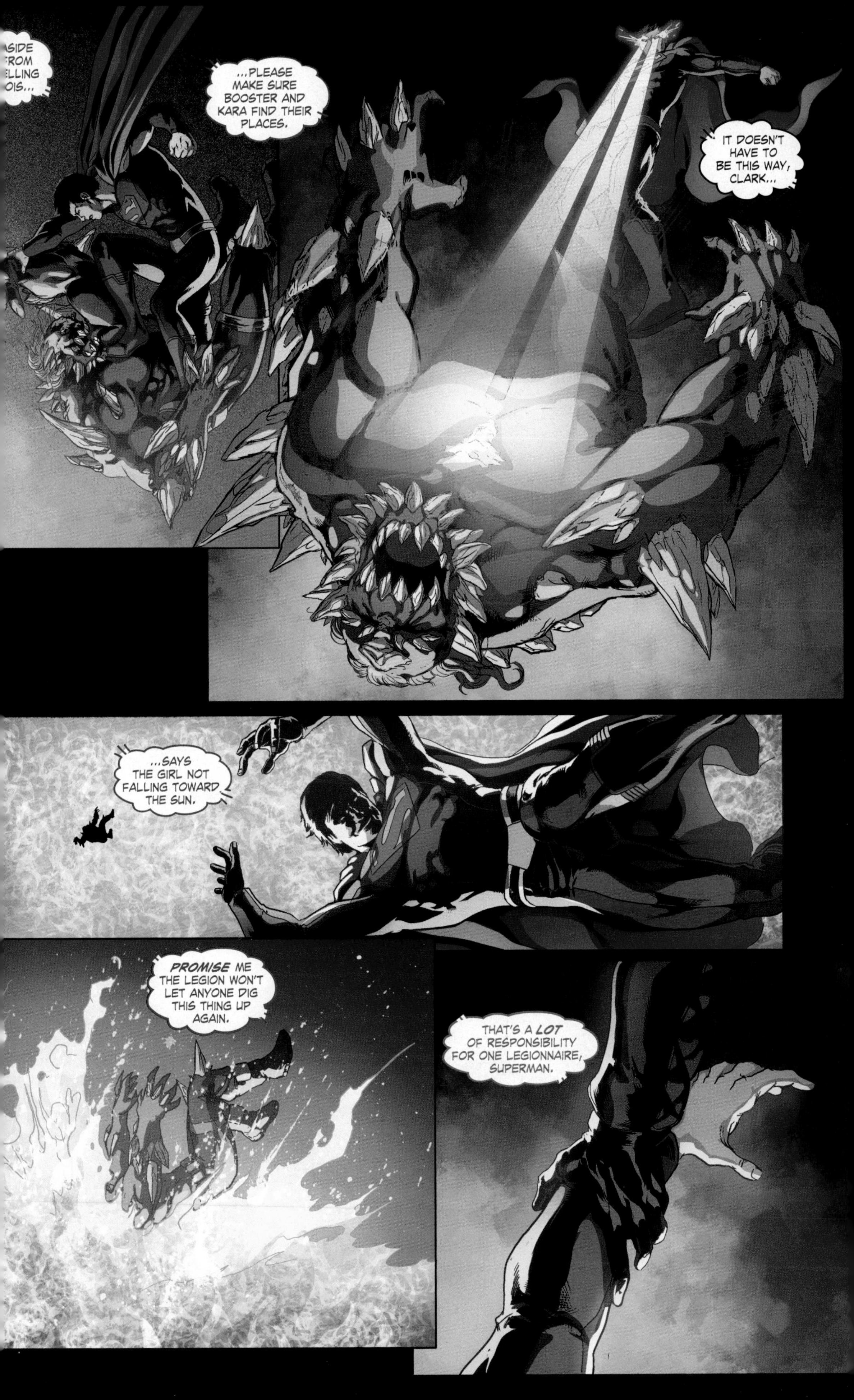

ASIDE FROM ...ELLING ...OIS...
...PLEASE MAKE SURE BOOSTER AND KARA FIND THEIR PLACES.
IT DOESN'T HAVE TO BE THIS WAY, CLARK...
...SAYS THE GIRL NOT FALLING TOWARD THE SUN.
PROMISE ME THE LEGION WON'T LET ANYONE DIG THIS THING UP AGAIN.
THAT'S A LOT OF RESPONSIBILITY FOR ONE LEGIONNAIRE, SUPERMAN.

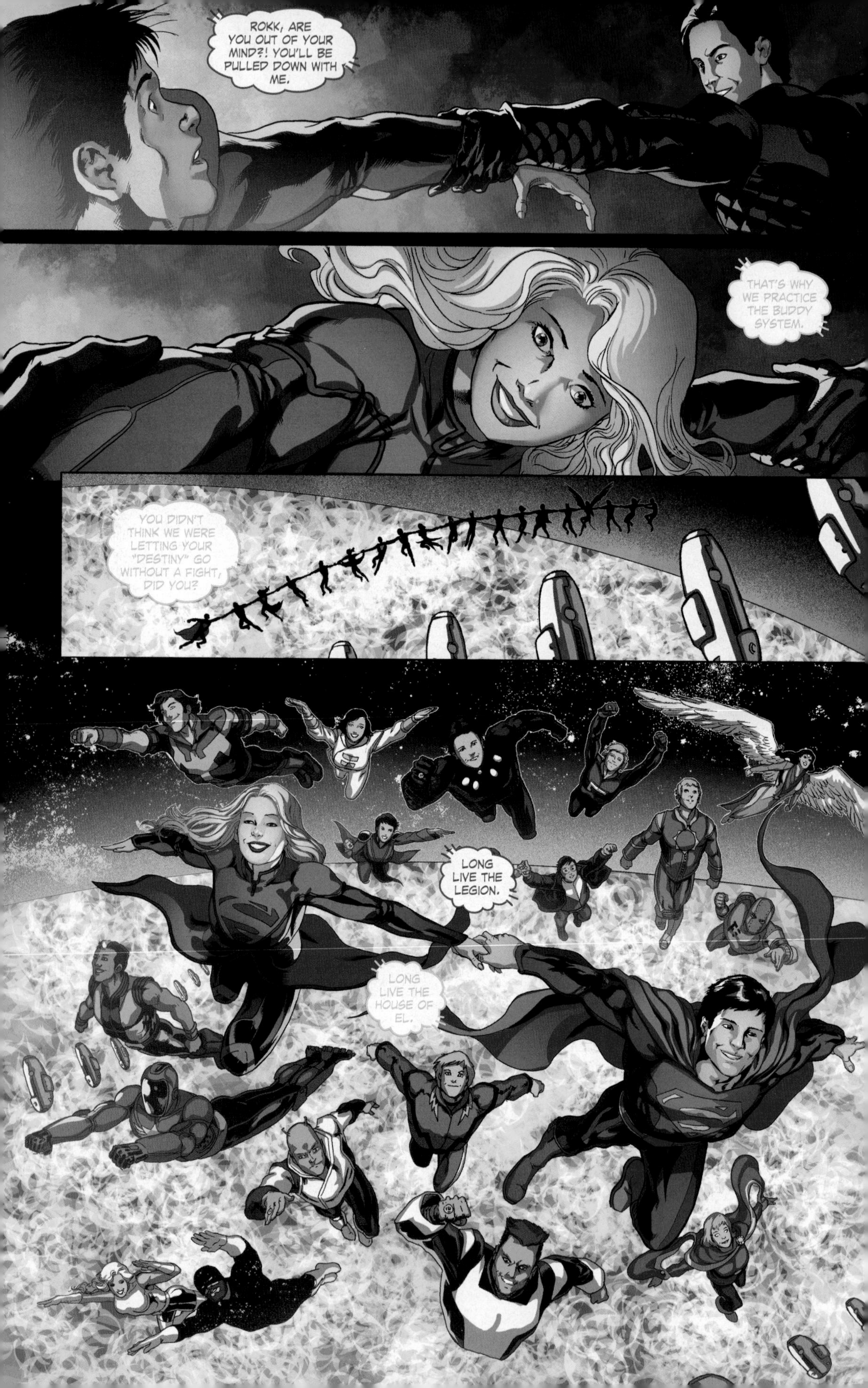
ROKK, ARE YOU OUT OF YOUR MIND?! YOU'LL BE PULLED DOWN WITH ME.
THAT'S WHY WE PRACTICE THE BUDDY SYSTEM.
YOU DIDN'T THINK WE WERE LETTING YOUR "DESTINY" GO WITHOUT A FIGHT, DID YOU?
LONG LIVE THE LEGION.
LONG LIVE THE HOUSE OF EL.

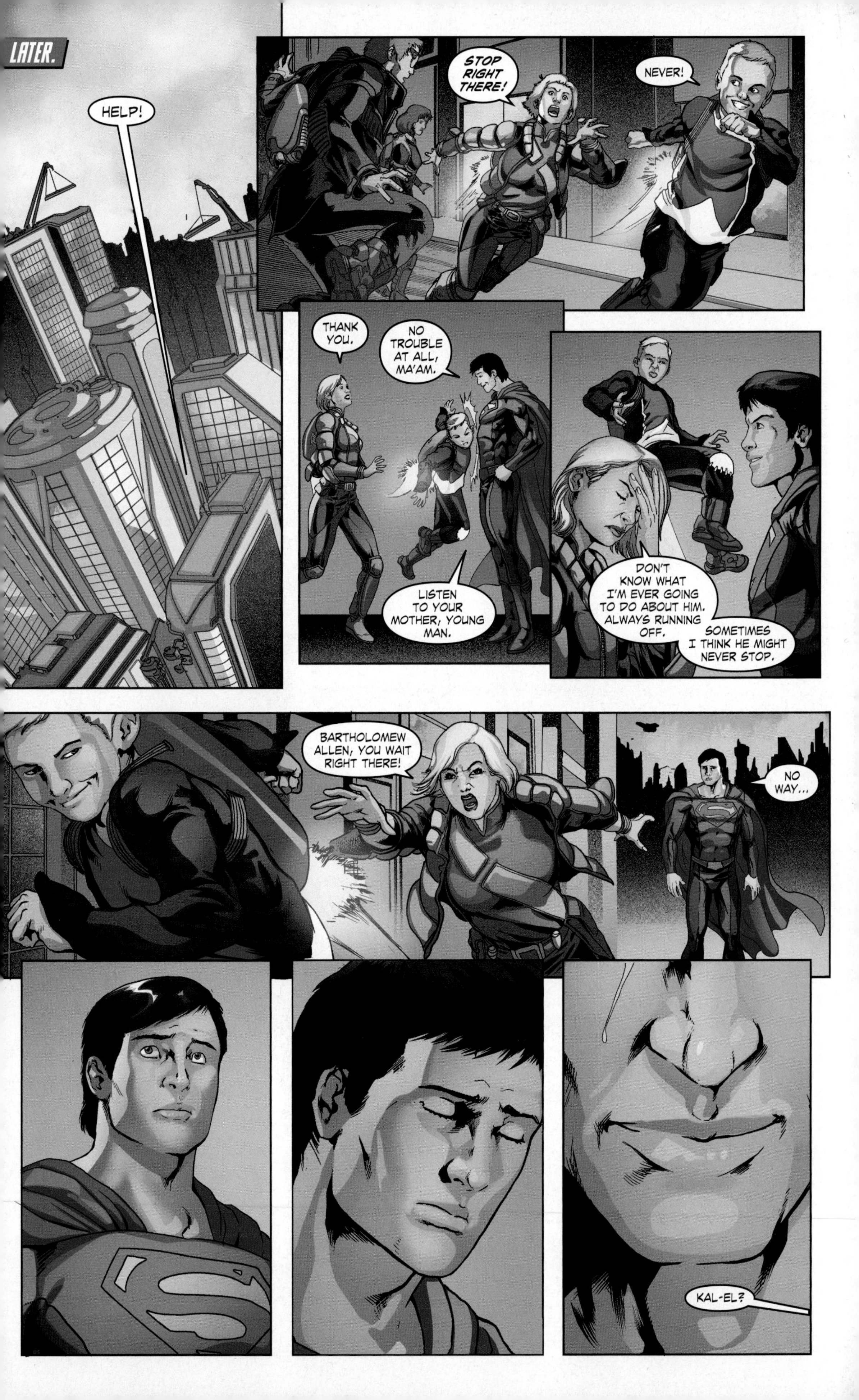
LATER.
HELP!
STOP RIGHT THERE!
NEVER!
THANK YOU.
NO TROUBLE AT ALL, MA'AM.
LISTEN TO YOUR MOTHER, YOUNG MAN.
DON'T KNOW WHAT I'M EVER GOING TO DO ABOUT HIM. ALWAYS RUNNING OFF.
SOMETIMES I THINK HE MIGHT NEVER STOP.
BARTHOLOMEW ALLEN, YOU WAIT RIGHT THERE!
NO WAY...
KAL-EL?

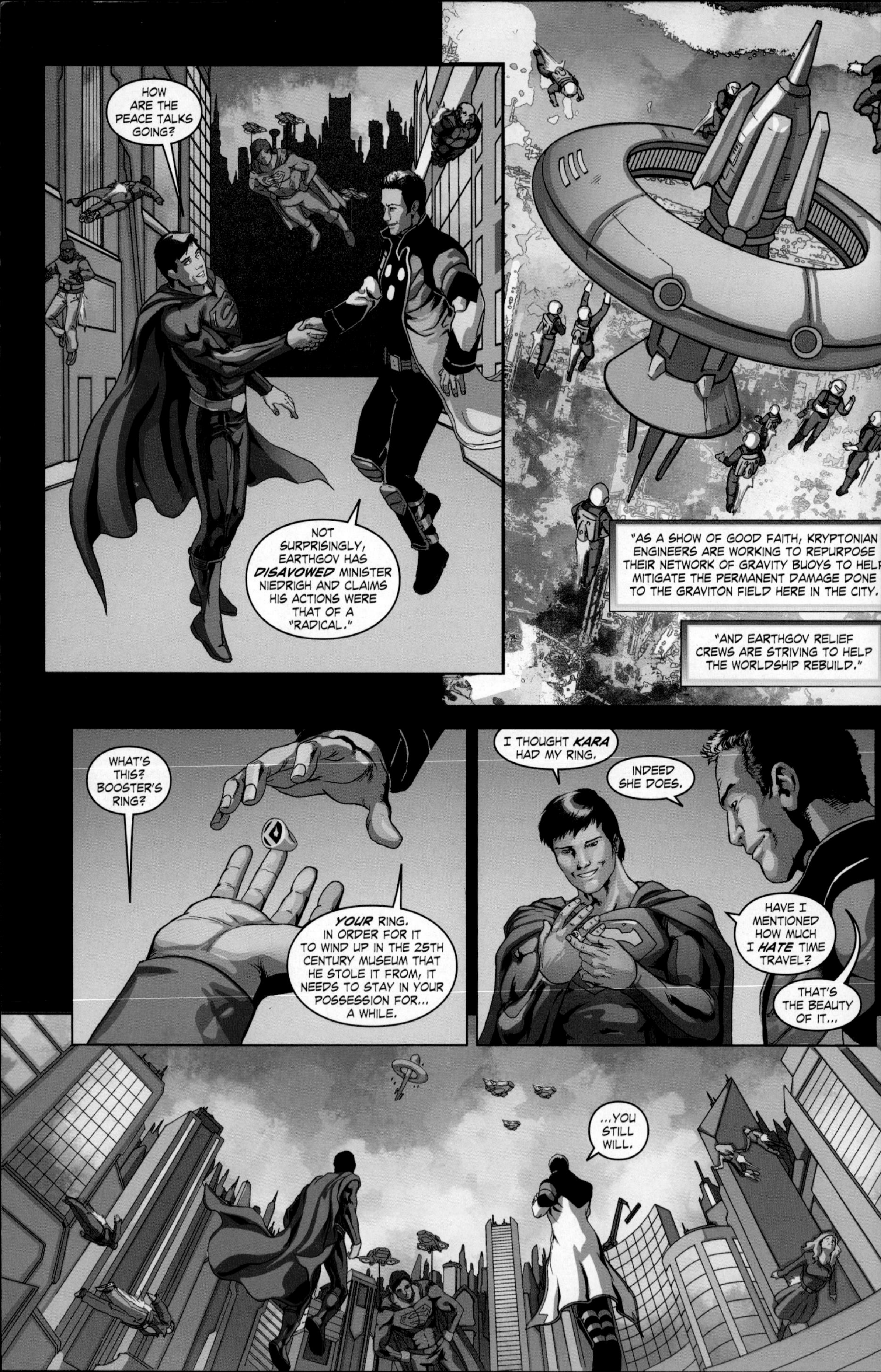
HOW ARE THE PEACE TALKS GOING?
NOT SURPRISINGLY, EARTHGOV HAS DISAVOWED MINISTER NIEDRIGH AND CLAIMS HIS ACTIONS WERE THAT OF A "RADICAL."
"AS A SHOW OF GOOD FAITH, KRYPTONIAN ENGINEERS ARE WORKING TO REPURPOSE THEIR NETWORK OF GRAVITY BUOYS TO HELP MITIGATE THE PERMANENT DAMAGE DONE TO THE GRAVITON FIELD HERE IN THE CITY.
"AND EARTHGOV RELIEF CREWS ARE STRIVING TO HELP THE WORLDSHIP REBUILD."
WHAT'S THIS? BOOSTER'S RING?
YOUR RING. IN ORDER FOR IT TO WIND UP IN THE 25TH CENTURY MUSEUM THAT HE STOLE IT FROM, IT NEEDS TO STAY IN YOUR POSSESSION FOR... A WHILE.
I THOUGHT KARA HAD MY RING.
INDEED SHE DOES.
HAVE I MENTIONED HOW MUCH I HATE TIME TRAVEL?
THAT'S THE BEAUTY OF IT...
...YOU STILL WILL.

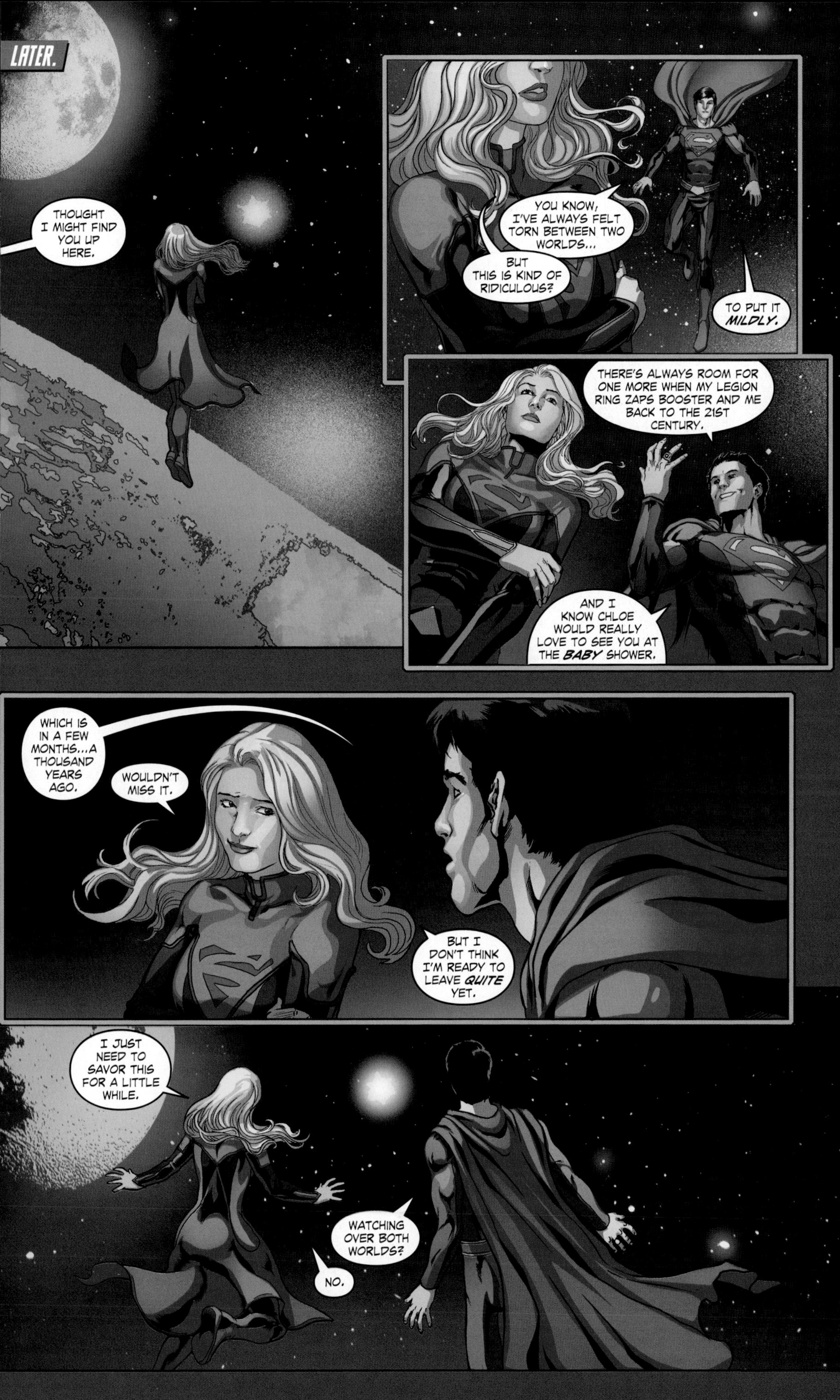
LATER.
THOUGHT I MIGHT FIND YOU UP HERE.
YOU KNOW, I'VE ALWAYS FELT TORN BETWEEN TWO WORLDS...
BUT THIS IS KIND OF RIDICULOUS?
TO PUT IT *MILDLY*.
THERE'S ALWAYS ROOM FOR ONE MORE WHEN MY LEGION RING ZAPS BOOSTER AND ME BACK TO THE 21ST CENTURY.
AND I KNOW CHLOE WOULD REALLY LOVE TO SEE YOU AT THE *BABY* SHOWER.
WHICH IS IN A FEW MONTHS...A THOUSAND YEARS AGO.
WOULDN'T MISS IT.
BUT I DON'T THINK I'M READY TO LEAVE *QUITE* YET.
I JUST NEED TO SAVOR THIS FOR A LITTLE WHILE.
WATCHING OVER BOTH WORLDS?
NO.

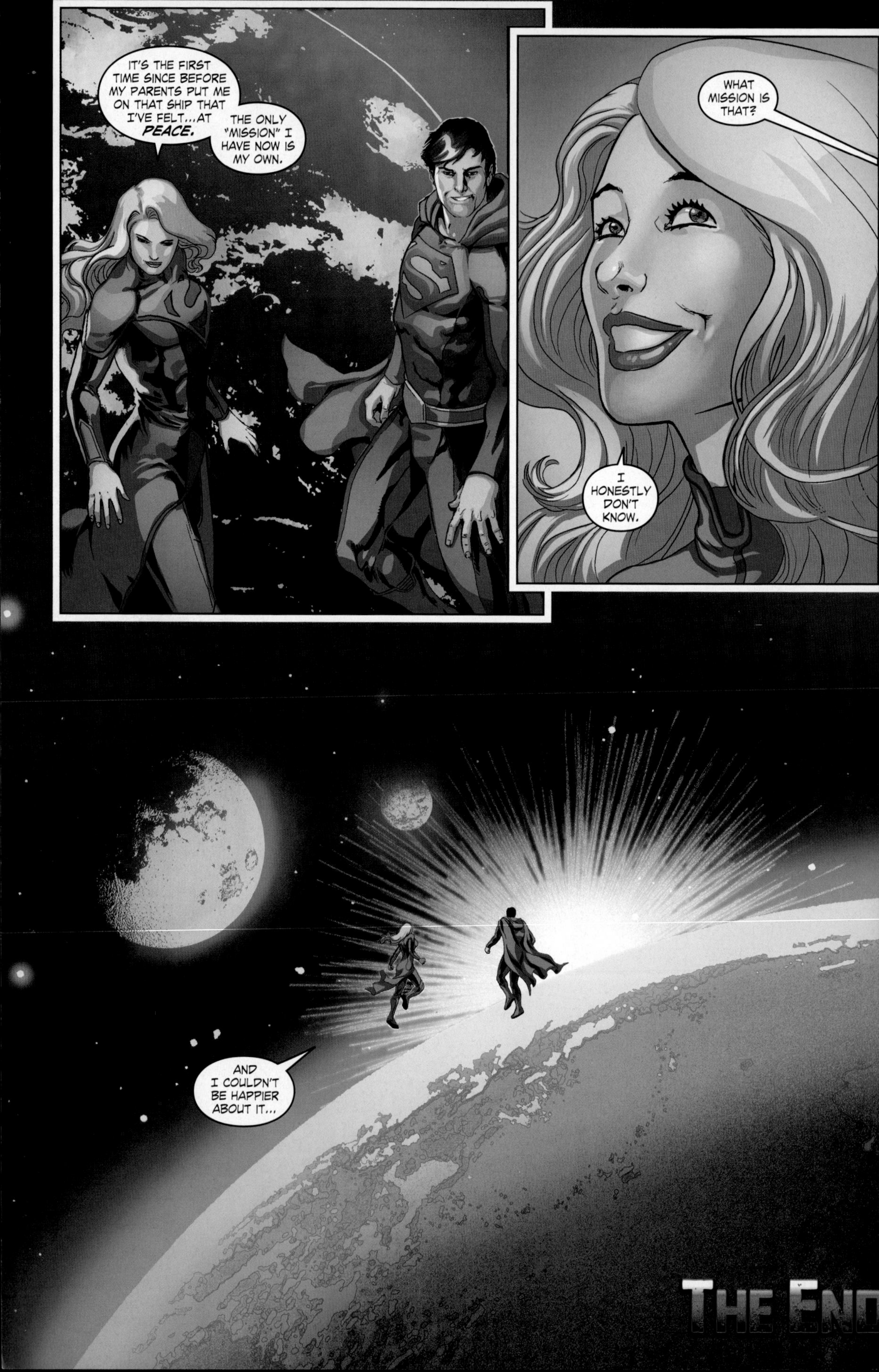
IT'S THE FIRST TIME SINCE BEFORE MY PARENTS PUT ME ON THAT SHIP THAT I'VE FELT...AT PEACE.
THE ONLY "MISSION" I HAVE NOW IS MY OWN.
WHAT MISSION IS THAT?
I HONESTLY DON'T KNOW.
AND I COULDN'T BE HAPPIER ABOUT IT...
THE END

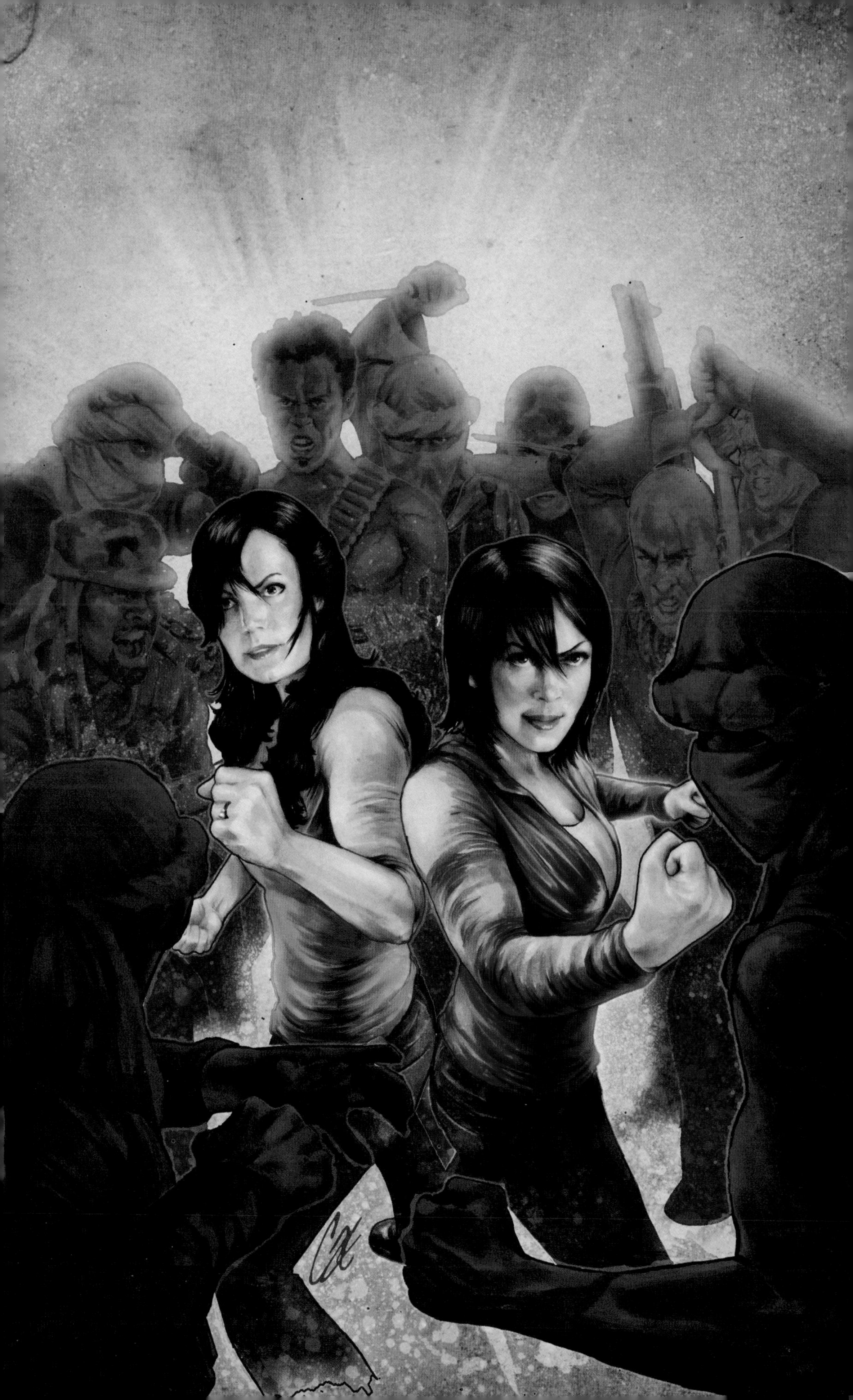

VALKYRIE

COVER BY CAT STAGGS

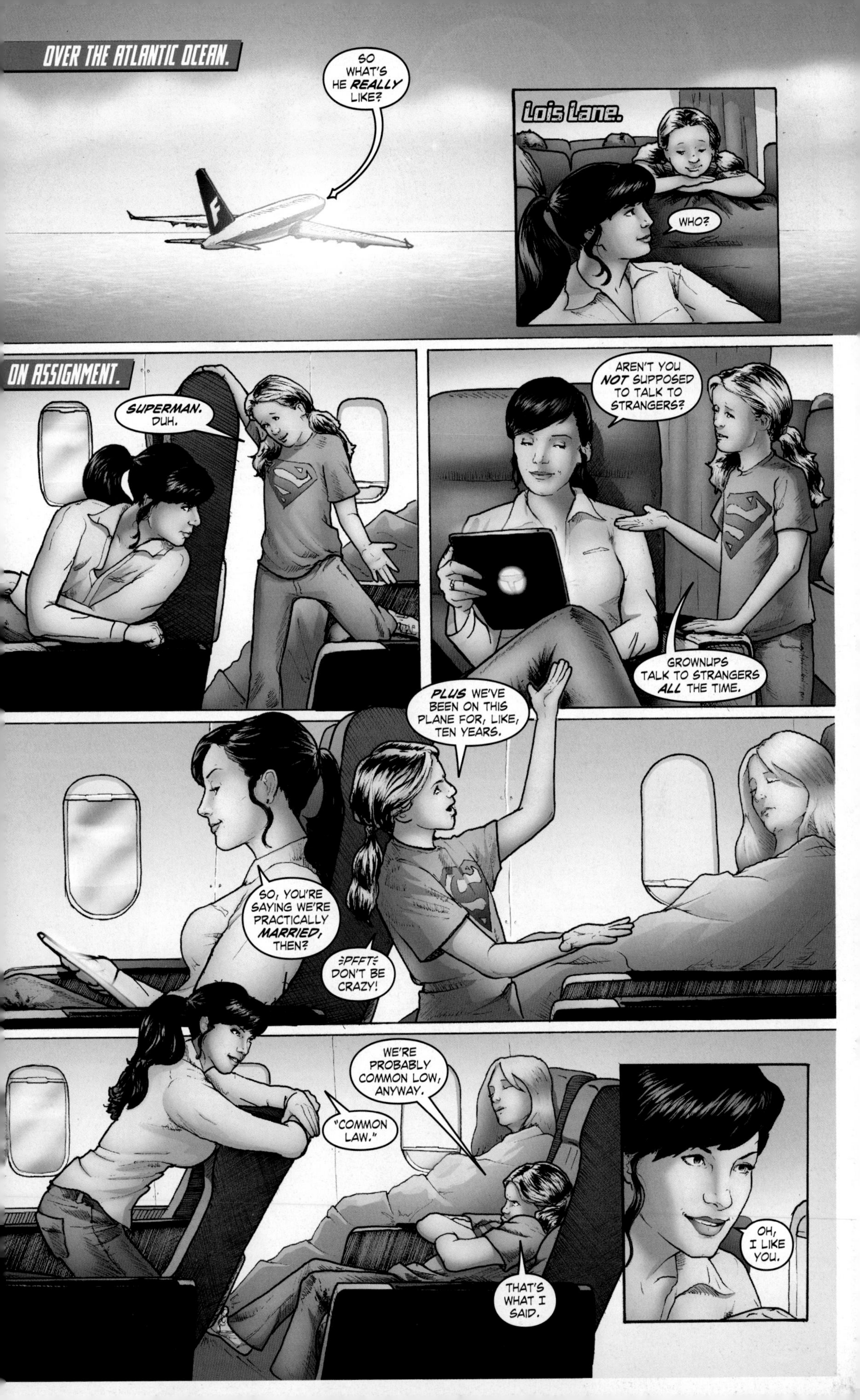
OVER THE ATLANTIC OCEAN.
SO WHAT'S HE *REALLY* LIKE?
Lois Lane.
WHO?
ON ASSIGNMENT.
SUPERMAN. DUH.
AREN'T YOU *NOT* SUPPOSED TO TALK TO STRANGERS?
GROWNUPS TALK TO STRANGERS *ALL* THE TIME.
PLUS WE'VE BEEN ON THIS PLANE FOR, LIKE, TEN YEARS.
SO, YOU'RE SAYING WE'RE PRACTICALLY *MARRIED,* THEN?
=PFFT= DON'T BE CRAZY!
WE'RE PROBABLY COMMON LOW, ANYWAY.
"COMMON LAW."
THAT'S WHAT I SAID.
OH, I LIKE YOU.

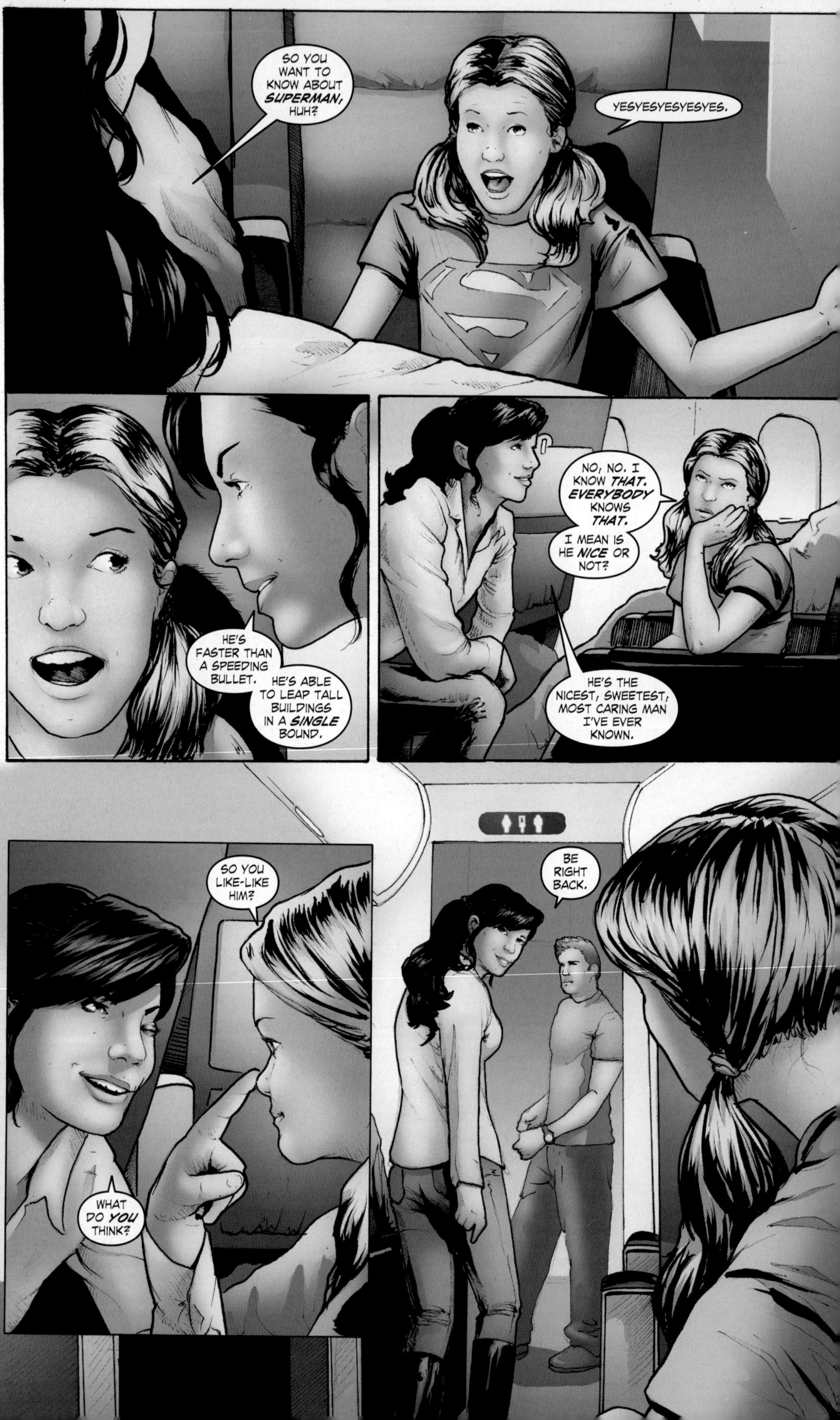
SO YOU WANT TO KNOW ABOUT SUPERMAN, HUH?
YESYESYESYESYESYES.
HE'S FASTER THAN A SPEEDING BULLET.
HE'S ABLE TO LEAP TALL BUILDINGS IN A SINGLE BOUND.
NO, NO. I KNOW THAT. EVERYBODY KNOWS THAT.
I MEAN IS HE NICE OR NOT?
HE'S THE NICEST, SWEETEST, MOST CARING MAN I'VE EVER KNOWN.
SO YOU LIKE-LIKE HIM?
WHAT DO YOU THINK?
BE RIGHT BACK.

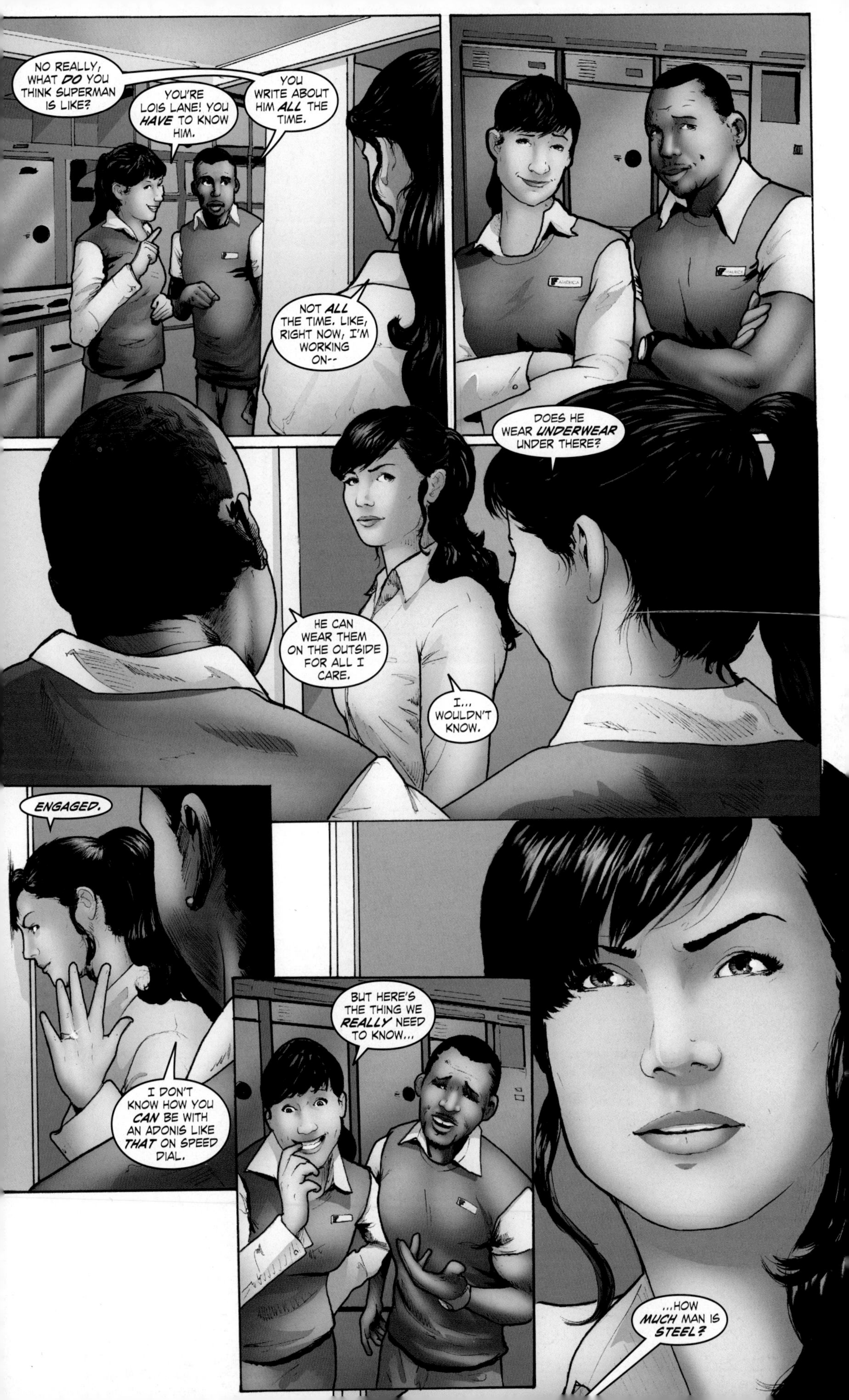
NO REALLY, WHAT DO YOU THINK SUPERMAN IS LIKE?
YOU'RE LOIS LANE! YOU HAVE TO KNOW HIM.
YOU WRITE ABOUT HIM ALL THE TIME.
NOT ALL THE TIME. LIKE, RIGHT NOW, I'M WORKING ON--
DOES HE WEAR UNDERWEAR UNDER THERE?
HE CAN WEAR THEM ON THE OUTSIDE FOR ALL I CARE.
I... WOULDN'T KNOW.
ENGAGED.
I DON'T KNOW HOW YOU CAN BE WITH AN ADONIS LIKE THAT ON SPEED DIAL.
BUT HERE'S THE THING WE REALLY NEED TO KNOW...
...HOW MUCH MAN IS STEEL?

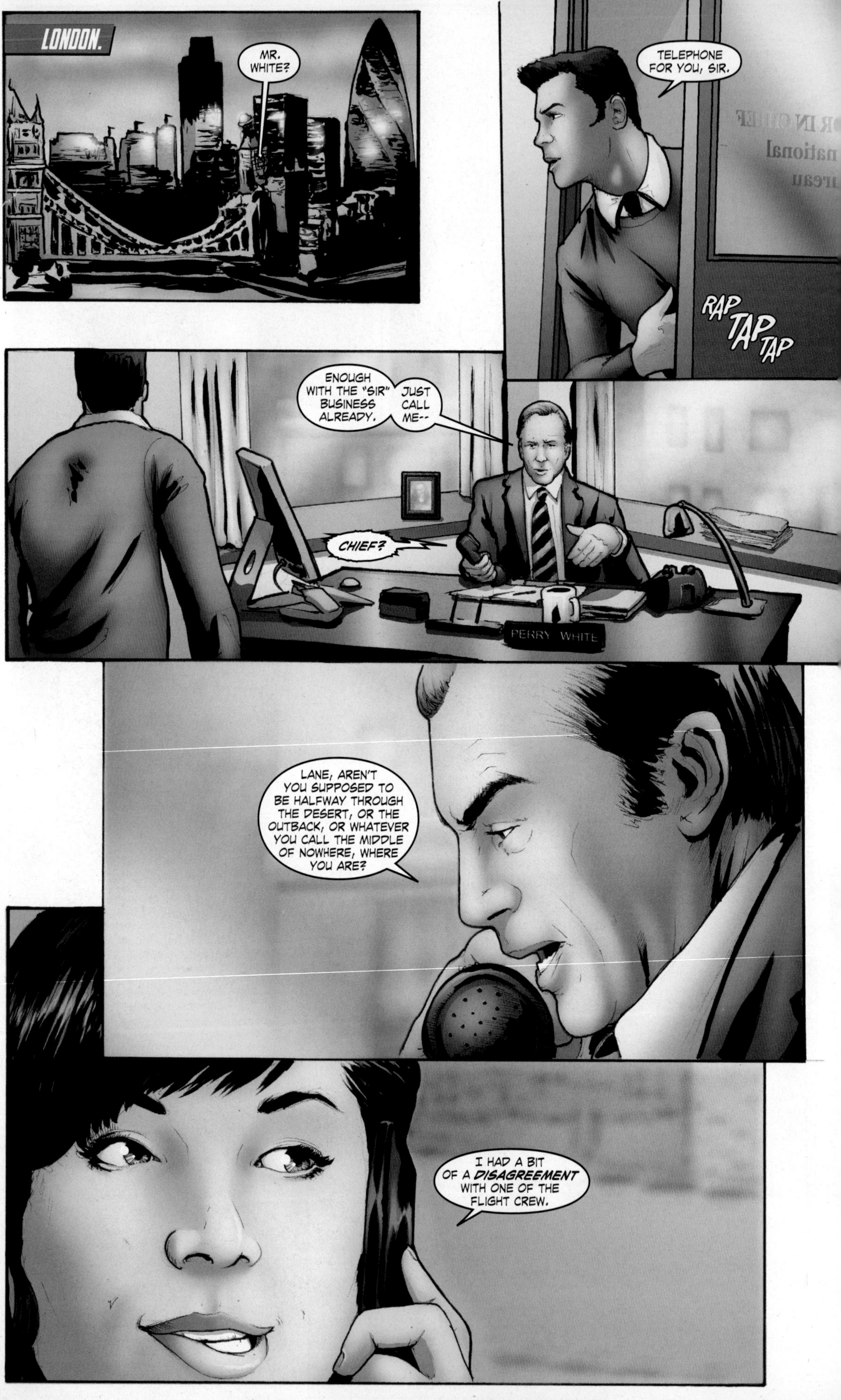
LONDON.
MR. WHITE?
TELEPHONE FOR YOU, SIR.
RAP TAP TAP
ENOUGH WITH THE "SIR" BUSINESS ALREADY.
JUST CALL ME--
CHIEF?
PERRY WHITE
LANE, AREN'T YOU SUPPOSED TO BE HALFWAY THROUGH THE DESERT, OR THE OUTBACK, OR WHATEVER YOU CALL THE MIDDLE OF NOWHERE, WHERE YOU ARE?
I HAD A BIT OF A DISAGREEMENT WITH ONE OF THE FLIGHT CREW.

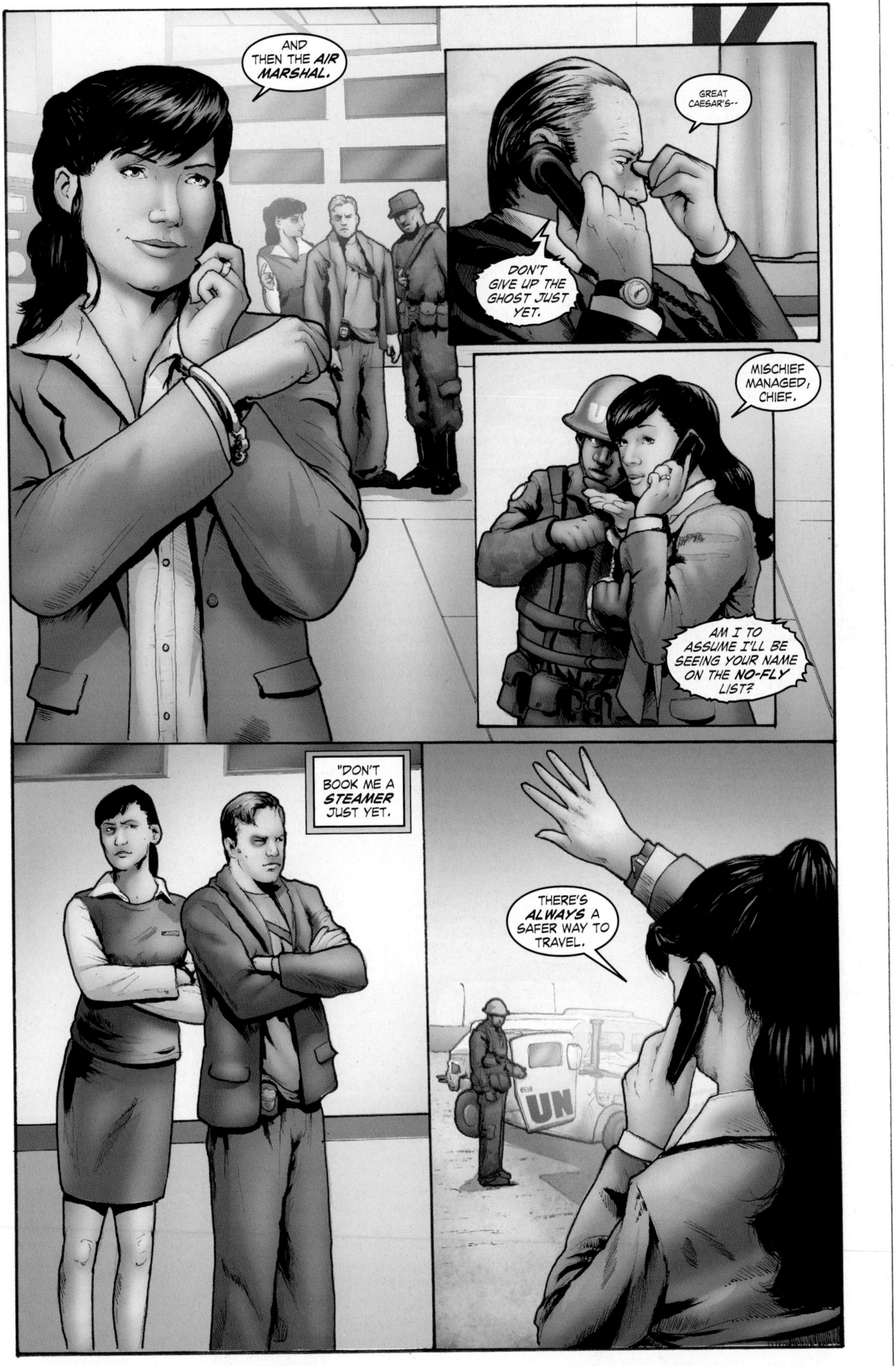
AND THEN THE AIR MARSHAL.
GREAT CAESAR'S--
DON'T GIVE UP THE GHOST JUST YET.
MISCHIEF MANAGED, CHIEF.
AM I TO ASSUME I'LL BE SEEING YOUR NAME ON THE NO-FLY LIST?
"DON'T BOOK ME A STEAMER JUST YET.
THERE'S ALWAYS A SAFER WAY TO TRAVEL.
UN

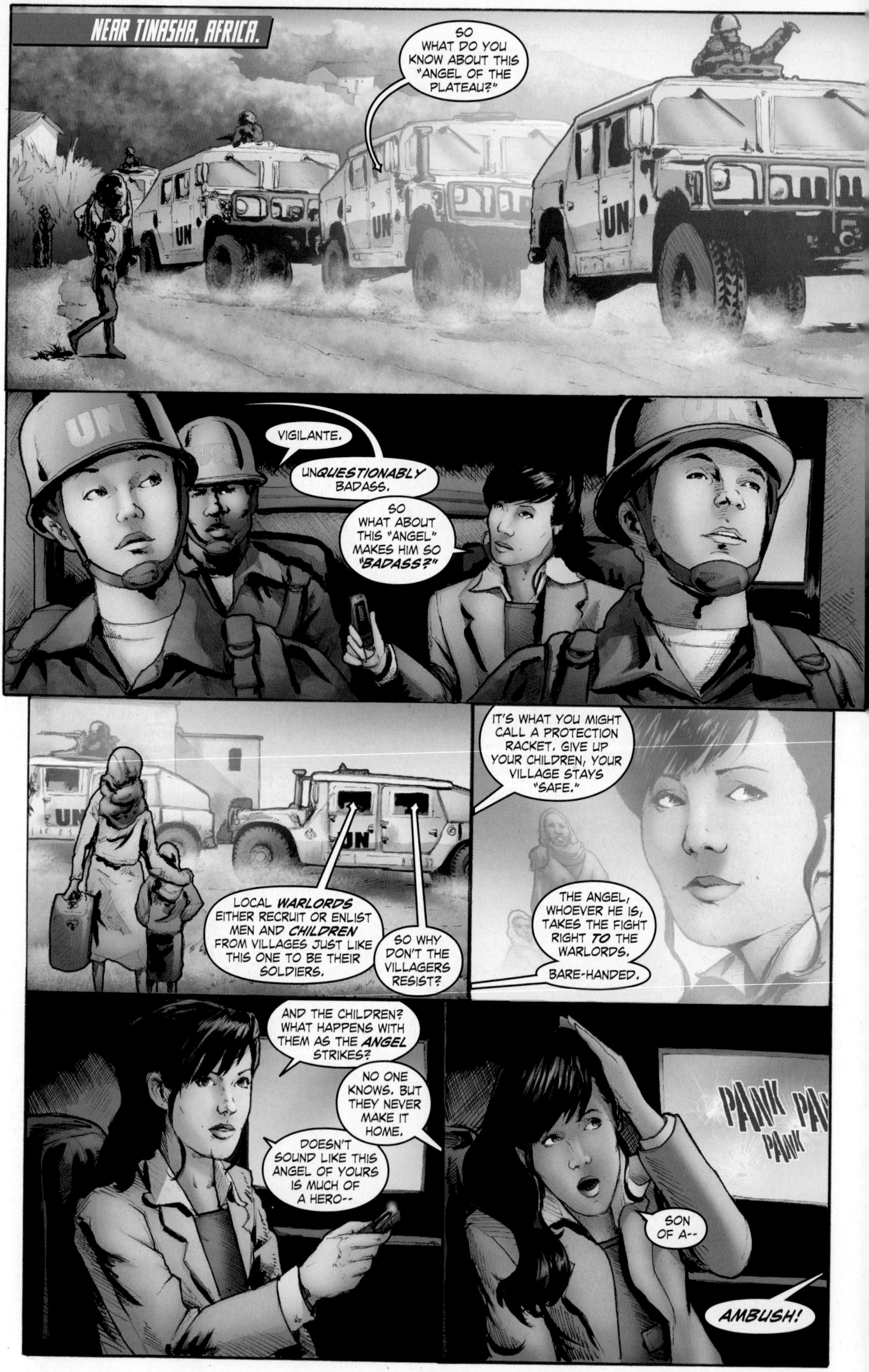
NEAR TINASHA, AFRICA.
SO WHAT DO YOU KNOW ABOUT THIS "ANGEL OF THE PLATEAU?"
VIGILANTE.
UNQUESTIONABLY BADASS.
SO WHAT ABOUT THIS "ANGEL" MAKES HIM SO "BADASS?"
IT'S WHAT YOU MIGHT CALL A PROTECTION RACKET. GIVE UP YOUR CHILDREN, YOUR VILLAGE STAYS "SAFE."
LOCAL WARLORDS EITHER RECRUIT OR ENLIST MEN AND CHILDREN FROM VILLAGES JUST LIKE THIS ONE TO BE THEIR SOLDIERS.
SO WHY DON'T THE VILLAGERS RESIST?
THE ANGEL, WHOEVER HE IS, TAKES THE FIGHT RIGHT TO THE WARLORDS.
BARE-HANDED.
AND THE CHILDREN? WHAT HAPPENS WITH THEM AS THE ANGEL STRIKES?
NO ONE KNOWS. BUT THEY NEVER MAKE IT HOME.
DOESN'T SOUND LIKE THIS ANGEL OF YOURS IS MUCH OF A HERO--
PANK PANK
SON OF A--
AMBUSH!

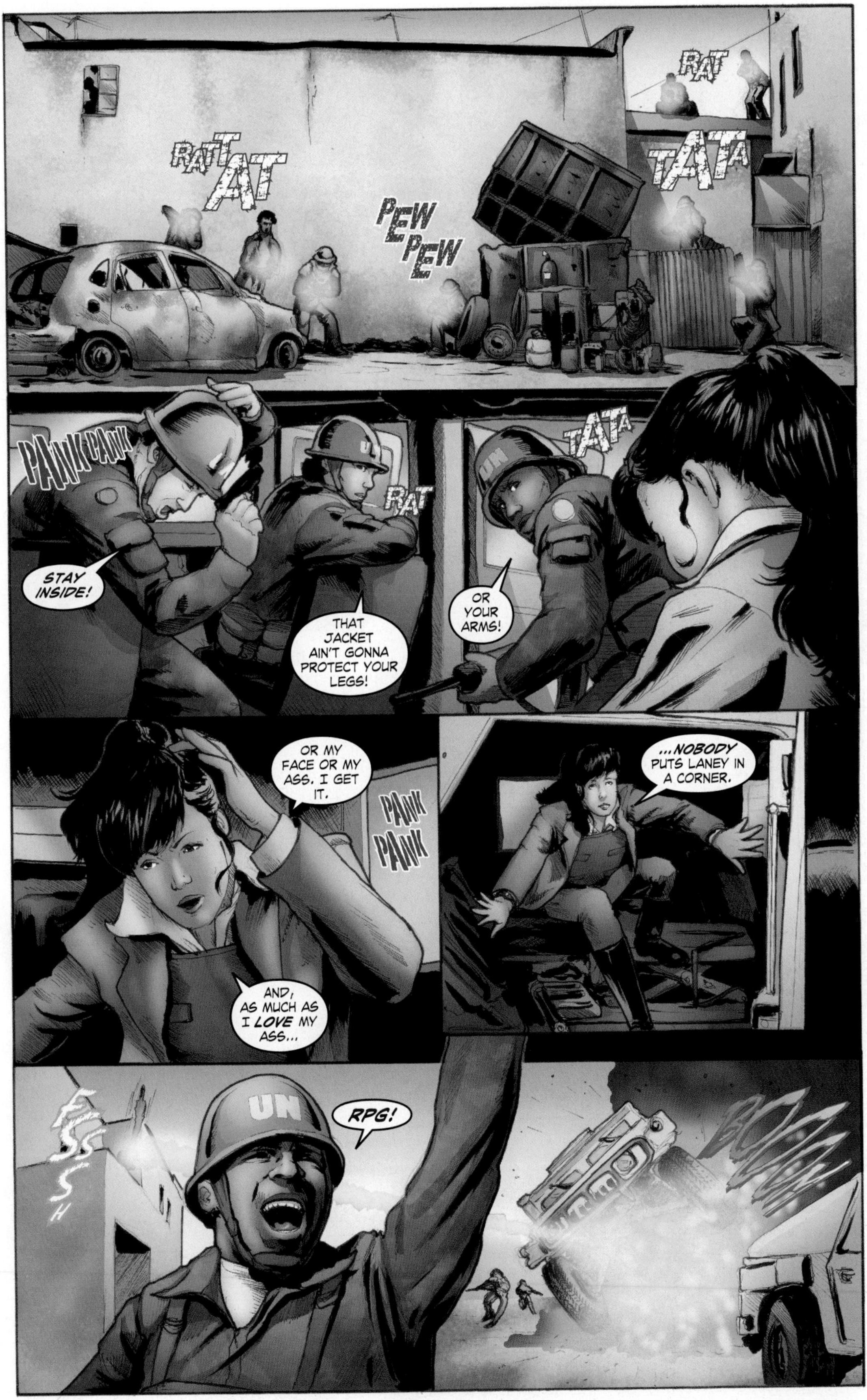
RATTAT
PEW PEW
RAT
TATA
PANK PANK
RAT
TATA
STAY INSIDE!
THAT JACKET AIN'T GONNA PROTECT YOUR LEGS!
OR YOUR ARMS!
OR MY FACE OR MY ASS. I GET IT.
PANK PANK
AND, AS MUCH AS I *LOVE* MY ASS...
...*NOBODY* PUTS LANEY IN A CORNER.
FSSSH
RPG!
BOOM

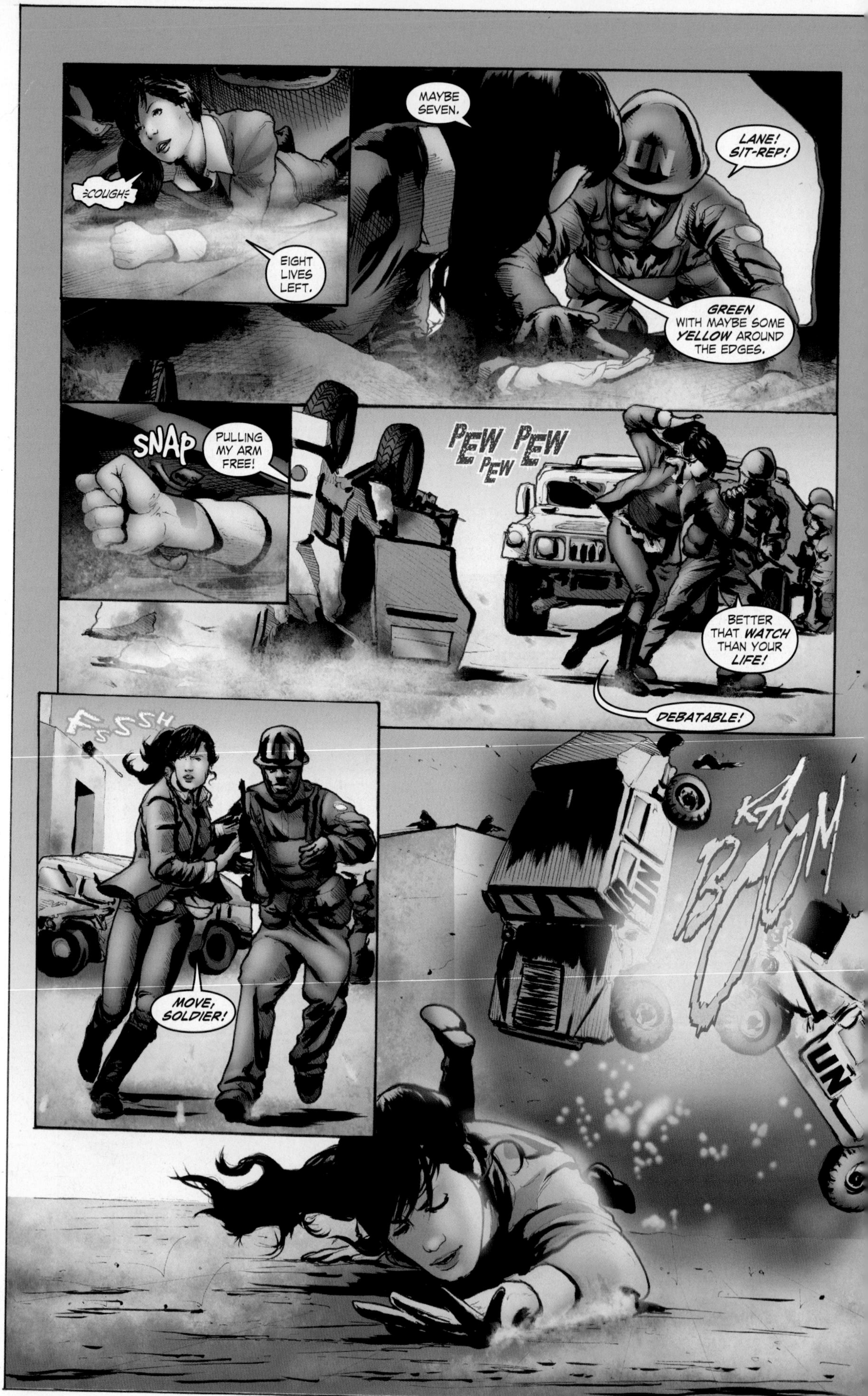

=COUGH=
EIGHT LIVES LEFT.
MAYBE SEVEN.
LANE! SIT-REP!
GREEN WITH MAYBE SOME YELLOW AROUND THE EDGES.
SNAP
PULLING MY ARM FREE!
PEW PEW PEW PEW
BETTER THAT WATCH THAN YOUR LIFE!
DEBATABLE!
FSSSH
MOVE, SOLDIER!
KA BOOM
UN

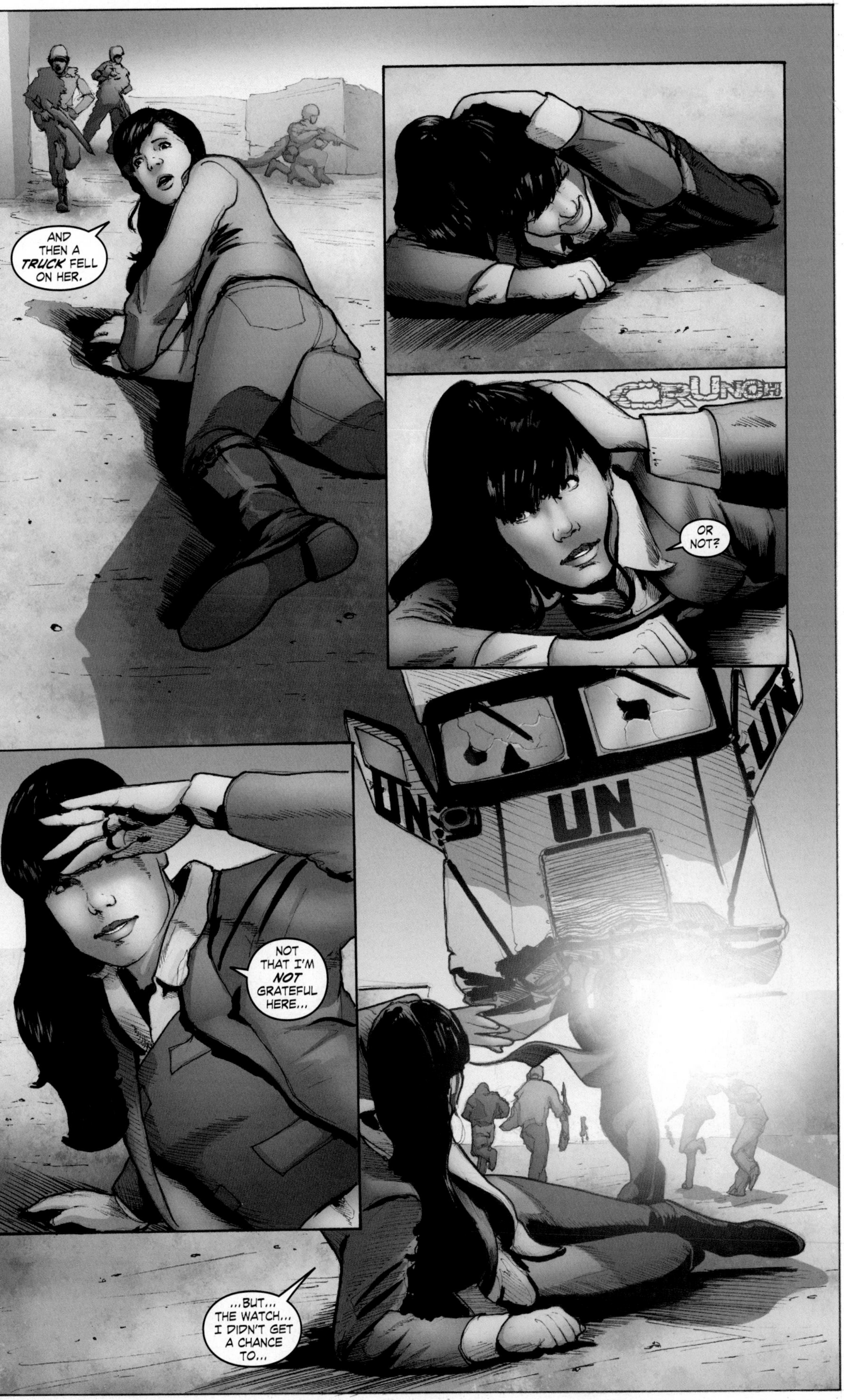
AND THEN A *TRUCK* FELL ON HER.
CRUNCH
OR NOT?
NOT THAT I'M *NOT* GRATEFUL HERE...
...BUT... THE WATCH... I DIDN'T GET A CHANCE TO...
UN
UN
UN

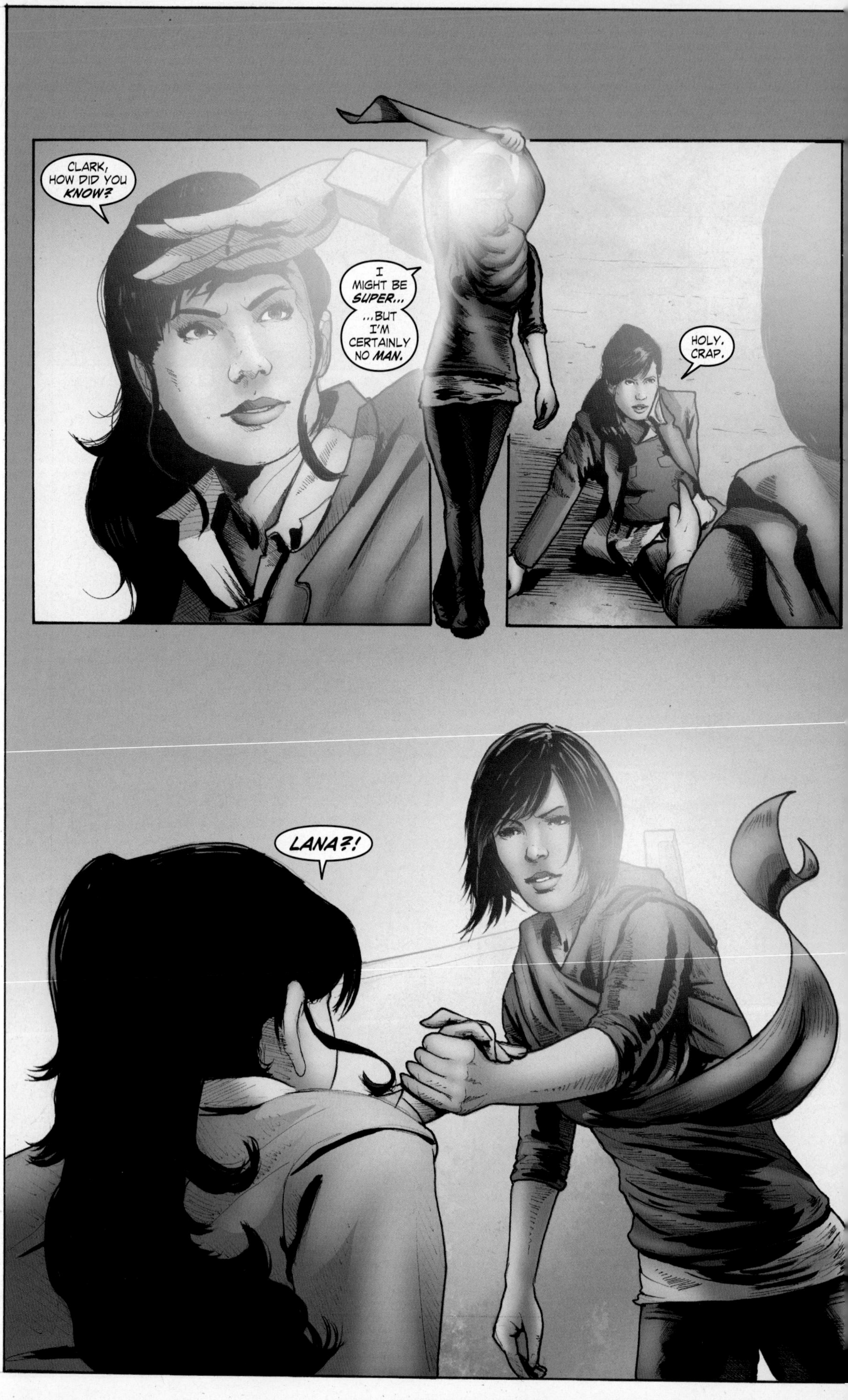
CLARK, HOW DID YOU KNOW?
I MIGHT BE SUPER...
...BUT I'M CERTAINLY NO MAN.
HOLY. CRAP.
LANA?!

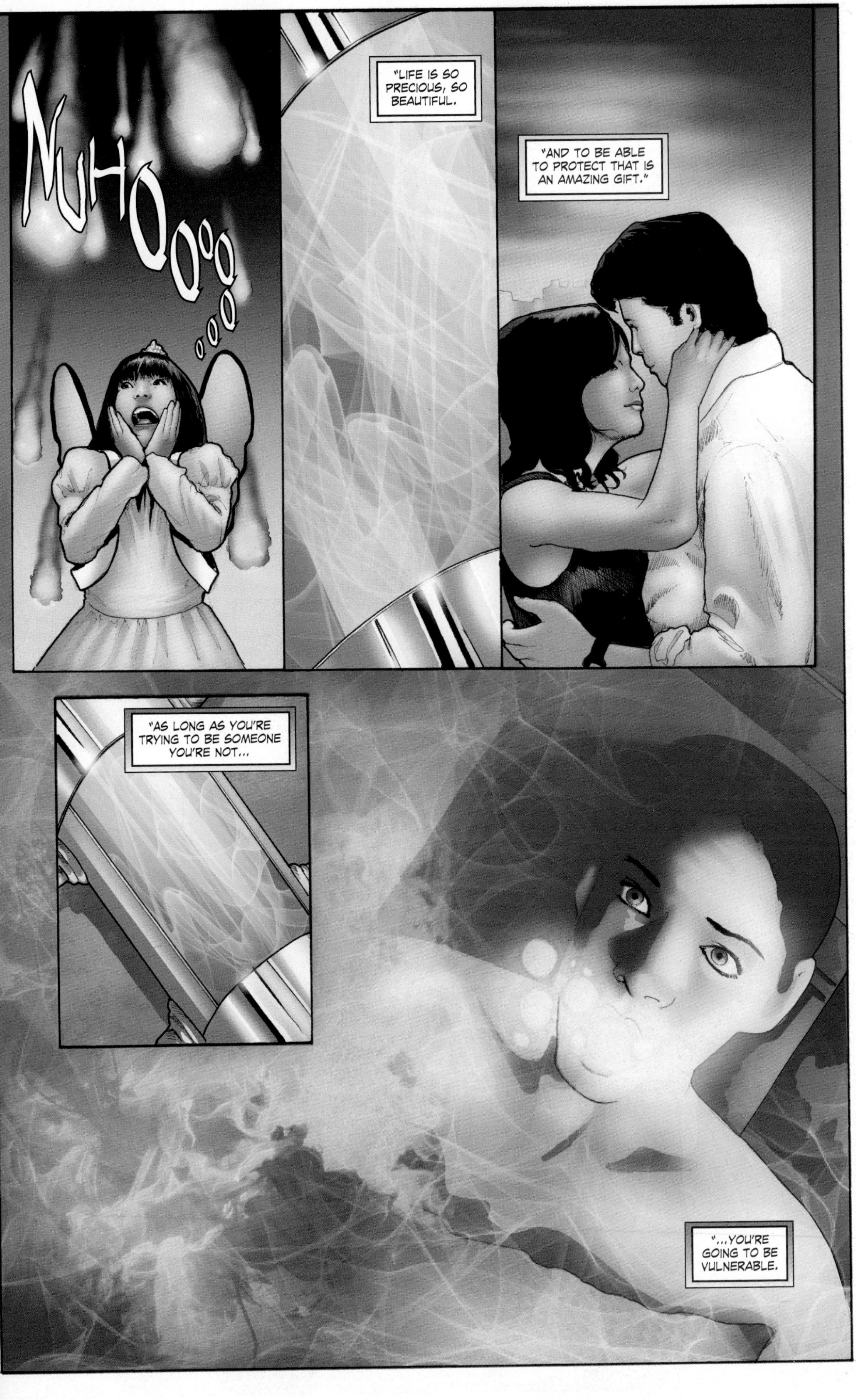
NUHOOooooo
"LIFE IS SO PRECIOUS, SO BEAUTIFUL.
"AND TO BE ABLE TO PROTECT THAT IS AN AMAZING GIFT."
"AS LONG AS YOU'RE TRYING TO BE SOMEONE YOU'RE NOT...
"...YOU'RE GOING TO BE VULNERABLE.

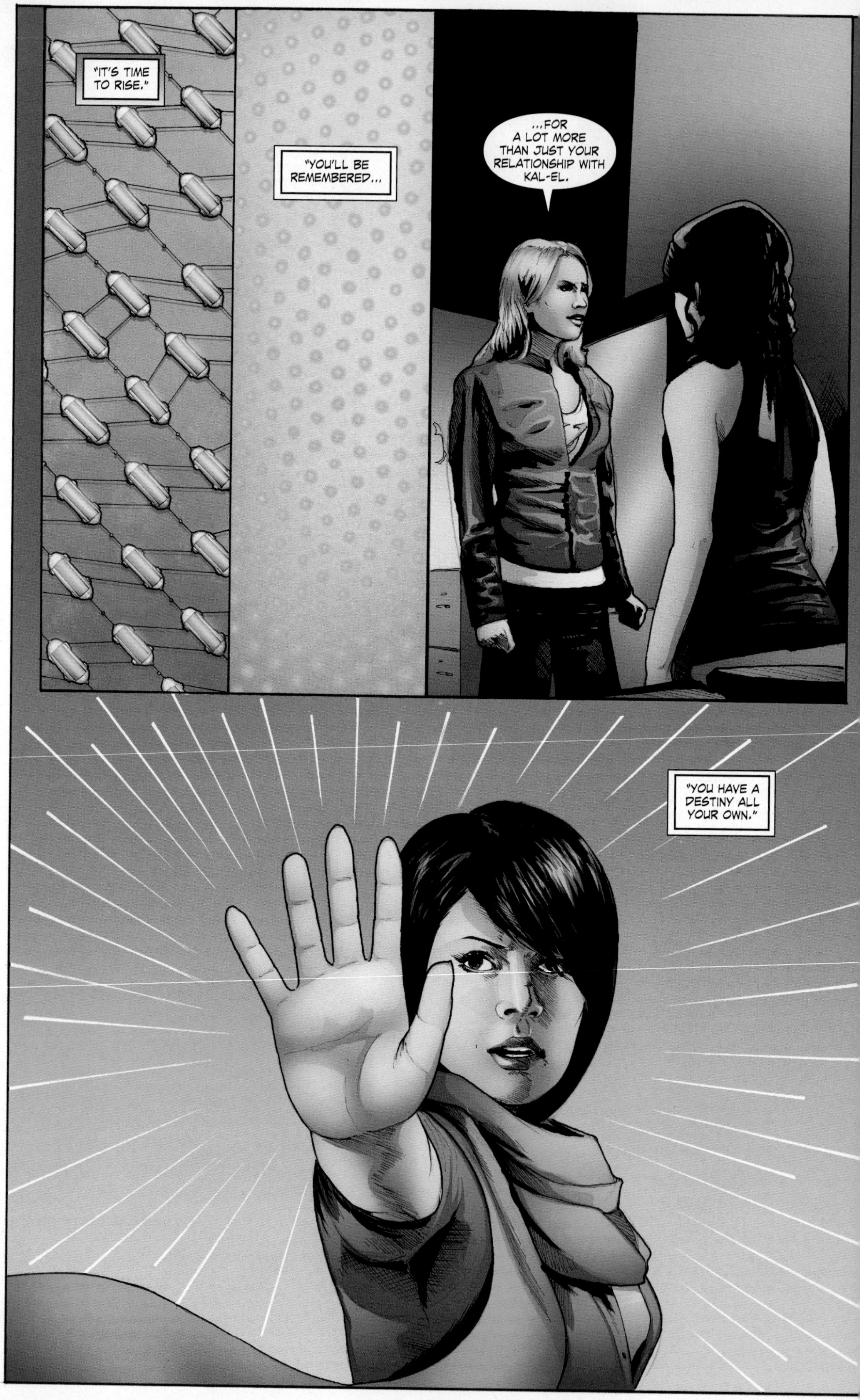
"IT'S TIME TO RISE."
"YOU'LL BE REMEMBERED...
...FOR A LOT MORE THAN JUST YOUR RELATIONSHIP WITH KAL-EL.
"YOU HAVE A DESTINY ALL YOUR OWN."

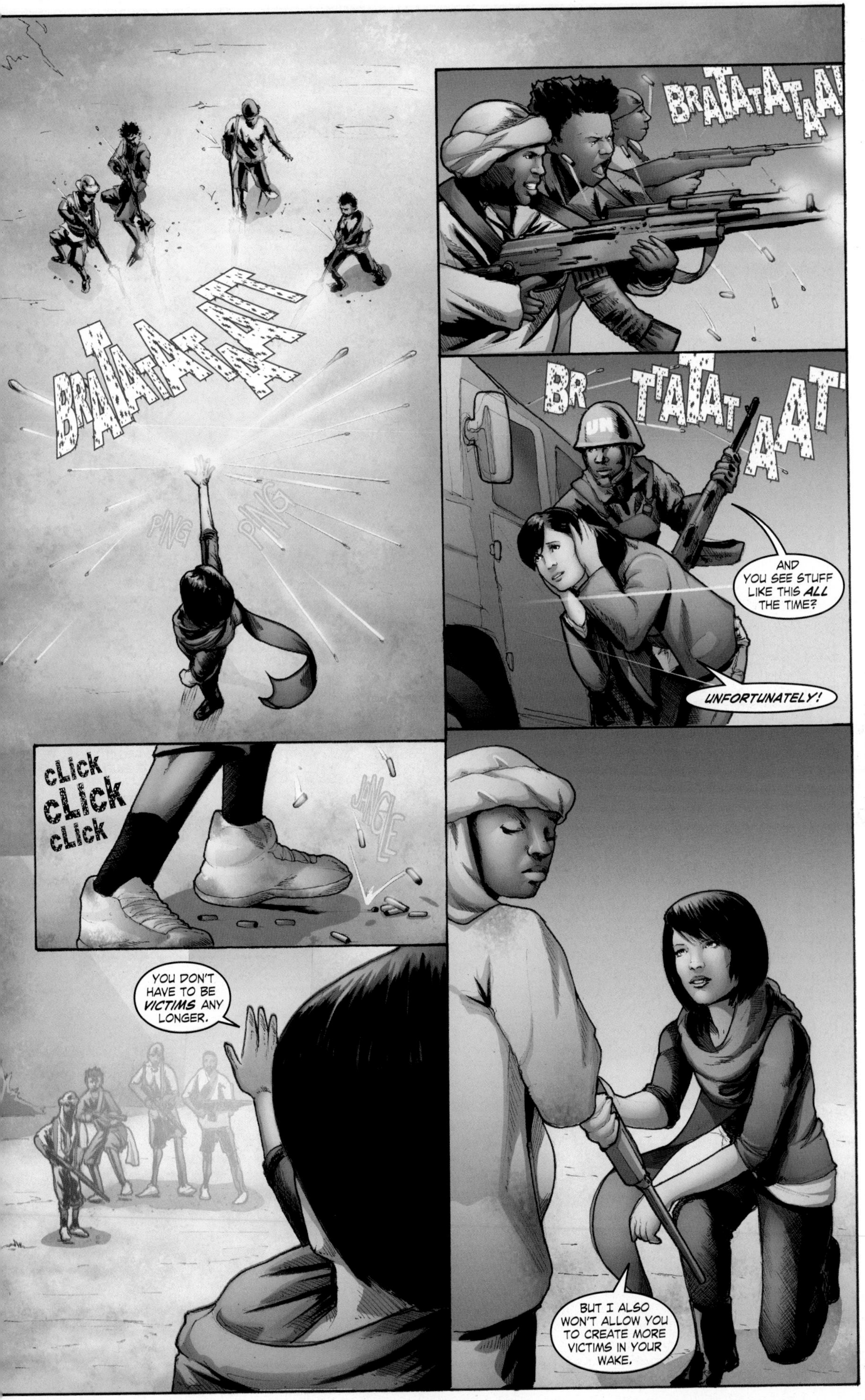
BRATATATAA!
BRATATATATAAT
PING
PING
BR TTATAT AAT
AND YOU SEE STUFF LIKE THIS ALL THE TIME?
UNFORTUNATELY!
cLick
cLick
cLick
JANGLE
YOU DON'T HAVE TO BE VICTIMS ANY LONGER.
BUT I ALSO WON'T ALLOW YOU TO CREATE MORE VICTIMS IN YOUR WAKE.

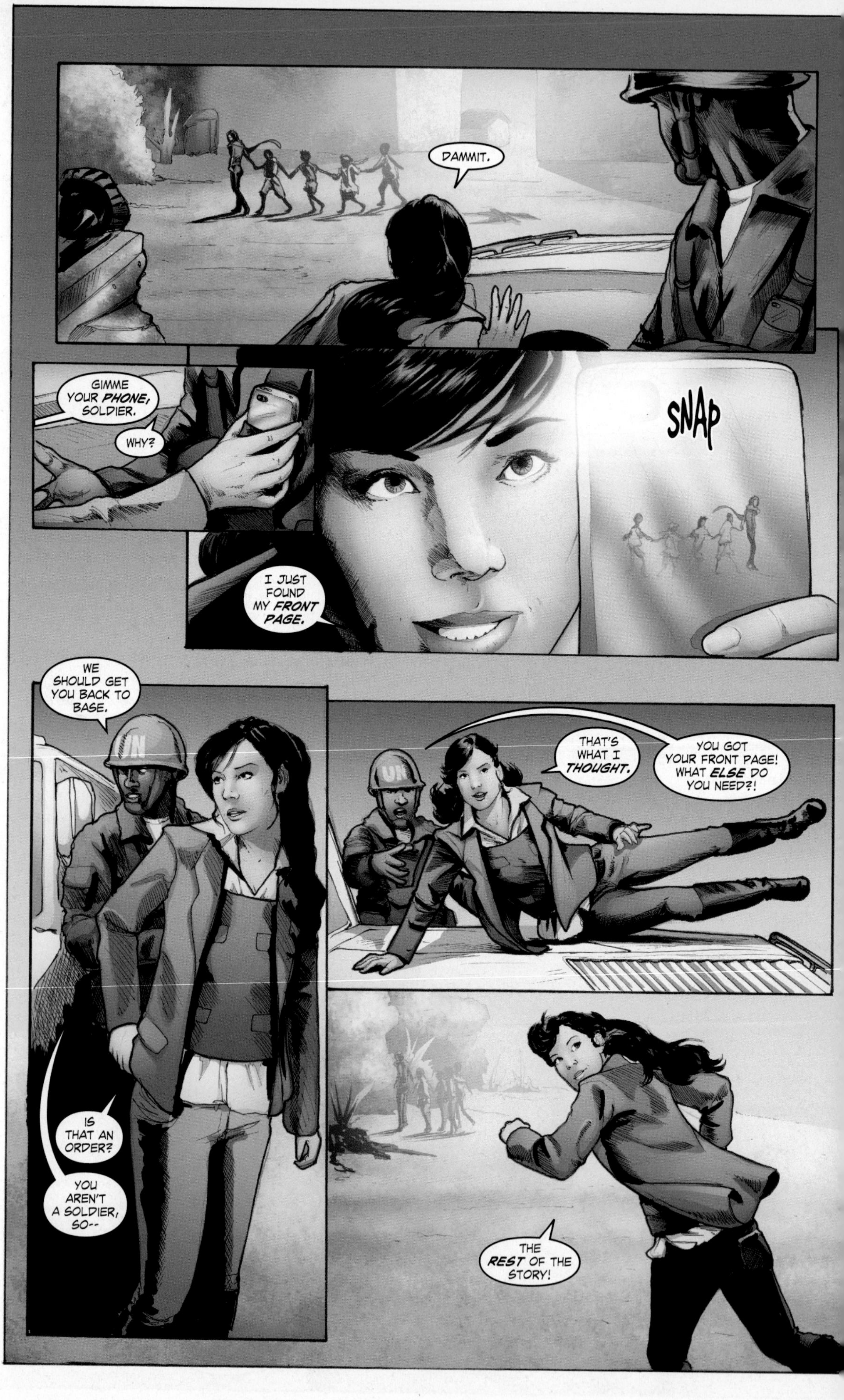
DAMMIT.
GIMME YOUR PHONE, SOLDIER.
WHY?
SNAP
I JUST FOUND MY FRONT PAGE.
WE SHOULD GET YOU BACK TO BASE.
IS THAT AN ORDER?
YOU AREN'T A SOLDIER, SO--
THAT'S WHAT I THOUGHT.
YOU GOT YOUR FRONT PAGE! WHAT ELSE DO YOU NEED?!
THE REST OF THE STORY!

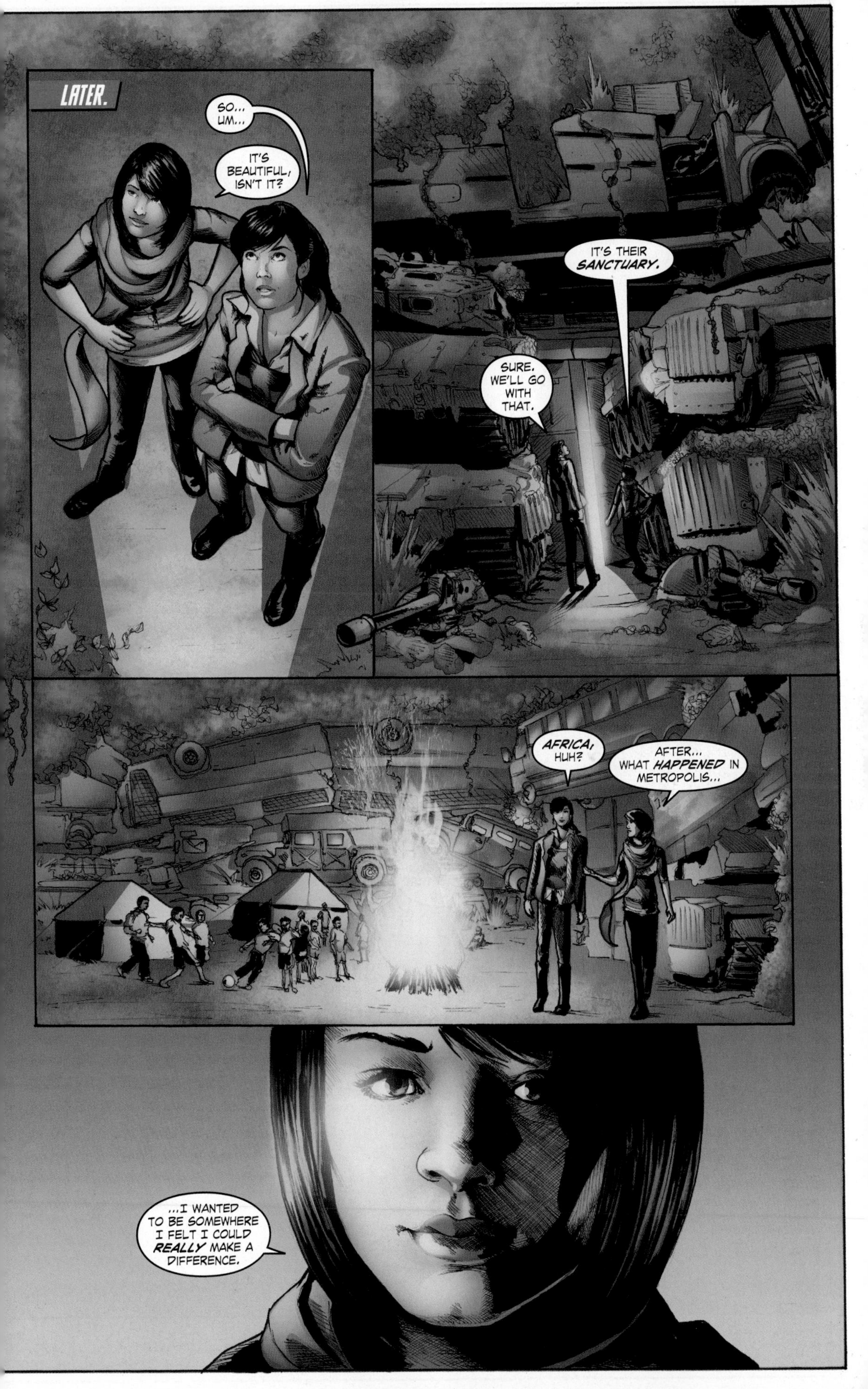
LATER.
SO... UM...
IT'S BEAUTIFUL, ISN'T IT?
IT'S THEIR SANCTUARY.
SURE. WE'LL GO WITH THAT.
AFRICA, HUH?
AFTER... WHAT HAPPENED IN METROPOLIS...
...I WANTED TO BE SOMEWHERE I FELT I COULD REALLY MAKE A DIFFERENCE.

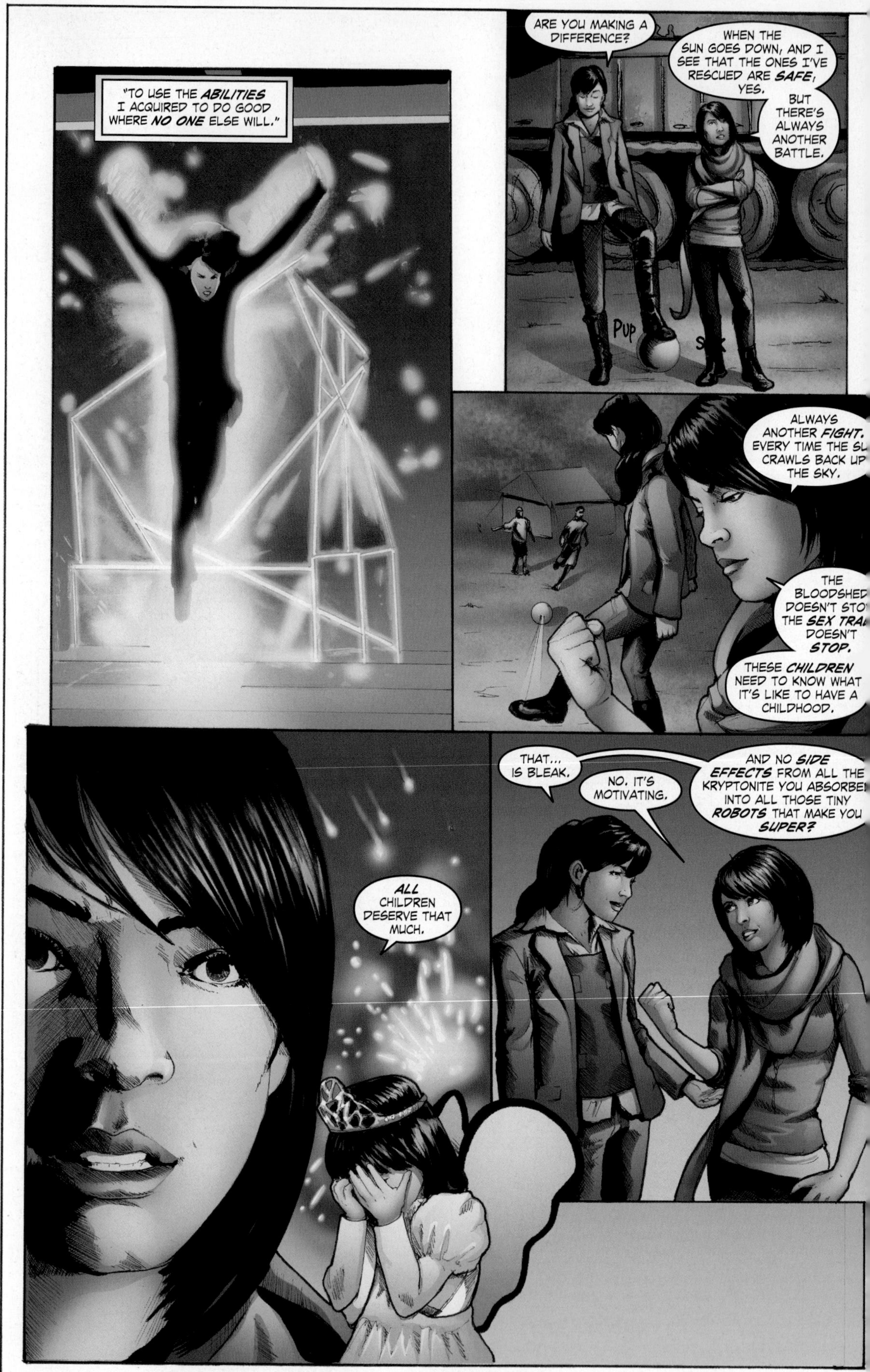
"TO USE THE ABILITIES I ACQUIRED TO DO GOOD WHERE NO ONE ELSE WILL."
ARE YOU MAKING A DIFFERENCE?
WHEN THE SUN GOES DOWN, AND I SEE THAT THE ONES I'VE RESCUED ARE SAFE, YES.
BUT THERE'S ALWAYS ANOTHER BATTLE.
PUP
ALWAYS ANOTHER FIGHT. EVERY TIME THE SL CRAWLS BACK UP THE SKY.
THE BLOODSHED DOESN'T STO THE SEX TRA DOESN'T STOP.
THESE CHILDREN NEED TO KNOW WHAT IT'S LIKE TO HAVE A CHILDHOOD.
ALL CHILDREN DESERVE THAT MUCH.
THAT... IS BLEAK.
NO. IT'S MOTIVATING.
AND NO SIDE EFFECTS FROM ALL THE KRYPTONITE YOU ABSORBE INTO ALL THOSE TINY ROBOTS THAT MAKE YOU SUPER?

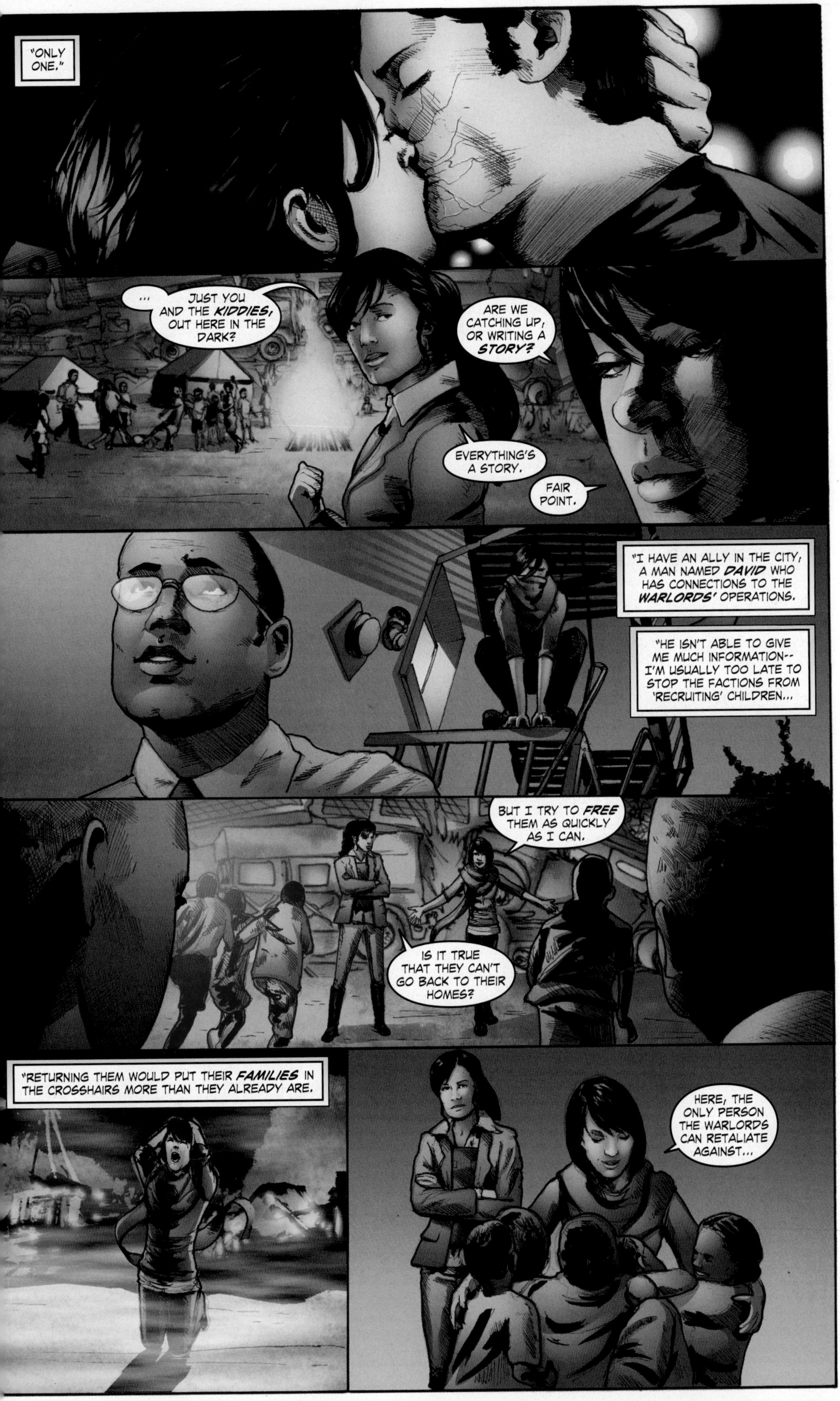
"ONLY ONE."
... JUST YOU AND THE KIDDIES, OUT HERE IN THE DARK?
ARE WE CATCHING UP, OR WRITING A STORY?
EVERYTHING'S A STORY.
FAIR POINT.
"I HAVE AN ALLY IN THE CITY, A MAN NAMED DAVID WHO HAS CONNECTIONS TO THE WARLORDS' OPERATIONS.
"HE ISN'T ABLE TO GIVE ME MUCH INFORMATION-- I'M USUALLY TOO LATE TO STOP THE FACTIONS FROM 'RECRUITING' CHILDREN...
BUT I TRY TO FREE THEM AS QUICKLY AS I CAN.
IS IT TRUE THAT THEY CAN'T GO BACK TO THEIR HOMES?
"RETURNING THEM WOULD PUT THEIR FAMILIES IN THE CROSSHAIRS MORE THAN THEY ALREADY ARE.
HERE, THE ONLY PERSON THE WARLORDS CAN RETALIATE AGAINST...

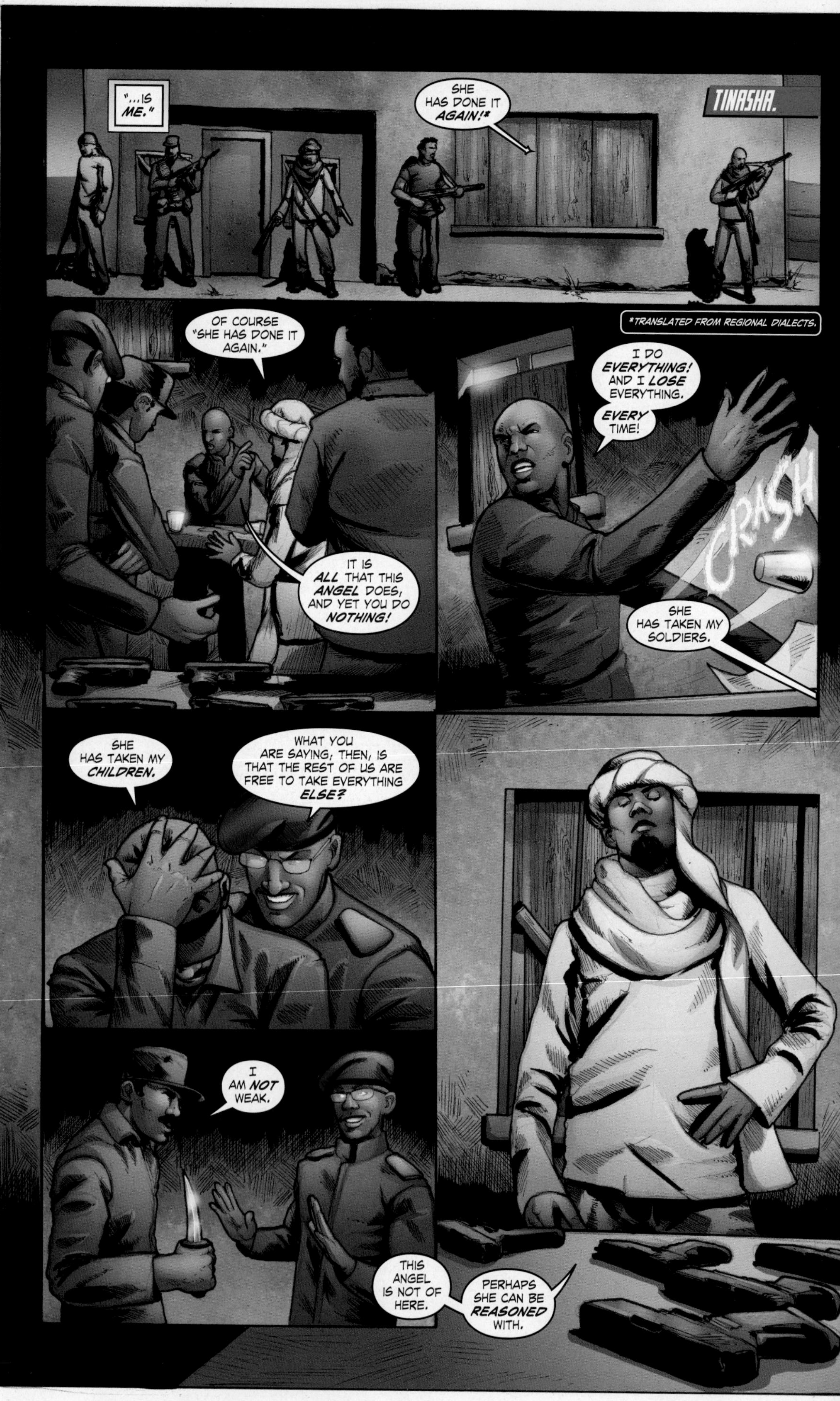
"...IS ME."
SHE HAS DONE IT AGAIN!*
TINASHA.
*TRANSLATED FROM REGIONAL DIALECTS.
OF COURSE "SHE HAS DONE IT AGAIN."
IT IS ALL THAT THIS ANGEL DOES, AND YET YOU DO NOTHING!
I DO EVERYTHING! AND I LOSE EVERYTHING.
EVERY TIME!
CRASH
SHE HAS TAKEN MY SOLDIERS.
SHE HAS TAKEN MY CHILDREN.
WHAT YOU ARE SAYING, THEN, IS THAT THE REST OF US ARE FREE TO TAKE EVERYTHING ELSE?
I AM NOT WEAK.
THIS ANGEL IS NOT OF HERE.
PERHAPS SHE CAN BE REASONED WITH.

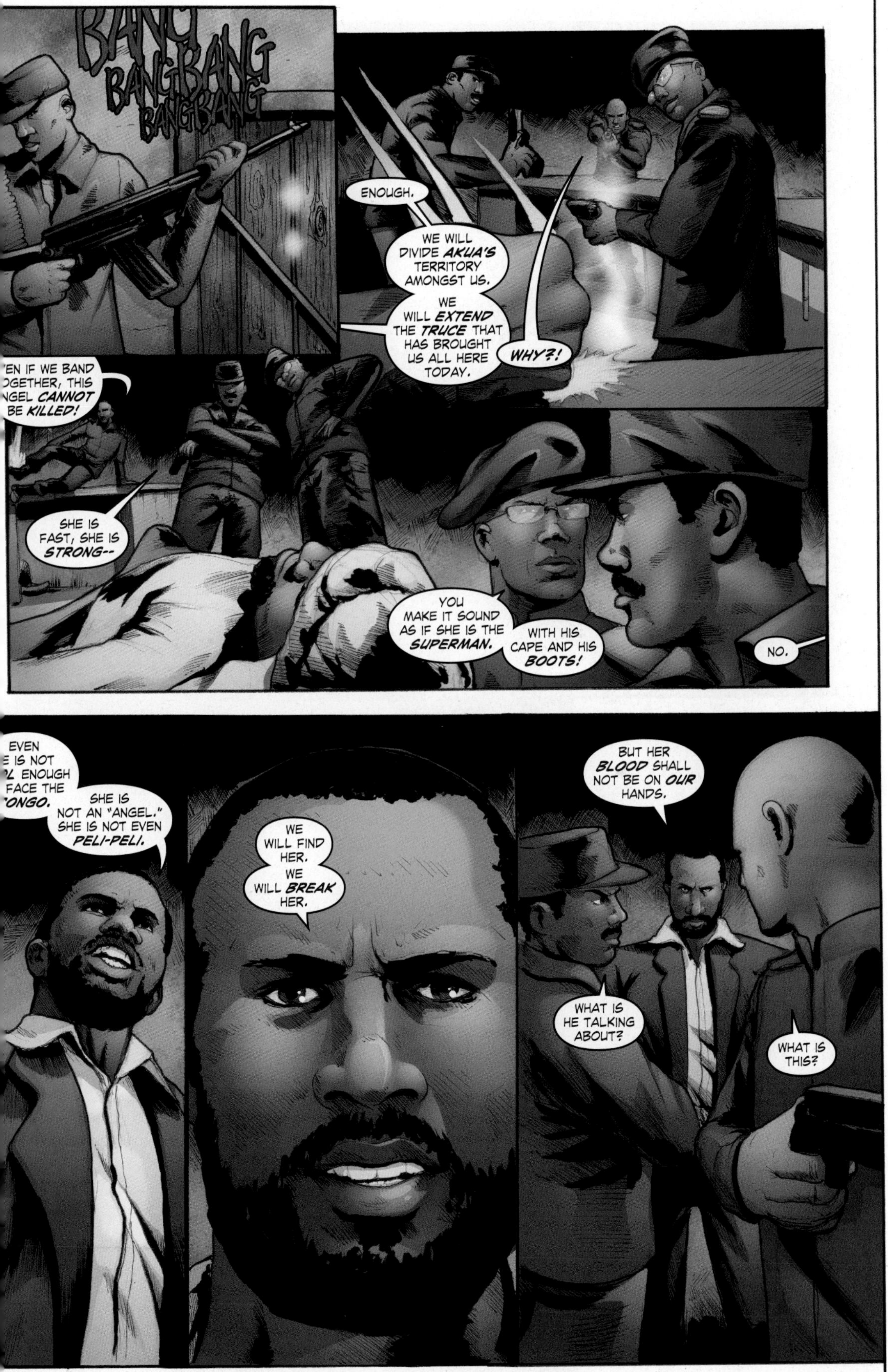

BANG
BANGBANG
BANGBANG
ENOUGH.
WE WILL DIVIDE AKUA'S TERRITORY AMONGST US.
WE WILL EXTEND THE TRUCE THAT HAS BROUGHT US ALL HERE TODAY.
WHY?!
'EN IF WE BAND OGETHER, THIS NGEL CANNOT BE KILLED!
SHE IS FAST, SHE IS STRONG--
YOU MAKE IT SOUND AS IF SHE IS THE SUPERMAN.
WITH HIS CAPE AND HIS BOOTS!
NO.
EVEN E IS NOT L ENOUGH FACE THE ONGO.
SHE IS NOT AN "ANGEL." SHE IS NOT EVEN PELI-PELI.
WE WILL FIND HER. WE WILL BREAK HER.
BUT HER BLOOD SHALL NOT BE ON OUR HANDS.
WHAT IS HE TALKING ABOUT?
WHAT IS THIS?

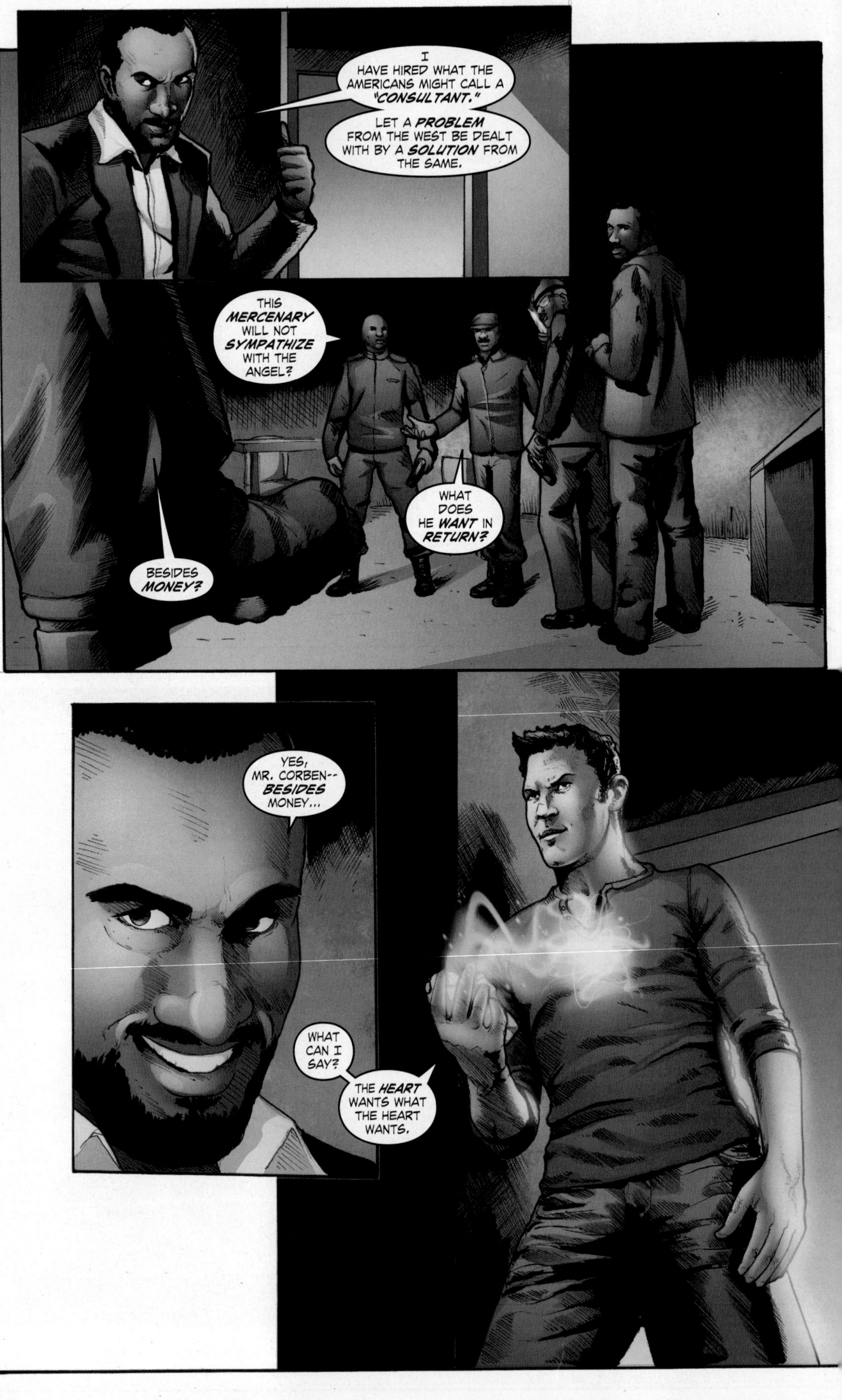
I HAVE HIRED WHAT THE AMERICANS MIGHT CALL A "CONSULTANT."
LET A PROBLEM FROM THE WEST BE DEALT WITH BY A SOLUTION FROM THE SAME.
THIS MERCENARY WILL NOT SYMPATHIZE WITH THE ANGEL?
WHAT DOES HE WANT IN RETURN?
BESIDES MONEY?
YES, MR. CORBEN-- BESIDES MONEY...
WHAT CAN I SAY?
THE HEART WANTS WHAT THE HEART WANTS.

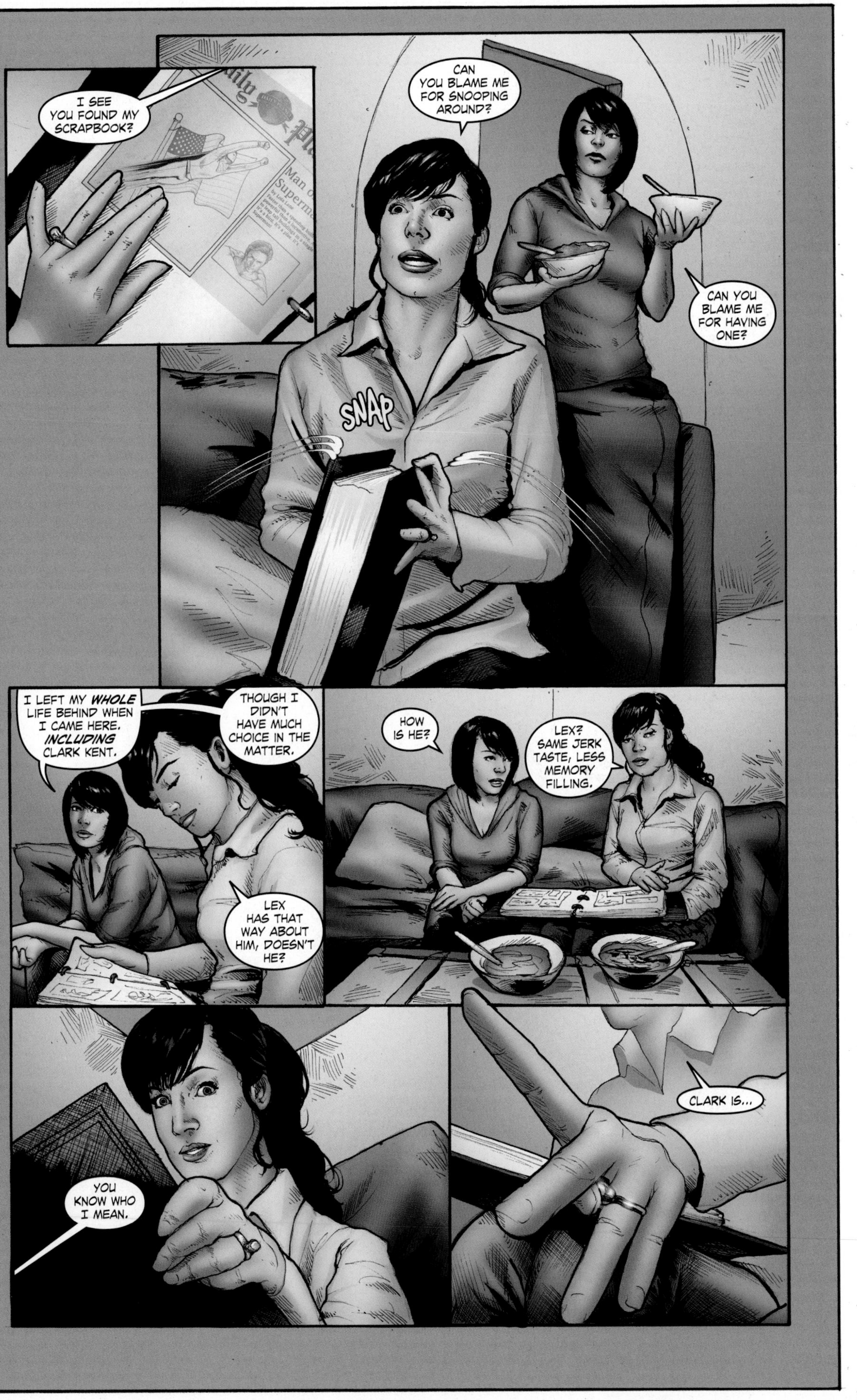
I SEE YOU FOUND MY SCRAPBOOK?
CAN YOU BLAME ME FOR SNOOPING AROUND?
CAN YOU BLAME ME FOR HAVING ONE?
SNAP
I LEFT MY *WHOLE* LIFE BEHIND WHEN I CAME HERE. *INCLUDING* CLARK KENT.
THOUGH I DIDN'T HAVE MUCH CHOICE IN THE MATTER.
LEX HAS THAT WAY ABOUT HIM, DOESN'T HE?
HOW IS HE?
LEX? SAME JERK TASTE, LESS MEMORY FILLING.
YOU KNOW WHO I MEAN.
CLARK IS...

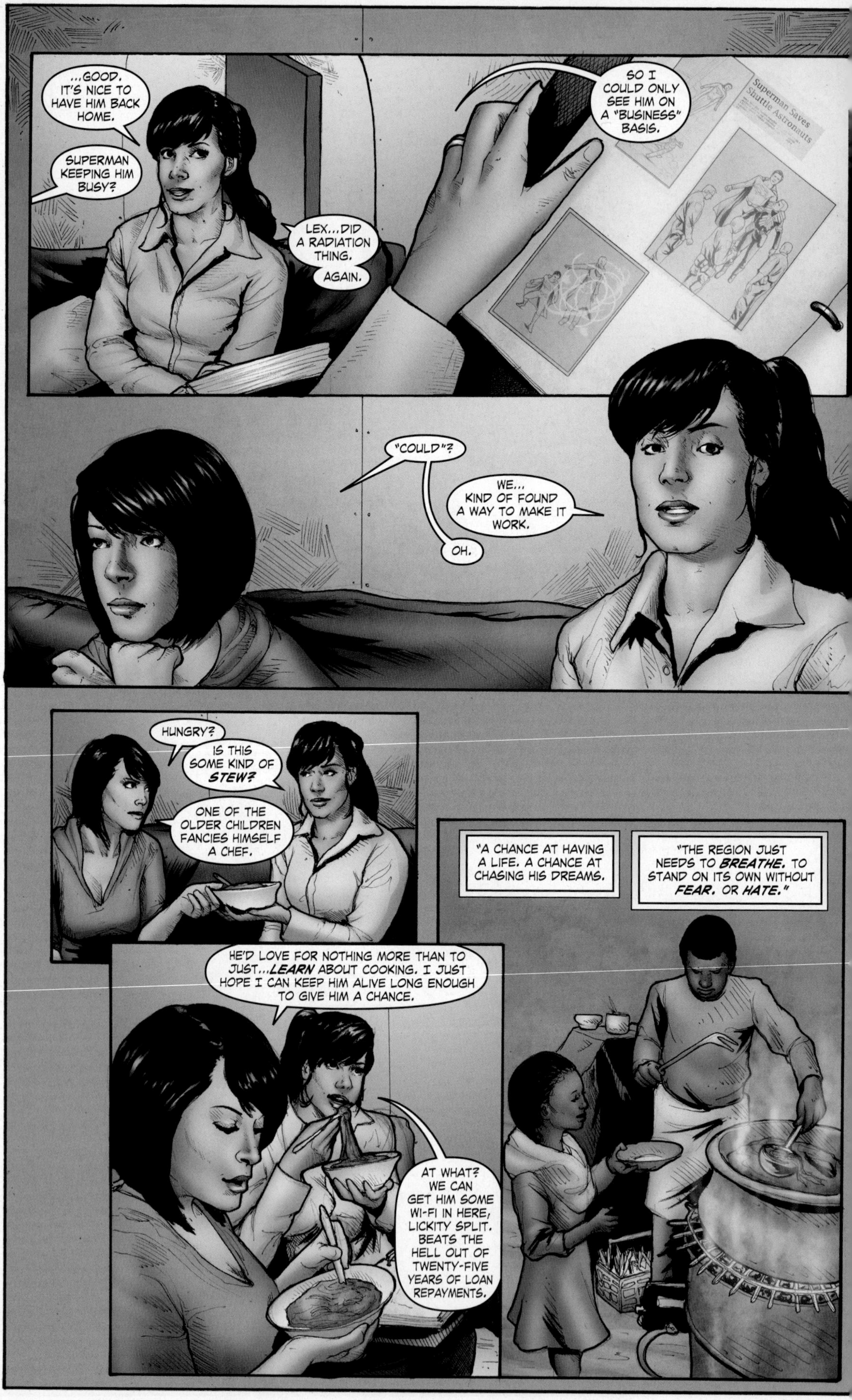

...GOOD. IT'S NICE TO HAVE HIM BACK HOME.
SUPERMAN KEEPING HIM BUSY?
LEX...DID A RADIATION THING.
AGAIN.
SO I COULD ONLY SEE HIM ON A "BUSINESS" BASIS.
Superman Saves Shuttle Astronauts
"COULD"?
WE... KIND OF FOUND A WAY TO MAKE IT WORK.
OH.
HUNGRY?
IS THIS SOME KIND OF STEW?
ONE OF THE OLDER CHILDREN FANCIES HIMSELF A CHEF.
HE'D LOVE FOR NOTHING MORE THAN TO JUST...LEARN ABOUT COOKING. I JUST HOPE I CAN KEEP HIM ALIVE LONG ENOUGH TO GIVE HIM A CHANCE.
AT WHAT? WE CAN GET HIM SOME WI-FI IN HERE, LICKITY SPLIT. BEATS THE HELL OUT OF TWENTY-FIVE YEARS OF LOAN REPAYMENTS.
"A CHANCE AT HAVING A LIFE. A CHANCE AT CHASING HIS DREAMS.
"THE REGION JUST NEEDS TO BREATHE. TO STAND ON ITS OWN WITHOUT FEAR. OR HATE."

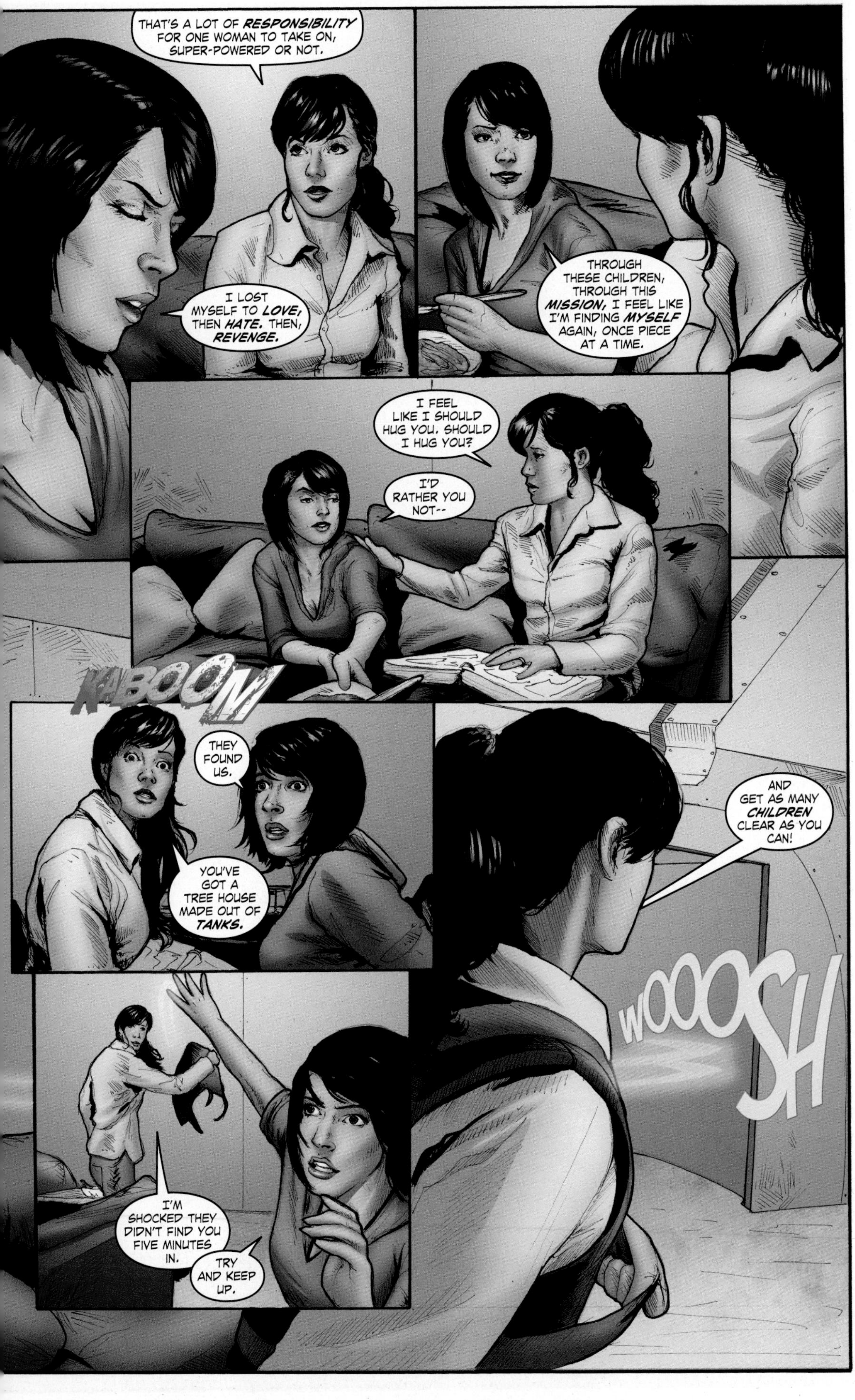
THAT'S A LOT OF RESPONSIBILITY FOR ONE WOMAN TO TAKE ON, SUPER-POWERED OR NOT.
I LOST MYSELF TO LOVE, THEN HATE. THEN, REVENGE.
THROUGH THESE CHILDREN, THROUGH THIS MISSION, I FEEL LIKE I'M FINDING MYSELF AGAIN, ONCE PIECE AT A TIME.
I FEEL LIKE I SHOULD HUG YOU. SHOULD I HUG YOU?
I'D RATHER YOU NOT--
KABOOM
THEY FOUND US.
YOU'VE GOT A TREE HOUSE MADE OUT OF TANKS.
I'M SHOCKED THEY DIDN'T FIND YOU FIVE MINUTES IN.
TRY AND KEEP UP.
AND GET AS MANY CHILDREN CLEAR AS YOU CAN!
WOOOSH

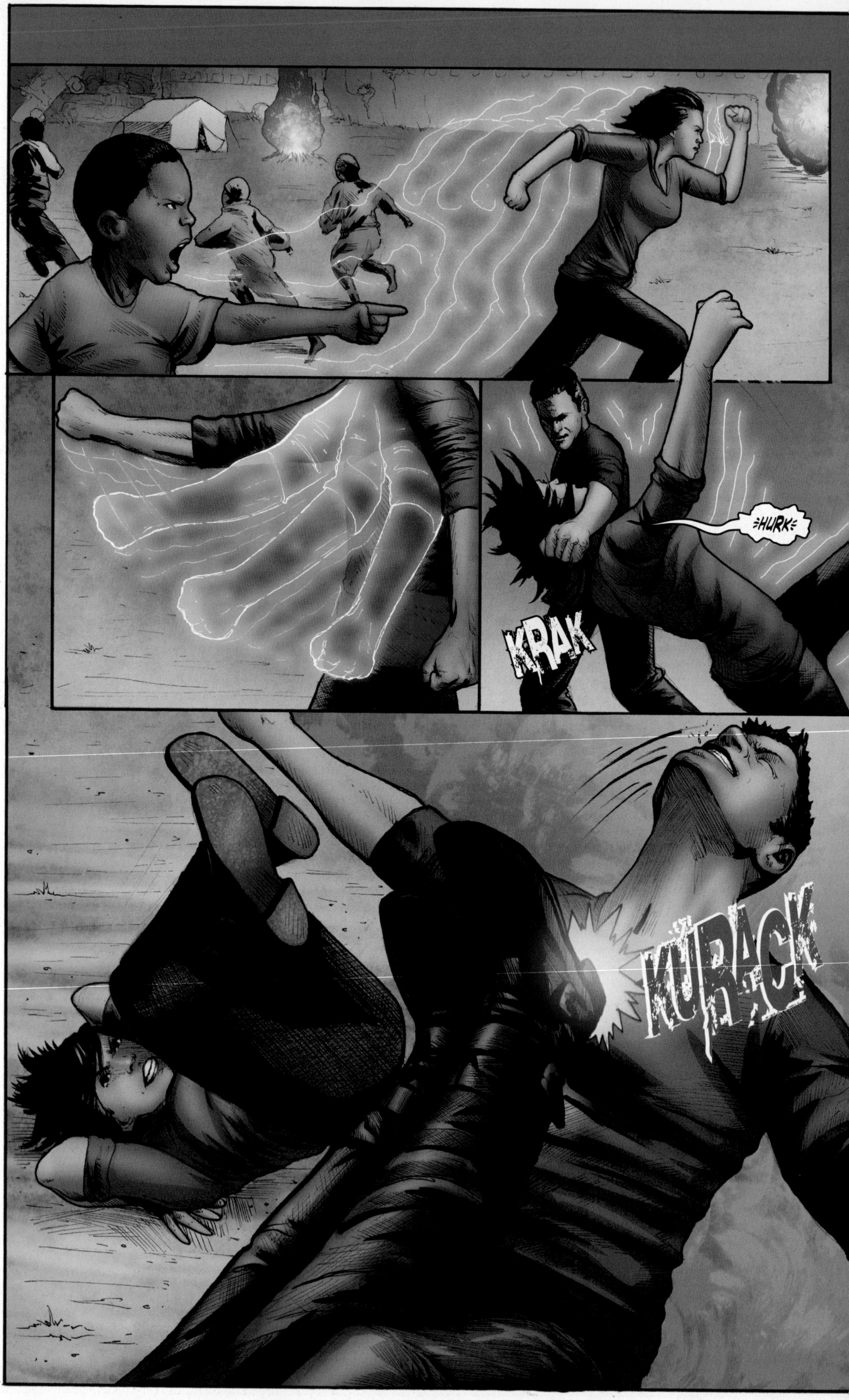
HURK
KRAK
KURACK

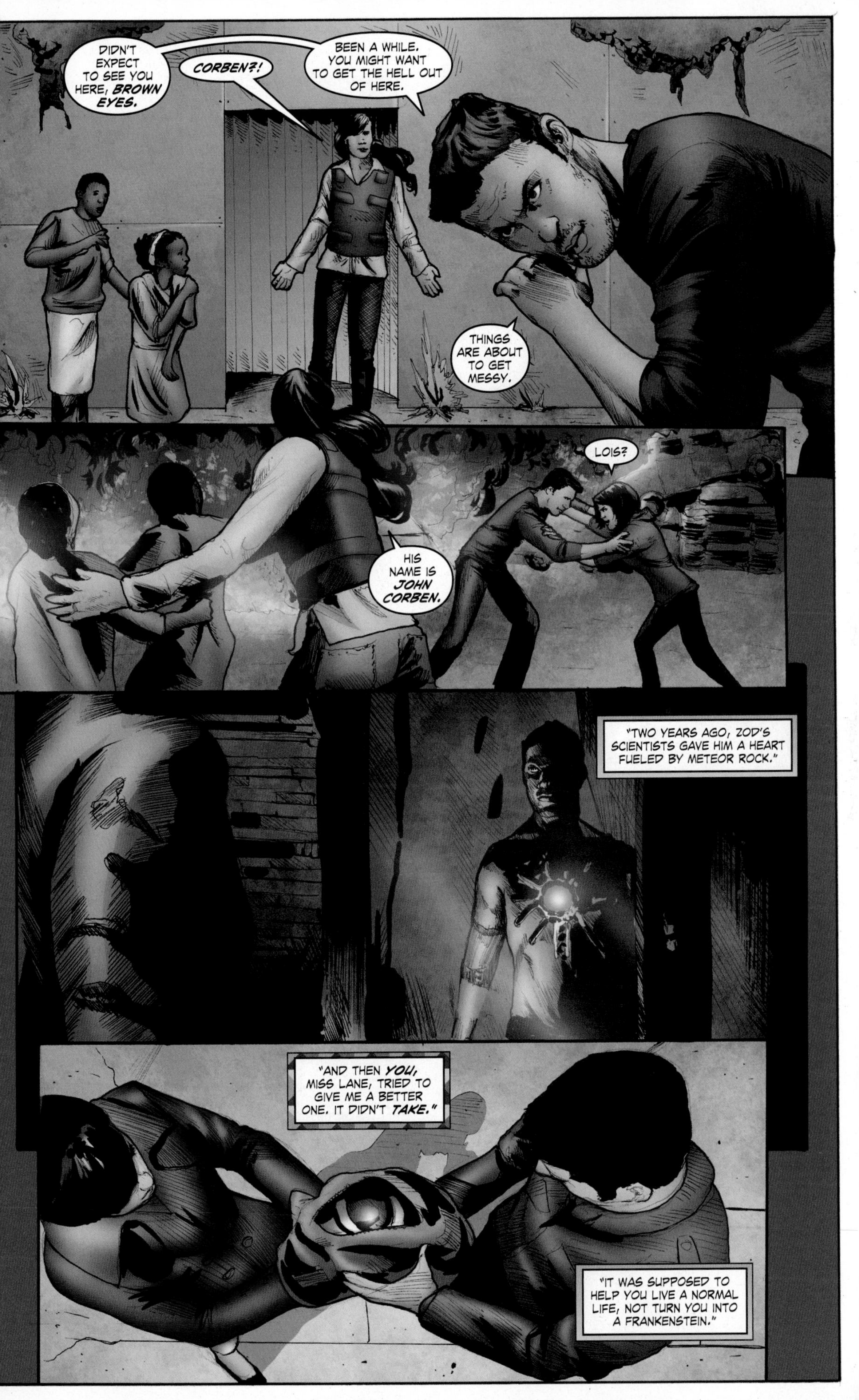
DIDN'T EXPECT TO SEE YOU HERE, BROWN EYES.
CORBEN?!
BEEN A WHILE. YOU MIGHT WANT TO GET THE HELL OUT OF HERE.
THINGS ARE ABOUT TO GET MESSY.
LOIS?
HIS NAME IS JOHN CORBEN.
"TWO YEARS AGO, ZOD'S SCIENTISTS GAVE HIM A HEART FUELED BY METEOR ROCK."
"AND THEN YOU, MISS LANE, TRIED TO GIVE ME A BETTER ONE. IT DIDN'T TAKE."
"IT WAS SUPPOSED TO HELP YOU LIVE A NORMAL LIFE, NOT TURN YOU INTO A FRANKENSTEIN."

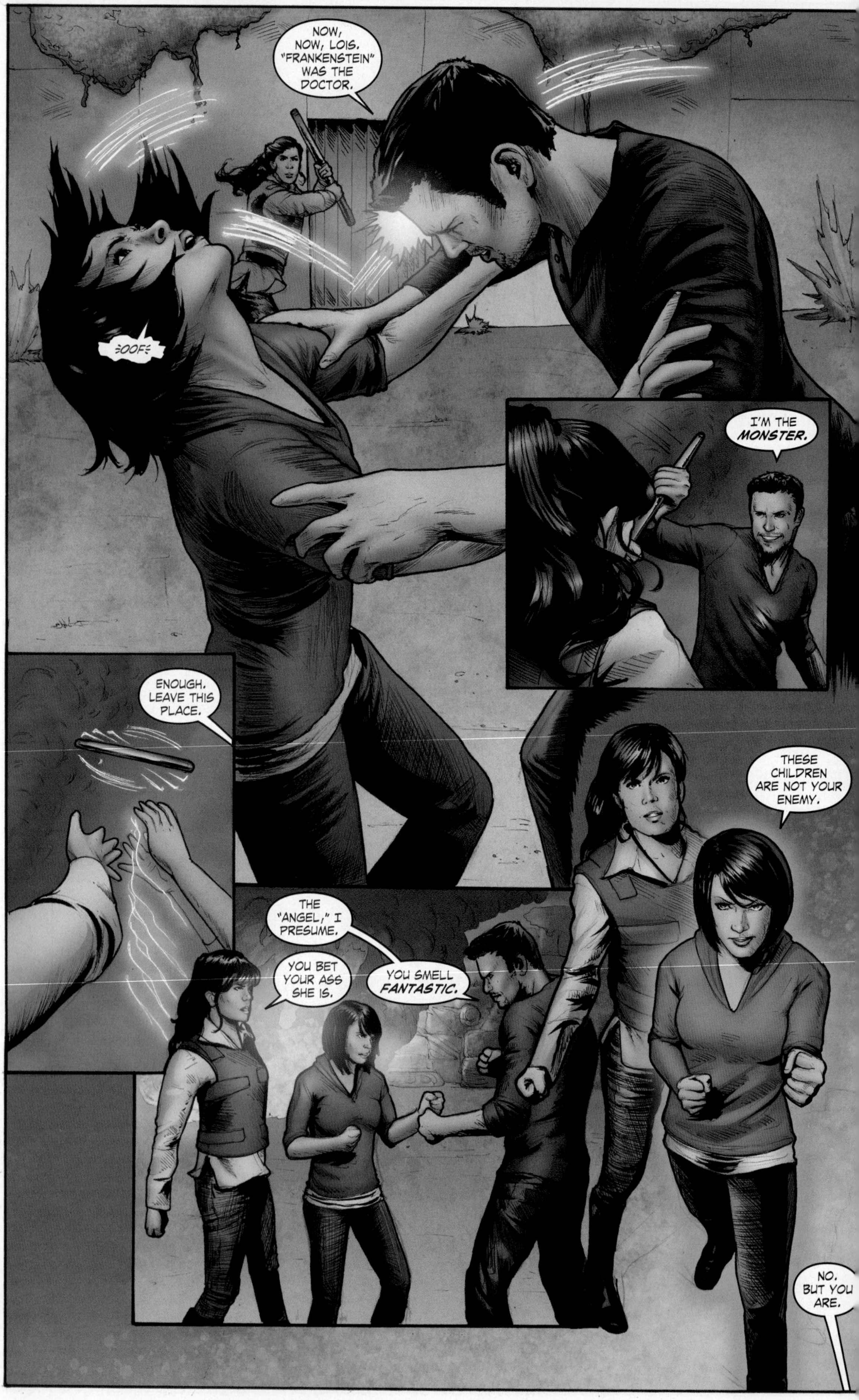
NOW, NOW, LOIS. "FRANKENSTEIN" WAS THE DOCTOR.
OOF
I'M THE MONSTER.
ENOUGH. LEAVE THIS PLACE.
THESE CHILDREN ARE NOT YOUR ENEMY.
THE "ANGEL," I PRESUME.
YOU BET YOUR ASS SHE IS.
YOU SMELL FANTASTIC.
NO. BUT YOU ARE.

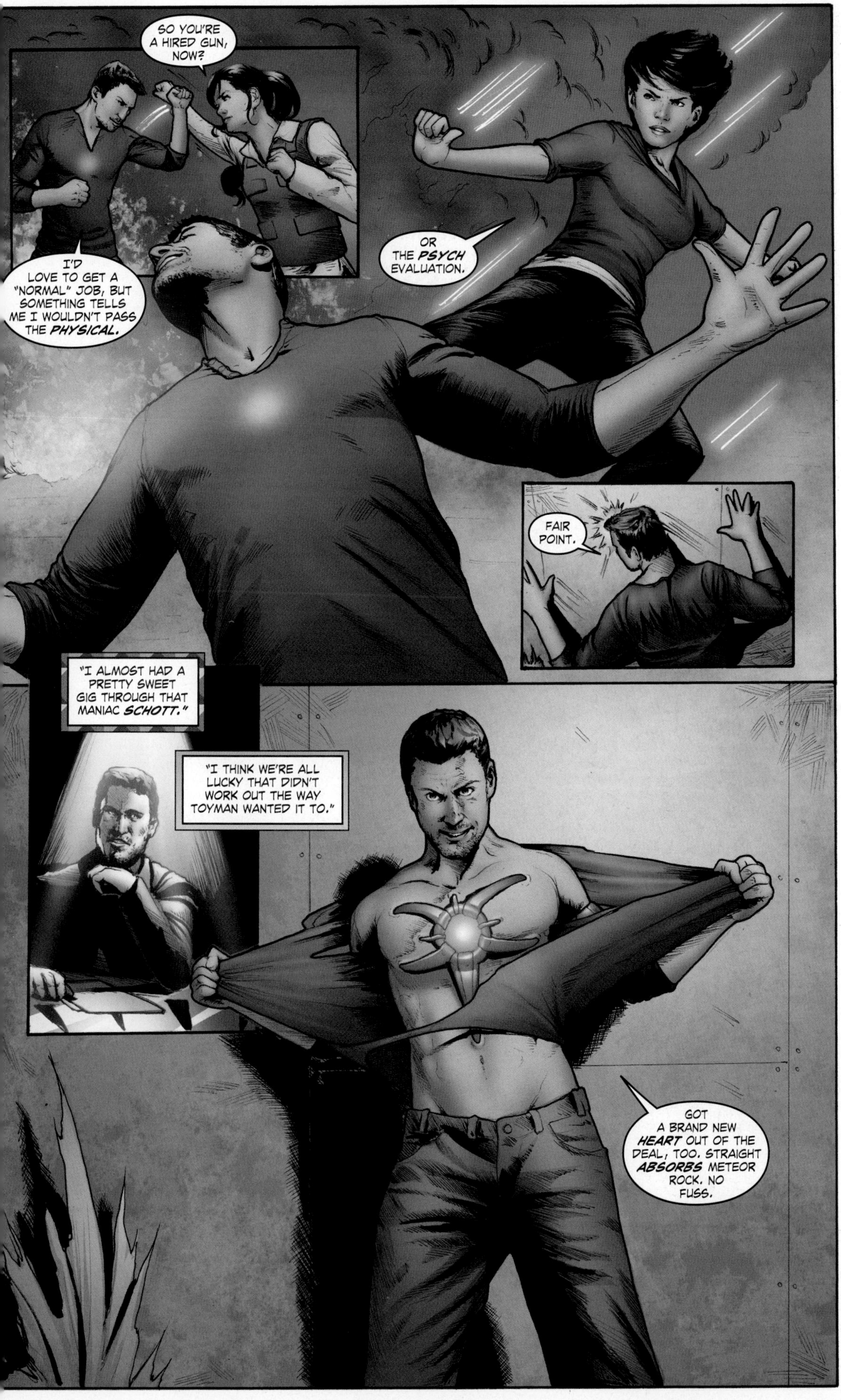
SO YOU'RE A HIRED GUN, NOW?
I'D LOVE TO GET A "NORMAL" JOB, BUT SOMETHING TELLS ME I WOULDN'T PASS THE PHYSICAL.
OR THE PSYCH EVALUATION.
FAIR POINT.
"I ALMOST HAD A PRETTY SWEET GIG THROUGH THAT MANIAC SCHOTT."
"I THINK WE'RE ALL LUCKY THAT DIDN'T WORK OUT THE WAY TOYMAN WANTED IT TO."
GOT A BRAND NEW HEART OUT OF THE DEAL, TOO. STRAIGHT ABSORBS METEOR ROCK. NO FUSS.

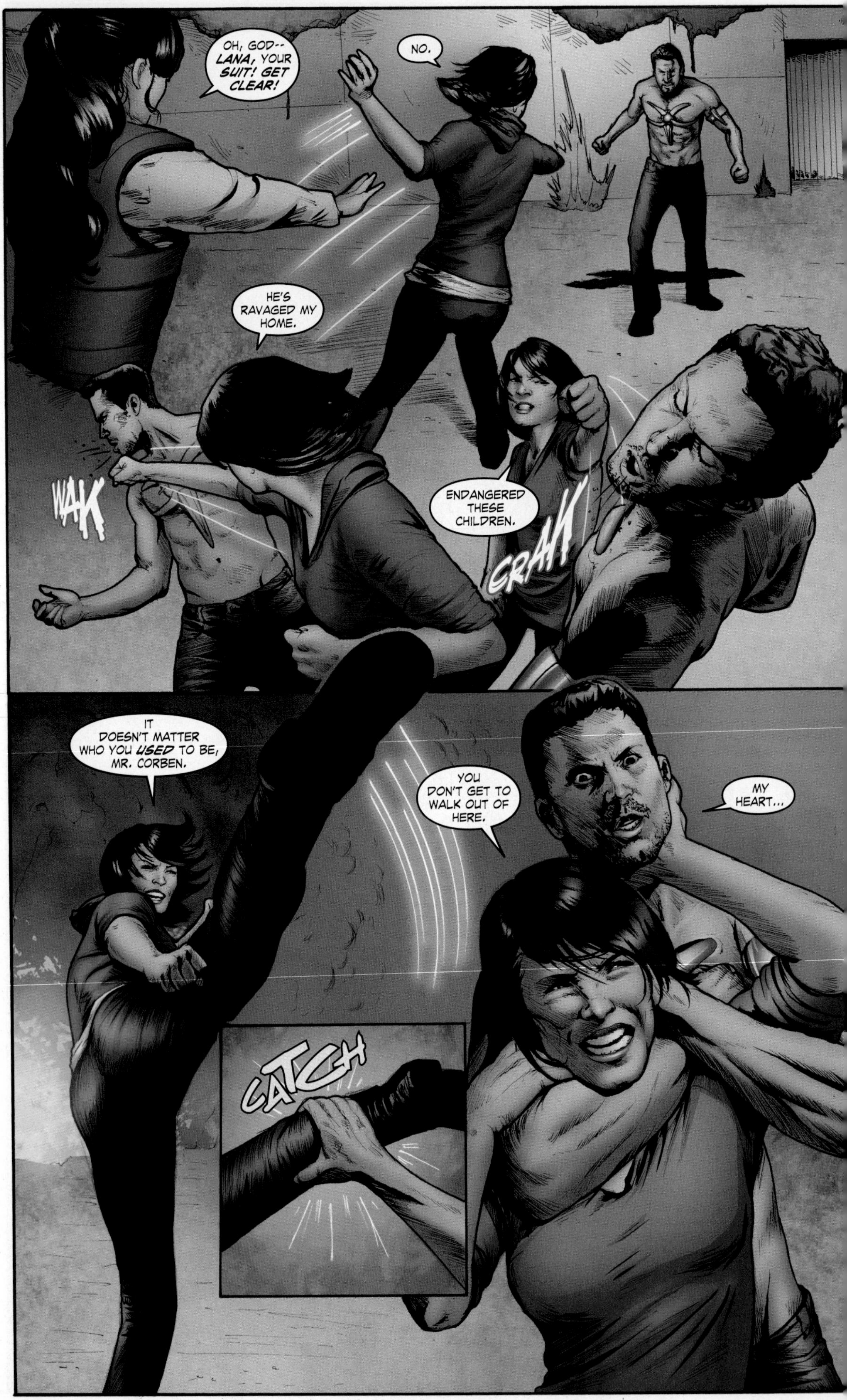
OH, GOD-- LANA, YOUR SUIT! GET CLEAR!
NO.
HE'S RAVAGED MY HOME.
WAK
ENDANGERED THESE CHILDREN.
CRAK
IT DOESN'T MATTER WHO YOU USED TO BE, MR. CORBEN.
YOU DON'T GET TO WALK OUT OF HERE.
MY HEART...
CATCH

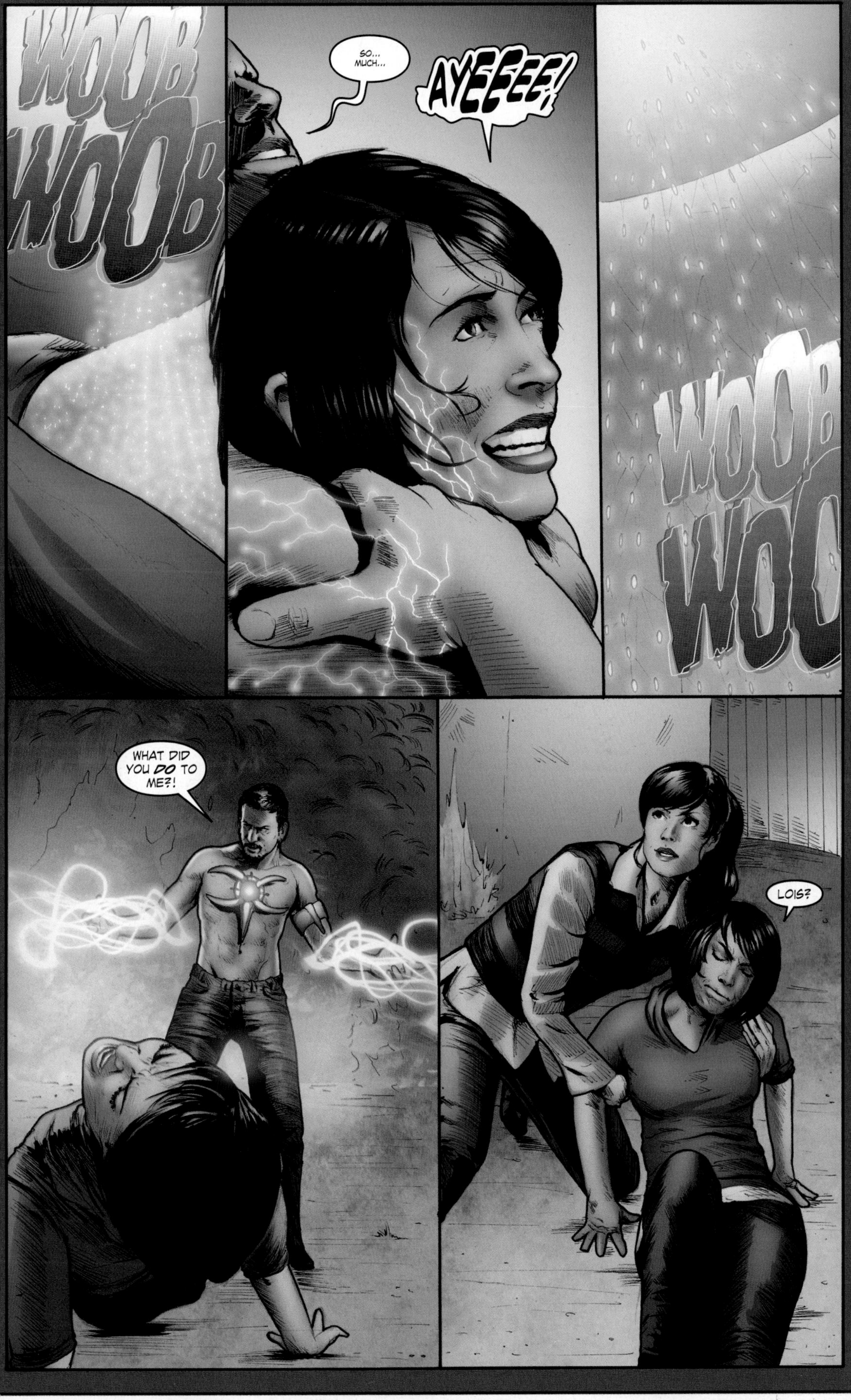
WOOB WOOB
SO... MUCH...
AYEEEEE!
WOOB WOOB
WHAT DID YOU DO TO ME?!
LOIS?

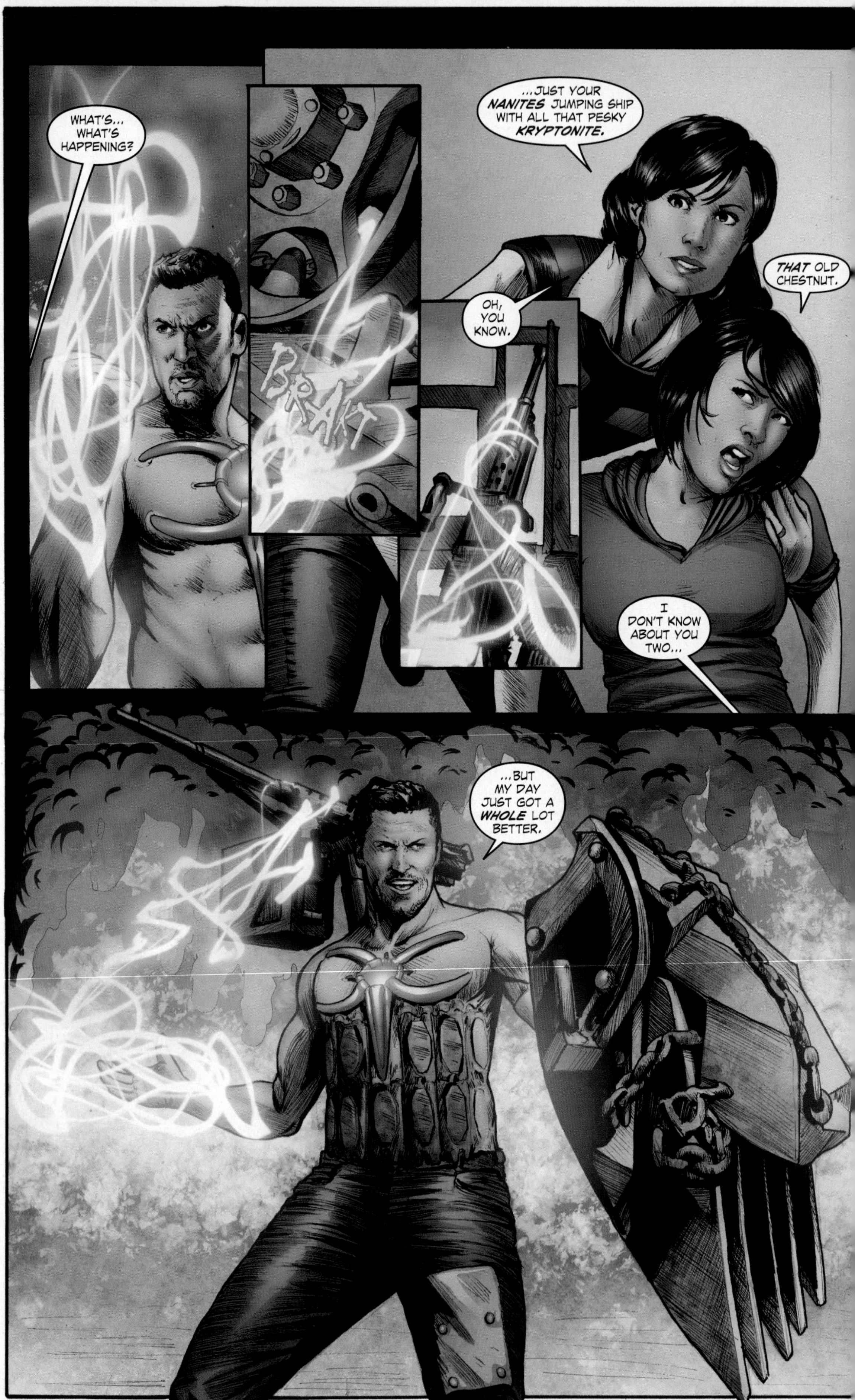
WHAT'S... WHAT'S HAPPENING?
BRAKT
...JUST YOUR NANITES JUMPING SHIP WITH ALL THAT PESKY KRYPTONITE.
OH, YOU KNOW.
THAT OLD CHESTNUT.
I DON'T KNOW ABOUT YOU TWO...
...BUT MY DAY JUST GOT A WHOLE LOT BETTER.

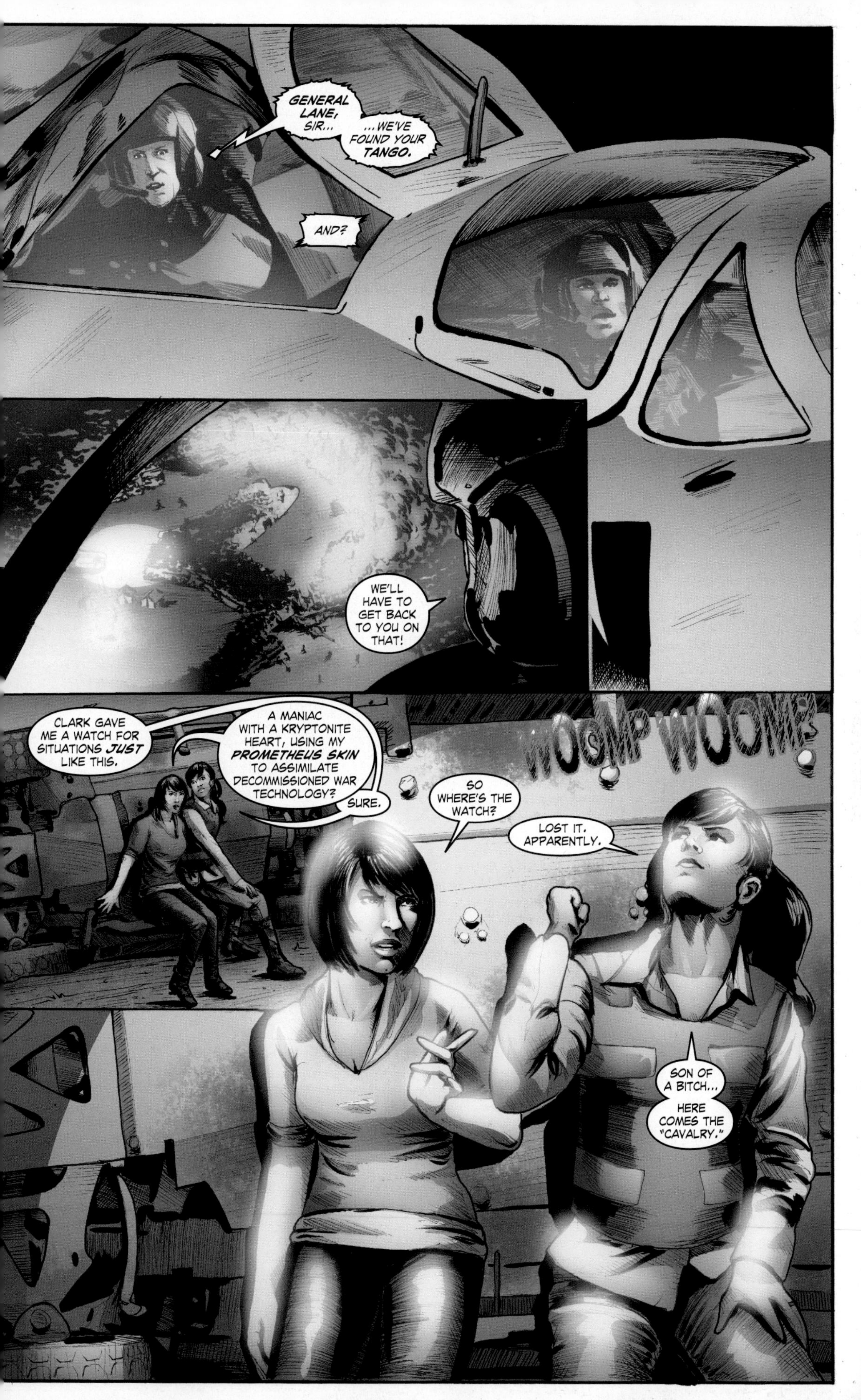
GENERAL LANE, SIR...
...WE'VE FOUND YOUR TANGO.
AND?
WE'LL HAVE TO GET BACK TO YOU ON THAT!
WOOMP WOOMP
CLARK GAVE ME A WATCH FOR SITUATIONS JUST LIKE THIS.
A MANIAC WITH A KRYPTONITE HEART, USING MY PROMETHEUS SKIN TO ASSIMILATE DECOMMISSIONED WAR TECHNOLOGY?
SURE.
SO WHERE'S THE WATCH?
LOST IT. APPARENTLY.
SON OF A BITCH...
HERE COMES THE "CAVALRY."

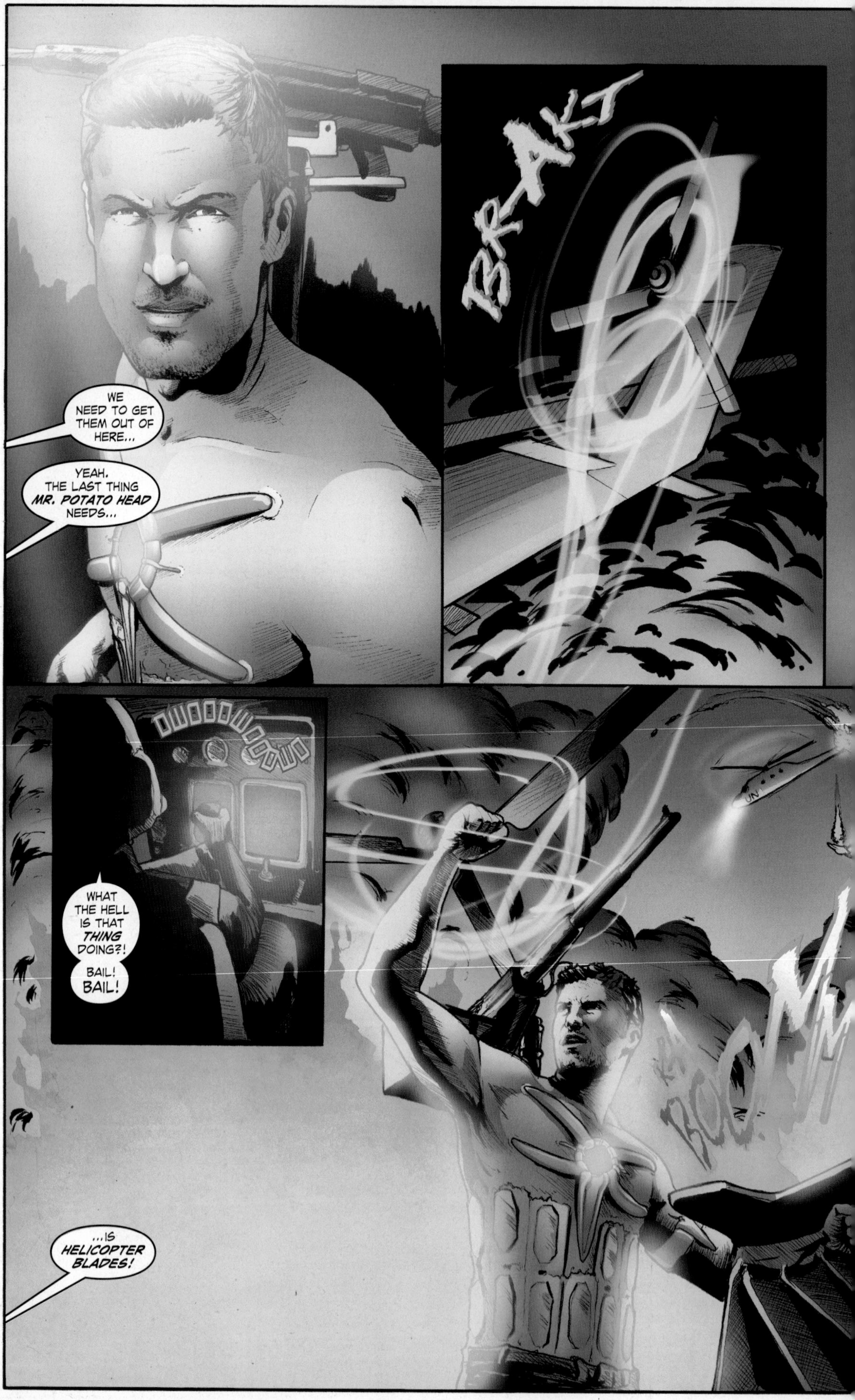
WE NEED TO GET THEM OUT OF HERE...
YEAH. THE LAST THING *MR. POTATO HEAD* NEEDS...
BR-AKT
WHAT THE HELL IS THAT *THING* DOING?!
BAIL! BAIL!
...IS *HELICOPTER BLADES!*

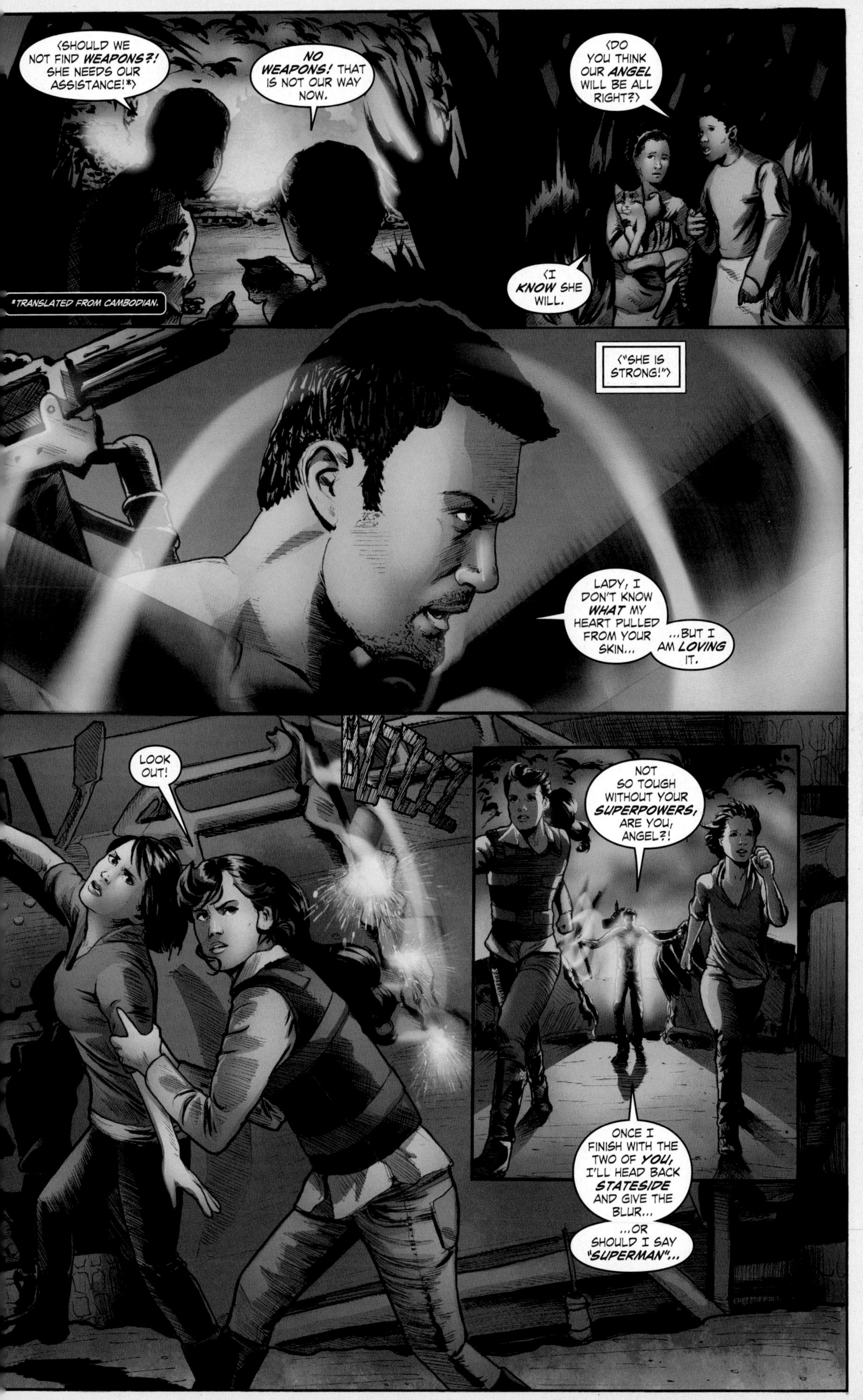

‹SHOULD WE NOT FIND **WEAPONS?!** SHE NEEDS OUR ASSISTANCE!*›
NO WEAPONS! THAT IS NOT OUR WAY NOW.
‹DO YOU THINK OUR **ANGEL** WILL BE ALL RIGHT?›
‹I **KNOW** SHE WILL.
*TRANSLATED FROM CAMBODIAN.
‹"SHE IS STRONG!"›
LADY, I DON'T KNOW **WHAT** MY HEART PULLED FROM YOUR SKIN...
...BUT I AM **LOVING** IT.
LOOK OUT!
NOT SO TOUGH WITHOUT YOUR **SUPERPOWERS,** ARE YOU, ANGEL?!
ONCE I FINISH WITH THE TWO OF **YOU,** I'LL HEAD BACK **STATESIDE** AND GIVE THE BLUR...
...OR SHOULD I SAY **"SUPERMAN"...**

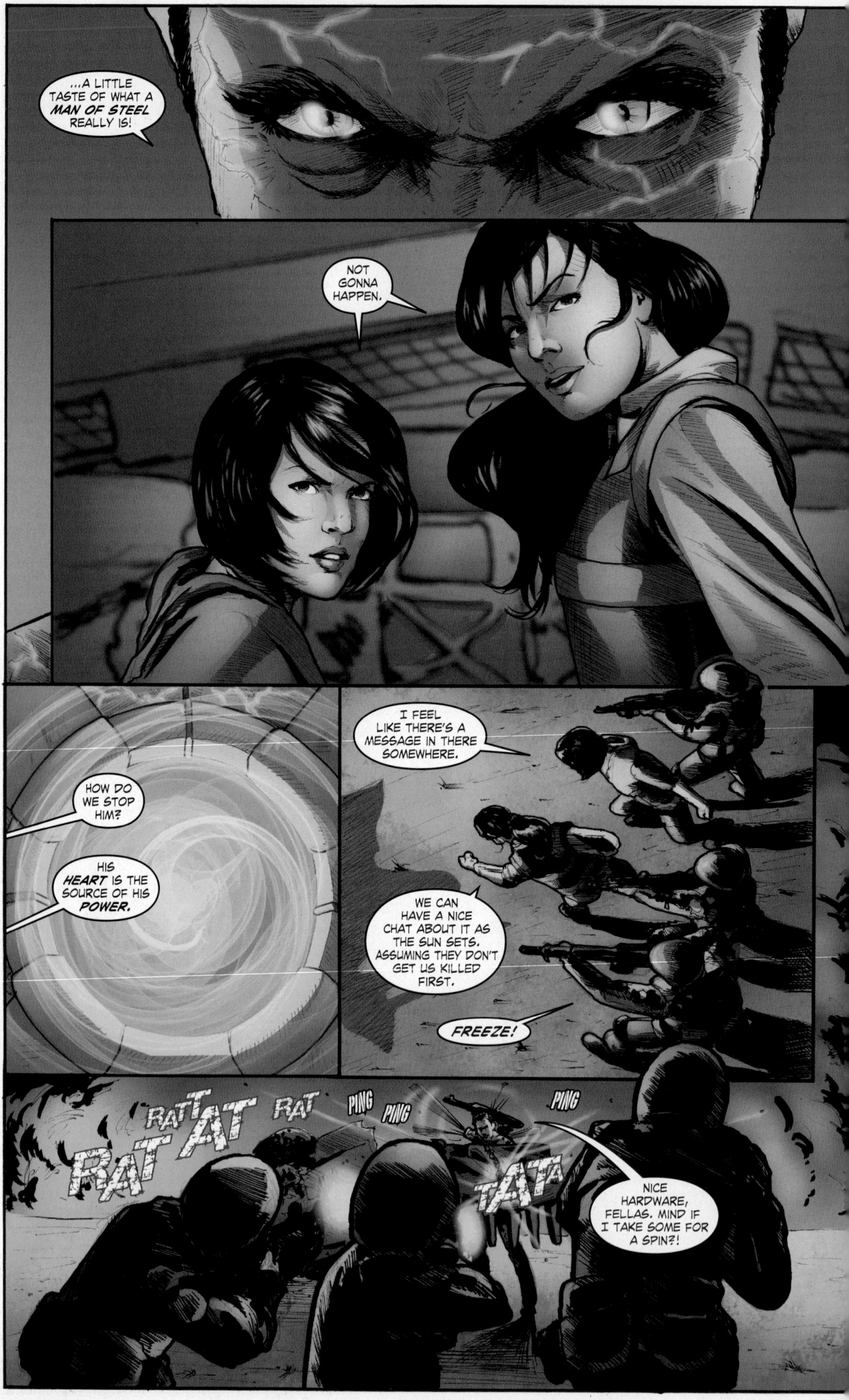
...A LITTLE TASTE OF WHAT A MAN OF STEEL REALLY IS!
NOT GONNA HAPPEN.
HOW DO WE STOP HIM?
HIS HEART IS THE SOURCE OF HIS POWER.
I FEEL LIKE THERE'S A MESSAGE IN THERE SOMEWHERE.
WE CAN HAVE A NICE CHAT ABOUT IT AS THE SUN SETS. ASSUMING THEY DON'T GET US KILLED FIRST.
FREEZE!
RAT RATTAT RAT
PING PING PING
TATA
NICE HARDWARE, FELLAS. MIND IF I TAKE SOME FOR A SPIN?!

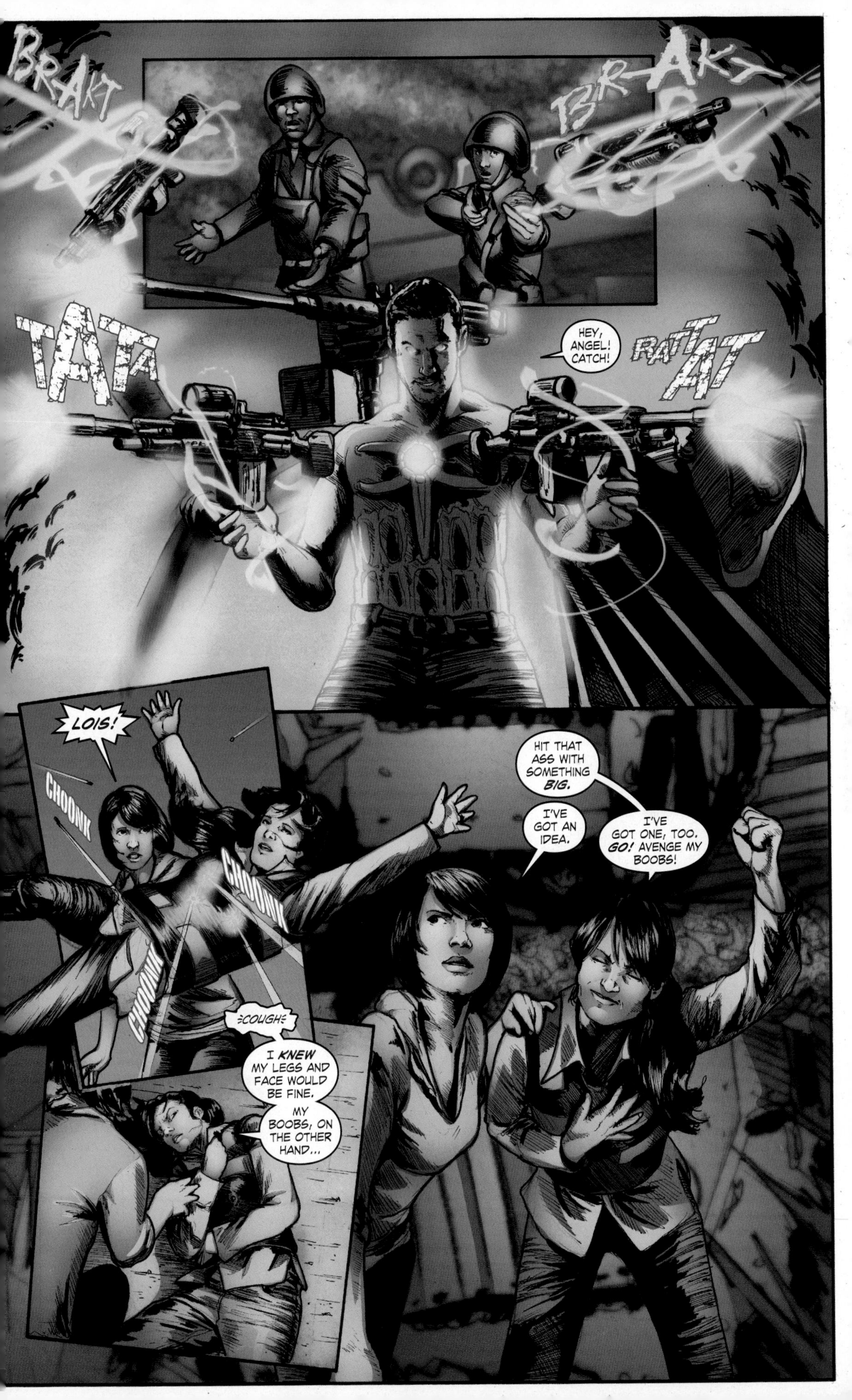
BRAKT
BR-AKT
TATA
HEY, ANGEL! CATCH!
RATTAT
LOIS!
CHOONK
CHOONK
CHOONK
HIT THAT ASS WITH SOMETHING *BIG.*
I'VE GOT AN IDEA.
I'VE GOT ONE, TOO. *GO!* AVENGE MY BOBS!
COUGH
I *KNEW* MY LEGS AND FACE WOULD BE FINE.
MY BOOBS, ON THE OTHER HAND...

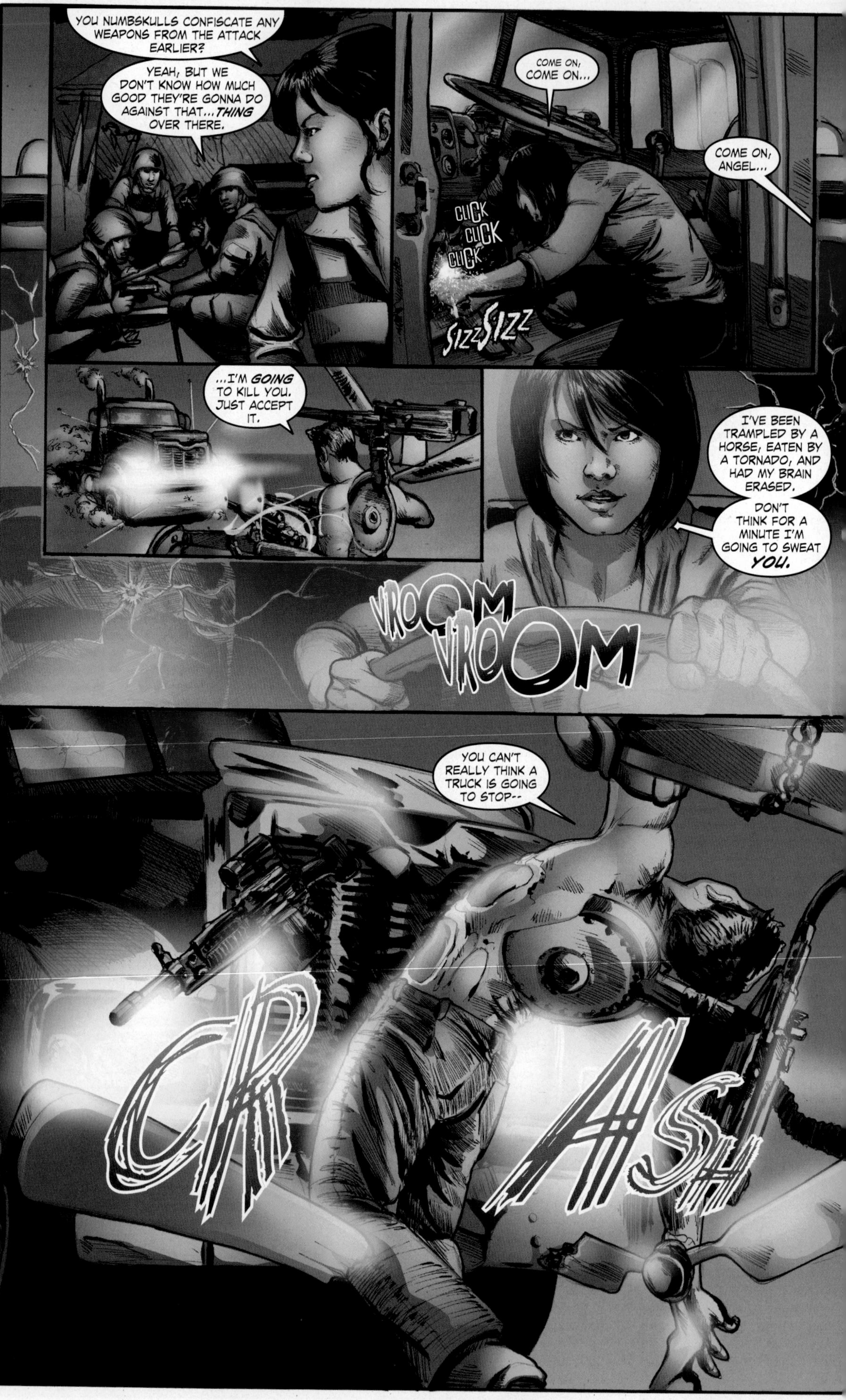
YOU NUMBSKULLS CONFISCATE ANY WEAPONS FROM THE ATTACK EARLIER?
YEAH, BUT WE DON'T KNOW HOW MUCH GOOD THEY'RE GONNA DO AGAINST THAT... *THING* OVER THERE.
COME ON, COME ON...
COME ON, ANGEL...
CLICK CLICK CLICK
SIZZ SIZZ
...I'M *GOING* TO KILL YOU. JUST ACCEPT IT.
I'VE BEEN TRAMPLED BY A HORSE, EATEN BY A TORNADO, AND HAD MY BRAIN ERASED.
DON'T THINK FOR A MINUTE I'M GOING TO SWEAT ***YOU.***
VROOM VROOM
YOU CAN'T REALLY THINK A TRUCK IS GOING TO STOP--
CRASH

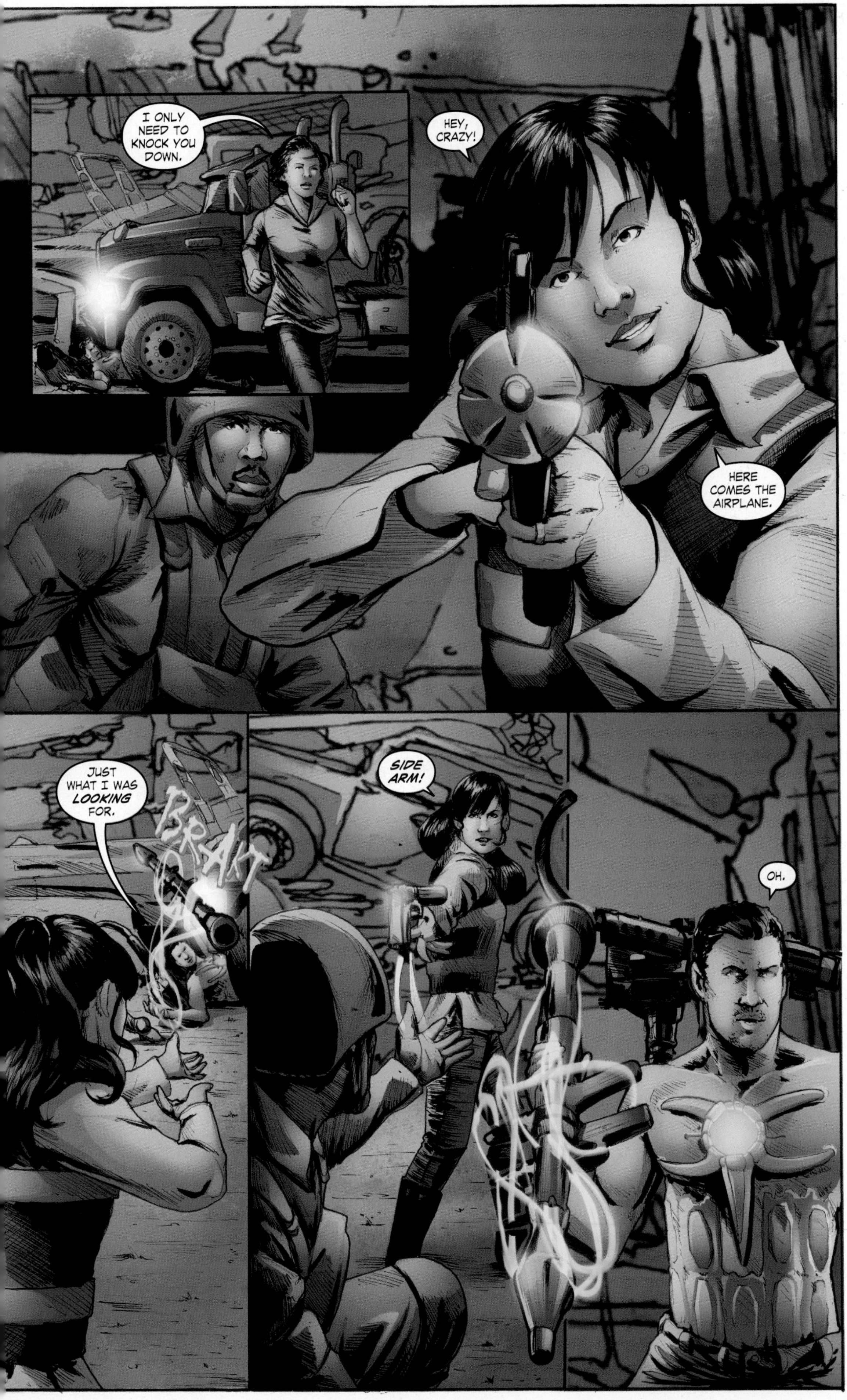
I ONLY NEED TO KNOCK YOU DOWN.
HEY, CRAZY!
HERE COMES THE AIRPLANE.
JUST WHAT I WAS LOOKING FOR.
BRAKT
SIDE ARM!
OH.

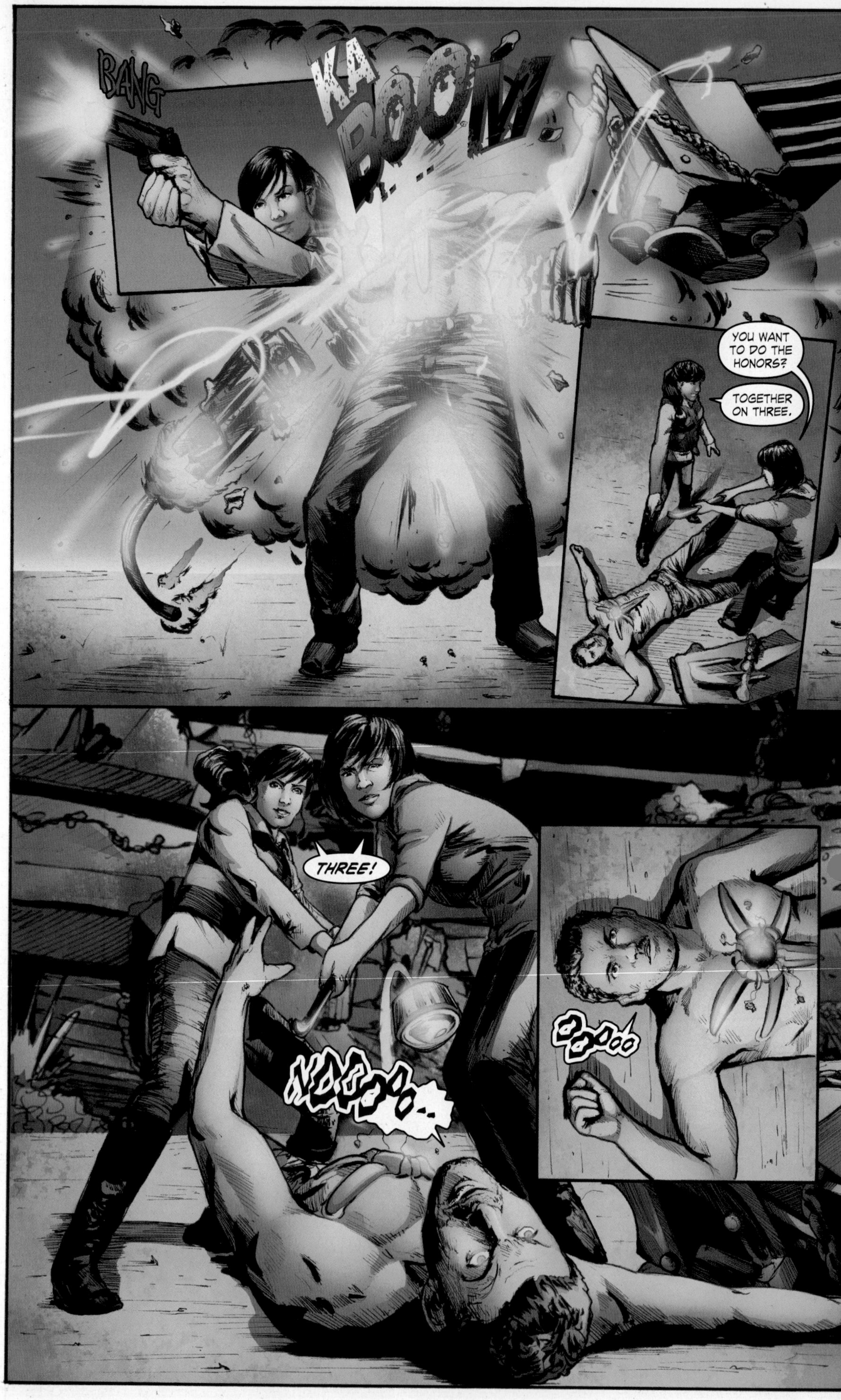
BANG
KA BOOM
YOU WANT TO DO THE HONORS?
TOGETHER ON THREE.
THREE!
NOOOOO--
OOOOO

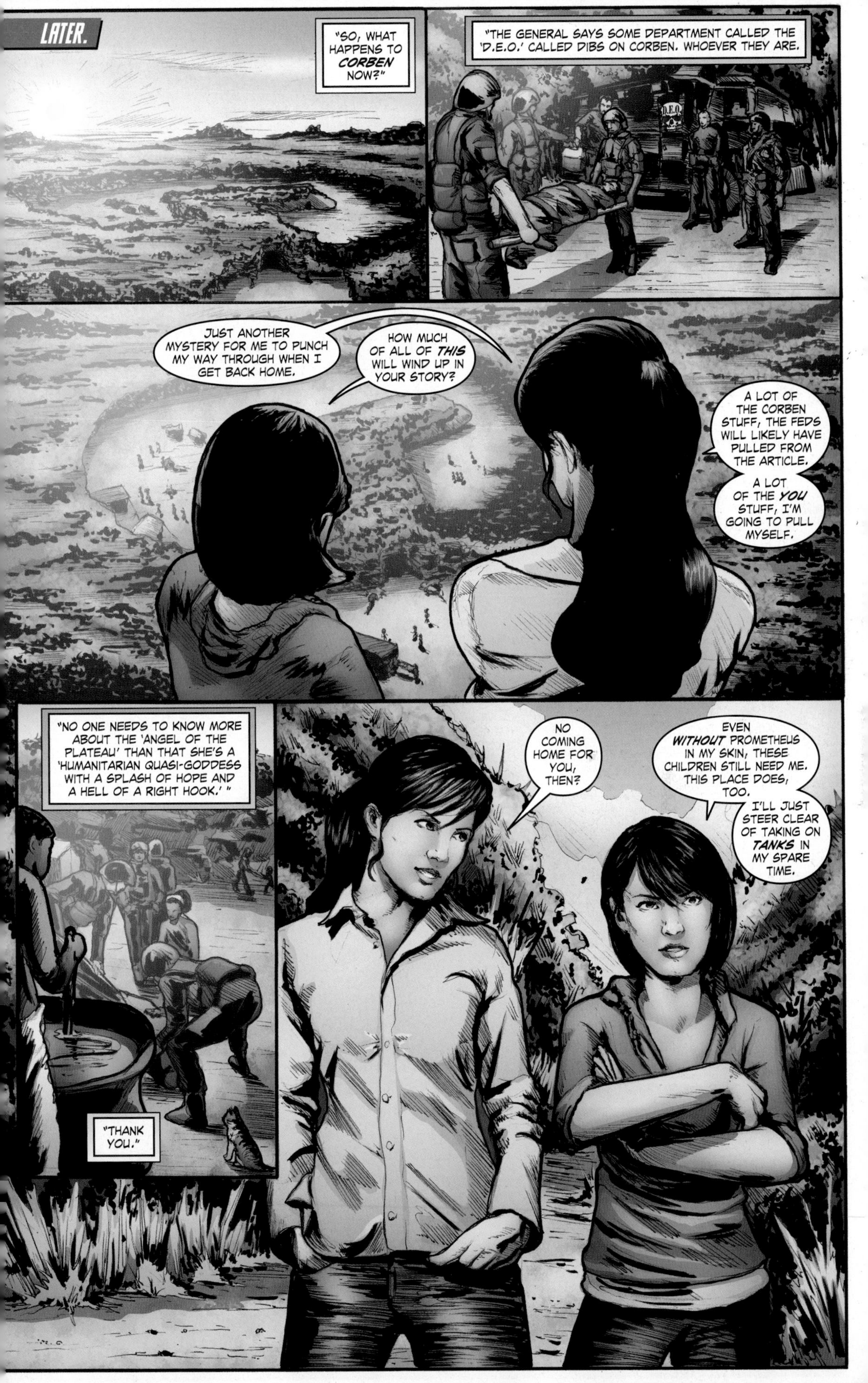
LATER.
"SO, WHAT HAPPENS TO CORBEN NOW?"
"THE GENERAL SAYS SOME DEPARTMENT CALLED THE 'D.E.O.' CALLED DIBS ON CORBEN. WHOEVER THEY ARE.
D.E.O.
JUST ANOTHER MYSTERY FOR ME TO PUNCH MY WAY THROUGH WHEN I GET BACK HOME.
HOW MUCH OF ALL OF THIS WILL WIND UP IN YOUR STORY?
A LOT OF THE CORBEN STUFF, THE FEDS WILL LIKELY HAVE PULLED FROM THE ARTICLE.
A LOT OF THE YOU STUFF, I'M GOING TO PULL MYSELF.
"NO ONE NEEDS TO KNOW MORE ABOUT THE 'ANGEL OF THE PLATEAU' THAN THAT SHE'S A 'HUMANITARIAN QUASI-GODDESS WITH A SPLASH OF HOPE AND A HELL OF A RIGHT HOOK.' "
"THANK YOU."
NO COMING HOME FOR YOU, THEN?
EVEN WITHOUT PROMETHEUS IN MY SKIN, THESE CHILDREN STILL NEED ME. THIS PLACE DOES, TOO.
I'LL JUST STEER CLEAR OF TAKING ON TANKS IN MY SPARE TIME.

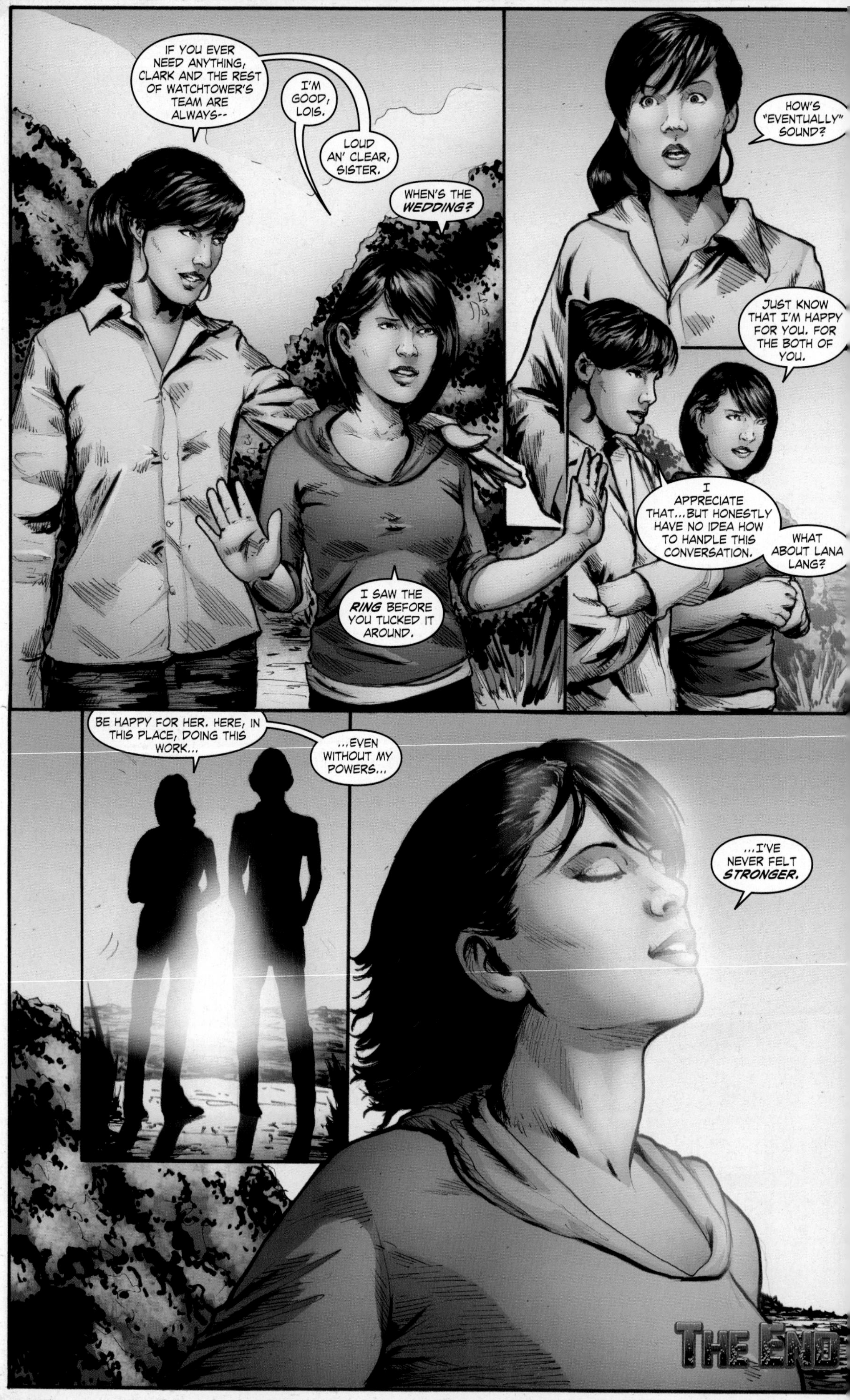
IF YOU EVER NEED ANYTHING, CLARK AND THE REST OF WATCHTOWER'S TEAM ARE ALWAYS--
I'M GOOD, LOIS.
LOUD AN' CLEAR, SISTER.
WHEN'S THE WEDDING?
I SAW THE RING BEFORE YOU TUCKED IT AROUND.
HOW'S "EVENTUALLY" SOUND?
JUST KNOW THAT I'M HAPPY FOR YOU. FOR THE BOTH OF YOU.
I APPRECIATE THAT...BUT HONESTLY HAVE NO IDEA HOW TO HANDLE THIS CONVERSATION.
WHAT ABOUT LANA LANG?
BE HAPPY FOR HER. HERE, IN THIS PLACE, DOING THIS WORK...
...EVEN WITHOUT MY POWERS...
...I'VE NEVER FELT STRONGER.
THE END

SMALLVILLE: SEASON ELEVEN Chapters 42-44 digital cover by **CAT STAGGS**

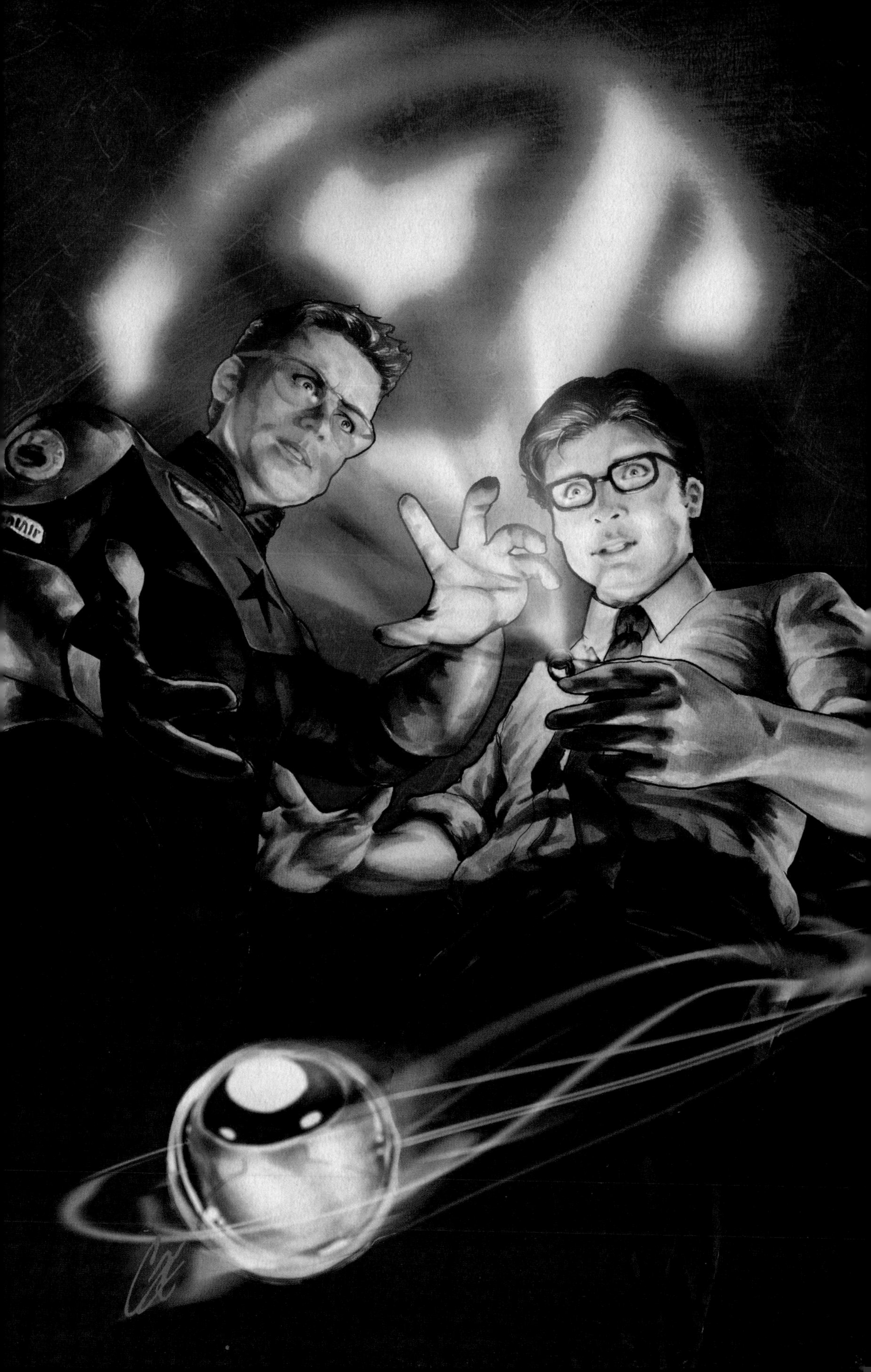

SMALLVILLE: SEASON ELEVEN Chapters 47-49 digital cover by **CAT STAGGS**

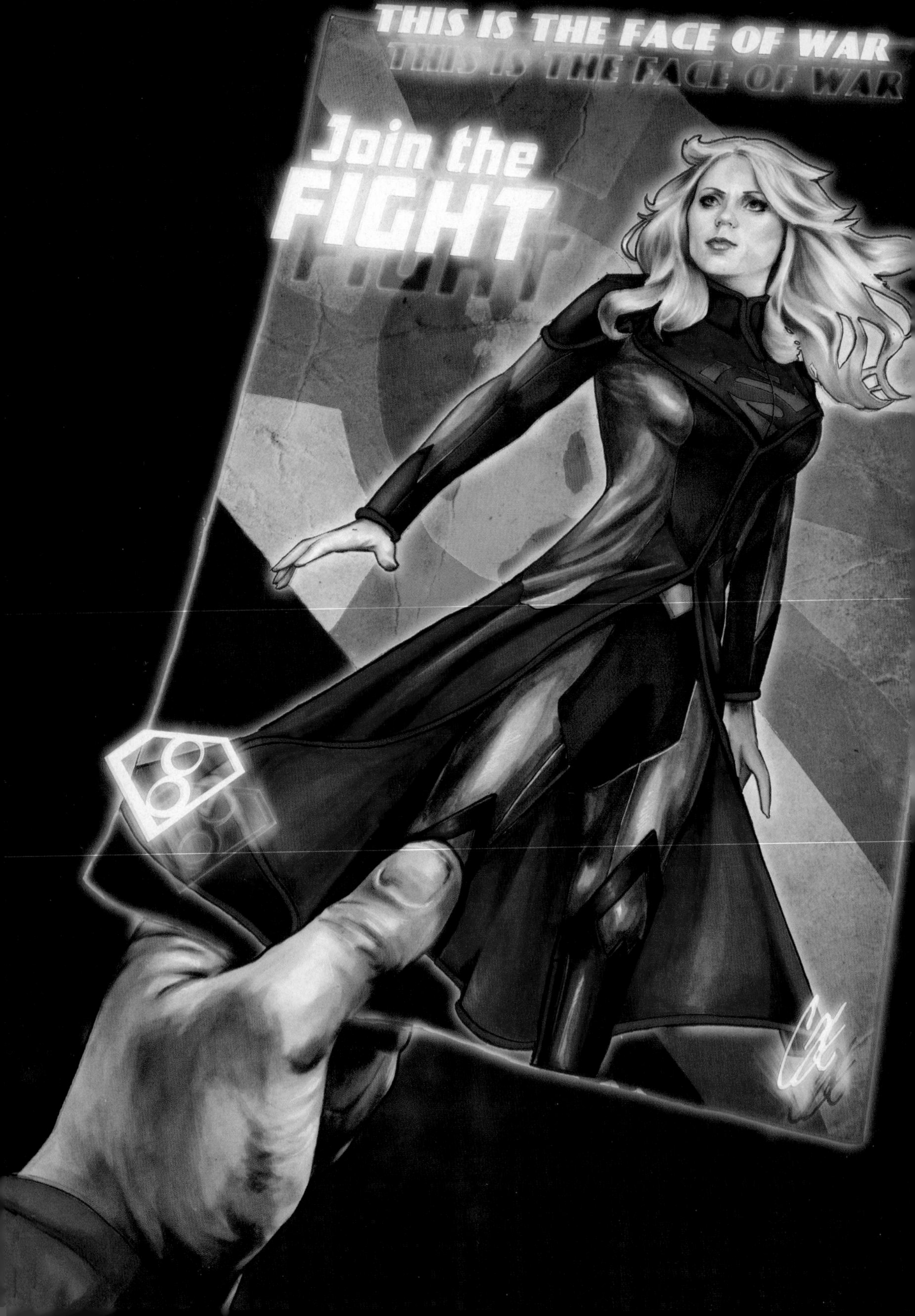
THIS IS THE FACE OF WAR
Join the FIGHT

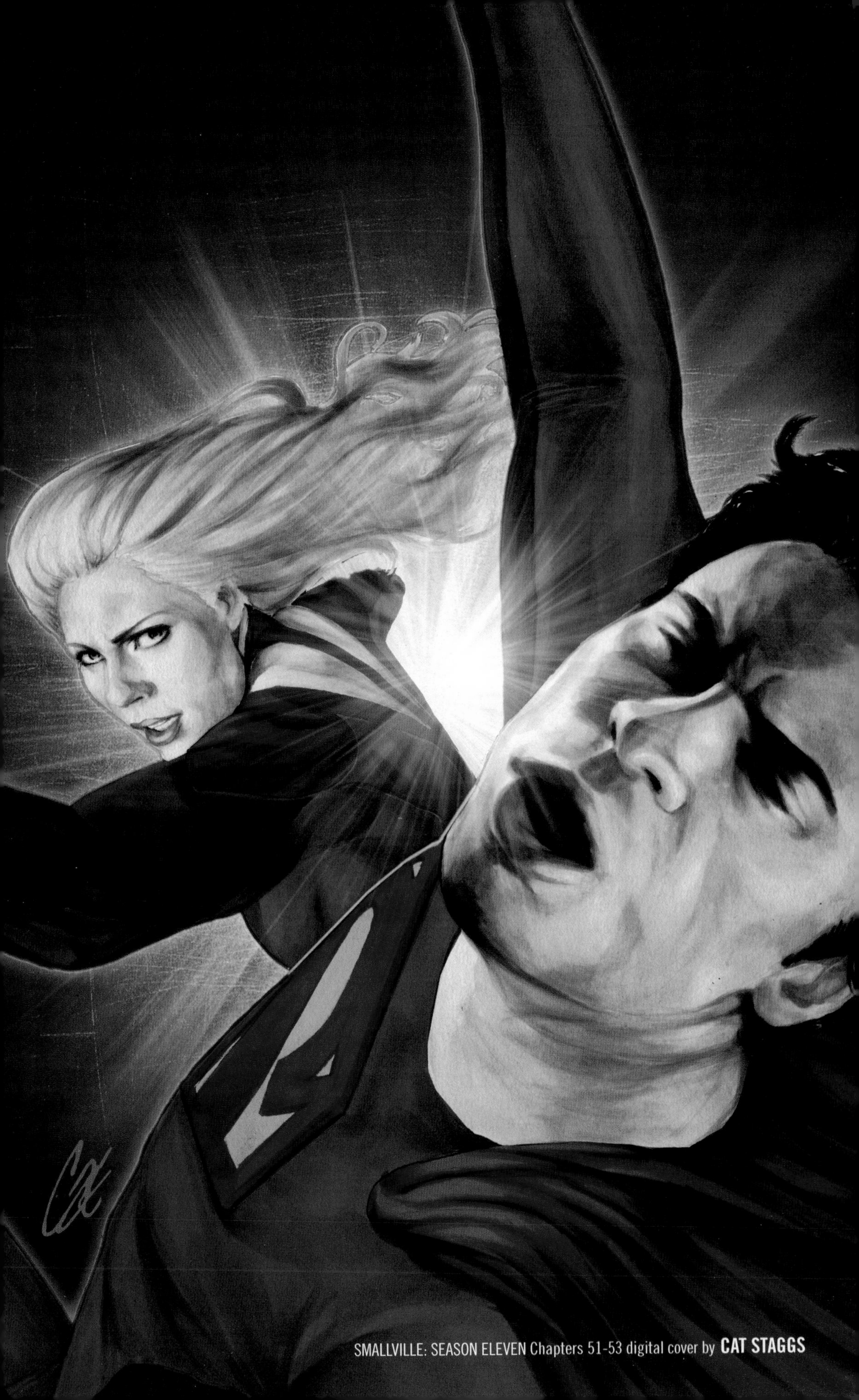

SMALLVILLE: SEASON ELEVEN Chapters 51-53 digital cover by **CAT STAGGS**

SMALLVILLE: SEASON ELEVEN Chapters 41, 45, 46 & 50 digital cover by **CAT STAGGS**

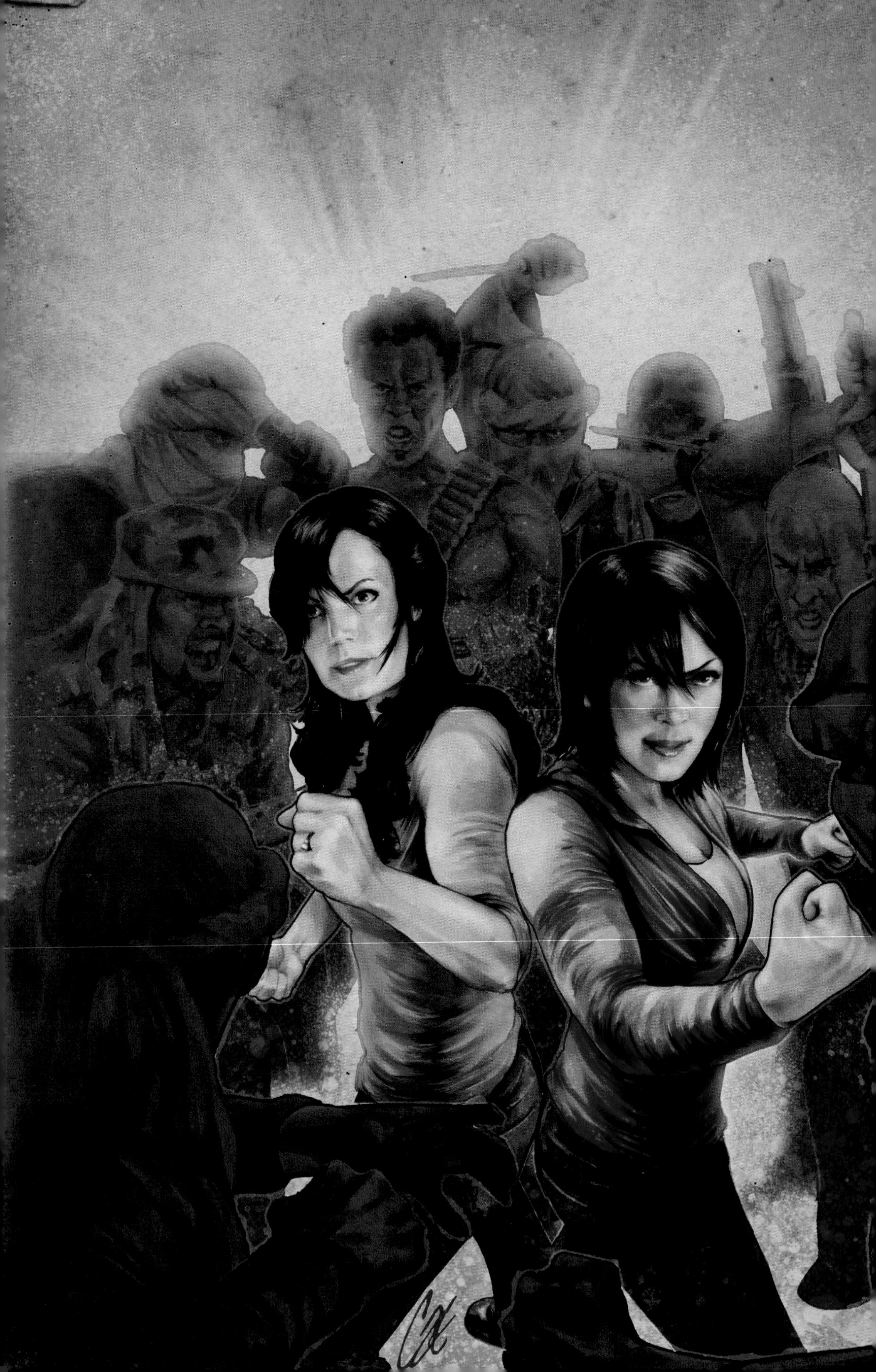

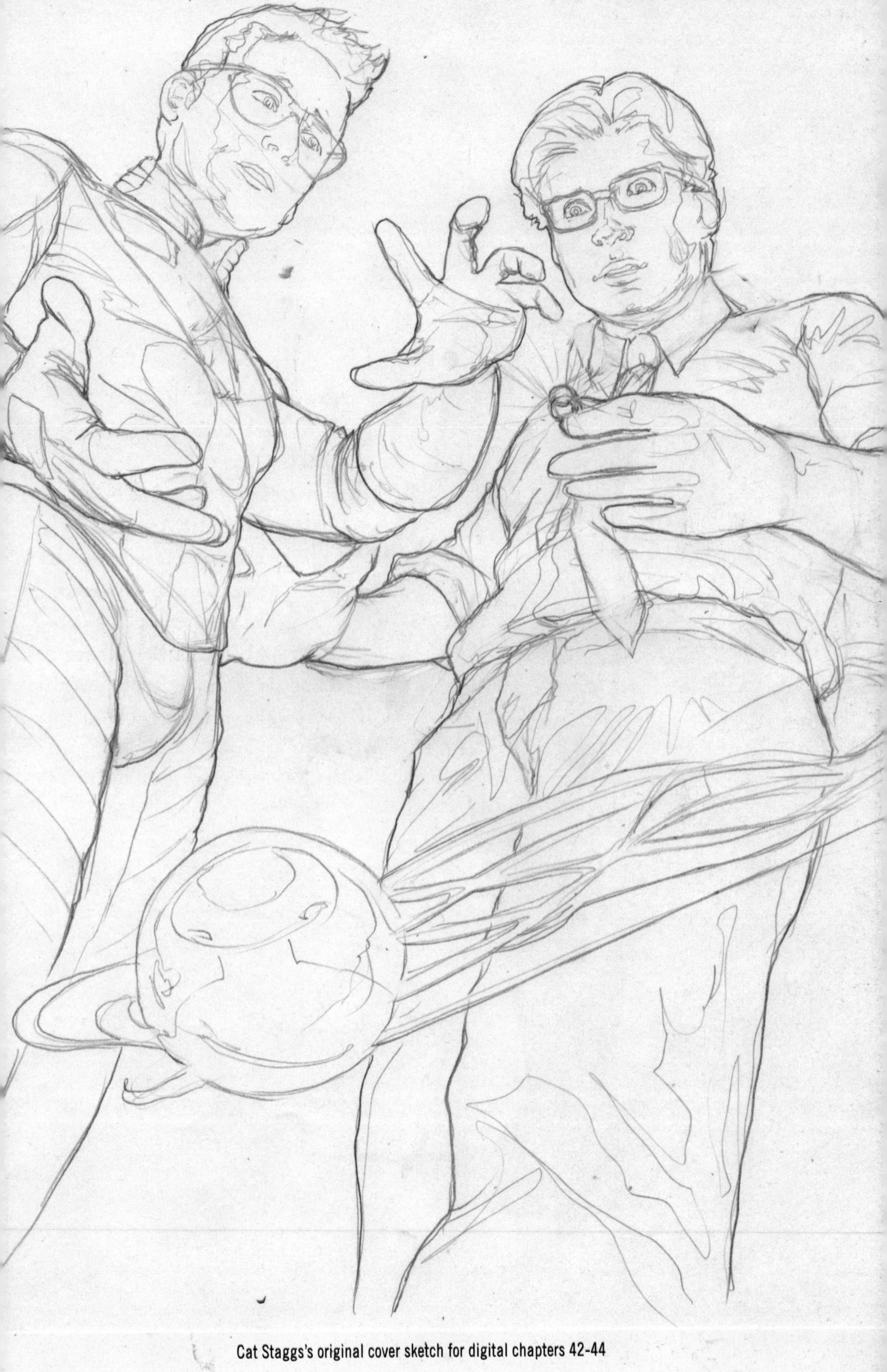

Cat Staggs's original cover sketch for digital chapters 42-44

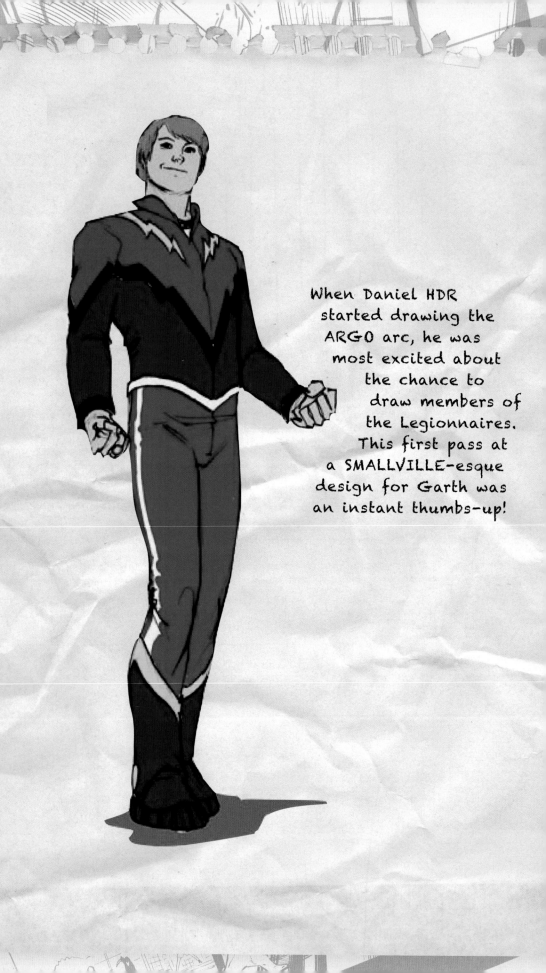

When Daniel HDR started drawing the ARGO arc, he was most excited about the chance to draw members of the Legionnaires. This first pass at a SMALLVILLE-esque design for Garth was an instant thumbs-up!

Brainiac, however, was a little too much in the first pass. As you can see in the sketch above, the pink shirt under the purple trench coat was a lot of look, even for the 31st Century.

CONCEPT DESIGN

Daniel's final version maintained the trench coat, slightly toned down, with an all-black suit underneath for contrast. We also asked for the simplest possible symbol: just the 3 orbs, no number five at all!

FINAL DESIGN

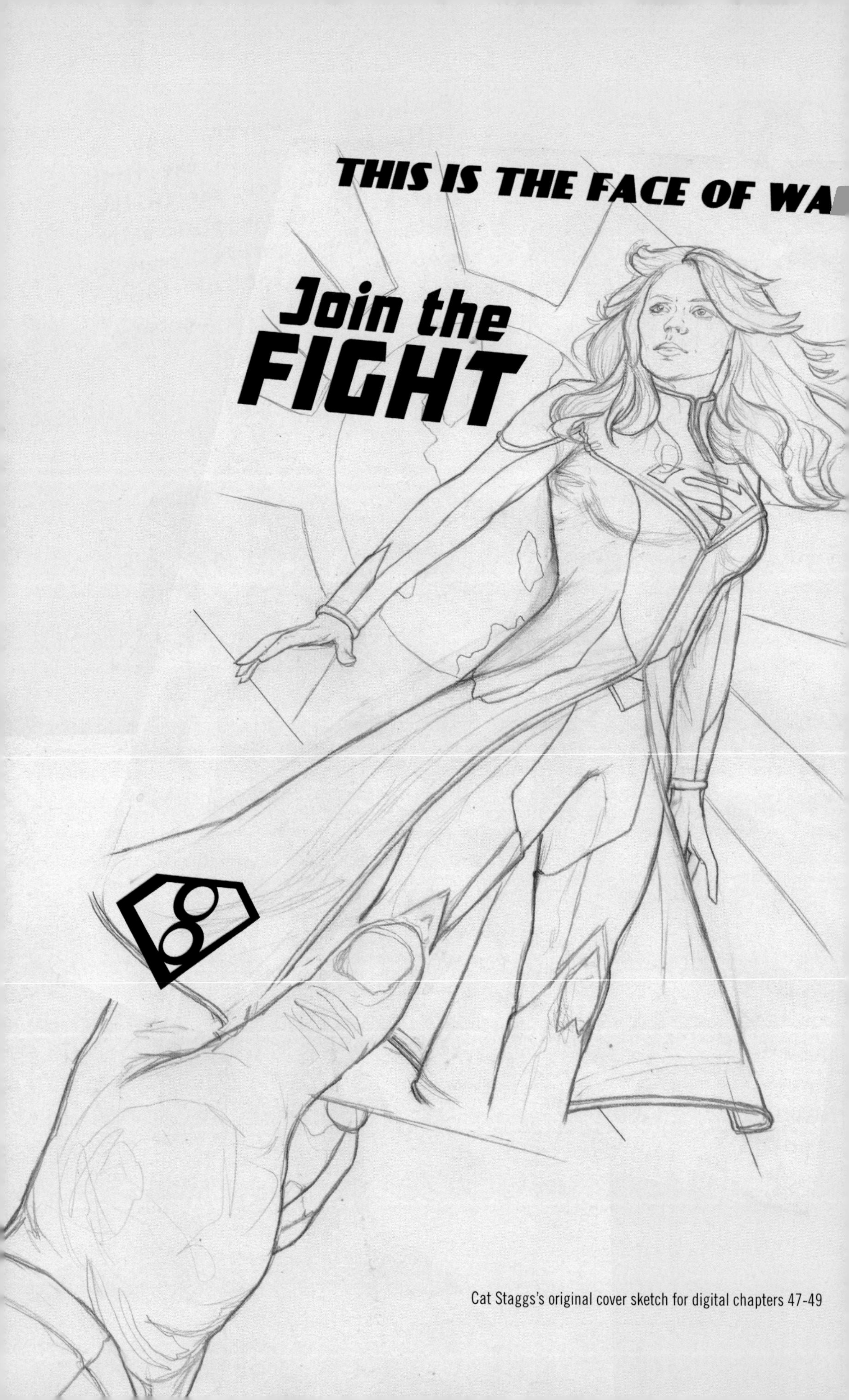
THIS IS THE FACE OF WA
Join the
FIGHT

Cat Staggs's original cover sketch for digital chapters 47-49

After we saw Pete Woods' sketches for the cover to issue #14, we knew we needed to go with option C and focus on Kara. But we didn't have a final design yet, so we turned to Cat Staggs.

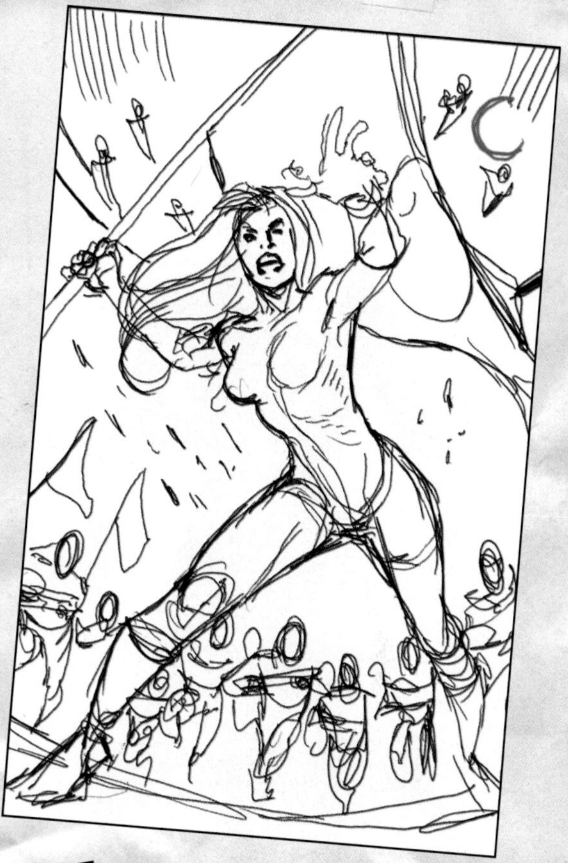
C

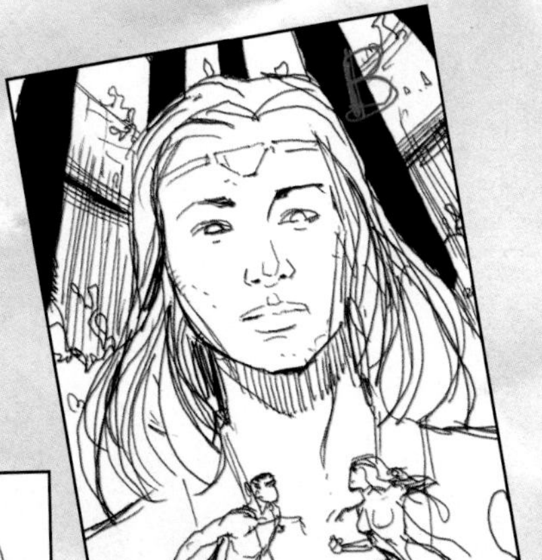
B

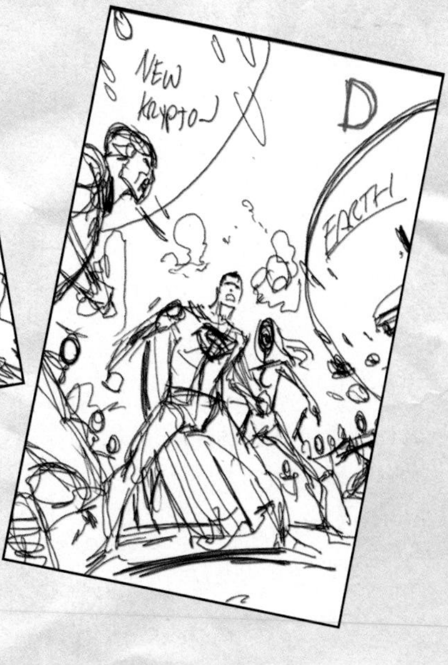
NEW KRYPTON
D
EARTH

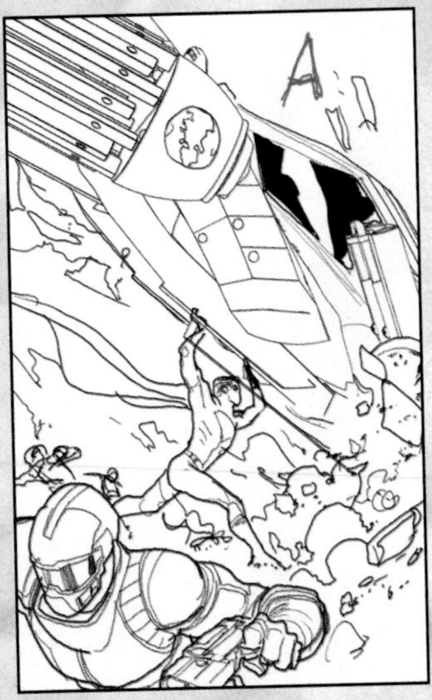
A

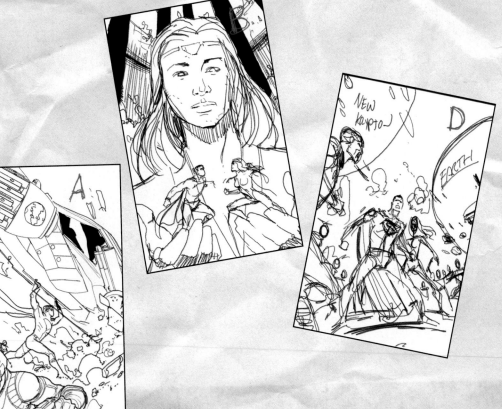

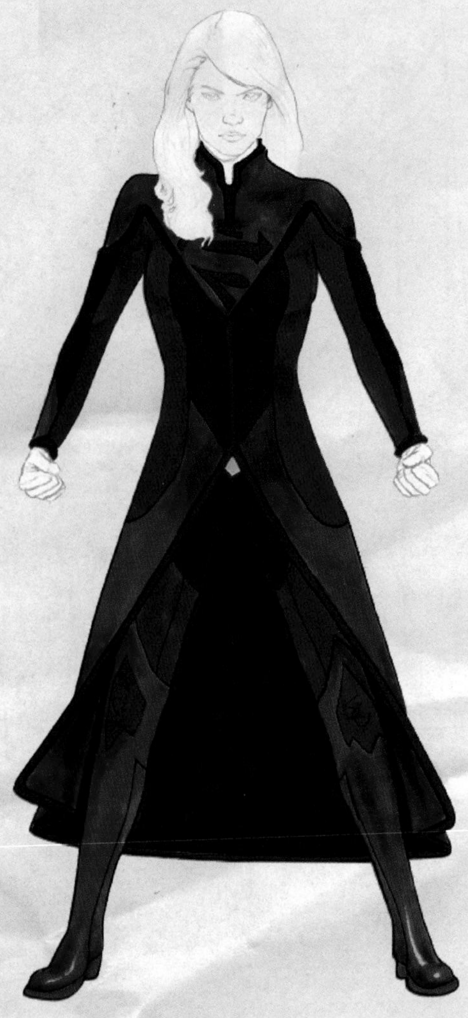

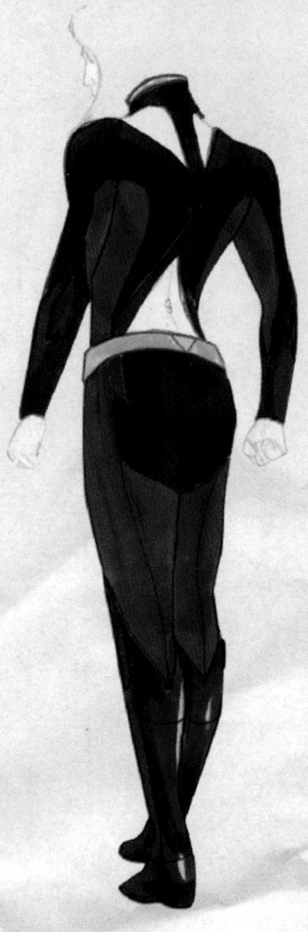

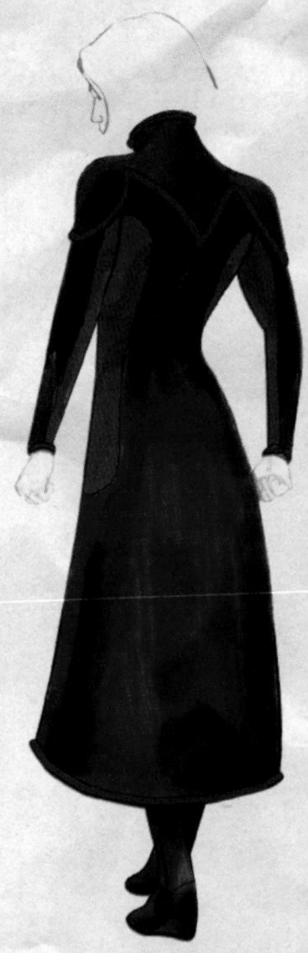

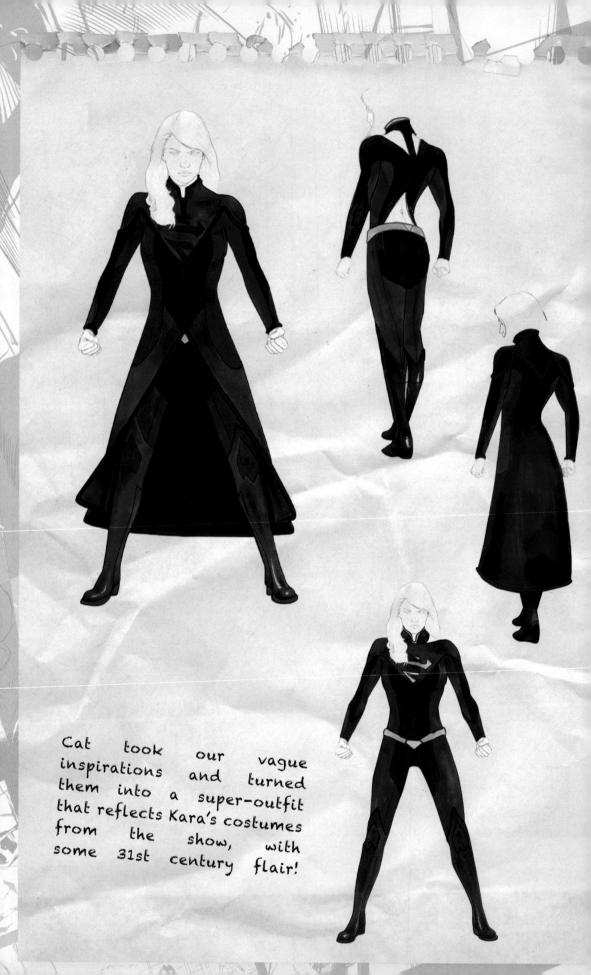

Cat took our vague inspirations and turned them into a super-outfit that reflects Kara's costumes from the show, with some 31st century flair!

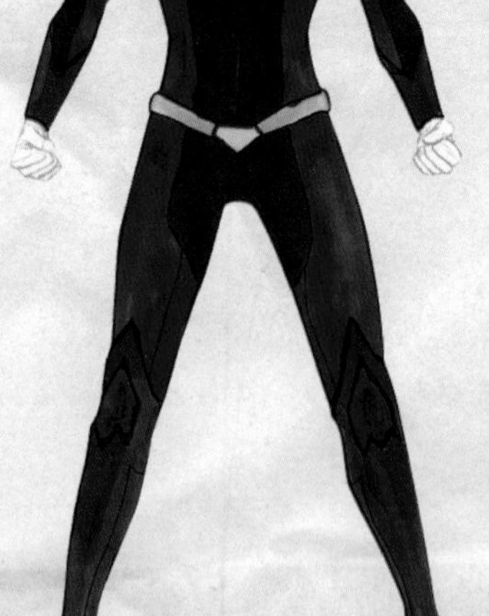

The big deal this issue is the fight with Kara and Clark, so I played on that. I threw in one Legion group cover for good measure.
-Cat

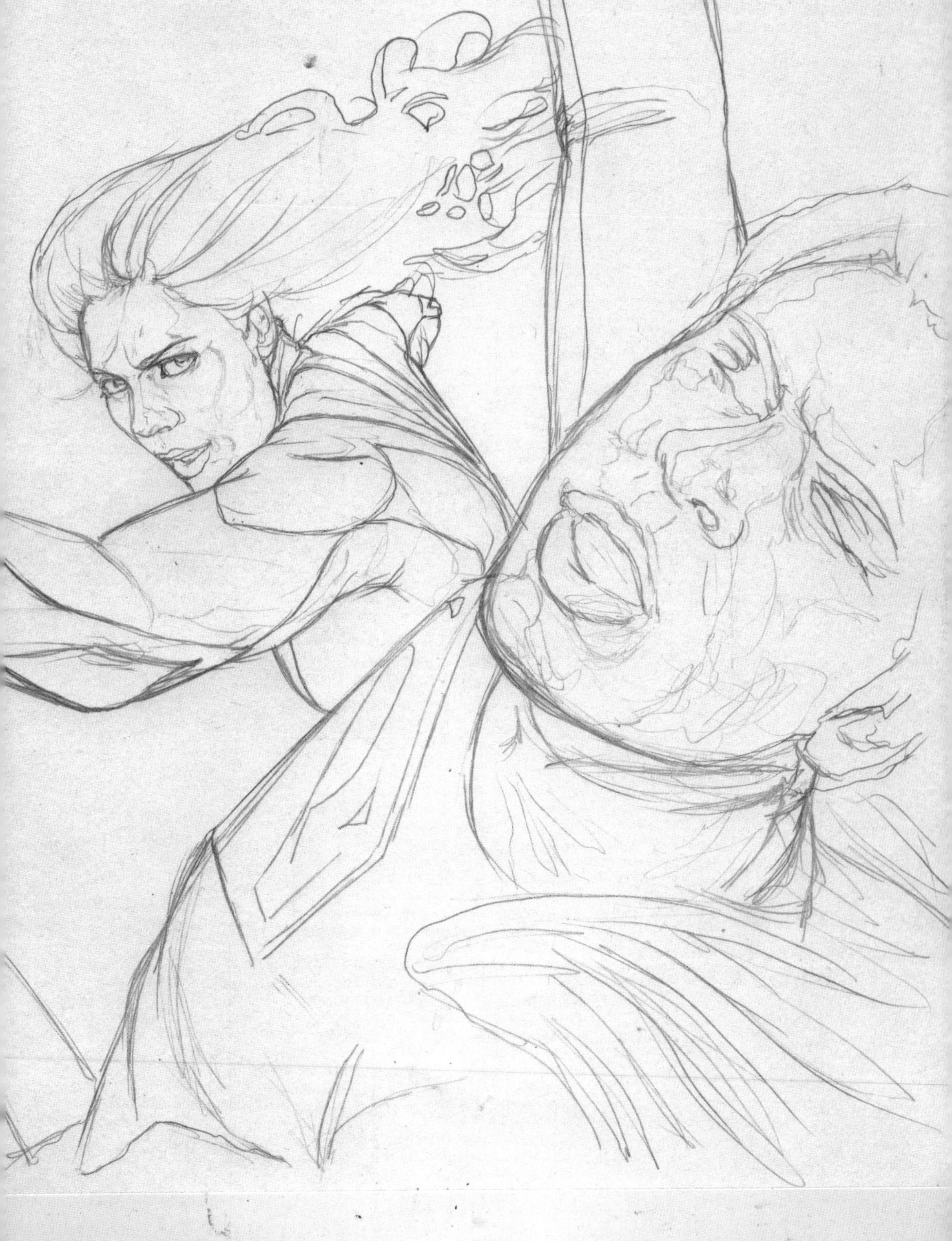

CONCEPT SKETCHES

THUMBNAIL SKETCHES

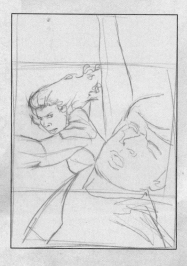

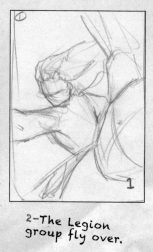

1-Kara punches Clark, spinning him around. This seems like a pretty badass Supergirl moment.

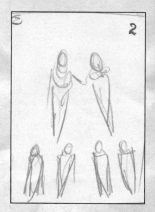

2-The Legion group fly over.

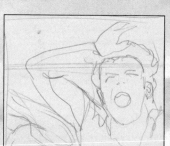

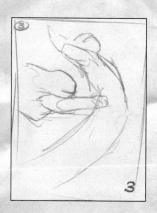

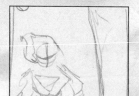

3 & 4-Two angles on Kara punching Clark in the back.

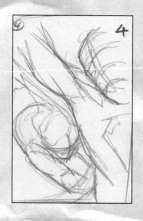

5-Kara charging Clark. I also thought this could be a standoff as well, Old West style.

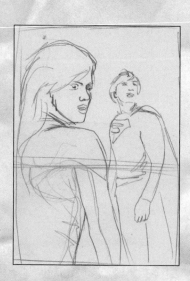

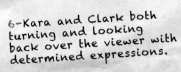

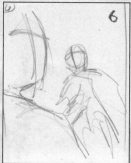

6-Kara and Clark both turning and looking back over the viewer with determined expressions.

Cat Staggs's cover sketch for "Valkyrie"

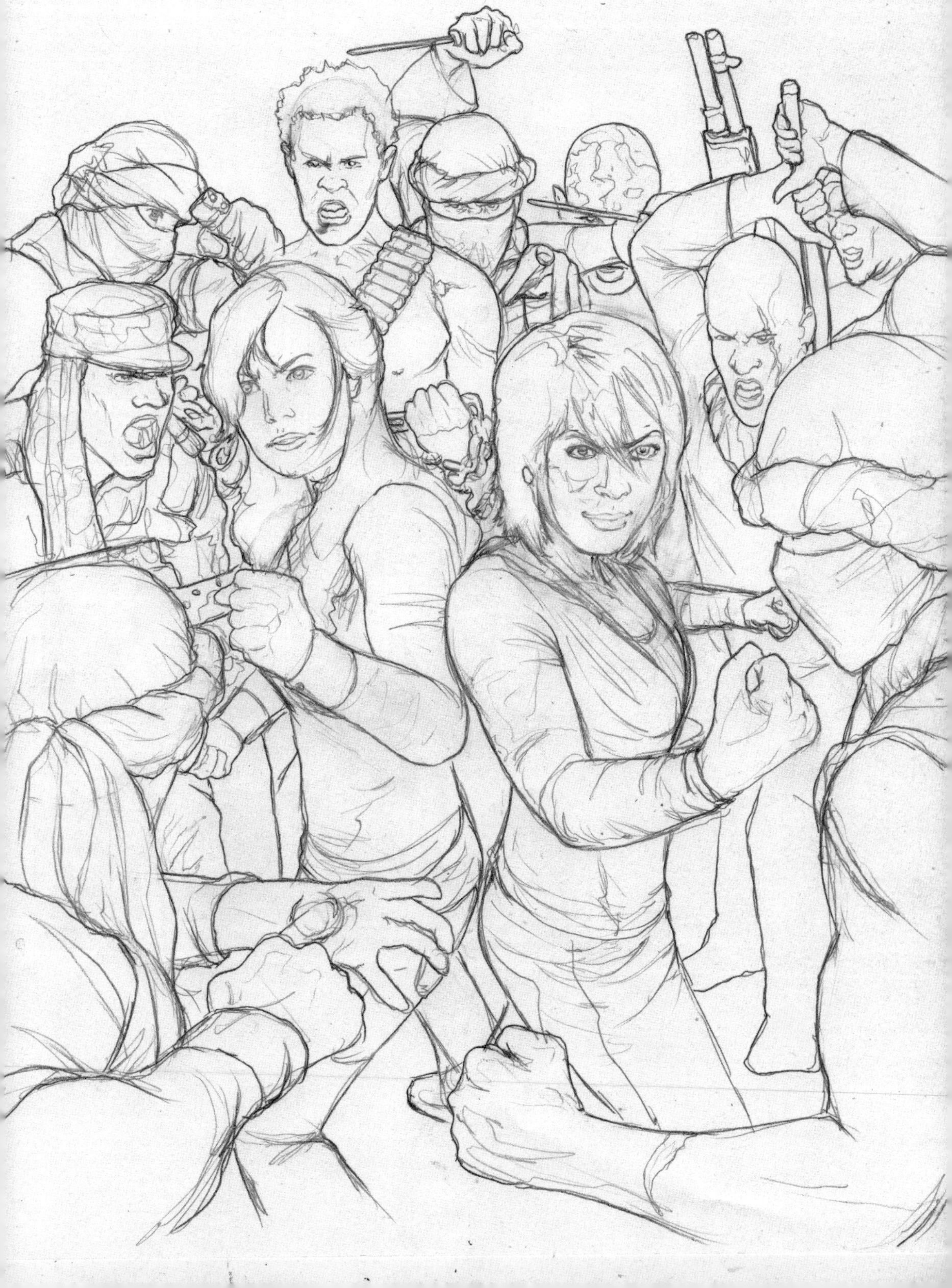

Cat Staggs's step-by-step progressions from pencils to inks to under color
for the first and last pages of digital chapter #41

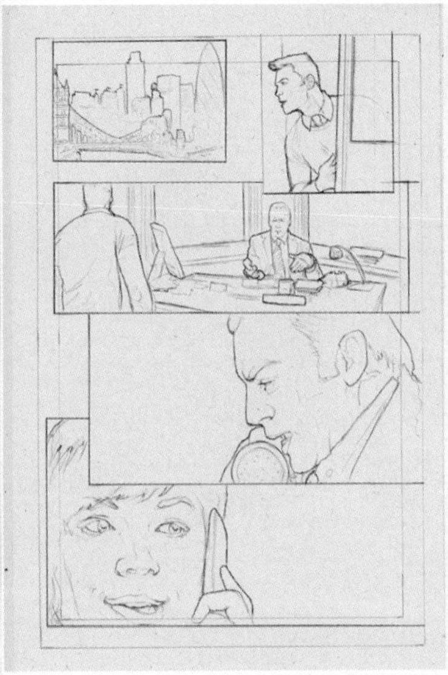

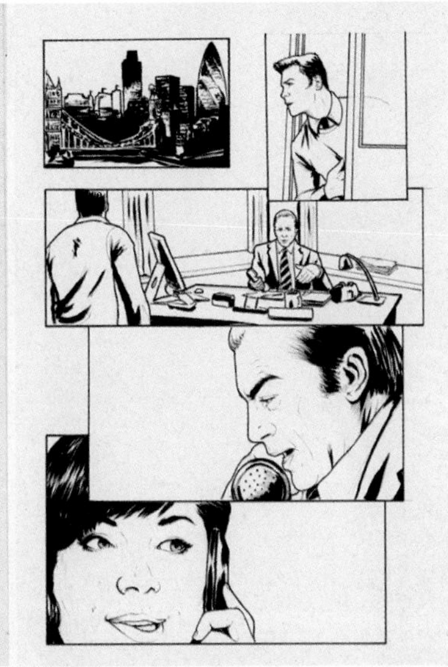

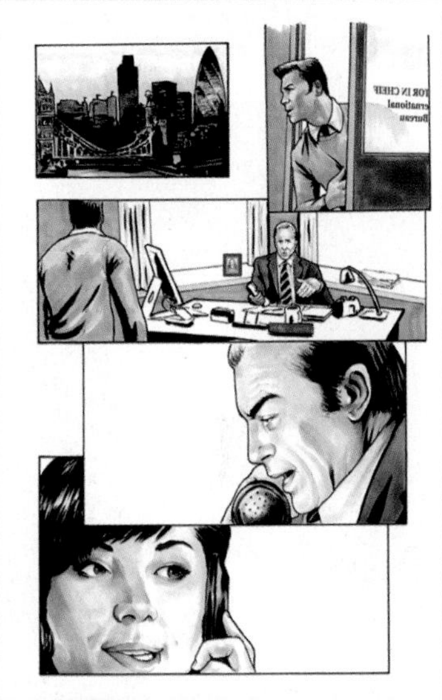

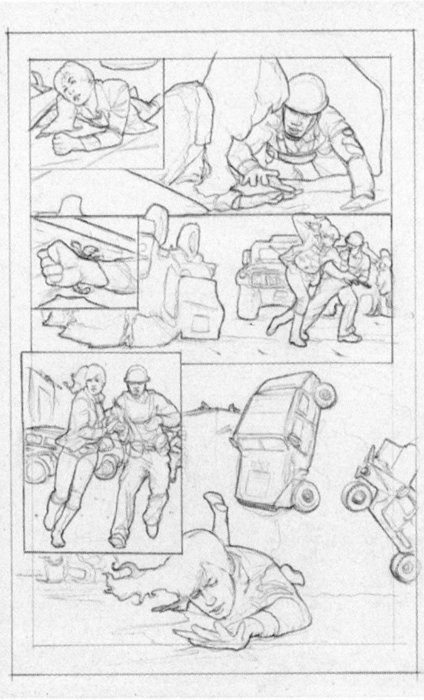

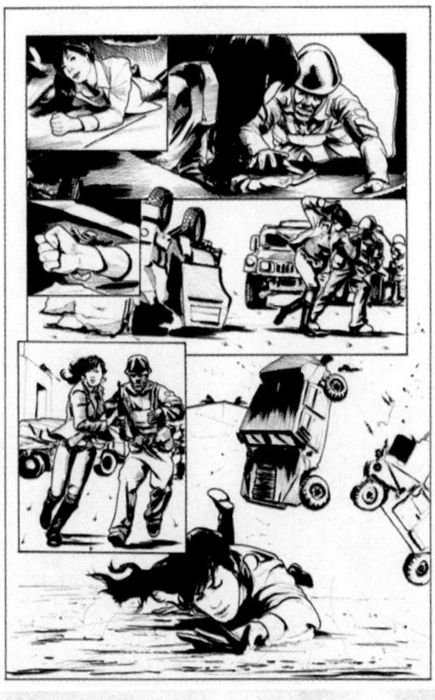

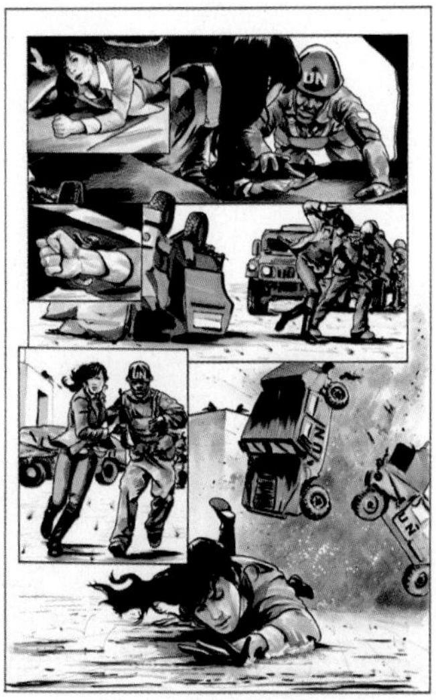
UN

Cat Staggs's under color on covers for “Argo” and “Valkyrie”

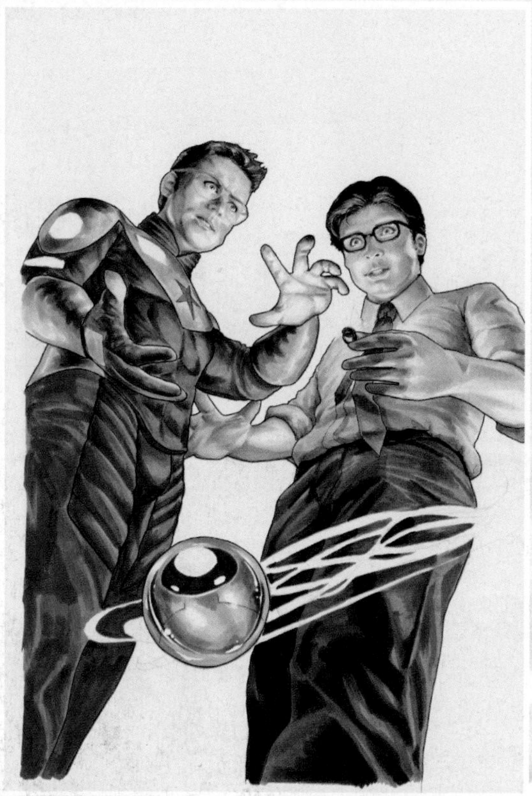

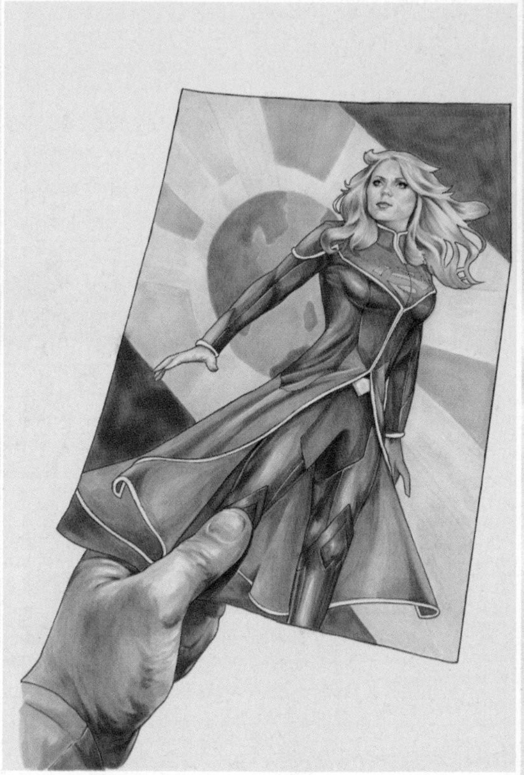

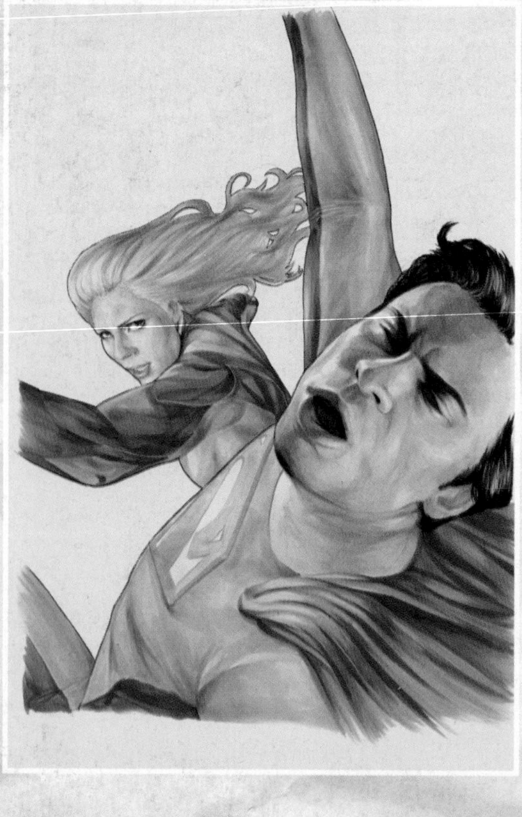

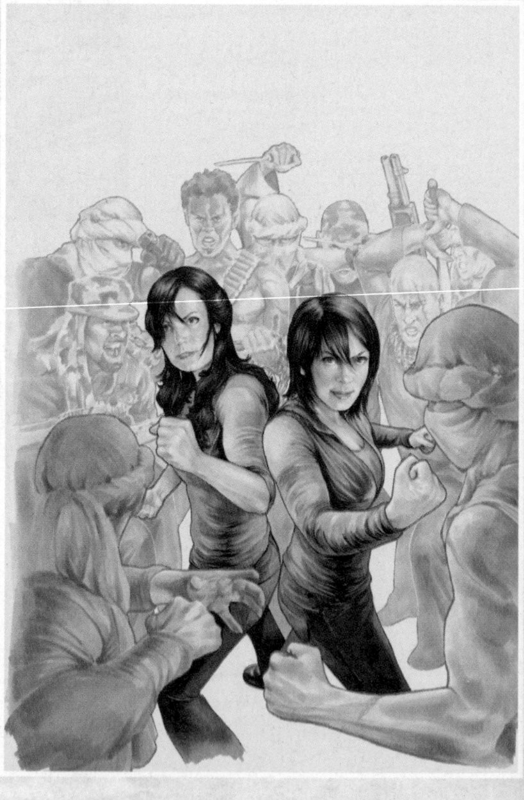

START AT THE BEGINNING!

SUPERMAN: ACTION COMICS VOLUME 1: SUPERMAN AND THE MEN OF STEEL

SUPERMAN VOLUME 1: WHAT PRICE TOMORROW?

SUPERGIRL VOLUME 1: THE LAST DAUGHTER OF KRYPTON

SUPERBOY VOLUME 1: INCUBATION

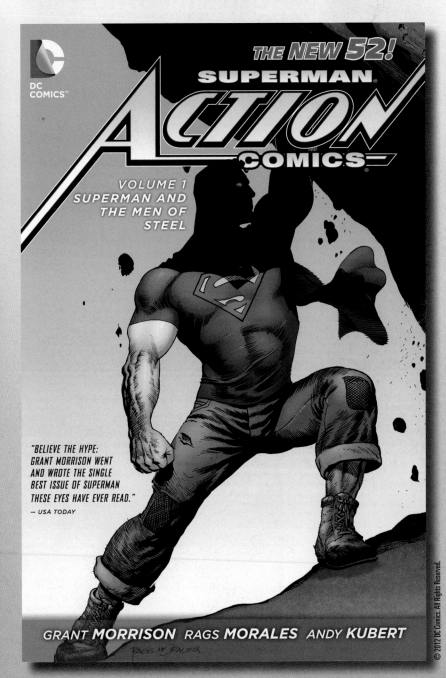

GRANT **MORRISON** RAGS **MORALES** ANDY **KUBERT**